APPROACHES
TO DEVIANCE

ACC SOCIOLOGY SERIES
John F. Cuber, *Editor*
Alfred C. Clarke, *Associate Editor*

APPROACHES
TO DEVIANCE
Theories, Concepts, and Research Findings

Edited by

Mark Lefton

James K. Skipper, Jr.

Charles H. McCaghy

All of Case Western Reserve University

New York / APPLETON-CENTURY-CROFTS

Division of Meredith Corporation

PRINTED IN THE UNITED STATES OF AMERICA

E 54900

Preface

The range of interest which characterizes the social scientific study of deviants and their behavior is broad. Social scientists conceptualize, theorize, and conduct research on: (1) individuals defined by various frames of reference as deviants, (2) the actual deviant acts which these individuals commit, and (3) the reactions of the general society (or some significant portion of it) to these people and their deviant actions. Of primary concern is the delineation of the social and psychological factors which may aid in understanding who becomes deviant, when and why deviant acts take place, and by whom individuals and their actions are labeled deviant. Traditionally, in American sociology the study of deviance has focussed on criminals, juvenile delinquents, prostitutes, suicides, the mentally ill, drug users and drug addicts, homosexuals, and political and religious radicals. Thus far no common frame of reference has been devised which will adequately account for any one of these types of behavior, let alone a rubric which would encompass all of them. Furthermore, these behaviors are not at all casually regarded by the public at large and, hence, it seems reasonable to assume that any useful frame of reference would have to include social values, norms, mores, and folkways as integral components.

Words can be deceptively simple. For while we may be permitted to describe in gross and abstract terms the content of a particular area of study, the portrait soon may become a caricature when other kinds of questions are posed. For example, what do we actually know about causes, reactions, interpretations; and just how strategic and heuristic is the work in deviance behavior for general sociology or social psychology? In short, knowledge is most decidedly different from intentions, although both are critical ingredients forming the substance of any given scientific endeavor.

In an important sense that message reflects the aim of this book. The selection of articles was chosen with essentially two major themes in mind. First, to indicate the conceptual shape of the field to the student by exposing him to several major efforts at delineating appropriate levels and units of analysis; attempts to specify key relationships between and among relevant factors, conditions, and variables; and significant questions dealing with the practical implications of scientific efforts to understand deviance in our society. The second, and by no means an independent theme, is reflected in articles which in our judgment represent significant attempts at empirical research in this difficult and complex field. They have produced new facts, demonstrable relationships, and more sharply defined hypotheses—all of which are essential in order to establish the guidelines for further understanding.

While the articles comprising this book reflect the scope and diversity of interests in the field of deviance, they have been organized to emphasize four major points of reference.

Part I, "Toward Defining the Field," consists of seven articles designed to introduce the study of deviant behavior in terms of three separate aspects: (1) the influence of traditional sociological concern with social problems in general, (2) several contemporary attempts at specifying the proper scope and limitations of the field for social scientific study, and (3) an indication that the problems of theory and conceptualization have a definite bearing on some severe practical dilemmas of our day.

Each of the seven articles in Part II, "The Sociological Approach," reflects a sociological stance with respect to one or more aspects of deviant behavior. These research papers provide the reader with insights into the way that the sociologist utilizes his distinctive perspective to formulate problems, to specify units for analysis, and to discover in what sense deviant behavior is social behavior.

Part III, "The Social Psychological Approach," consists of six readings designed to inform the student that, while the empirical referent appears to be similar (e.g., criminal behavior, alcholism, mental illness), the social psychology of deviance represents a perspective decidedly distinct from that which characterizes the sociological approach. These articles indicate that the deviant *actor* is clearly as important to the social psychologist as is his *behavior*.

Part IV, "Societal Reaction and Functions of Deviance," is distinct from the substantive materials of Parts II and III. The concern is not with etiological or otherwise explanatory models for the existence or emergence of deviant behavior, but rather with its consequences for the system in which it occurs, for the significant other persons who must necessarily react, and finally, for the deviant himself.

Like any collection of readings this one is representative or partial, rather than exhaustive. The viewpoint expressed is entirely that of social scientists. With these caveats in mind it is our contention that this book of readings provides a sound introduction to the field of deviant behavior in that it forces the student to recognize not only the complexity of the realities involved but the range of scholarly effort put forth to meet that challenge.

We wish to express our appreciation to the authors and publishers who gave us permission to reprint their works. We wish also to thank Mrs. Gloria Sterin for her able editorial assistance in handling a number of the necessary but often thankless details accompanying the task of making a book out of a group of articles. A special note of appreciation is due Stuart Schoenfeld who provided us with keen insights regarding the ordering of articles and for his participation in the preparation of materials for the introductory comments preceding each section. Finally, we acknowledge and gratefully appreciate the patience of our wives, Eva, Joan, and Dawn for allowing us to complete this project during the last days of a summer's vacation.

M. L.

J. K. S., Jr.

C. H. M.

Contributors

Shirley S. Angrist, Department of Sociology, Carnegie Institute of Technology
Richard A. Ball, Department of Sociology, University of West Virginia
Lee L. Bean, Department of Sociology, Yale University
James H. Bryan, Department of Psychology, Northwestern University
John P. Clark, Department of Sociology, University of Illinois
Lewis A. Coser, Department of Sociology, Brandeis University
Arlene K. Daniels, Department of Sociology, San Francisco State College
Richard R. Daniels, Sequoia Hospital, Redwood City, California
Howard Davidman, M.D., The New York School of Psychiatry
Simon Dinitz, Department of Sociology, The Ohio State University
John H. Gagnon, Institute for Sex Research, Indiana University
Jack P. Gibbs, Department of Sociology, Washington State University
Peter M. Hall, Department of Sociology, University of California at Santa
    Barbara
Richard Jessor, Institute of Behavioral Science, University of Colorado
Theodore D. Kemper, Department of Sociology, Rutgers University
Mark Lefton, Department of Sociology, Case Western Reserve University
Edwin M. Lemert, Department of Sociology, University of California at Davis
Walter T. Martin, Department of Sociology, University of Oregon
Arden E. Melzer, School of Social Work, University of Pittsburgh
Robert K. Merton, Department of Sociology, Columbia University
Lloyd Miller, Department of Sociology, Case Western Reserve University
C. Wright Mills, Late of Columbia University
Ephraim H. Mizruchi, Department of Sociology, Syracuse University
Jerome K. Myers, Department of Sociology, Yale University
Benjamin Pasamanick, M.D., Dean, The New York School of Psychiatry
Max P. Pepper, M.D., School of Medicine, Yale University
Robert Perrucci, Department of Sociology, Purdue University
Edward Preble, The New York School of Psychiatry
Albert J. Reiss, Department of Sociology, University of Michigan
Gary B. Rush, Department of Sociology, Simon Fraser University
William Simon, Institute for Sex Research, Indiana University
James K. Skipper, Jr., Department of Sociology, Case Western Reserve University
Thomas S. Szasz, M.D., College of Medicine, State University of New York
Austin T. Turk, Department of Sociology, Indiana University
Ralph H. Turner, Department of Sociology, University of California at Los
    Angeles
Martin S. Weinberg, Department of Sociology, Rutgers University
Eugene P. Wenninger, Department of Sociology, Kent State University
George H. Wolkon, School of Applied Social Sciences, Case Western Reserve
    University

viii

Contents

APPROACHES
TO DEVIANCE

I

Toward Defining the Field

Perhaps one of the more frustrating problems confronting students of social science is the challenge of discerning the criteria by which special fields, areas, or even disciplines are differentiated one from the other. There is so much obvious overlap between and among the substantive branches of sociology and social psychology that labels often appear to be more the result of convenient jurisdictional treaties than outcomes of a logically ordered classification. Neither extreme is correct —nor is the search for "hard" criteria necessarily fruitful. The matter of defining fields of study is best viewed as a dynamic process involving shifting interests, foci, and perspectives and a constant recognition of potential contributions from a diversity of sources. Each article in this part represents a distinctly different facet of the study of deviance, but taken together they provide a sense of the process involved in defining the field.

C. Wright Mills' "The Professional Ideology of Social Pathologists" was published initially in 1943. The article is both a review and an indictment of the study of deviant behavior to that time. In objecting to the value bias attending the conceptualization of deviance as social pathology, Mills' arguments regarding normative judgments are as relevant today as they were 25 years ago.

The concept of "social disorganization" has played a vital role in sociological theories on deviance behavior and has been instrumental in prompting definitions of deviance as violations of social norms and expectations. The selection by Turner, however, suggests that conceptualizing social behavior as conformity to or as deviations from norms is analytically restricting. He argues that far greater attention must be paid to the *values* that are held by actors in given situations.

In a critical sense Robert K. Merton's "Social Structure and Anomie" provided the theoretical antidote for the difficulties which the Mills' article articulated. In this now classic essay, Merton forcefully showed how deviant behavior may be explained as a function of the properties of social systems rather than as the exclusive manifestation of personal or psychological maladjustments.

In recent years key formulations of the dimensions of deviance have

1

tended to eschew earlier concerns with questions of etiology and have tended instead to place great emphasis on the importance of viewing deviants and deviant behavior as products of social definition or labeling. Although he acknowledges the importance of such notions, Jack P. Gibbs warns against the premature translation of concepts into explanatory theories.

The selection by Albert J. Reiss pursues still another direction for the study of deviance by cogently pointing to and well supporting the proposition that the deviant behavior of *organizations* is perhaps a more appropriate sociological interest than the traditional concern with deviant patterns of individuals.

The final two selections in this part are concerned with a specific type of deviant behavior—mental illness—and serve to indicate not only the relevance of theories and conceptualizations for real and major social problems but also the great disparity between and among the theorists themselves. Shirley S. Angrist is concerned with the special contribution the sociology of deviance might make to a better understanding of mental illness while Thomas S. Szasz, a psychiatrist, dramatically proposes that the concept of mental illness is mythical and ought to be abandoned altogether.

1

C. Wright Mills

The Professional Ideology of Social Pathologists

An analysis of textbooks in the field of social disorganization reveals a common style of thought which is open to social imputation. By grasping the social orientation of this general perspective we can understand why thinkers in this field should select and handle problems in the manner in which they have.

By virtue of the mechanism of sales and distribution, textbooks tend to embody a content agreed upon by the academic group using them. In some cases texts have been written only after an informal poll was taken of professional opinion as to what should be included, and other texts are consulted in the writing of a new one. Since one test of their success is wide adoption, the very spread of the public for which they are written tends to insure a textbook tolerance of the commonplace. Although the conceptual framework of a pathologist's textbook is not usually significantly different from that of such monographs as he may write, this essay is not concerned with the "complete thought" or with the "intentions" of individual authors; it is a study of a professional ideology variously exhibited in a set of textbooks.[1] Yet, because

Reprinted from *The American Journal of Sociology,* Vol 49, September 1943, pp. 165–180, by permission of The University of Chicago Press. Copyright 1943 by the University of Chicago Press.
[1] No attempt has been made to trace specific concepts to their intellectual origins. Only elements admitted into the more stable textbook formulations have come within my view: the aim is to grasp typical perspectives and key concepts. Hence, no one of the texts to be quoted exemplifies *all* the concepts analyzed; certain elements are not so visible in given texts as in others, and some elements are not evidenced in certain texts at all. In general, the documentary quotations which follow in footnotes are from the later editions of the following books: W. G. Beach and E. E. Walker, *American Social Problems* (1934); J. H. S. Bossard, (*a*) *Social Change and Social*

of its persistent importance in the development of American sociology
and its supposed proximity to the social scene, "social pathology" seems
an appropriate point of entry for the examination of the style of reflection and the social-historical basis of American sociology.

The level of abstraction which characterizes these texts is so low
that often they seem to be empirically confused for lack of abstraction
to knit them together.[2] They display bodies of meagerly connected
facts, ranging from rape in rural districts to public housing, and intellectually sanction this low level of abstraction.[3] The "informational" character of social pathology is linked with a failure to consider total social
structures. Collecting and dealing in a fragmentary way with scattered
problems and facts of milieux, these books are not focused on larger
stratifications or upon structured wholes. Such an omission may not be
accounted for merely in terms of a general "theoretical weakness." Such
structural analyses have been available; yet they have not been attended to or received into the tradition of this literature. American sociologists have often asserted an interest in the "correlation of the social

---

Problems (1934) and (b) Problems of Social Well-Being (1927); C. H. Cooley, (a)
The Social Process (1918), (b) Human Nature and the Social Order (1902, 1922),
(c) Social Organization (1909); Edward T. Devine, (a) The Normal Life (1915,
1924), (b) Progressive Social Action (1933); R. C. Dexter, Social Adjustment (1927);
G. S. Dow, Society and Its Problems (1920, 1929); M. A. Elliott and F. E. Merrill,
Social Disorganization (1934, 1941); C. A. Ellwood, (a) The Social Problem, a Constructive Analysis (1915, 1919); (b) Sociology and Modern Social Problems (1910–35);
H. P. Fairchild, Outline of Applied Sociology (1916, 1921); M. P. Follett, (a) The
New State (1918), (b) Creative Experience (1924); James Ford, Social Deviation
(1939); J. M. Gillette and J. M. Reinhardt, Current Social Problems (1933, 1937);
J. L. Gillin, (a) Poverty and Dependence (1921, 1926, 1937), (b) Social Pathology
(1933, 1939); J. L. Gillin, C. G. Dittmer, and R. J. Colbert, Social Problems (1928,
1932); E. C. Hayes, editor's introductions to texts in the "Lippincott Series"; W. J.
Hayes and I. V. Shannon, Visual Outline of Introductory Sociology (1935); G. B.
Mangold, Social Pathology (1932, 1934); H. A. Miller, Races, Nations, and Classes
(1924); H. W. Odum, Man's Quest for Social Guidance: The Study of Social Problems
(1927); Maurice Parmelee, Poverty and Social Progress (1916); H. A. Phelps, Contemporary Social Problems (1932, 1933, 1938); S. A. Queen and J. R. Gruener, Social
Pathology (1940); S. A. Queen, W. B. Bodenhafer, and E. B. Harper, Social Organization and Disorganization (1935); C. M. Rosenquist, Social Problems (1940); U. G.
Weatherly, Social Progress (1926).

[2] See Read Bain, "The Concept of Complexity," Social Forces, VIII, pp. 222 and 369.
K. Mannheim has called this type "isolating empiricism" ("German Sociology," Politica,
February, 1934, p. 30).

[3] H. P. Fairchild, p. vii: "Dealing with applied sociology [this book] devotes itself
to facts rather than to theories." James H. S. Bossard (a), p. xi: "In [Problems of
Social Well-Being] an effort was made to consider chiefly in a factual vein, certain
elements which seemed of basic importance. . . ." G. B. Mangold, p. viii: "The author
has tried to select that which [of factual material] best illustrates problems and practical situations."

The quotations in the footnotes are merely indications of what is usual. The
imputations presented must be held against the reader's total experience with the
literature under purview.

sciences;" nevertheless, academic departmentalization may well have been instrumental in atomizing the problems which they have addressed.[4] Sociologists have always felt that "not many representatives of the older forms of social science are ready to admit that there is a function for sociology."[5] However, neither lack of theoretical ability nor restrictive channeling through departmentalization constitutes a full explanation of the low level of abstraction and the accompanying failure to consider larger problems of social structure.

If the members of an academic profession are recruited from similar social contexts and if their backgrounds and careers are relatively similar, there is a tendency for them to be uniformly set for some common perspective. The common conditions of their profession often seem more important in this connection than similarity of extraction. Within such a generally homogeneous group there tend to be fewer divergent points of view which would clash over the meaning of facts and thus give rise to interpretations on a more theoretical level.[6]

The relatively homogeneous extraction and similar careers of American pathologists is a possible factor in the low level of abstraction characterizing their work. All the authors considered[7] (except one, who was foreign born) were born in small towns, or on farms near small towns, three-fourths of which were in states not industrialized during the youth of the authors. The social circles and strata in which they have severally moved are quite homogeneous; all but five have participated in similar "reform" groups and "societies" of the professional and business classes. By virtue of their being college professors (all but three are known to have the Ph.D.), of the similar type of temporary positions (other than academic) which they have held, of the sameness of the "societies" to which they have belonged and of the social positions of the persons whom they have married, the assertion as regards general

[4] In Germany the academic division of specialties prior to the rise of sociology channeled sociological work into a formal emphasis. In America a somewhat comparable situation led to a fragmentalization of empirical attention and especially to a channeling of work into "practical problems."

[5] A. W. Small, *American Journal of Sociology*, May, 1916, p. 785, citing an editorial in the *American Journal of Sociology*, 1907.

[6] Such "homogeneity" is not, however, the only condition under which some common style of thought is taken on by a group of thinkers. Compare the formal conception of "points of coincidence" advanced by H. H. Gerth in *Die sozialgeschichtliche Lage der burgerlichen Intelligenz um die Wende des 18 Jahrhunderts* (diss., Frankfurt A.M.) (V.D.I-Verlag, G.m.b.H. Berlin, N.W. 7). The entire question of the grounding of imputations in terms of social extraction and career-lines is an unfinished set of methodological issues. In this paper the major imputations advanced do *not* proceed upon career data as much as upon the social orientation implied by general perspectives and specific concepts, and by the selection of "problems."

[7] Information concerning twenty-four of the thirty-two authors was full enough to be considered. Five of the eight not considered were junior authors collaborating with persons who are included.

similarity of social extraction, career, and circles of contact seems justified.[8]

A further determinant of the level of abstraction and lack of explicit systematization (beyond which the mentality we are examining does not easily or typically go) is the immediate purpose and the type of public for which they have presumably written. They have been teachers and their specific public has been college students: this had influenced the content and direction of their intellectual endeavors.[9] Teaching is a task which requires a type of systematization to which the textbook answers. Most of the "systematic" or "theoretical" work in "social pathology" has been performed by teachers in textbooks for academic purposes.[10] The fact that sociology often won its academic right to existence in opposition to other departments may have increased the necessity for *textbook* systematization. Such systematization occurs in a context of presentation and of justification rather than within a context of discovery.[11] The textbook writing and the academic profession of the writers thus figure in the character and function of systematic theory within the field.[12] Systematization of facts for the purpose of making them accessible to collegiate minds is one thing; systematization which is oriented toward crucial growing-points in a research process is quite another. An attempt to systematize on the level of the textbook makes for a taxonomic gathering of facts and a systematization of them under concepts that have already been logically defined.[13] The research possibilities

[8] The order of their respective experience has not been systematically considered. All career data on contemporary persons should be held tentatively: open to revision by knowledge not now publicly available.

[9] See above. A. W. Small, p. 754: ". . . the mental experience of the teacher-explorer in the course of arriving at the present outlook of sociologists . . . has also been due to the fact that many of the advances in perception or expression have been in the course of attempts to meet students' minds at their precise point of outlook." See C. Wright Mills, "Language, Logic, and Culture," *American Sociological Review*, October, 1939, for mechanisms involved in such determinations of the thinker by his public.

[10] This statement, as is widely recognized, holds in a measure for all American sociology. Cf., e.g., Pitirim Sorokin, "Some Contrasts in Contemporary European and American Sociology," *Social Forces*, September, 1929, pp. 57–58. "In America sociology has grown as a child nursed by the universities and colleges. . . . American literature in sociology has been composed largely out of textbooks."

[11] Cf. Hans Reichenbach, *Experience and Prediction*, chap. i. See P. Sorokin's comment, *op. cit.*, p. 59.

[12] J. L. Gillin (a), p. v: "My years of experience as a social worker and teacher have gone into the content and method of presentation." J. H. S. Bossard (a), p. 759: "In the preceding chapters, problems have been grouped on the basis of one underlying fact or condition. Obviously, this is an arbitrary procedure which can be justified only on the basis of pedagogical experience"; p. xi: "The . . . is the method followed. . . . By way of defense, this seems simpler and pedagogically preferable"; p. xii: "The decision to omit them was made . . . second, because in an increasing number of colleges and universities, these particular fields are dealt with in separate courses."

[13] Cf. Fritz Mauthner, *Aristotle*, for the pedagogic character of the taxonomic logic of Aristotle. H. P. Fairchild, pp. 6–7: ". . . the essential features of the scientific

of concepts are not as important as is the putting of the accumulated factual details into some sort of order.

But, even though the perspectives of these texts are usually not explicit, the facts selected for treatment are not "random." One way to grasp the perspective within which they do lie is to analyze the scope and character of their problems. What, then, are the selecting and organizing principles to be extracted from the range and content of these texts? What types of fact come within their field of attention?

The direction is definitely toward particular "practical problems"— problems of "everyday life."[14] The ideal of practicality, of not being "utopian," operated, in conjunction with other factors, as a polemic against the "philosophy of history" brought into American sociology by men trained in Germany; this polemic implemented the drive to lower levels of abstraction. A view of isolated and immediate problems as the "real" problems may well be characteristic of a society rapidly growing and expanding, as America was in the nineteenth century and, ideologically, in the early twentieth century. The depictive mode of speech and the heavy journalistic "survey" are intellectual concomitants of an expanding society in which new routines are rising and cities are being built.[15] Such an approach is then sanctioned with canons of what constitutes real knowledge; the practice of the detailed and complete empiricism of the survey is justified by an epistemology of gross description. These norms of adequate knowledge linger in an academic

method . . . are three in number. First, the accumulation of facts. . . . Second, the arrangement or classification of these facts according to some predetermined logical basis of classification. . . ." J. H. S. Bossard (a), p. 34: "It is the present contention that the scientific study of social problems which confines itself to mere description and classification serves a useful purpose."

14 M. A. Elliott, *American Sociological Review*, June, 1941, p. 317: "The only problems which need concern the sociologists' theories and research are the real, practical problems of everyday living." Queen and Gruener, p. 42: "[In contradistinction to scientific problems] social problems . . . pertain directly to everyday life. . . . Their concern is usually 'practical,' and often personal." J. H. S. Bossard (a), p. 32: "Frankly, applied sociology is utilitarian. It is concerned with practical problems and purposes." Gillette and Reinhardt, p. 22: "The study of social problems constitutes the heart of sociology as a science. . . . Even so-called 'pure' sociology, or theoretical sociology, more and more devotes itself to these practical problems of society."

On the other hand, such writers as Ellwood, rising to a *very* high level of abstraction, conceive *formally* of "the social problem." C. A. Ellwood (a), pp. 13–14: "Some of us, at least, are beginning to perceive that the social problem is now, what it has been in all ages, namely, *the problem of the relations of men to one another*. It is the problem of human living together, and cannot be confined to any statement in economic, eugenic or other one-sided terms . . . it is as broad as humanity and human nature. . . . Such a statement [in terms of one set of factors] obscures the real nature of the problem, and may lead to dangerous, one-sided attempts at its solution." In terms of social and intellectual orientation, both ways of conceiving of "social problems" are similar in that neither is of a sort usable in collective action which proceeds against, rather than well within, more or less tolerated channels.

15 See H. D. Lasswell, *Politics* (1936), p. 148; K. Mannheim, *op. cit.*, pp. 30–31; and *Ideology and Utopia*, pp. 228–29.

tradition to mold the work of its bearers. The emphasis upon fragmentary,[16] practical problems tends to atomize social objectives. The
studies so informed are not integrated into designs comprehensive
enough to serve collective action, granted the power and intent to realize such action.

One of the pervasive ways of defining "problems" or of detecting
"disorganization" is in terms of *deviation from norms*. The "norms" so
used are usually held to be the standards of "society." Later we shall
see to what type of society they are oriented. In the absence of studies
of specific norms themselves this mode of problematization shifts the responsibility of "taking a stand" away from the thinker and gives a
"democratic" rationale to his work.[17] Rationally, it would seem that
those who accept this approach to "disorganization" would immediately
examine these norms themselves. It is significant that, given their interest in reforming society, which is usually avowed, these writers typically assume the norms which they use and often tacitly sanction
them.[18] There are few attempts to explain deviations from norms in
terms of the norms themselves, and no rigorous facing of the implications of the fact that social transformations would involve shifts *in them*.

The easy way to meet the question of why norms are violated is in
terms of biological impulses which break through "societal restrictions."
A paste-pot eclectic psychology provides a rationale for this facile analy-

[16] Gillin, Dittmer, and Colbert, p. 44: "There are hundreds of social problems,
big and little." Queen and Gruener, p. 171: "We present here some of the problems
of day by day living encountered by diabetics and cardiacs." J. H. S. Bossard (a),
p. 33: "Certain particular social problems are coming to be reserved for applied
sociology. Their selection has been determined less by logic or principle than by
accident and historical development"; p. 44: "The more one deals with life's problems
at first hand, the more one is impressed with their concreteness, their specificity, and
their infinite variety." Gillette and Reinhardt, p. 14: "From almost any point of view
there must be a large number of social problems today"; p. 15: "This book is a treatise
on a large number of social problems. It does not claim to consider them all. It repeatedly recognizes the plurality of problems in its treatment of the great problems."
[17] C. M. Rosenquist, p. 19: ". . . popular recognition of any social condition or
process as bad, followed by any attempt to eliminate or cure it, serves as a criterion for
its inclusion in a study of social problems. The writer merely accepts the judgment
of public opinion. This is the method to be followed in this book." E. T. Devine (a),
in Note to the Second Edition: "The object of Social Economy is that each shall be
able to live as nearly as possible a normal life according to the standard of the period
and the community."
[18] C. M. Rosenquist, p. 19: "Perhaps we may be on solid ground through a
recognition of the capitalist system and its accompaniments as normal. We may then
deal with its several parts, treating as problems those which do not function smoothly.
This, it seems, is what the more reputable sociologist actually does." H. P. Fairchild,
p. 59: ". . . some of the social conditions which are the natural and consistent outcome
of an individualistic-capitalistic organization of industry, and hence are to be considered as normal in modern societies." Examination of discussions of such items as
poverty in most of the texts confirms this assertion. J. L. Gillin (a), p. 495: "For
serious depressions carefully planned unemployment relief schemes should be formulated before the depression is felt."

sis.[19] Thus, more comprehensive problematization is blocked by a biological theory of social deviation. And the "explanation" of deviations can be put in terms of a requirement for more "socialization." "Socialization" is either undefined, used as a moral epithet, or implies norms which are themselves without definition. The focus on "the facts" takes no cognizance of the normative structures within which they lie.

The texts tend either to be "apolitical"[20] or to aspire to a "democratic" opportunism.[21] When the political sphere is discussed, its pathological phases are usually stated in terms of "the anti-social," or of "corruption," etc.[22] In another form the political is tacitly identified with the proper functioning of the current and unexamined political order; it is especially likely to be identified with a legal process or the administration of laws.[23] If the "norms" were examined, the investigator would perhaps be carried to see total structures of norms and to relate these to distributions of power. Such a structural point of sight is not usually achieved. The level of abstraction does not rise to permit examination of these normative structures themselves, or of why they

[19] That is, an eclecticism that does not analyze in any adequate way the elements and theories which it seeks to combine. Cf. Reuter's critique, *American Journal of Sociology,* November, 1940, pp. 293–304.

[20] E. C. Hayes in the Introduction to H. A. Miller, p. x: "Not political action, the inadequacy of which Professor Eldridge (*Political Action*) has shown, nor revolution, the pathological character of which Professor Sorokin has demonstrated, but social interaction, the causal efficiency of human relationships, is the predominant factor in securing both order and progress."

[21] J. H. S. Bossard (a), pp. 14–15: "The constructive approach . . . may be summarized in one sentence: It is always possible to do something. . . . Such an approach represents in welfare work that hopelessly incurable optimism which in political life we call democracy." Gillette and Reinhardt, pp. 16–17: "There are no certain rules to be followed step by step in the discovery of the solution. Our best recourse is to employ scientific methods rigidly at every step . . . because of uncertain factors always present, we never can be sure that our conclusions are more than approximations of the truth. . . . Since we cannot completely control their activities . . . our cures must be partial and approximate." One type of link between democratic ideology and social pathology is shown in the following quotation, wherein a condition that deviates from the former is called pathological; the quotation also indicates a typical shying-away from all orders of domination other than that type legitimated traditionally, which is left open: H. A. Miller, p. 32: "When certain . . . psycho-pathological conditions are found, we may postulate an abnormal relationship as a cause . . . the particular form of pathology which is involved in our problem may be called the *oppression psychosis.* Oppression is the domination of one group by another." G. V. Price, reviewing Queen and Gruener, *Social Forces,* May, 1941, p. 566: "Without using the word democracy in the doctrinal sense the authors have shown what its utilities are in reducing pathologies."

[22] M. A. Elliott and F. Merrill, p. 28: "The pathological phases of the political process include such anti-social behavior as delinquency, crime, disorder, revolt, and revolution. Corrupt political activity is an important example of such malfunctioning."

[23] Note the identification of "political action" with legislation: Gillin, Dittmer, and Colbert, p. 94: "It is an American practice to attempt to solve any and every sort of social problem through political action. As a result, our statute-books are loaded with 'dead-letter' laws that are not enforced simply because public opinion does not respect them, nor does it feel responsible for them."

come to be transgressed, or of their political implications. Instead, this literature discusses many kinds of apparently unrelated "situations."

About the time W. I. Thomas stated the vocabulary of the situational approach, a social worker was finding it congenial and useful. In M. E. Richmond's influential *Social Diagnosis* (1917) we gain a clue as to why pathologists tend to slip past structure to focus on isolated situations, why there is a tendency for problems to be considered as problems of individuals,[24] and why sequences of situations were not seen as linked into structures:

> Social diagnosis . . . . may be described as the attempt to make as exact a definition as possible of the situation and personality of a human being in some social need—of his situation and personality, that is, in relation to the other human beings upon whom he in any way depends or who depend upon him, and in relation also to the social institutions of his community.[25]

This kind of formulation has been widely applied to isolated "problems" addressed by sociologists.[26] And the "situational approach" has an affinity with other elements which characterize their general perspective.[27]

Present institutions train several types of persons—such as judges and social workers—to think in terms of "situations."[28] Their activities and mental outlook are set within the existent norms of society; in their professional work they tend to have an occupationally trained incapacity to rise above series of "cases." It is in part through such concepts as "situation" and through such methods as "the case approach"[29] that social pathologists have been intellectually tied to social work with its occupational position and political limitations. And, again, the similarity of origin and the probable lack of any continuous "class experience" of the group of thinkers decrease their chances to see social structures rather than a scatter of situations. The mediums of experience and

[24] J. L. Gillin (*a*), p. 13: "Experience shows that rehabilitation is possible only when each case of poverty or dependency is taken separately and its difficulties handled with strict regard for all the attendant circumstances. . . . It must be done in terms of the individual, for . . . it cannot be done *en masse.*"

[25] Richmond, p. 357; see also pp. 51 and 62.

[26] J. H. S. Bossard (*a*), p. 3: "Social problems consist of (*a*) a social situation, (*b*) which are . . . a product of group life." Gillette and Reinhardt, p. 15: "A social problem is a situation, confronting a group. . . ."

[27] J. H. S. Bossard (*a*), p. 57: ". . . the emphasis in our social thinking upon the situation as a unit of experience, as 'an aggregate of interactive and interdependent factors of personality and circumstance' is in essence a recognition of the idea of the emergent. . . . Queen recognizes the implications of the situational approach very clearly in these words: 'For purposes of sociological analysis, a situation consists in relationships between persons viewed as a cross section of human experience, constantly changing. . . . Thus we make of the concept "situation" an intellectual tool' " (S. Queen, "Some Problems of the Situational Approach," *Social Forces,* June, 1931, p. 481).

[28] See K. Mannheim, *Man and Society,* p. 305.

[29] Queen, Bodenhafer, and Harper, p. viii: Editor's Note by S. Eldridge: "The present volume . . . features the case approach to social problems."

orientation through which they respectively view society are too similar, too homogeneous, to permit the clash of diverse angles which, through controversy, might lead to the construction of a whole.

The paramount fact of immigration in American culture, with each wave of immigrants displacing the lower-class position of former waves and raising the position of the earlier immigrants, also tends to obscure structural and class positions.[30] Thus, instead of positional issues, pathologists typically see problems in terms of an individual, such as an immigrant, "adjusting" to a milieu[31] or being "assimilated" or Americanized. Instead of problems of class structure involving immigration, the tendency has been to institute problems in terms of immigration involving the nationalist assimilation of individuals. The fact that some individuals have had opportunities to rise in the American hierarchy decreases the chance fully to see the ceilings of class. Under these conditions such structures are seen as fluctuating and unsubstantial and are likely to be explained not in terms of *class position* but in terms of *status attitudes*.[32]

Another element that tends to obviate an analytic view of structure is the emphasis upon the "processual" and "organic" character of society. In Cooley, whose influence on these books is decisive, one gets a highly formal, many-sided fluidity where "nothing is fixed or independent, everything is plastic and takes influence as well as gives it."[33] From the standpoint of political action, such a view may mean a reformism dealing with masses of detail and furthers a tendency to be apolitical. There can be no bases or points of entry for larger social action in a structureless flux. The view is buttressed epistemologically with an emotionalized animus against "particularism" and with the intense approval of the safe, if colorless, "multiple-factor" view of causation.[34] The liberal "multiple-factor" view does not lead to a conception of causation which would permit points of entry for broader types of action, especially political action.[35] No set of underlying structural shifts is given which might be open to manipulation, at key points, and which, like the fact of private property in a corporate economy, might be

30 Note the lack of structure in the conception of "class": Gillette and Reinhardt, p. 177: "Viewing the matter historically, then, it appears that the chief cause of rigid *class systems* of society with their attendant evils is the prolonged concentration of wealth in the hands of a relatively few persons."

31 See below, the concept of "adjustment."

32 Gillin, Dittmer, and Colbert, p. 59: "The most fundamental cause of class and group conflict is the attitude of superiority on the part of one class, or group, toward another."

33 *The Social Process*, pp. 44–45.

34 Elliott and Merrill, p. 38: "One of the most significant concepts in the understanding of social problems is the idea of multiple causation."

35 See above comments on political relevance. C. A. Ellwood (*b*) p. 324: "We may, perhaps, sum up this chapter by saying that it is evident that the cure of poverty is not to be sought merely in certain economic rearrangements, but in scientific control

seen as efficacious in producing many "problems." If one fragmentalizes society into "factors," into elemental bits, naturally one will then need quite a few of them to account for something,[36] and one can never be sure they are all in. A formal emphasis upon "the whole" plus lack of total structural consideration plus a focus upon scattered situations does not make it easy to reform the status quo.

The "organic" orientation of liberalism has stressed all those social factors which tend to a harmonious balance of elements.[37] There is a minimization of chances for action in a social milieu where "there is always continuity with the past, and not only with any one element only of the past, but with the whole interacting organism of man."[38] In seeing everything social as continuous process, changes in pace and revolutionary dislocations are missed[39] or are taken as signs of the "pathological." The formality and the assumed unity implied by "the mores" also lower the chances to see social chasms and structural dislocations.

Typically, pathologists have not attempted to construct a structural whole. When, however, they do consider totalities, it is in terms of such concepts as "society," "the social order," or "the social organization," "the mores and institutions," and "American culture." Four things should be noted about their use of such terms: (a) The terms represent undifferentiated entities. Whatever they may indicate, it is systematically homogeneous. Uncritical use of such a term as "the" permits a writer the hidden assumption in politically crucial contexts of a homogeneous and harmonious whole.[40] The large texture of "the society" will take care of itself, it is somehow and in the long run harmonious,[41] it has

---

of the whole life process of human society. This means that in order to get rid of poverty, the defects in education, in government, in religion and morality, in philanthropy, and even in physical heredity, must be got rid of. Of course, this can only be done when there is a scientific understanding of the conditions necessary for normal human social life."

[36] J. L. Gillin (a), pp. 51–128: ". . . the modern theory of the causes of poverty has passed beyond any one-sided explanation to a many-sided theory." The following conditions of poverty and dependence are discussed: poor natural resources, adverse climate, adverse weather, insect pests, disasters, illness and diseases, physical inheritance, mental inheritance, adverse surroundings of children, death or disability of the earner, unemployment, lack of proper wages, traditions, customs, habits, advertising and installment buying, fluctuations between costs of living and income, inequitable distribution of wealth and income, family marital relations, political conditions, unwise philanthropy, etc. After these discussions, *family cases* are presented as ". . . studies in causation."

[37] Whereas many socialist theories have tended to overlook the elastic elements that do exist in a society. Cf. K. Mannheim, *Politica*, pp. 25–26.

[38] C. H. Cooley (a), p. 46.

[39] See Max Lerner, *It Is Later than You Think*, pp. 14–15; and *Encyclopaedia of the Social Sciences*, article "Social Process." See documentation and consequences below.

[40] Gillin, Dittmer, and Colbert, p. 11: "All this group life is nicely woven into a system that we call society. . . ."

[41] *Ibid.*, p. 15: "But the aim of society is ever directed to the task of bringing uniform advantages to all." C. A. Ellwood (b), p. 395: "Social organization may refer

a "strain toward consistency" running through it;[42] or, if not this, then only the co-operation of all is needed,[43] or perhaps even a right moral feeling is taken as a solution.[44] (b) In their formal emptiness these terms are commensurate with the low level of abstration. Their *formality* facilitates the empirical concern with "everyday" problems of (community) milieu. (c) In addition to their "descriptive" use, such terms are used normatively. The "social" becomes a good term when it is used in ethical polemics against "individualism" or against such abstract moral qualities as "selfishness," lack of "altruism," or of "antisocial" sentiments.[45] "Social" is conceived as a "co-operative" "sharing" of something or as "conducive to the general welfare."[46] The late eighteenth-century use of "society" as against "state" by the rising bourgeoisie had

---

to any condition or relation of the elements of a social group; but by social order we mean a settled and harmonious relation between the individuals or the parts of a society. The problem of social order is then the problem of harmonious adaptation among the individuals of the group. . . ."

[42] It is significant that it was Summer, with his tacit belief in "natural" order, who set forth the phrase and what it implies.

[43] Gillin, Dittmer, and Colbert, p. 13: "Since a community is made up of a number of neighborhoods, it is necessary that all cooperate in order to secure better schools, improved. . . ."

[44] J. L. Gillin (a), p. 133: "Only as a passion for social righteousness takes the place of an imperative desire for selfish advantage . . . will society do away with the conditions that now depress some classes of the population and exhalt others."

[45] C. A. Ellwood (b), p. 84: ". . . increasing altruism is necessary for the success of those more and more complex forms of cooperation which characterize higher civilization and upon which it depends." G. B. Mangold, p. 17: "Without the spirit of altruism society would be but a sorry exhibition of the collective humanity that we believe has been made in the image of God." Conversely, the "anti-social" is held to include certain abstract, moral traits of individuals. Elliott and Merrill, p. 43: "An analysis of the disorganization process suggests two types of anti-social forces: (1) the consciously directed anti-social forces and (2) the impersonal organic forces which are an outgrowth of the formalism discussed above . . . to advance their own selfish ends. These men are thoroughly aware of their anti-social attitudes. Social values have no meaning for them. . . . There has often been no socializing influence in the lives of those men. . . . Cooperation, or 'mutual aid,' the implicit counterpart of effective social organization. . . . Vice areas . . . function because of human appetites, because individual desires are more deeply rooted than any sense of the social implications. . . . The prostitute exists only because she is a means to man's sensual pleasure and satiety"; p. 44: "Sin, vice, crime, corruption, all consciously directed anti-social forces, offer a primrose. . . ." G. B. Mangold, p. 59: "Unsocial habits lead to poverty; particularly do they degrade poverty into dependency. Chief among these vices is intemperance. Before the advent of prohibition it was. . . ." Queen, Bodenhafer, and Harper, p. 4: "When there is . . . characterized by harmony, teamwork, understanding, approval, and the like, we may speak of organization. When the opposite is true and there is a . . . marked by tension, conflict, or drifting apart, we may speak of disorganization."

[46] Gillin, Dittmer, and Colbert, p. 5: " 'The word [social] means conducive to the collective welfare, and thus becomes nearly equivalent to moral' [Cooley, *Human Nature and the Social Order*, p. 4] . . . it is this . . . meaning that comes closest to our interpretation . . . —'conducive to the collective welfare'—relationships, and products of relationships that are believed to foster and promote *group life,* and to insure *group survival.*"

already endowed "society" with a "democratic" tinge which this literature transmits. (*d*) There is a strong tendency for the term "society"
to be practically assimilated to, or conceived largely in terms of, primary
groups and small homogeneous communities. Such a conception typically characterizes the literature within our purview.[47] In explaining it,
we come upon an element that is highly important in understanding the
total perspective.

The basis of "stability," "order," or "solidarity" is not typically analyzed in these books, but a conception of such a basis is implicitly used
and sanctioned,[48] for some normative conception of a socially "healthy"
and stable organization is involved in the determination of "pathological"
conditions. "Pathological" behavior is not discerned in a *structural* sense
(i.e., as incommensurate with an existent structural type) or in a *statistical* sense (i.e., as deviations from central tendencies). This is evidenced by the regular assertion that pathological conditions *abound*
in the city.[49] If they *"abound"* therein, they cannot be "abnormal" in the

[47] J. L. Gillin (*b*), p. 313: ". . . personal relationships . . . are the most important
ties in the social organization. . . ." C. A. Ellwood (*b*), pp. 3–4: "The tendency in
the best sociological thinking is to emphasize the importance, for the understanding of
our social life, of 'primary' or face-to-face groups"; p. 77: "Primary groups . . . are
of most interest sociologically, because they exhibit social life at its maximum intensity,
and because they are the bearers of the most vital elements in social life, especially
the traditions of civilization"; pp. 79–80: "The chief importance of primary groups
in our social life, however, is that they . . . furnish the 'patterns' which we attempt
to realize in our social life in general"; pp. 84–85: "All human history has, from one
point of view, been a struggle to transfer altruism and solidarity of the family to
successively larger and larger groups of men"; pp. 90–91: "Primary, or face-to-face
groups are the key to the understanding of our social life. . . ." Gillin, Dittmer,
Colbert, p. 282: ". . . the home is probably our most fundamental social institution. . . ."; p. 285: "Anything that endangers the stability of the family endangers
society." J. H. S. Bossard (*a*), p. 555: "Family life is the focal point of virtually all of
our social problems."

[48] C. A. Ellwood (*b*), pp. 79–80: "The very ideal of social solidarity itself comes
from the unity experienced in such [primary] groups." Elliott and Merrill, p. 581:
"An ever-increasing number of persons living in the giant cities has become completely deracinated, cut off from all stable primary ties. They have lost not only their
physical home, but often their spiritual home as well. Social disorganization breeds in
these unattached masses of the urban proletariat. They furnish willing nuclei for robbery, brigandage, and revolution."

[49] J. L. Gillin (*b*), p. 411: "In the city we have a greater degree of disorganization
in the sense in which we use that term"; p. 410: ". . . in the simple and well-organized
ties of country life . . ."; p. 409: "Recreation in the country is largely homemade. . . .
In the city it is professional. . . . The patterns of behavior . . . are here again disorganized and new patterns have to be found." Gillette and Reinhardt, p. 116: "Cities
exhibit all the social problems, save those peculiar to agricultural extractive pursuits."
H. P. Fairchild, p. 304: "Since there are no *natural* facilities available to the majority
of the *denizens* of cities for the gratification of the desire for dancing, it inevitably follows that provision is made on a commercial basis" (my italics). C. M. Rosenquist,
p. 47: "The controls which were effective in the small, settled farm community no
longer suffice in . . . the city. To this fact may be traced many of the conditions we
speak of as social problems. . . ." W. G. Beach and E. E. Walker, pp. 102–3: ". . . men
find their life interests and values in group membership and participation. The most

statistical sense and are not likely to prevail in the structural sense. It may be proposed that the norms in terms of which "pathological" conditions are detected are "humanitarian ideals." But we must then ask for the social orientation of such ideals.[50] In this literature the operating criteria of the pathological are typically *rural* in orientation and extraction.[51]

Most of the "problems" considered arise because of the urban deterioration of certain values which can live genuinely only in a relatively homogeneous and primary rural milieu. The "problems" discussed typically concern urban behavior. When "rural problems" are discussed, they are conceived as due to encroaching urbanization.[52] The notion of disorganization is quite often merely the absence of that *type* of organization associated with the stuff of primary-group communities having Christian and Jeffersonian legitimations.[53]

influential groups are those which provide intimate, face-to-face relationships, as the family, the playground, the club, the neighborhood, and the small community. . . . Any wholesome and satisfying life must provide for a continuation of such small groups and institutional forms. . . . One of the most elusive and challenging problems arising from the growth of cities is that of preventing the complete disorganization of essential social groups. In the rural community. . . ." J. H. S. Bossard (a), p. 113: "The marked trend of population to the city and the rapid rise of large urban centers, together with their reflex upon the rural regions, constitute the basis of virtually every problem to be discussed in this volume."

[50] This is what Waller does *not* do in his provocative discussion of "humanitarian" and "organizing mores" ("Social Problems and the Mores," *American Sociological Review*, December, 1936, pp. 922–33).

[51] J. L. Gillin (b), p. 407: The home "developing as . . . rural" is considered "disorganized" in the city; p. 409: "[In the city] it is only the rebel, unable and unwilling to adjust himself to machine and organization, who retains personal independence. . . . The farmer, conscious that he lives by his own thinking . . . responds to his environment with a feeling of independence—a normal response. The city worker has no keen perception of his dependence upon nature." Elliott and Merrill, p. 32: "However different their approach, the basic dilemma of civilization is the fundamental disparity of values and standards of universally accepted definitions of the situation."

[52] C. A. Ellwood (b), p. 281: "The reflex of the city problem is the rural problem." J. L. Gillen (b), p. 429: "[Urbanization] which has modified the solidarity of the rural family. . . ." W. J. Hayes and I. V. Shannon, p. 22: "Contacts . . . emancipate individuals from control of primary groups . . . this leads to setting up personal norms of behavior instead of conforming to group standards." (Implies no conception of *urban* types of norms.)

[53] The intellectual consequences of the rural to urban drift are much wider than the perspectives noted in the literature of pathology. In more general American sociology the writings of a man like E. A. Ross are to be understood in terms of a reaction of those oriented to a farmer's democracy against the growth of big business, in its control of railroads, etc. Another division of American sociology in which America's rural past is *intellectually* evident is "rural sociology" itself. This field shows the positive side of the matter, for here the yearning for the values associated with rural simplicity and neighborliness is even more noticeable. In this literature a primary, rural heritage is taken as the source of "stability" and is conceived as the reservoir of "values." Such straddling concepts as "urban" function to limit recognition of the urban character of dominant contemporary social structures. In a historical sense we need not argue with these emphases: the underlying form of American democracy and

Cooley, the local colorist of American sociology, was the chief pub-
licist of this conception of normal organization. He held "the great
historical task of mankind" to be the more effective and wider organization of that moral order and pattern of virtues developed in primary
groups and communities.[54] Cooley took the idealists' absolute[55] and
gave it the characteristics of an organic village; all the world should be
an enlarged, Christian-democratic version of a rural village. He practically assimilated "society" to this primary-group community, and he
blessed it emotionally and conceptually.[56] "There is reflected here," says
T. V. Smith of Cooley—and what he says will hold for the typical social
pathologist—"what is highly common in our culture, an ideal of intimacy short of which we do not rest satisfied where other people are
concerned. Social distance is a dire fate, achieved with difficulty and
lamented as highly unideal, not to say as immoral, in our Christian
traditions. It is not enough to have saints; we must have "communion"
of the saints. In order to have social relations, we must nuzzle one
another."[57]

The aim to preserve rurally oriented values and stabilities is indicated by the implicit model which operates to detect urban disorganization; it is also shown by the stress upon *community* welfare. The
community is taken as a major unit, and often it sets the scope of concern
and problematization.[58] It is also within the framework of ideally demo-

---

religion, e.g., has drawn much from the dominance of a rural society. And a rapid
urbanization may well be only a veneer upon masses of rurally oriented personalities.
But the kind of structural stability in America which grew from rural patterns is
historical. In the world today the kind of stability that can—indeed, in part has—
emerged from the hunger for those primary contacts historically associated with ties
of blood and closeness to soil is a streamlined variety.

[54] *Social Organization,* chap. v.

[55] G. H. Mead, "Cooley's Contribution to American Social Thought," *American
Journal of Sociology,* XXXV, 701: "Cooley was Emersonian in finding the individual
self in an oversoul." Cf. G. W. F. Hegel, *Lectures on the Philosophy of History* (London: Geo. Bell & Sons, 1884) , especially pp. 39–44.

[56] Note the common association of urban "impersonality" and "formalism" with
"disorganization." Elliott and Merrill, p. 16: ". . . lack of harmony between the various
units of the social order is in a sense . . . exemplified by the impersonal nature of the
social organization and the consequent process of social disorganization . . . [cf. C. H.
Cooley, *Social Process,* pp. 3–29]"; p. 574: "There is a very close relationship between
formalism and disorganization, although at first glance the two states appear to be
opposite poles in the social process. They are in reality sequential steps in the same
great movement of disorganization, which grows out of formalism. . . ."

[57] *Beyond Conscience,* p. 111.

[58] C. A. Ellwood (b) , p. 12: "All forms of association are of interest to the sociologist, though not all are of equal importance. The natural, genetic social groups, which
we may call 'communities,' serve best to exhibit sociological problems. Through the
study of such simple and primary groups as the family and the neighborhood group,
for example, the problems of sociology can be much better attacked than through the
study of society at large or association in general"; pp. 76–77: ". . . natural groupings,
such as the family, the neighborhood, the city, the state or province, and the nation.
They may be, and usually are, called *communities,* since they are composed of indi-

cratic communities that proposed solutions are to be worked out.[59] It should be noted that sometimes, although not typically or exclusively, solutions are conceived as dependent upon abstract moral traits or democratic surrogates of them, such as a "unanimous public will."[60]

"Cultural lag" is considered by many pathologists to be the concept with which many scattered problems may be detected and systematized. Whereas the approach by deviation from norms is oriented "ideologically" toward a rural type of order and stability, the cultural-lag model is tacitly oriented in a "utopian"[61] and progressive manner toward changing some areas of the culture or certain institutions so as to "integrate" them with the state of progressive technology.[62] We must analyze the use made by pathologists of "lag" rather than abstract formulations of it.[63]

Even though all the situations called "lags" *exist* in the present, their functional realities are referred back, away from the present. Evaluations are thus translated into a time sequence; cultural lag is an assertion of unequal "progress." It tells us what changes are "called for," what changes "ought" to have come about and didn't. In terms of

---

viduals who carry on all phases of a common life. Voluntary, purposive associations always exist within some community, whether large or small. Groups which we call 'communities' are, therefore, more embracing, more stable, less artificial and specialized than purely voluntary groups. For this reason communities are of more interest to the sociologist than specialized voluntary groups, and sociology is in a peculiar sense a study of the problems of community life." J. H. S. Bossard (*a*), pp. 49–50: "Acceptance of the community as a definite unit in social work and in social theory has become general during the past fifteen years. American participation in the World War was an important factor in bringing this about, first because the community constituted the basic expression of that democratic spirit which the war engendered, and second, the community was seized upon by the various war-time activities and drives as the most effective unit for the mobilization of the spirit and resources of the nation."

59 Gillin, Dittmer, and Colbert, p. 15: ". . . *social work,* which means, scientifically developing and adjusting human relations in a way that will secure normal life to individuals and communities and encourage individual and community progress"; p. 47: ". . . it is important to keep in mind that the central problem is that of adjusting our social life and our social institutions, so that, as individuals and as communities, we may use and enjoy the largest measure of civilization possible, and promote further progress." M. P. Follett (*a*), Part III, has suggested that neighborhood groups be organized into political units. This would permit the expression of daily life and bring to the surface live needs that they may become the substance of politics. The neighborhood as a political unit would make possible friendly acquaintance; it would socialize people and would make for "the realization of oneness."

60 J. L. Gillin (*b*), p. 97: "The 'liquor problem' is as acute in the United States today as it ever was in the past, perhaps even more so"; p. 101: "The solution must spring from an aroused and unanimous public will."

61 Cf. K. Mannheim, *Ideology and Utopia,* for definitions of these terms.

62 However, "lag" and "norms" are not unrelated: Queen, Bodenhafer, and Harper, p. 437: "Much of the discussion of cultural lags in the family assumes some kind of normal pattern which is commonly believed to have permanent validity because of the functions performed."

63 See examples given in J. W. Woodard's "Critical Notes on the Cultural Lag Concept," *Social Forces,* March, 1934, p. 388.

various spheres of society it says what progress is, tells us how much we have had, ought to have had, didn't have, and when and where we didn't have it. The imputation of "lag" is complicated by the historical judgment in whose guise it is advanced and by the programmatic content being shoved into pseudo-objective phrases, as, for example, "called for."

It is not enough to recognize that the stating of problems in terms of cultural lag involves evaluations, however disguised. One must find the general loci of this kind of evaluation and then explain why just this form of evaluation has been so readily accepted and widely used by pathologists. The model in which institutions lag behind technology and science involves a positive evaluation of natural science and of orderly progressive change. Loosely, it derives from a liberal continuation of the enlightenment with its full rationalism, its messianic and now politically naïve admiration of physical science as a kind of thinking and activity, and with its concept of time as progress. This notion of progress was carried into American colleges by the once prevalent Scottish moral philosophy. From after the Civil War through the first two or three decades of the twentieth century the expanding business and middle classes were taking over instruments of production, political power, and social prestige; and many of the academic men of the generation were recruited from these rising strata and/or actively mingled with them. Notions of progress are congenial to those who are rising in the scale of position and income.

Those sociologists who think in terms of this model have not typically focused upon the conditions and interest groups underlying variant "rates of change" in different spheres. One might say that in terms of the rates of change at which sectors of culture *could* move, it is technology that is "lagging," for the specific reason of the control of patents, etc., by intrenched interests.[64] In contrast to the pathologists' use, Veblen's use of "lag, leak, and friction" is a structural analysis of industry versus business enterprise.[65] He focused on where "the lag" seemed to pinch; he attempted to show how the trained incapacity of legitimate business-men acting within entrepreneurial canons would result in a commercial sabotage of production and efficiency in order to augment profits within a system of price and ownership. He did not like this "unworkman-like result," and he detailed its mechanism. In the pathologists' usage the conception has lost this specific and structural anchorage: it has been generalized and applied to everything fragmentarily. This generalization occurs with the aid of such blanket terms as "adaptive

[64] See, e.g., B. J. Stern's article in *Annals of the American Academy of Political and Social Science,* November, 1938.
[65] *The Engineers and the Price System; The Theory of Business Enterprise.*

culture" and "material culture."[66] There is no specific focus for a program of action embodied in the application of such terms.

Another model in terms of which disorganizations are instituted is that of "social change" itself.[67] This model is not handled in any one typical way, but usually it carries the implicit assumption that human beings are "adjusted" satisfactorily to any social condition that has existed for a long time and that, when some aspect of social life changes, it may lead to a social problem.[68] The notion is oriented ideologically and yet participates in assumptions similar to those of cultural lag, which, indeed, might be considered a variant of it. Such a scheme for problematization buttresses and is buttressed by the idea of continuous process, commented on above; but here the slow, "evolutionary" pace of change is taken explicitly as normal and organized,[69] whereas "discontinuity" is taken as problematic.[70] The orientation to "rural" types of organization should be recalled. In line with the stress on continuous process, the point where sanctioned order meets advisable change is not typically or structurally drawn.[71] A conception of "balance" is usual and

66 J. H. S. Bossard (a), p. 5: ". . . as Ogburn put it [W. F. Ogburn, *Social Change* (1922)] to the extent that the adaptive culture has not kept pace with the material culture, the amount of social ill-being has increased relatively."

67 J. L. Gillin (b), p. 416: "Social disorganization is a function of rapidly changing conditions in people's lives." W. J. Hayes and I. V. Shannon, p. 20: "Social disorganization is an abrupt break in the existing social arrangements or a serious alteration in the routine of group life causing maladjustment." H. W. Odum, p. 100: ". . . if one reviews the general categories of social problems already listed in previous chapters, it must be clear that most of them or their present manifestations are due to or accentuated by the process of social change."

68 The point is made and acutely discussed by Rosenquist, pp. 8–10.

69 Gillin, Dittmer, and Colbert, p. 48: "Social life and its products require long periods of time to develop and ripen. . . ." Gillette and Reinhardt, p. 13: "The larger proportion of social changes are small and simple, and resemble osmosis in the field of physics and organic life." This gradualism is related to the orientation to primary group relations and experiences and hence to the "sharing" conception of the social. E.g., Elliott and Merrill, p. 11: "Assimilation, on the other hand, is gradual and depends upon some degree of contact and communication, if there is to be any vital sharing of common experience (Cf. M. P. Follett, *Creative Experience*). . . ."

70 Gillette and Reinhardt, p. 30: ". . . the need for thought about discontinuity in industry or education and about our dependence on proper training to keep society stabilized and progressive should be emphasized"; p. 21: "The habitual, daily, routine, conventional activities of life fortunately make up the greater part of life, most of the time. Often, however, they are broken across by social breakdowns, disturbances, and dislocations and the appearance of troublesome classes of persons." C. A. Ellwood (a), p. 230: ". . . revolution is not a *normal* method of social change; . . . it marks the breakdown of the normal means of social development; . . . it is not inevitable, but may easily be avoided by plasticity in social institutions and in the mental attitudes of classes and individuals. . . ."

71 The notion of temporal contingency, at times extended to the point of historical irrationality, plays into the processual, nonstructural characteristics of the perspective; notice also its commensurability with the apolitical and one-thing-at-a-time reformism. Elliott and Merrill, p. 3: "Life is dynamic. Life is ceaseless, bewildering change, and

sometimes is explicitly sanctioned.[72] The question, "Changes in what spheres induce disorganization?" is left open; the position taken is usually somewhere between extremes, both of which are held to be bad.[73] This comes out in the obvious fact that what a conservative calls *dis*organization, a radical might well call *re*organization. Without a construction of total social structures that are actually emerging, one remains caught between simple evaluations.

Besides deviation from norms, orientation to rural principles of stability, cultural lag, and social change, another conception in terms of which "problems" are typically discussed is that of adaptation or "adjustment" and their opposites.[74] The pathological or disorganized is the maladjusted. This concept, as well as that of the "normal," is usually left empty of concrete, social content;[75] or its content is, in effect, a propaganda for conformity to those norms and traits ideally associated with small-town, middle-class milieux.[76] When it is an individual who is thought to be maladjusted, the "social type" within which he is maladjusted is not stated. Social and moral elements are masked by a quasi-

---

man, armed though he is with the experience of the past, can never be certain of the future. He must recognize that the immediate present is a constantly changing frame of reference and that future problems are a matter of chance for which the past offers no sure panacea."

[72] E. C. Hayes' Editor's Introduction to U. G. Weatherly, p. xii: "Realization that progressive change is not likely to be less in the generation next to come . . . and determination . . . to promote progress, is the normal attitude for every person who is animated by generous loyalty and. . . ." Weatherly, p. 138: "Both innovation and conservatism have their value, and the balance between them, which is an ideal attitude. . . ."; p. 380: "Discipline and liberation are not two antagonistic processes; they are complimentary parts of the same process, which is social equilibration. They illustrate the law of physics . . . stability is reached only by a balance of forces."

[73] A. Ellwood (a), p. vii: "The aim of the book is to indicate the direction which our social thinking must take if we are to avoid revolution, on the one hand, and reactions, on the other."

[74] H. P. Fairchild, p. 35: ". . . it can be safely said that maladjustments are among the most numerous and important of all forms of abnormality, frequently being so extensive as to include entire social groups or classes."

[75] Gillin, Dittmer, and Colbert, p. 536: "All social problems grow out of *the* social problem—the problem of the adjustment of man to his universe, and of the social universe to man. The maladjustments in these relationships give us all our social problems. . . ." H. P. Fairchild, p. 16: "While the word 'normal' carries a fairly definite and, for the most part, accurate implication to the mind of any intelligent person, it is nevertheless extremely difficult to define in concrete terms. . . . As commonly used to convey a definite idea, the word 'normal' means that which is in harmony with the general make-up and organization of the object under discussion—that which is consistent with other normal factors."

[76] Elliott and Merrill, p. 17, correctly assert that in "Edward T. Divine's discussion of 'the normal life' the norm is the healthy and uneventful life cycle of the average middle-class man or woman. These persons are never subjected to the temptations of great wealth. Neither do they come in contact with poverty, crime, vice, and other unpleasantly sordid aspects of life [*The Normal Life*, pp. 5–8]. His discussion is thus a consideration of the 'normal standards' for the several ages of the bourgeoisie. . . ."

biological meaning of the term "adaptation"[77] with an entourage of apparently socially bare terms like "existence" and "survival," which seem still to draw prestige from the vogue of evolutionism.[78] Both the quasi-biological and the structureless character of the concept "adjustment" tend, by formalization, to universalize the term, thus again obscuring specific social content. Use of "adjustment" accepts the goals and the means of smaller community milieux.[79] At the most, writers using these terms suggest techniques or means believed to be less disruptive than others to attain the goals that are given. They do not typically consider whether or not certain groups or individuals caught in economically underprivileged situations can possibly obtain the current goals without drastic shifts in the basic institutions which channel and promote them. The idea of adjustment seems to be most directly applicable to a social scene in which, on the one hand, there is a society and, on the other, an individual immigrant.[80] The immigrant then "ad-

[77] When it is so hidden; but note the heavily sentimental endowment the term may receive: R. C. Dexter, p. 408: ". . . few of the present generation of little ones, and fewer still of the next, will never see the sun or the green grass because of the sins of their parents or the carelessness of their physician; and thanks to our increasing provisions of free public education, more and more adapted to the needs of the individual child, thousands of boys and girls will become intelligent, responsible citizens, worthy of a free nation, instead of pawns for unscrupulous politicians. All this and much more is due to social adjustments, made by the unceasing effort and sacrifice of men and women who. . . ."

[78] J. L. Gillin (b), p. 4: "Social pathology . . . is the study of the social patterns and processes involved in man's failure to adjust himself and his institutions to the necessities of existence to the end that he may survive and satisfy the felt needs of his nature."

[79] J. L. Gillin (b), p. 8: "An individual who does not approximate these [socially approved] standards is said to be unadjusted. If he does not concern himself with living up to them, he is said to be demoralized or disorganized." R. C. Dexter, p. 407: "In this book the term Social Adjustment has been . . . used as applying to . . . the necessary task of smoothing-off the rough edges and softening the sledge-hammer blows of an indifferent social system. The term . . . is practically synonymous with social adaptation—the fitting of man to his complete environment, physical and social alike. Until the present it has been the especially maladjusted individual or group who has received the service of 'straighteners.' " (Note ideological orientation of concept.)

[80] H. P. Fairchild, p. 34: "The other form of incompetence, which may be called 'maladjustment,' does not imply any lack on the part of the individual himself. . . . The man is all right, but he is not in the right place. Our immigrants furnish abundant examples of this form of incompetence. . . . But the foreigner is not by any means the sole example of maladjustment. Our modern life, particularly our modern city life, teems with cases of this sort." J. H. S. Bossard (a), p. 110 (under "The Immigrant's Problem of Adjustment"): "To most persons, life consists in large measure of habitual responses to the demands of a fairly fixed environment. When man changes his environment, new and perhaps untried responses are called for. New adjustments must be made, as we say." J. L. Gillin (b), p. 10: "Social pathology . . . arises out of the maladjustment between the individual and the social structure." Elliott and Merrill, p. 22: "Just as an effective social organization implies a harmony between individual and social interests, so a disorganized social order must involve a conflict between individual and social points of view."

justs" to the new environment. The "immigrant problem" was early in
the pathologist's center of focus, and the concepts used in stating it
may have been carried over as the bases for a model of experience and
formulations of other "problems." *The Polish Peasant* (1918), which
has had a very strong influence on the books under consideration, was
empirically focused upon an immigrant group.

In approaching the notion of adjustment, one may analyze the specific
illustrations of maladjustment that are given and from these instances
infer a type of social person who in this literature is evaluated as "adjusted." The ideally adjusted man of the social pathologists is "socialized." This term seems to operate ethically as the opposite of "selfish";[81]
it implies that the adjusted man conforms to middle-class morality and
motives and "participates" in the gradual progress of respectable institutions. If he is not a "joiner," he certainly gets around and into many
community organizations.[82] If he is socialized, the individual thinks of
others and is kindly toward them. He does not brood or mope about but
is somewhat extravert, eagerly participating in his community's institutions. His mother and father were not divorced, nor was his home
ever broken. He is "successful"—at least in a modest way—since he is
ambitious; but he does not speculate about matters too far above his
means, lest he become "a fantasy thinker," and the little men don't
scramble after the big money. The less abstract the traits and fulfilled
"needs" of "the adjusted man" are, the more they gravitate toward the

[81] Gillin, Dittmer, and Colbert, pp. 16–17: "By *socialization* we mean the directing of human motives toward giving to 'even the least' of the members of the social
whole the benefits of cultural development. Socialization is thus practically the opposite to *aloofness, selfishness, greed, exploitation,* and *profiteering.* It causes the individual and the group to *feel* their *oneness* with the social whole. . . . In brief, what
society regards as *moral,* i.e., good for the whole, becomes the aim of socialized individuals and groups. This being true, the improvement of society rests to a very large
extent upon *moral progress.*"

[82] See Queen and Gruener, *Social Pathology: Obstacles to Social Participation.*
These authors would deny this mode of statement, but such verbal denials must be
tested against what they have done and the framework they have actually employed
in defining pathologies. Their criterion of the pathological is correctly indicated in the
subtitle of their book. Elliott and Merrill, p. 580: "There are various criteria by which
the degree of individual participation may be measured roughly . . . whether or not
he votes at elections . . . the individual's ownership of real or personal property . . .
the degree of specific interest in community activities may be roughly measured by the
number and character of the institutions to which the individual belongs, as well as
the voluntary community activities in which he participates. Communities in which
there is a high percentage of individuals with a positive rating on the items listed
above are logically those which are the most highly organized and efficient." (Note the
character of the institutions, participation in which is defined as organized.)

norms of independent middle-class persons verbally living out Protestant
ideals in the small towns of America.[83]

[83] See above documentation; notice the Protestant ethical accent on *utility* and
what it will do for one, apparently irrespective of social fact: Gillin, Dittmer, and
Colbert, p. 106: "People who are useful, no matter what happens to be their race or
color, come to be liked and respected. Consequently, the central aim of a sound educational program should be to teach people to be useful. (Hart, Hornell, *The Science of
Social Relations*, 1927, pp. 521–524.) " In the following, note the norm of competitive-
ness; Elliott and Merrill, pp. 29–30: "Often, however, the individual cannot or will not
compete. We then have the following pathological manifestations: '. . . the *dependent*
. . . who is unable to compete; the *defective* . . . who is, if not unable, at least handicapped in his efforts to compete. The *criminal*, on the other hand, . . . who is perhaps unable, but at any rate refuses, to compete according to the rules which society
lays down.' (Park and Burgess, *Introduction to the Science of Sociology*, p. 560)."
Among the traits thought to characterize "the good life from the standpoint of the
individual," Odum, pp. 50–51, cites: "patience," "specialized knowledge of some particular thing," "skill," "optimism," "love of work," "dynamic personality," "modera-
tion," "trained will power," etc. Cf., in this connection, K. Davis, "Mental Hygiene and
the Class Structure," *Psychiatry: Journal of the Biology and Pathology of Interpersonal
Relations*, February, 1938, pp. 55–65.

2

Ralph H. Turner

Value-Conflict in Social Disorganization

The idea of value-conflict has played an important part in thinking about social disorganization for several years.[1] At the same time, it has remained an imprecise notion, and the implications of its use as an organizing concept in the study of social disorganization have been little developed. This paper will propose some clarification of the nature of value-conflict, with a view toward rendering it a more effective tool of theory and research.

Before exploring value-conflict, we need to note some distinctive aspects of the social disorganization approach of which it is a part. Social disorganization focuses attention on the harmonious and inharmonious aspects of the structure of society, as such. It is concerned with the ways and degrees to which the activities implicit in the organization of the society are mutually reinforcing or mutually contradictory. Consequently, its concern with the individual is incidental, and individual satisfactions, while they may turn out to be important symptomatically, do not constitute the major criteria of social organization. In the same way, social disorganization is differentiated from the study of conformity and deviancy in individuals, or the degree to which the social norms are effectively followed in individual behavior (social control).

The activities which represent the social structure are most frequently described in terms of "norms" and "values." Social disorganization may

From *Sociology and Social Research*, **38** (May–June 1954), 301–308, by permission of the author and publisher.

[1] Since Lawrence K. Frank's classic statement in "Social Problems," *American Journal of Sociology*, **30**: 462–73, 1925, nearly all sociological writings on the subject have made use of the idea of value-conflict.

then be conceptualized in terms of some conflicts among norms and values in a society. Social disorganization deals with ways in which activities which are in some sense the product of, and legitimatized by, the social structure conflict with one another. Much the same results are obtained by stressing either conflicts among norms or conflicts among values, but it is useful to make a distinction between these two concepts.

Social norms are prescriptions regarding behavior and belief and prohibitions against certain patterns of behavior and belief. They are statements that certain types of behavior and belief should be followed or avoided when such statements are generally accepted in a society and when each individual has the sense that they are generally accepted by others.

Social norms do not generally exist in an unequivocal sense for most activities in the society. What we conceive ideally as social norms tend in practice to be "short-circuited" into social values. Social values are objects which are regarded favorably or unfavorably, in the same manner as described for norms. As objects, values refer to something which can be secured or attained. They constitute attributes or end products of activity. Thus, the usual way of saying that one should tell the truth (norm) is to say that honesty (value) is a good thing.

Values and norms are obverse aspects of the same thing, and in some sense alternative ways of conveying the same meanings. But there are at least two important differences. First, there is generally greater agreement on values in a society than on norms, but the specific behavior meaning of values is less well defined. Thus, there will be general agreement that health, beauty, "character," and money are good things (positive values), but considerable confusion exists over what constitutes beauty and character and what particular responsibilities are imposed on the individual for the attainment of those positive values of health and money.

Second, the concept of social value is somewhat more inclusive than that of social norm. An object may be regarded as worthy of attainment, bringing its possessor social approbation, without there being any sense that others ought to pursue it. One may achieve recognition for special achievements and special attributes of personality because these are regarded as good things by the society. But it would be hard to find a norm declaring that one should develop skill at playing baseball or collecting rare manuscripts, to correspond with the value which these activities constitute.

We shall choose to consider social disorganization primarily as conflict of values, rather than of norms. We gain thereby a more inclusive framework and one closer to the reality of the loose ordering of even the society with the least number of cultural "alternatives."

Conflict of Values: Difficulties of Application

Social disorganization may be conceived as a state of conflict among
social values.[2] This means that certain socially sanctioned values are
unattainable in practice without violation or interference with the attainment of other social values, also socially sanctioned. Such conflicts
exist either among values adhered to by all members and groups in the
society or among values belonging to different subgroups in the society.
In the latter instance, different groups within the society may seek
values which are mutually contradictory, so that the activities of each
group are interfered with by the activities of other groups. The clearest
example of this type of conflict may be found in the existence of ethnic
groups with diverse values and of economic classes with values which
contradict those of other classes. But values which are generally accepted by most members and groups within the society may also come
in conflict, as in the general acceptance of individualistic competition
as a positive good at the same time that humanitarian cooperation is
also regarded as a positive value in American society.[3] The problem in
this instance is not that one group is exclusively identified with one
of these values and another group with the other, but rather that all
groups accept both values in general.

Confusion immediately arises in applying the value-conflict framework, however, if the sense in which values come into conflict is not
clarified. We must distinguish between *logical* incompatibility of values
and incompatibility in *application*. A subject for adolescent debate is the
supposed conflict between the values of honesty and humanitarianism
when the doctor gives a patient a rosier picture of his health than the
facts justify. It is argued that complete honesty might kill the patient
and that humanitarian values require dishonesty. One must violate
one value in adhering to the other. But such discussions are purely
recreational. The normally socialized person in our society encounters
such a situation with no sense of having to make a crucial choice, nor
does he feel guilt over having violated his values of honesty. The approved course of action is clear, the individual experiences no conflicting
imperatives or indecision, and there is no major group sanction for the
course of pure honesty in this situation. Thus, there is certainly a logical
contradiction between these values in such a situation, but there is no
contradiction in application. The orderly functioning of the society is not

[2] The present discussion should be compared with Robert C. Angell's treatment of
"moral integration" in terms of compatibility and adequacy of social norms. Angell
does not escape the difficulties discussed below, however. See Robert C. Angell, *The
Moral Integration of American Cities* (Chicago: University of Chicago Press, 1951),
especially pp. 115–22.

[3] Kingsley Davis, Harry C. Bredemeier, and Marion J. Levy, Jr., *Modern American
Society* (New York: Rinehart and Company, Inc., 1948), pp. 705–06.

perceptibly disturbed by such a logical contradiction, and so the latter cannot be equated with social disorganization.

Only when social values may be called upon to support contradictory patterns of behavior in actual situations can we speak of social disorganization. Thus, Myrdal's famous study of the American Negro problem is not framed as a study of social disorganization.[4] He poses, as the "American dilemma," a logical contradiction between the "American Creed" and "the Negro's place." But it does not necessarily follow from the logical contradiction that most people in American society perceive any dilemma here. In fact, the overenthusiastic student of race relations may be distressed to find how many people and groups sincerely feel no disloyalty to democratic ideals in their support of segregation and discrimination.

How is it possible, then, for values to be in logical contradiction without coming into contradiction in application? One answer may be attempted by borrowing an idea from the study of personal disorganization. Values are not all equal in importance. Rather, they fall in hierarchies. So long as such hierarchies are clearly understood, logical conflicts of values may be easily resolved in practice in favor of the more important value. Thus, the humanitarian value may be regarded as more important than honesty, so that the individual resolves the foregoing dilemma on this basis.

While such a formulation is of some help in understanding value-conflicts, it has clear limitations. The weighing of alternative values and selection of the more important does not actually seem to take place in most situations. Furthermore, choices are not always consistent with the notion that the more important value predominates. The police officer may provoke, with public approval, a high-speed chase on crowded highways, which endangers many lives, in order to capture someone violating a relatively minor traffic rule. Yet the policeman and the public would certainly rank protection of human life a higher value than punishment for the particular minor traffic offense.

Another formulation which is a special variant of the value-conflict position is the statement of *anomie* by Robert Merton.[5] By dichotomizing values into means and ends, he observes that either means or ends may become unduly stressed in a society so that the one is not adequately qualified by the other. Money is pursued in American society as an end frequently without attention to the socially approved means for its attainment. Or it is possible for a society to become excessively

---

[4] Gunnar Myrdal, *An American Dilemma* (New York: Harper & Brothers, 1944), especially pp. xlv–lii. Myrdal's entire introductory statement rests implicitly on the assumption that a logical contradiction of norms must be disturbing to the general population in America.

[5] Robert K. Merton, "Social Structure and Anomie," *American Sociological Review*, October 1938, pp. 672–82.

formalized, emphasizing means so rigidly that they cease to be tested against ends achieved. Anomie is thus conceived as a special form of value-conflict. Socially approved means constitute limitations on socially approved ends, and vice versa, but value-conflict in a meaningful sense exists only when the balance between the two is lost.

This scheme is difficult to apply, however, since the distinctions between means and ends are not easily made in practice. Values become means or ends only in the context of a particular act in progress, and there are no values which constitute ends all of the time or means all of the time. To apply the scheme requires that the investigator determine what are really ends—a highly dubious process. Thus, in American society the pursuit of money (an end) without respect to the approved means can be called an excessive emphasis on goals. But it is equally logical to insist that money is regarded as a means toward more ultimate goals such as happiness, and that the excessive pursuit of money is a concentration on means at the expense of ends.

THE EMPIRICAL NATURE OF VALUES

Part of our problem may be that the nature of a social value has not been sufficiently clarified. Values are a product of ongoing behavior. While values, once conceptualized, acquire an existence prior to and partly independent of the activities to which they are applied, their general vagueness leaves much room for specific application to be adapted to the nature of the ongoing activity and to change as the activity proceeds.

Values are generalizations, through which different acts can be related and through which a particular activity may be seen as part of a larger setting. Since every activity is unique in many respects, values are necessarily quite incomplete designators for any particular activity.

Values are conceptualizations. But the conceptualization is often misleading. Values are generally conceptualized in absolute terms, but applied with distinct situational limitations. Freedom of speech, whether presented as a value to be upheld or a norm (as in the American Constitution) is formulated in absolute terms. And yet there are laws against profanity, disturbance of the peace, libel, plagiarism, advocating overthrow of the government by violence, and laws which designate the times and places at which certain utterances are permissible. These laws do not generally trouble people as inconsistencies. Occasional discussions of this point are largely recreational; that is, they are not taken as serious discussions which should lead to rectifying action. Challenges are normally met by the statement that these are not the things which are meant by freedom of speech, or that these are not inconsistent with the *spirit* of free speech. Such answers are disturbing to the logical purist, but they accurately reflect the societal consensus.

Before we conclude summarily that people are inconsistent, we need to recognize that social values have two aspects which we may call the explicit and the implicit. The absolute conceptualization of the value is a symbol, an incomplete representation standing for a body of understandings regarding the value. This body of understandings defines the application of the value in different kinds of situations. We may speak of these understandings as the implicit limitations on the applications of values. On the basis of normal exposure to the culture in question, the individual acquires these understandings. They constitute the empirical content of a value. But they are not logically coherent and hence are not subject to neat summarization.

Both in the social development of values and in the individual learning of values, the experience of a multitude of specific situations precedes the generalized value statement. As conditions change, large bodies of people sense that a particular course of action in a certain type of situation is rewarding or unsatisfactory. Into such a situation comes the ideologist, who offers a formulation of an established value in such a way that it sanctions the preferred course of action.

Similarly, no learning of the symbolic value formulations can be a guide to behavior in a society. The "stranger" may indeed find it more difficult to learn the effective values of a culture to the degree to which he has prepared himself with a systematic learning of the explicit value formulations. The explicit formulations are effective guides only to those who have already so fully internalized the multitude of situational directives that they have become dulled to the perception of the logical implications of the explicit value statements of the society.

The confusion arising over apparent contradictions of values which do not seem to constitute contradictions in application comes out of mistaking the absolute formulation typical of values for the actual behaviorally relevant content of the values. In fact, it is likely that the absolute logical extension of any accepted value to correspond with its conceptual formulation would necessarily bring it into conflict with many or most other values.

For the most part, the arraying of values in hierarchies of importance is an effort to conceive in rational terms the situational specificity of values. In some few ill-defined situations in which ongoing activity does not dictate the choice, the tendency to think of values in hierarchies may determine choice. Or in the case of some individuals who value an intellectual approach to situations more than do most, choice may be on this basis. Conceptualization of values into hierarchies is most frequently a technique for supporting an action under way

whose legitimacy is challenged by some groups who contend that a
different value is applicable to the situation in question. Thus, condemnation proceedings are justified by calling community welfare a
higher value than private property. But the interest groups supporting
such a definition do not support the same value-primacy in other
situations and would not define the situation in this manner were not a
sufficiently powerful opposition able to insist on the applicability of the
value of private property in this situation.

DISORGANIZATION AND THE IMPLICIT CONTENT OF VALUES

While there are some values held by subgroups in a society which
are not recognized as legitimate by others, most disorganization consists of conflicting interpretations of the application of certain values.
There is agreement on the symbolic level of the value, but there is disagreement regarding its applicability to situations. In a smooth-functioning society, there is consensus concerning value applications, and
logically contradictory values (which will always be present) are well
"insulated" from one another in practice through their situational applications.

This formulation is consistent with the way in which people and
organizations, in practice, deal with the logically possible application
of two different values to a single situation. Rather than make judgments
by weighing the importance of one value against the other, individuals
and organizations make choices as to *which one* applies. Thus, the
minister in a businessman's church who makes suggestions about em-
ployer-employee relations is not told that profits are more important
than religious values. He is told, rather, that the subject matter is business, and hence is not the sphere to which religious values apply. Such
partitionings of the areas which belong to different sets of values seem
to be the stuff of which a smooth-functioning social order is made. The
breakdown of these partitions, and the erection of different partitions
by different subgroups within the society, seem to constitute most of
social disorganization.

The processes of establishing and maintaining the partitioning of
situations to which different values apply should accordingly be one of
the major areas of investigation in the study of social disorganization.
For example, in the maintenance of the separation between values which
might conflict logically, certain types of imagery may be important. Thus
the stereotype, as a type of imagery, may function to preserve the
separation between values of racial inequality and values of general
equality. The stereotype of the happy, carefree Negro plantation worker
renders the value of general equality inapplicable and the value of
subordination innocuous in its application.

The circumstances under which a subgroup within a society comes to sponsor a different understanding concerning the application of certain values from that held by other groups in the society should be another central concern of the study of social disorganization. The place of segmentalization of activities in the society, the limitation of communication between groups, and the tendency for organizations to be conceived as the sponsors of particular values apply here. Within the academic world, for example, the scientific method tends to be exalted and extended in its application beyond that approved elsewhere. Scientific method is a positive value throughout the society, but divergence develops regarding the situations to which it applies. Some of the conflict between educational institutions and the rest of society seems to revolve about this sort of divergence.

Such conditions as the foregoing, which signalize disorganization in some degree, need to be differentiated from the kind of organization through which a specialized group is shielded from interaction with the rest of society at a value level. In scientific research organizations, for example, the extensive application of scientific method may prevail. Interaction with the general public, however, is not on the basis of scientific method as a value, but solely on the basis of the product of the method, which is favorably evaluated in the society. This type of value divergence does not become value-conflict and social disorganization.

Finally, social change can be meaningfully related to social disorganization by a study of its impact on the implicit or situational aspect of values. Shifts in intergroup relations, such as those accompanying war and economic dislocation, alter the significance of traditional courses of action. Instead of relinquishing the old explicit value formulations which legitimized these outmoded courses of action, people become receptive to reinterpretation of the values. A situation is thus created in which social values do not constitute effective directives to consistent action within the society. At the same time, differential interest positions and differential willingness to make reinterpretations foster group alignments about alternative definitions of the situational applications of values. The resulting state is one of value-conflict, and a degree of social disorganization characterizes the society.

3

Robert K. Merton

Social Structure and Anomie

There persists a notable tendency in sociological theory to attribute the malfunctioning of social structure primarily to those of man's imperious biological drives which are not adequately restrained by social control. In this view, the social order is solely a device for "impulse management" and the "social processing" of tensions. These impulses which break through social control, be it noted, are held to be biologically derived. Nonconformity is assumed to be rooted in original nature.[1] Conformity is by implication the result of an utilitarian calculus or unreasoned conditioning. This point of view, whatever its other deficiencies, clearly begs one question. It provides no basis for determining the non-biological conditions which induce deviations from prescribed patterns of conduct. In this paper, it will be suggested that certain phases of social structure generate the circumstances in which infringement of social codes constitutes a "normal" response.[2]

The conceptual scheme to be outlined is designed to provide a coherent, systematic approach to the study of socio-cultural sources of

From *American Sociological Review*, 3 (October, 1938), 672–682, by permission of the author and the American Sociological Association.

[1] E.g., Ernest Jones, *Social Aspects of Psychoanalysis*, 28, London, 1924. If the Freudian notion is a variety of the "original sin" dogma, then the interpretation advanced in this paper may be called the doctrine of "socially derived sin."

[2] "Normal" in the sense of a culturally oriented, if not approved, response. This statement does not deny the relevance of biological and personality differences which may be significantly involved in the *incidence* of deviate conduct. Our focus of interest is the social and cultural matrix; hence we abstract from other factors. It is in this sense, I take it, that James S. Plant speaks of the "normal reaction of normal people to abnormal conditions." See his *Personality and the Cultural Pattern*, 248, New York, 1937.

deviate behavior. Our primary aim lies in discovering how some social structures *exert a definite pressure* upon certain persons in the society to engage in nonconformist rather than conformist conduct. The many ramifications of the scheme cannot all be discussed; the problems mentioned outnumber those explicitly treated.

Among the elements of social and cultural structure, two are important for our purposes. These are analytically separable although they merge imperceptibly in concrete situations. The first consists of culturally defined goals, purposes, and interests. It comprises a frame of aspirational reference. These goals are more or less integrated and involve varying degrees of prestige and sentiment. They constitute a basic, but not the exclusive, component of what Linton aptly has called "designs for group living." Some of these cultural aspirations are related to the original drives of man, but they are not determined by them. The second phase of the social structure defines, regulates, and controls the acceptable modes of achieving these goals. Every social group invariably couples its scale of desired ends with moral or institutional regulation of permissible and required procedures for attaining these ends. These regulatory norms and moral imperatives do not necessarily coincide with technical or efficiency norms. Many procedures which from the standpoint of *particular individuals* would be most efficient in securing desired values, e.g., illicit oil-stock schemes, theft, fraud, are ruled out of the institutional area of permitted conduct. The choice of expedients is limited by the institutional norms.

To say that these two elements, culture goals and institutional norms, operate jointly is not to say that the ranges of alternative behaviors and aims bear some constant relation to one another. The emphasis upon certain goals may vary independently of the degree of emphasis upon institutional means. There may develop a disproportionate, at times, a virtually exclusive, stress upon the value of specific goals, involving relatively slight concern with the institutionally appropriate modes of attaining these goals. The limiting case in this direction is reached when the range of alternative procedures is limited only by technical rather than institutional considerations. Any and all devices which promise attainment of the all important goal would be permitted in this hypothetical polar case.[3] This constitutes one type of cultural

[3] Contemporary American culture has been said to tend in this direction. See André Siegfried, *America Comes of Age*, 26–37, New York, 1927. The alleged extreme(?) emphasis on the goals of monetary success and material prosperity leads to dominant concern with technological and social instruments designed to produce the desired result, inasmuch as institutional controls become of secondary importance. In such a situation, innovation flourishes as the *range of means* employed is broadened. In a sense, then, there occurs the paradoxical emergence of "materialists" from an "idealistic" orientation. Cf. Durkheim's analysis of the cultural conditions which predispose toward crime and innovation, both of which are aimed toward efficiency, not moral norms. Durkheim was one of the first to see that "contrairement aux idées courantes le

malintegration. A second polar type is found in groups where activities originally conceived as instrumental are transmuted into ends in themselves. The original purposes are forgotten and ritualistic adherence to institutionally prescribed conduct becomes virtually obsessive.[4] Stability is largely ensured while change is flouted. The range of alternative behaviors is severely limited. There develops a tradition-bound, sacred society characterized by neophobia. The occupational psychosis of the bureaucrat may be cited as a case in point. Finally, there are the intermediate types of groups where a balance between culture goals and institutional means is maintained. These are the significantly integrated and relatively stable, though changing, groups.

An effective equilibrium between the two phases of the social structure is maintained as long as satisfactions accrue to individuals who conform to both constraints, viz., satisfactions from the achievement of the goals and satisfactions emerging directly from the institutionally canalized modes of striving to attain these ends. Success, in such equilibrated cases, is twofold. Success is reckoned in terms of the product and in terms of the process, in terms of the outcome and in terms of activities. Continuing satisfactions must derive from sheer *participation* in a competitive order as well as from eclipsing one's competitors if the order itself is to be sustained. The occasional sacrifices involved in institutionalized conduct must be compensated by socialized rewards. The distribution of statuses and roles through competition must be so organized that positive incentives for conformity to roles and adherence to status obligations are provided *for every position* within the distributive order. Aberrant conduct, therefore, may be viewed as a symptom of dissociation between culturally defined aspirations and socially structured means.

Of the types of groups which result from the independent variation of the two phases of the social structure, we shall be primarily concerned with the first, namely, that involving a disproportionate accent on goals. This statement must be recast in a proper perspective. In no group is there an absence of regulatory codes governing conduct, yet groups do vary in the degree to which these folkways, mores, and institutional controls are effectively integrated with the more diffuse goals which are part of the culture matrix. Emotional convictions may cluster

criminel n'apparait plus comme un être radicalement insociable, comme une sorte d'elément parasitaire, de corps étranger et inassimilable, introduit au sein de la société; c'est un agent régulier de la vie sociale." See *Les Règles de la Méthode Sociologique,* 86–89, Paris, 1927.

[4] Such ritualism may be associated with a mythology which rationalizes these actions so that they appear to retain their status as means, but the dominant pressure is in the direction of strict ritualistic conformity, irrespective of such rationalizations. In this sense, ritual has proceeded farthest when such rationalizations are not even called forth.

about the complex of socially acclaimed ends, meanwhile shifting their support from the culturally defined implementation of these ends. As we shall see, certain aspects of the social structure may generate counter-mores and antisocial behavior precisely because of differential emphases on goals and regulations. In the extreme case, the latter may be so vitiated by the goal-emphasis that the range of behavior is limited only by considerations of technical expediency. The sole significant question then becomes, which available means is most efficient in netting the socially approved value?[5] The technically most feasible procedure, whether legitimate or not, is preferred to the institutionally prescribed conduct. As this process continues, the integration of the society becomes tenuous and anomie ensues.

Thus, in competitive athletics, when the aim of victory is shorn of its institutional trappings and success in contests becomes construed as "winning the game" rather than "winning through circumscribed modes of activity," a premium is implicitly set upon the use of illegitimate but technically efficient means. The star of the opposing football team is surreptitiously slugged; the wrestler furtively incapacitates his opponent through ingenious but illicit techniques; university alumni covertly subsidize "students" whose talents are largely confined to the athletic field. The emphasis on the goal has so attenuated the satisfactions deriving from sheer participation in the competitive activity that these satisfactions are virtually confined to a successful outcome. Through the same process, tension generated by the desire to win in a poker game is relieved by successfully dealing oneself four aces, or, when the cult of success has become completely dominant, by sagaciously shuffling the cards in a game of solitaire. The faint twinge of uneasiness in the last instance and the surreptious nature of public delicts indicate clearly that the institutional rules of the game *are known* to those who evade them, but that the emotional supports of these rules are largely vitiated by cultural exaggeration of the success-goal.[6] They are microcosmic images of the social macrocosm.

---

[5] In this connection, one may see the relevance of Elton Mayo's paraphrase of the title of Tawney's well known book. "Actually the problem *is not that of the sickness of an acquisitive society; it is that of the acquisitiveness of a sick society.*" *Human Problems of an Industrial Civilization*, 153, New York, 1933. Mayo deals with the process through which wealth comes to be a symbol of social achievement. He sees this as arising from a state of anomie. We are considering the unintegrated monetary-success goal as an element in producing anomie. A complete analysis would involve both phases of this system of interdependent variables.

[6] It is unlikely that interiorized norms are completely eliminated. Whatever residuum persists will induce personality tensions and conflict. The process involves a certain degree of ambivalence. A manifest rejection of the institutional norms is coupled with some latent retention of their emotional correlates. "Guilt feelings," "sense of sin," "pangs of conscience" are obvious manifestations of this unrelieved tension; symbolic adherence to the nominally repudiated values or rationalizations constitute a more subtle variety of tensional release.

Of course, this process is not restricted to the realm of sport. The process whereby exaltation of the end generates a *literal demoralization*, i.e., a deinstitutionalization, of the means is one which characterizes many[7] groups in which the two phases of the social structure are not highly integrated. The extreme emphasis upon the accumulation of wealth as a symbol of success[8] in our own society militates against the completely effective control of institutionally regulated modes of acquiring a fortune.[9] Fraud, corruption, vice, crime, in short, the entire catalogue of proscribed behavior, becomes increasingly common when the emphasis on the *culturally induced* success-goal becomes divorced from a coordinated institutional emphasis. This observation is of crucial theoretical importance in examining the doctrine that antisocial behavior most frequently derives from biological drives breaking through the restraints imposed by society. The difference is one between a strictly utilitarian interpretation which conceives man's ends as random and an analysis which finds these ends deriving from the basic values of the culture.[10]

Our analysis can scarcely stop at this juncture. We must turn to other aspects of the social structure if we are to deal with the social genesis of the varying rates and types of deviate behavior characteristic of different societies. Thus far, we have sketched three ideal types of social orders constituted by distinctive patterns of relations between culture ends and means. Turning from these types of *culture patterning*, we find five logically possible, alternative modes of adjustment or adaptation *by individuals* within the culture-bearing society or group.[11] These are schematically presented in the following table, where (+)

7 "Many," and not all, unintegrated groups, for the reason already mentioned. In groups where the primary emphasis shifts to institutional means, i.e., when the range of alternatives is very limited, the outcome is a type of ritualism rather than anomie.

8 Money has several peculiarities which render it particularly apt to become a symbol of prestige divorced from institutional controls. As Simmel emphasized, money is highly abstract and impersonal. However acquired, through fraud or institutionally, it can be used to purchase the same goods and services. The anonymity of metropolitan culture, in conjunction with this peculiarity of money, permits wealth, the sources of which may be unknown to the community in which the plutocrat lives, to serve as a symbol of status.

9 The emphasis upon wealth as a success-symbol is possibly reflected in the use of the term "fortune" to refer to a stock of accumulated wealth. This meaning becomes common in the late sixteenth century (Spenser and Shakespeare). A similar usage of the Latin *fortuna* comes into prominence during the first century B.C. Both these periods were marked by the rise to prestige and power of the "bourgeoisie."

10 See Kingsley Davis, "Mental Hygiene and the Class Structure," *Psychiatry*, 1928, I, esp. 62–63; Talcott Parsons, *The Structure of Social Action*, 59–60, New York, 1937.

11 This is a level intermediate between the two planes distinguished by Edward Sapir; namely, culture patterns and personal habit systems. See his "Contribution of Psychiatry to an Understanding of Behavior in Society," *Amer. J. Sociol.*, 1937, 42:862–70.

signifies "acceptance," (—) signifies "elimination" and (±) signifies "rejection and substitution of new goals and standards."

	Culture Goals	Institutionalized Means
I. Conformity	+	+
II. Innovation	+	—
III. Ritualism	—	+
IV. Retreatism	—	—
V. Rebellion[12]	±	±

Our discussion of the relation between these alternative responses and other phases of the social structure must be prefaced by the observation that persons may shift from one alternative to another as they engage in different social activities. These categories refer to role adjustments in specific situations, not to personality *in toto*. To treat the development of this process in various spheres of conduct would introduce a complexity unmanageable within the confines of this paper. For this reason, we shall be concerned primarily with economic activity in the broad sense, "the production, exchange, distribution and consumption of goods and services" in our competitive society, wherein wealth has taken on a highly symbolic cast. Our task is to search out some of the factors which exert pressure upon individuals to engage in certain of these logically possible alternative responses. This choice, as we shall see, is far from random.

In every society, Adaptation I (conformity to both culture goals and means) is the most common and widely diffused. Were this not so, the stability and continuity of the society could not be maintained. The mesh of expectancies which constitutes every social order is sustained by the modal behavior of its members falling within the first category. Conventional role behavior oriented toward the basic values of the group is the rule rather than the exception. It is this fact alone which permits us to speak of a human aggregate as comprising a group of society.

Conversely, Adaptation IV (rejection of goals and means) is the least common. Persons who "adjust" (or maladjust) in this fashion are, strictly speaking, *in* the society but not *of* it. Sociologically, these constitute the true "aliens." Not sharing the common frame of orientation,

---

12 This fifth alternative is on a plane clearly different from that of the others. It represents a *transitional* response which seeks to *institutionalize* new procedures oriented toward revamped cultural goals shared by the members of the society. It thus involves efforts to *change* the existing structure rather than to perform accommodative actions *within* this structure, and introduces additional problems with which we are not at the moment concerned.

they can be included within the societal population merely in a fictional sense. In this category are *some* of the activities of psychotics, psycho-neurotics, chronic autists, pariahs, outcasts, vagrants, vagabonds, tramps, chronic drunkards and drug addicts.[13] These have relinquished, in certain spheres of activity, the culturally defined goals, involving complete aim-inhibition in the polar case, and their adjustments are not in accord with institutional norms. This is not to say that in some cases the source of their behavioral adjustments is not in part the very social structure which they have in effect repudiated nor that their very existence within a social area does not constitute a problem for the socialized population.

This mode of "adjustment" occurs, as far as structural sources are concerned, when both the culture goals and institutionalized procedures have been assimilated thoroughly by the individual and imbued with affect and high positive value, but where those institutionalized proce-dures which promise a measure of successful attainment of the goals are not available to the individual. In such instances, there results a two-fold mental conflict insofar as the moral obligation for adopting insti-tutional means conflicts with the pressure to resort to illegitimate means (which may attain the goal) and inasmuch as the individual is shut off from means which are both legitimate *and* effective. The competitive order is maintained, but the frustrated and handicapped individual who cannot cope with the order drops out. Defeatism, quietism and resig-nation are manifested in escape mechanisms which ultimately lead the individual to "escape" from the requirements of the society. It is an expedient which arises from continued failure to attain the goal by legit-imate measures and from an inability to adopt the illegitimate route be-cause of internalized prohibitions and institutionalized compulsives, *during which process the supreme value of the success-goal has as yet not been renounced.* The conflict is resolved by eliminating *both* pre-cipitating elements, the goals and means. The escape is complete, the conflict is eliminated and the individual is asocialized.

Be it noted that where frustration derives from the inaccessibility of effective institutional means for attaining economic or any other type of highly valued "success," that Adaptations II, III and V (innovation, ritualism and rebellion) are also possible. The result will be determined by the particular personality, and thus, the *particular* cultural back-ground, involved. Inadequate socialization will result in the innovation response whereby the conflict and frustration are eliminated by relin-

---

[13] Obviously, this is an elliptical statement. These individuals may maintain some orientation to the values of their particular differentiated groupings within the larger society or, in part, of the conventional society itself. Insofar as they do so, their conduct cannot be classified in the "passive rejection" category (IV). Nels Anderson's descrip-tion of the behavior and attitudes of the bum, for example, can readily be recast in terms of our analytical scheme. See *The Hobo*, 93–98, *et passim*, Chicago, 1923.

quishing the institutional means and retaining the success-aspiration; an extreme assimilation of institutional demands will lead to ritualism wherein the goal is dropped as beyond one's reach but conformity to the mores persists; and rebellion occurs when emancipation from the reigning standards, due to frustration or to marginalist perspectives, leads to the attempt to introduce a "new social order."

Our major concern is with the illegitimacy adjustment. This involves the use of conventionally proscribed but frequently effective means of attaining at least the simulacrum of culturally defined success,—wealth, power, and the like. As we have seen, this adjustment occurs when the individual has assimilated the cultural emphasis on success without equally internalizing the morally prescribed norms governing means for its attainment. The question arises, Which phases of our social structure predispose toward this mode of adjustment? We may examine a concrete instance, effectively analyzed by Lohman,[14] which provides a clue to the answer. Lohman has shown that specialized areas of vice in the near north side of Chicago constitute a "normal" response to a situation where the cultural emphasis upon pecuniary success has been absorbed, but where there is little access to conventional and legitimate means for attaining such success. The conventional occupational opportunities of persons in this area are almost completely limited to manual labor. Given our cultural stigmatization of manual labor, and its correlate, the prestige of white collar work, it is clear that the result is a strain toward innovational practices. The limitation of opportunity to unskilled labor and the resultant low income cannot compete *in terms of conventional standards of achievement* with the high income from organized vice.

For our purposes, this situation involves two important features. First, such antisocial behavior is in a sense "called forth" by certain conventional values of the culture *and* by the class structure involving differential access to the approved opportunities for legitimate, prestige-bearing pursuit of the culture goals. The lack of high integration between the means-and-end elements of the cultural pattern and the particular class structure combine to favor a heightened frequency of antisocial conduct in such groups. The second consideration is of equal significance. Recourse to the first of the alternative responses, legitimate effort, is limited by the fact that actual advance toward desired success-symbols through conventional channels is, despite our persisting open-class ideology,[15] relatively rare and difficult for those handicapped by

14 Joseph D. Lohman, "The Participant Observer in Community Studies," *Amer. Sociol. Rev.,* 1937, 2:890–98.

15 The shifting historical role of this ideology is a profitable subject for exploration. The "office-boy-to-president" stereotype was once in approximate accord with the facts. Such vertical mobility was probably more common then than now, when the class structure is more rigid. (See the following note.) The ideology largely persists,

little formal education and few economic resources. The dominant pressure of group standards of success is, therefore, on the gradual attenuation of legitimate, but by and large ineffective, strivings and the increasing use of illegitimate, but more or less effective, expedients of vice and crime. The cultural demands made on persons in this situation are incompatible. On the one hand, they are asked to orient their conduct toward the prospect of accumulating wealth and on the other, they are largely denied effective opportunities to do so institutionally. The consequences of such structural inconsistency are psychopathological personality, and/or antisocial conduct, and/or revolutionary activities. The equilibrium between culturally designated means and ends becomes highly unstable with the progressive emphasis on attaining the prestige-laden ends by any means whatsoever. Within this context, Capone represents the triumph of amoral intelligence over morally prescribed "failure," when the channels of vertical mobility are closed or narrowed[16] *in a society which places a high premium on economic affluence and social ascent for* all *its members.*[17]

This last qualification is of primary importance. It suggests that other phases of the social structure besides the extreme emphasis on pecuniary success, must be considered if we are to understand the social sources of antisocial behavior. A high frequency of deviate behavior is not generated simply by "lack of opportunity" or by this exaggerated

---

however, possibly because it still performs a useful function for maintaining the *status quo*. For insofar as it is accepted by the "masses," it constitutes a useful sop for those who might rebel against the entire structure, were this consoling hope removed. This ideology now serves to lessen the probability of Adaptation V. In short, the role of this notion has changed from that of an approximately valid empirical theorem to that of an ideology, in Mannheim's sense.

[16] There is a growing body of evidence, though none of it is clearly conclusive, to the effect that our class structure is becoming rigidified and that vertical mobility is declining. Taussig and Joslyn found that American business leaders are being *increasingly* recruited from the upper ranks of our society. The Lynds have also found a "diminished chance to get ahead" for the working classes in Middletown. Manifestly, these objective changes are not alone significant; the individual's subjective evaluation of the situation is a major determinant of the response. The extent to which this change in opportunity for social mobility has been recognized by the least advantaged classes is still conjectural, although the Lynds present some suggestive materials. The writer suggests that a case in point is the increasing frequency of cartoons which observe in a tragi-comic vein that "my old man says everybody can't be President. He says if ya can get three days a week steady on W.P.A. work ya ain't doin' so bad either." See F. W. Taussig and C. S. Joslyn, *American Business Leaders*, New York, 1932; R. S. and H. M. Lynd, *Middletown in Transition*, 67 ff., chap. 12, New York, 1937.

[17] The role of the Negro in this respect is of considerable theoretical interest. Certain elements of the Negro population have assimilated the dominant caste's values of pecuniary success and social advancement, but they also recognize that social ascent is at present restricted to their own caste almost exclusively. The pressures upon the Negro which would otherwise derive from the structural inconsistencies we have noticed are hence not identical with those upon lower class whites. See Kingsley Davis, *op. cit.*, 63; John Dollard, *Caste and Class in a Southern Town*, 66 ff., New Haven, 1936; Donald Young, *American Minority Peoples*, 581, New York, 1932.

pecuniary emphasis. A comparatively rigidified class structure, a feudalistic or caste order, may limit such opportunities far beyond the point which obtains in our society today. [It is only when a system of cultural values extols, virtually above all else, certain *common* symbols of success *for the population at large* while its social structure rigorously restricts or completely eliminates access to approved modes of acquiring these symbols *for a considerable part of the same population*, that antisocial behavior ensues on a considerable scale.] In other words, our egalitarian ideology denies by implication the existence of noncompeting groups and individuals in the pursuit of pecuniary success. The same body of success-symbols is held to be desirable for all. These goals are held to *transcend class lines*, not to be bounded by them, yet the actual social organization is such that there exist class differentials in the accessibility of these *common* success-symbols. Frustration and thwarted aspiration lead to the search for avenues of escape from a culturally induced intolerable situation; or unrelieved ambition may eventuate in illicit attempts to acquire the dominant values.[18] The American stress on pecuniary success and ambitiousness for all thus invites exaggerated anxieties, hostilities, neuroses and antisocial behavior.

This theoretical analysis may go far toward explaining the varying correlations between crime and poverty.[19] Poverty is not an isolated variable. It is one in a complex of interdependent social and cultural variables. When viewed in such a context, it represents quite different states of affairs. [Poverty as such, and consequent limitation of opportunity, are not sufficient to induce a conspicuously high rate of criminal behavior.] Even the often mentioned "poverty in the midst of plenty" will not necessarily lead to this result. Only insofar as poverty and associated disadvantages in competition for the culture values approved for *all* members of the society is linked with the assimilation of a cultural emphasis on monetary accumulation as a symbol of success is antisocial conduct a "normal" outcome. Thus, poverty is less highly correlated with crime in southeastern Europe than in the United States.

---

[18] The psychical coordinates of these processes have been partly established by the experimental evidence concerning *Anspruchsniveaus* and levels of performance. See Kurt Lewin, *Vorsatz, Wille und Bedurfnis,* Berlin, 1926; N. F. Hoppe, "Erfolg und Misserfolg," *Psychol. Forschung,* 1930, 14:1–63; Jerome D. Frank, "Individual Differences in Certain Aspects of the Level of Aspiration," *Amer. J. Psychol.,* 1935, 47:119–28.

[19] Standard criminology texts summarize the data in this field. Our scheme of analysis may serve to resolve some of the theoretical contradictions which P. A. Sorokin indicates. For example, "not everywhere nor always do the poor show a greater proportion of crime . . . many poorer countries have had less crime than the richer countries. . . . The [economic] improvement in the second half of the nineteenth century, and the beginning of the twentieth, has not been followed by a decrease of crime." See his *Contemporary Sociological Theories,* 560–61, New York, 1928. The crucial point is, however, that poverty has varying social significance in different social structures, as we shall see. Hence, one would not expect a linear correlation between crime and poverty.

The possibilities of vertical mobility in these European areas would seem to be fewer than in this country, so that neither poverty *per se* nor its association with limited opportunity is sufficient to account for the varying correlations. It is only when the full configuration is considered, poverty, limited opportunity and a commonly shared system of success symbols, that we can explain the higher association between poverty and crime in our society than in others where rigidified class structure is coupled with *differential class symbols of achievement.*

In societies such as our own, then, the pressure of prestige-bearing success tends to eliminate the effective social constraint over means employed to this end. "The-end-justifies-the-means" doctrine becomes a guiding tenet for action when the cultural structure unduly exalts the end and the social organization unduly limits possible recourse to approved means. Otherwise put, this notion and associated behavior reflect a lack of cultural coordination. In international relations, the effects of this lack of integration are notoriously apparent. An emphasis upon national power is not readily coordinated with an inept organization of legitimate, i.e., internationally defined and accepted, means for attaining this goal. The result is a tendency toward the abrogation of international law, treaties become scraps of paper, "undeclared warfare" serves as a technical evasion, the bombing of civilian populations is rationalized,[20] just as the same societal situation induces the same sway of illegitimacy among individuals.

The social order we have described necessarily produces this "strain toward dissolution." The pressure of such an order is upon outdoing one's competitors. The choice of means within the ambit of institutional control will persist as long as the sentiments supporting a competitive system, i.e., deriving from the possibility of outranking competitors and hence enjoying the favorable response of others, are distributed throughout the entire system of activities and are not confined merely to the final result. A stable social structure demands a balanced distribution of affect among its various segments. When there occurs a shift of emphasis from the satisfactions deriving from competition itself to almost exclusive concern with successful competition, the resultant stress leads to the breakdown of the regulatory structure.[21] With the resulting attenuation of the institutional imperatives, there occurs an approximation of the situation erroneously held by utilitarians to be typical of society generally wherein calculations of advantage and fear of punishment are the sole regulating agencies. In such situations, as

[20] See M. W. Royse, *Aerial Bombardment and the International Regulation of War,* New York, 1928.
[21] Since our primary concern is with the socio-cultural aspects of this problem, the psychological correlates have been only implicitly considered. See Karen Horney, *The Neurotic Personality of Our Time,* New York, 1937, for a psychological discussion of this process.

Hobbes observed, force and fraud come to constitute the sole virtues in view of their relative efficiency in attaining goals,—which were
for him, of course, not culturally derived.

It should be apparent that the foregoing discussion is not pitched
on a moralistic plane. Whatever the sentiments of the writer or reader
concerning the ethical desirability of coordinating the means-and-goals
phases of the social structure, one must agree that lack of such coordination leads to anomie. Insofar as one of the most general functions of
social organization is to provide a basis for calculability and regularity of
behavior, it is increasingly limited in effectiveness as these elements
of the structure become dissociated. At the extreme, predictability
virtually disappears and what may be properly termed cultural chaos
or anomie intervenes.

This statement, being brief, is also incomplete. It has not included
an exhaustive treatment of the various structural elements which predispose toward one rather than another of the alternative responses open
to individuals; it has neglected, but not denied the relevance of, the
factors determining the specific incidence of these responses; it has not
enumerated the various concrete responses which are constituted by
combinations of specific values of the analytical variables; it has omitted,
or included only by implication, any consideration of the social functions performed by illicit responses; it has not tested the full explanatory power of the analytical scheme by examining a large number of
group variations in the frequency of deviate and conformist behavior; it
has not adequately dealt with rebellious conduct which seeks to re-
fashion the social framework radically; it has not examined the relevance
of cultural conflict for an analysis of culture-goal and institutional-means
malintegration. It is suggested that these and related problems may be
profitably analyzed by this scheme.

4

Jack P. Gibbs

Conceptions of Deviant Behavior:

The Old and the New

The ultimate end of substantive theory in any science is the formulation of empirical relations among classes of phenomena, e.g., X varies directly with Y, X is present if and only if Y is present. However, unless such propositions are arrived at by crude induction or sheer intuition, there is a crucial step before the formulation of a relational statement. This step can be described as the way the investigator comes to perceive or "think about" the phenomena under consideration. Another way to put it is the development of a "conception."

There is no clear cut distinction between, on the one hand, a conception of a class of phenomena and, on the other, formal definitions and substantive theory. Since a conception emphasizes the predominant feature of a phenomenon, it is not entirely divorced from a definition of it; but the former is not identical with the latter. Thus, for example, the notion of exploitation looms large in the Marxian conception of relations among social classes; but exploitation is or may be only one feature of class relations, and it does not serve as a formal definition of them. Further, in certain fields, particularly the social sciences, a conception often not only precedes but also gives rise to operational definitions. As the case in point, if an operational definition of social class relies on the use of "reputational technique," the investigator's conception of social class is in all probability non-Marxian.

What has been said of the distinction between definitions and conceptions holds also for the relation between the latter and substantive theory. A conception may generate a particular theory, but it is not

From *The Pacific Sociological Review,* **9** (Spring, 1966), 9–14, by permission of the author and the publishers.

identical with it. For one thing, a conception contains definitional elements and is therefore partially tautological, which means that in itself
a conception is never a clear-cut empirical proposition. Apart from its
tautological character, a conception is too general to constitute a testable
idea. Nonetheless, a conception may generate substantive theory, and
it is certainly true that theories reflect conceptions. Durkheim's work is
a classic illustration. His theory on suicide clearly reflects his view of
society and social life generally.

In a field without consensus as to operational definitions and little
in the way of systematic substantive theory, conceptions necessarily occupy a central position. This condition prevails in most of the social
sciences. There, what purports to be definitions of classes of phenomena
are typically general and inconsistent to the point of lacking empirical
applicability (certainly in the operational sense of the word). Moreover, what passes for a substantive theory in the social sciences is more
often than not actually a loosely formulated conception. These observations are not intended to deride the social sciences for lack of progress. All fields probably go through a "conceptions" stage; it is only
more apparent in some than in others.

Of the social sciences, there is perhaps no better clear-cut illustration of the importance of conceptions than in the field identified as
criminology and the study of deviant behavior. As we shall see, the history of the field can be described best in terms of changing conceptions
of crime, criminals, deviants, and deviation. But the purpose of this
paper is not an historical account of major trends in the field. If it
is true that conceptions give rise to formal definitions and substantive
theory, then a critical appraisal of conceptions is important in its own
right. This is all the more true in the case of criminology and the study
of deviant behavior, where conceptions are frequently confused with
substantive theories, and the latter so clearly reflect the former.

OLDER CONCEPTIONS

In recent years there has been a significant change in the prevailing
conception of deviant behavior and deviants. Prior to what is designated
here as the "new perspective," it commonly was assumed that there is
something inherent in deviants which distinguishes them from non-
deviants.[1] Thus, from Lombroso to Sheldon, criminals were viewed as
biologically distinctive in one way or another.[2] The inadequacies of this

[1] Throughout this paper crime is treated as a sub-class of deviant behavior. Particular issues may be discussed with reference to crime, but on the whole the observations apply to deviant behavior generally.

[2] Although not essential to the argument, it is perhaps significant that the alleged
biological differentiae of criminals have been consistently viewed as "pathological" in
one sense or another.

conception are now obvious. After decades of research, no biological characteristic which distinguishes criminals has been discovered, and this generalization applies even to particular types of criminals (e.g., murderers, bigamists, etc.). Consequently, few theorists now even toy with the notion that all criminals are atavistic, mentally defective, constitutionally inferior. But the rejection of the biological conception of crime stems from more than research findings. Even casual observation and mild logic cast doubt on the idea. Since legislators are not geneticists, it is difficult to see how they can pass laws in such a way as to create "born criminals." Equally important, since most if not all "normal" persons have violated a law at one time or another,[3] the assertion that criminals are so by heredity now appears most questionable.

Although the biological conception generally has been rejected, what is here designated as the analytic conception of criminal acts largely has escaped criticism. Rather than view criminal acts as nothing more or less than behavior contrary to legal norms, the acts are construed as somehow injurious to society. The shift from the biological to the analytical conception is thus from the actors to the characteristics of their acts, with the idea being that some acts are inherently "criminal" or at least that criminal acts share intrinsic characteristics in common.

The analytical conception is certainly more defensible than the biological view, but it is by no means free of criticism. Above all, the "injurious" quality of some deviant acts is by no means conspicuous, as witness Durkheim's observation:

. . . there are many acts which have been and still are regarded as criminal without in themselves being harmful to society. What social danger is there is touching a tabooed object, an impure animal or man, in letting the sacred fire die down, in eating certain meats, in failure to make the traditional sacrifice over the grave of parents, in not exactly pronouncing the ritual formula, in not celebrating holidays, etc.?[4]

Only a radical functionalism would interpret the acts noted by Durkheim as literally injuring society in any reasonable sense of the word. The crucial point is that, far from actually injuring society or sharing some intrinsic feature in common, acts may be criminal or deviant because and only because they are proscribed legally and/or socially. The proscription may be irrational in that members of the society cannot explain it, but it is real nonetheless. Similarly, a law may be "arbitrary" in that it is imposed by a powerful minority and, as a consequence, lacks popular support and is actively opposed. But if the

[3] See Edwin H. Sutherland and Donald R. Cressey, *Principles of Criminology*, 6th ed., Chicago: J. B. Lippincott, 1960, p. 39.

[4] Emile Durkheim, *The Division of Labor in Society*, trans. George Simpson, Glencoe, Illinois: The Free Press, 1949, p. 72.

law is consistently enforced (i.e., sanctions are imposed regularly on violators), it is difficult to see how it is not "real."

The fact that laws may appear to be irrational and arbitrary has prompted attempts to define crime independently of legal criteria, i.e., analytically. The first step in this direction was Garofalo's concept of natural crime—acts which violate prevailing sentiments of pity and probity.[5] Garofalo's endeavor accomplished very little. Just as there is probably no act which is contrary to law universally, it is equally true that no act violates sentiments of pity and probity in all societies. In other words, cultural relativity defeats any attempt to compile a list of acts which are crimes universally. Also, it is hard to see why the violation of a rigorously enforced traffic regulation is not a crime even though unrelated to sentiments of pity and probity. If it is not a crime, what is it?

The search for an analytic identification of crime continued in Sellin's proposal to abandon legal criteria altogether in preference for "conduct norms."[6] The rationale for the proposal is simple. Because laws vary and may be "arbitrary" in any one society, a purely legal definition of crime is not suited for scientific study. But Sellin's observations on the arbitrariness of laws apply in much the same way to conduct norms. Just as the content of criminal law varies from one society to the next and from time to time, so does the content of extra-legal norms. Further, the latter may be just as arbitrary as criminal laws. Even in a highly urbanized society such as the United States, there is evidently no rationale or utilitarian reason for all of the norms pertaining to mode of dress. True, there may be much greater conformity to conduct norms than to some laws, but the degree of conformity is hardly an adequate criterion of the "reality" of norms, legal or extra-legal. If any credence whatever can be placed in the Kinsey report, sexual taboos may be violated frequently and yet remain as taboos. As a case in point, even if adultery is now common in the United States, it is significant that the participants typically attempt to conceal their acts. In brief, just as laws may be violated frequently and are "unreal" in that sense, the same applies to some conduct norms; but in neither case do they cease to be norms. They would cease to be norms if and only if one defines deviation in terms of statistical regularities in behavior, but not even Sellin would subscribe to the notion that normative phenomena can or should be defined in statistical terms.

In summary, however capricious and irrational legal and extra-legal norms may appear to be, the inescapable conclusion is that some acts

[5] Raffaele Garofalo, *Criminology*, Boston: Little, Brown, and Co., 1914, Chapter I.
[6] Thorsten Sellin, *Culture Conflict and Crime*, New York: Social Science Research Council, Bulletin 41, 1938.

are criminal or deviant for the very simple reason that they are proscribed.

THE NEW CONCEPTION

Whereas both the pathological and the analytical conception of
deviation assume that some intrinsic feature characterizes deviants
and/or deviant acts, an emerging perspective in sociology flatly rejects
any such assumption. Indeed, as witness the following statements by
Kitsuse, Becker, and Erikson, exactly the opposite position is taken.

Kitsuse:
> Forms of behavior *per se* do not differentiate deviants from non-deviants;
> it is the responses of the conventional and conforming members of the society
> who identify and interpret behavior as deviant which sociologically transform
> persons into deviants.[7]

Erikson:
> From a sociological standpoint, deviance can be defined as conduct which
> is generally thought to require the attention of social control agencies—that is
> conduct about which 'something should be done.' Deviance is not a property
> *inherent* in certain forms of behavior; it is a property *conferred upon* these
> forms by the audiences which directly or indirectly witness them. Sociologically,
> then, the critical variable in the study of deviance is the social *audience* rather
> than individual *person*, since it is the audience which eventually decides
> whether or not any given action or actions will become a visible case of
> deviation.[8]

Becker:
> From this point of view, deviance is *not* a quality of the act a person
> commits, but rather a consequence of the application by others of rules and
> sanctions to an 'offender.' The deviant is one to whom that label has successfully
> been applied; deviant behavior is behavior that people so label.[9]

The common assertion in the above statements is that acts can be
identified as deviant or criminal only by reference to the character of
reaction to them by the public or by the official agents of a politically
organized society. Put simply, if the reaction is of a certain kind, then
and only then is the act deviant. The crucial point is that the essential
feature of a deviant or deviant act is *external* to the actor and the act.
Further, even if the act or actors share some feature in common other
than social reactions to them, the feature neither defines nor completely

---

[7] John I. Kitsuse, "Societal Reaction to Deviant Behavior: Problems of Theory
and Method," *Social Problems,* 9 (Winter, 1962), p. 253.

[8] Kai T. Erikson, "Notes on the Sociology of Deviance," *Social Problems,* 9
(Spring, 1962), p. 308.

[9] Howard S. Becker, *Outsiders,* New York: The Free Press of Glencoe, 1963, p. 9.

explains deviation. To take the extreme case, even if Lombroso had been correct in his assertion that criminals are biologically distinctive, the biological factor neither identifies the criminal nor explains criminality. Purely biological variables may explain why some persons commit certain acts, but they do not explain why the acts are crimes. Consequently, since criminal law is spatially and temporally relative, it is impossible to distinguish criminals from noncriminals (assuming that the latter do exist, which is questionable) in terms of biological characteristics. To illustrate, if act X is a crime in society A but not a crime in society B, it follows that, even assuming Lombroso to have been correct, the anatomical features which distinguish the criminal in society A may characterize the non-criminal in society B. In both societies some persons may be genetically predisposed to commit act X, but the act is a crime in one society and not in the other. Accordingly, the generalization that all persons with certain anatomical features are criminals would be, in this instance, false. True, one may assert that the "born criminal" is predisposed to violate the laws of his own society, but this assumes either that "the genes" know what the law is or that the members of the legislature are geneticists, (i.e., they deliberately enact laws in such a way that the "born criminal" will violate them). Either assumption taxes credulity.

The new perspective of deviant behavior contradicts not only the biological but also the analytical conception. Whereas the latter seeks to find something intrinsic in deviant or, more specifically, criminal acts, the new conception denies any such characterization. True, the acts share a common denominator—they are identified by the character of reaction to them—but this does not mean that the acts are "injurious" to society or that they are in any way inherently abnormal. The new conception eschews the notion that some acts are deviant or criminal in all societies. For that matter, the reaction which identifies a deviant act may not be the same from one society or social group to the next. In general, then, the new conception of deviant behavior is relativistic in the extreme.

CRITICISM OF THE NEW PERSPECTIVE

The new perspective of deviant behavior is much more consistent not only with what is known about deviant behavior but also with contemporary sociological principles generally. However, while containing a fundamentally sound idea, the new perspective leaves some crucial questions unanswered. For one thing, it is not clear whether the perspective is intended to be a "substantive theory" of deviant behavior (i.e., an explanation of the phenomenon) or a conceptual treatment of it. Consider, again, statements by Becker, Kitsuse, and Erikson:

Becker:

> . . . *social groups create deviance by making the rules whose infraction constitute deviance*, and by applying those rules to particular people and labeling them as outsiders.[10]

Kitsuse and Cicourel:

> . . . *rates of deviant behavior* are produced by *the actions taken by persons in the social system* which define, classify and record certain behaviors as deviant.[11]

Erikson:

> . . . transactions taking place between deviant persons on the one side and agencies on the other are boundary maintaining mechanisms. They mark the outside limits of the area in which the norm has jurisdiction, and in this way assert how much diversity and variability can be contained within the system before it begins to lose its distinct structure, its unique shape.[12]

Now these statements appear to be something more than definitions. However, if regarded as explanations of deviant behavior, these and other similar observations do not provide adequate answers to three major questions: (1) Why does the incidence of a particular act vary from one population to the next? (2) Why do some persons commit the act while others do not? (3) Why is the act in question considered deviant and/or criminal in some societies but not in others?

The assertion that deviation is created or produced by the character of reactions to behavior (see statements by Becker and Kitsuse above) implies an answer to the question on incidence. But are we to conclude that the incidence of a given act is in fact a constant in all populations and that the only difference is in the quality of reactions to the act? Specifically, given two populations with the same kind of reaction to a particular type of act, can the new perspective explain why the incidence of the act is greater in one population than in the other? Not at all! On the contrary, even if two populations have the same legal and social definition of armed robbery and even if instances of the crime are reacted to in exactly the same way, it is still possible for the armed robbery rate to be much higher in one population than in the other. Reaction to deviation may influence the rate of deviation in that certain kinds of reaction may have a deterrent effect, but the deterrent quality of reaction has not been examined systematically by Becker, Kitsuse, or Erikson, primarily because they view reaction in terms of *identifying* deviant behavior. Actually, apart from identifying deviation, the new conception presents a sophisticated framework for the study of

---

[10] *Op. cit.*, p. 9.
[11] John I. Kitsuse and Aaron Cicourel, "A Note on the Uses of Official Statistics," *Social Problems,* 11 (Fall, 1963) , p. 135.
[12] *Op. cit.*, p. 310.

deterrence as an aspect of reaction to deviant behavior. All three of the advocates are sensitive to the importance of the deviant's response to reaction, and it would not be inconsistent for them to devote more attention to the possibility that some kinds of reaction have consequences beyond identifying behavior as deviant.

What has been said of the new perspective with regard to explaining variation in the incidence of deviant acts also applies to the second major question: Why do some persons commit a given act while others do not? The point is that the new perspective does not generate an answer to this question. For example, the fact that the reaction to armed robbery may involve incarceration hardly explains why some but not all persons commit the act. Again, the quality of reaction (or the probability of reaction) may have a differential deterrent effect, a possibility which is relevant in attempting to answer the question; but, as noted before, the new perspective exhibits little concern not only with deterrence but also with etiological factors generally. The lack of concern with etiological factors suggests that Becker, Erikson, and Kitsuse actually are seeking a theory not about deviant behavior *per se* but rather about reactions to deviant behavior (i.e., why does the quality of reaction vary from place to place and time to time?). In any event, the three persons closely associated with the perspective have not explicitly stated that they are seeking such a theory.

It is not at all clear whether Becker is pursuing a theory about deviant behavior or a theory about reactions to deviation. If it is the latter, then his focus on deviants rather than reactors is puzzling. Kitsuse is concerned with reaction to deviant behavior as a process, but he views reaction not only as a criterion of deviant behavior but also (evidently) as the decisive factor in relation to incidence. As such, he is apparently seeking a theory about deviant behavior and not reactions to it. Erikson's "functionalist" position could be construed as a theory about deviant behavior, or reactions, or both. However, even if reactions to deviation do serve a "function"—boundary maintenance—a functional interpretation hardly explains why the quality of reaction varies from one society to the next. Further, with reference to incidence, are we to conclude that social boundaries are maintained or demarcated if and only if the rate of deviant behavior is high?

Even if deviant acts are defined in terms of reactions to behavior, the identification does not and cannot explain why a given act is considered deviant and/or criminal in some but not all societies (the third major question). After all, a certain kind of reaction may identify behavior as deviant, but it obviously does not explain why the behavior is deviant.

The danger in evaluating the work of Becker, Erikson, and Kitsuse is that of prematurely rejecting what is a most promising approach to the study of deviant behavior. The danger can be avoided if it is clearly understood that they have formulated what is essentially a conception. As such, it contains both definitions and elements of substantive theory, and the development of the latter would be furthered considerably by making the distinction explicit. Finally, since a conception precedes substantive theory, it would be most unrealistic to demand testable empirical propositions at this stage. The only justifiable criticism on this point is that the three men have not specified their goal adequately, i.e., whether they are seeking an explanation of deviant behavior or of reaction to it. The fact that it may be both testifies to the fertility of the conception, but it is all the more reason to treat the distinction seriously.

REACTION AS A CRITERION OF DEVIATION

The point stressed continually by the new perspective is that acts are identified as deviant by the character of reactions to them. Whatever the merits of this position, it is not free of criticism. For one thing, Becker, Erikson, and Kitsuse have never specified exactly what kind of reaction identifies deviant acts. Becker constantly refers to deviants as persons labelled as "outsiders," but this term is Becker's, not that of the man on the street. For that matter, the public may be more familiar with the meaning of the term "deviant" than with "outsider."

When we turn to concrete cases of reactions supposedly indicative of deviant acts, there are some rather curious results. Kitsuse, for example, found reactions of students to persons identified by the students as homosexuals to be "generally mild."[13] These reactions may or may not be representative of the public generally; nonetheless, two significant questions are posed. First, are we to conclude, because of the mildness of the reaction, that homosexuals are not deviants after all? Second, how "harsh" must the reaction be before the behavior is to be construed as deviant? More generally, since "mild" and "harsh" are subjective terms, exactly what "kind" of reaction identifies deviant acts or deviance? Some of Becker's observations are puzzling in this connection. As a case in point: "Whether an act is deviant, then, depends on how other people react to it. You can commit clan incest and suffer no more than gossip as long as no one makes a public accusation. . . ."[14] Why is it that gossip does not qualify as a reaction which identifies deviant behavior?

The failure of Becker, Erikson, and Kitsuse to specify the kind of reactions which identify deviation is further complicated by the contradictions in their own position. The contradictions stem from the fact

[13] *Op. cit.*, p. 256.
[14] *Op. cit.*, p. 11.

that a deviant act can be defined as behavior *which is contrary to a norm or rule.* One type of norm is simply what the members of a social unit think conduct "ought" or "ought not" be. For example, on this basis it is probably true that the act of joining the Communist party is "deviant" in American society, even though the quality of reaction to it in a particular instance may be problematical. This conception of deviation enables one to treat deviant acts and reactions to them as conceptually distinct. But this is not so from the viewpoint of Becker, Erikson, and Kitsuse, because deviant behavior for them *is defined in terms of reactions to it.* On the other hand, while advocates of the new perspective do recognize the "norm" conception of deviation, they do not consistently reject it. Witness, for example:

Becker:

An even more interesting kind of case is found at the other extreme of *secret deviance.* Here an improper act is committed, yet no one notices it or reacts to it as a violation of the rules.[15]

Kitsuse and Cicourel:

We wish to state explicitly that the interpretation of official statistics proposed here *does not* imply that the forms of behavior which the sociologist might define and categorize as deviant (e.g., Merton's modes of adaptation) have no factual basis or theoretical importance.[16]

Erikson:

There are societies in which deviance is considered a natural pursuit for the young, an activity which they can easily abandon when they move through defined ceremonies into adulthood. There are societies which give license to large groups of persons to engage in deviant behavior for certain seasons or on certain days of the year. And there are societies in which special groups are formed to act in ways 'contrary' to the normal expectations of the culture.[17]

Now all of these statements admit, in one way or another, that deviant behavior can be identified in terms of norms, but the authors do not come to grips with the problem and take a consistent stand on the issue. Thus, if deviant behavior is defined in terms of reactions to it, then Becker cannot speak properly of "secret deviance." If behavior defined as deviant by sociologists in reference to the prevailing social norms is "real," then in what sense can one maintain, as Kitsuse does elsewhere, that behavior is deviant if and only if there is a certain kind of reaction to it. Finally, in the case of Erikson, how can the behavior of "large groups of persons" be identified as deviant when they have been given a "license" to engage in it? To be consistent, Becker, Kitsuse, and Erikson would have to insist that behavior which is

15 *Op. cit.,* p. 20.
16 *Op. cit.,* pp. 138–139.
17 *Op. cit.,* p. 313.

contrary to a norm is not deviant unless it is discovered and there is a particular kind of reaction to it. Thus, if persons engage in adultery but their act is not discovered and reacted to in a certain way (by the members of the social unit), then it is not deviant! Similarly, if a person is erroneously thought to have engaged in a certain type of behavior and is reacted to "harshly" as a consequence, a deviant act has taken place!

The extreme position of Becker, Erikson, and Kitsuse is also apparent when attempting to explain why reaction to deviant behavior is not purely random and idiosyncratic. One could argue that a satisfactory explanation cannot be given without making reference to norms, but this concept evidently is not altogether welcome in the new perspective. Finally, apart from the issue of norms, the new perspective negates a significant empirical question: Why do reactions to deviant behavior vary from place to place and time to time? An answer to this question from the new perspective necessarily would be at least partially tautological because deviant behavior is defined in terms of reactions to it.

As the tone of the above criticism suggests, this writer differs with Becker, *et al.*, on the issue of identifying deviant behavior. My preference is to identify deviant acts by reference to norms, and treat reaction to deviation as a contingent property. However, this preference reflects nothing more than opinion, and the ultimate evaluation of the new conception on this point must await an assessment of substantive theory generated by it. Accordingly, no claim is made that Becker, Erikson, and Kitsuse are "wrong." Rather, the criticism is that (1) they have not specified exactly what kind of reaction identified behavior as deviant and (2) they have failed to take a consistent stand on a particular conceptual issue.

OVERVIEW

The major trend in the study of crime and deviant behavior has been in the direction of a distinctly "social" conception of the subject matter. Whereas Lombroso thought of criminals in biological terms and later positivists sought to discover intrinsic features of criminal acts, the new perspective conceives of both in terms of the quality of social reaction to behavior. Accordingly, whether or not a person or an act is criminal or deviant is a matter of the way in which the public and/or officials react.

The relativistic criterion of deviation introduced by the new perspective is in keeping with contemporary sociological principles. Further, a social conception of the phenomenon promises to generate substantive theories that are distinctly sociological in outlook. But the new conception has left at least four crucial questions unanswered. First, what elements in the scheme are intended to be definitions rather than substantive theory? Second, is the ultimate goal to explain deviant behavior or to explain reactions to deviation? Third, is deviant behavior to be identified exclusively in terms of reaction to it? Fourth, exactly what kind of reaction identifies behavior as deviant?

No claim is made that the advocates of the new conception are unable to answer the above questions, nor that their answers would be wrong. The only point is that the questions must be answered if the new conception is to develop and receive the constructive attention that it deserves.

5

Albert J. Reiss

The Study of Deviant Behavior: Where the Action Is*

The early American sociologists wrote unabashedly about social pathology and the action lay in social reform. Indeed it was not uncommon for sociologists at the turn of the century to be actively engaged in reform movements, often with only a second hand acquaintance with ideas concerning that which they would reform. Some were among the severest critics of the established order and a few lost their jobs to their principles.

But the scene changed and with it the action. Sociologists studied social problems and the more sophisticated wrote more or less dispassionately of social movements and of personal and social disorganization. Particularly within the Chicago school the action shifted to "making the scene." Sociologists made their naturalistic observations without quite going native. Though not without involvement in changing the established order, their analyses were cloaked within the terminology of personal and social reorganization and the stages of social movements. They were more likely than not to renounce reform.

Beginning in the mid-thirties the stage, the scene, and even to a degree the actors shifted. Interest in the study of social movements declined; almost disappeared. The action began to lie in a ". . . systematic approach to the analysis of social and cultural sources of deviant behavior."[1] Writing in 1938 Merton signaled the shift in action,

From *Ohio Valley Sociologist*, **32** (Autumn, 1966, 1–12, by permission of the author and the publishers.
* Presidential Address, Twenty-Eighth Annual Meeting of The Ohio Valley Sociological Society, Dayton, Ohio, April 29, 1966.
[1] Robert K. Merton, "Social Structure and Anomie," *American Sociological Review*, **3** (1938) 672–682, p. 672.

stating: "Our primary aim is to discover how some social structures exert a definite pressure upon certain persons in the society to engage in noncomformist rather than conformist conduct."[2] He argued that our sociological task was to explain variation in rates of deviant behavior, not its incidence, and he introduced functional theory by way of explanation.

While the action lay in investigating cultural and social structure, there is no mistaking the fact that deviance was defined as the behavior or conduct of people, their modes of adaptation to cultural goals and institutionalized means. Later developments of the theory while elaborating the theory of social structure emphasizing differential opportunities, and while elaborating the theory of cultural structure to emphasize subcultures have left the definition of deviance as behavior or conduct of people unchanged.

Beginning with the 60's there have been growing signs of dissatisfaction with both the definition of deviance and the explanatory variables. The main thrust of this criticism whether by Albert Cohen, Erving Goffman, or Howard Becker has been the failure of the theory to regard deviance as a process or persons becoming labeled as deviant and a concern with organizational responses or adaptation to deviance, an idea that earlier was central to the writings of Clifford Shaw.[3]

Becker's and Goffman's approaches to the study of deviance perhaps are the most serious attempt to redefine the action, both in their reformulation of the problem and in their call for sociologists who study deviance to once again "make the scene" in their investigations. Becker's definition of deviance is cited to illustrate the shift in action:

. . . social groups create deviance by making the rules whose infractions constitute deviance, and by *applying those rules to particular people* and labeling them as outsiders. From this point of view, deviance is not a quality of the act the person commits, but rather a consequence of the application by others of rules and sanctions to an *offender*.[4]

The action for Becker and others has shifted somewhat from the investigation of cultural and social structure *per se* to investigation of ". . . the process of interaction between people, some of whom in the service of their interests make and enforce rules which catch others who, in the service of their own interests, have committed acts which are labeled as deviant."[5]

[2] *Ibid.*, p. 72.
[3] Albert K. Cohen, "The Sociology of the Deviant Act: Anomie Theory and Beyond," *The American Sociological Review*, 30 (February, 1965) 5–14; Erving Goffman, *Asylums*, Garden City: Anchor Books, Doubleday and Co., Inc., 1961; Howard S. Becker, *Outsiders: Studies in The Sociology of Deviance*, The Free Press of Glencoe, 1963.
[4] *Ibid.*, p. 9.
[5] *Ibid.*, p. 163.

Added to the emphasis on interaction is one on enterprise in an organizational sense. As Becker states: ". . . whenever rules are created and applied, we expect that the process of enforcement will be shaped by the *complexity of the organization*, resting on a basis of shared understandings in simpler groups and resulting from political maneuvering and bargaining in *complex structures*.[6]

I would call your attention here to the development of the idea that organization is a crucial element both in the moral crusade and in shaping the process of rule enforcement. While the action then appears to have shifted to the investigation of interaction in an organizational context, there still is no mistaking the fact that deviance is defined in terms of the application of rules to *particular people* and a labeling of them as outsiders.

By now it should be apparent that although I have highlighted the shifts in where the action is in theory and research on deviance, I also have emphasized that the definition of deviance has focused on the behavior of *persons* who are defined or labeled as deviant. My purpose in doing so is to call attention to the fact that more is involved in the study of deviance than the explanation of variation in the rates of deviant behavior of persons or of the moral enterprise involved in the creation and enforcement of rules related to the behavior of persons. More is involved because deviance characterizes the actions of aggregates and organized groups and what we have come to call formal organizations quite apart from the defined deviance of individuals who comprise their membership or hold an official position in them. Though I dislike the term, I am referring to what sometimes is called the "behavior of organizations," activity that is evaluated by moral enterprise and labeled as deviant. It is to this matter that I now turn, suggesting that a more general theory will concern itself not only with the behavior of persons but of organizations.

What I shall say about organizational deviance first must be understood by discussing several forms of deviance that apparently are similar to, or an aspect of, organizational deviance. One of these is referred to as "institutionalized" or "patterned evasion."

Institutionalized or patterned evasion is said to occur in those cases ". . . where a publicly accepted norm is covertly violated on a large scale, with the tacit acceptance or even approval of the same society or group, at least so long as the violation is concealed."[7] Examples commonly referred to as patterned evasion are income tax evasion, sharp business practices, drinking wet and voting dry, and some of the patterns of sex behavior reported in the Kinsey studies. Common to all

6 *Ibid.*, p. 146, italics mine.
7 Robin Williams, *American Society*, New York: Alfred A. Knopf, revised edition, 1962, p. 379.

patterned evasion is the element of individual behavior deviating from norms and institutional support for the deviation so long as it is not processed before an open public.

Though this is not the place to develop the matter, I want to suggest that there are at least two major and different forms of patterned evasion. In the first type the patterning arises largely from an aggregative effect of individuals deviating from norms, their evasion carries relatively low risk of detection, and at least moderate cultural support if not publicly processed. There is relatively little by way of organized relations among the individuals who deviate, however, and even relatively little formal organizational implementation of the deviant action itself. This is true, for example, of much institutionalized income tax evasion, sharp business practices, cheating in the classroom, and some forms of sex deviation. Premarital sex relations, for example, are all right so long as you don't get pregnant or have a child out of wedlock.

The second type involves a more elaborate and complex organizational system that makes mass evasion possible. The organization itself may be more liable to negative sanctioning than the individuals who evade. Furthermore, individuals or organizations who cater to the interest of the mass who evade may need considerable organizational support in the form of bribes, fixes, and protection if they are to operate. This is true for much of the kind of deviance we call vice that is catered to by what is loosely referred to as organized crime. Much organized crime thrives on institutionalized evasion—buying liquor in a dry area or illegal betting for example. Indeed any form of mass evasion will necessarily be quite different if there is no organized vehicle for its practice.

Though the literature tends to confuse the matter, it is important in these cases to distinguish the deviance of the organization from the patterned deviance of the clients. They pose quite different problems for rule makers and enforcers in the system since the client system generally is only loosely integrated with the organized service system. Police action, for example, more generally is directed against the operators and their business rather than against the clients in most vice activity.

A word needs to be said, too, about what Edwin Sutherland defined as white-collar crime. Sutherland was acutely aware of the fact that what he termed white-collar crime involved organizations as well as individuals. His paper "Is 'White-Collar Crime' Crime?" published in 1945 analyzes the decisions by courts and commissions against the 70 latest industrial and mercantile corporations in the United States for four types of law.[8] Despite this organizational starting point, his primary concern in the paper is with white-collar criminals, particularly businessmen

[8] Edwin H. Sutherland, "Is 'White-Collar Crime' Crime?" *American Sociological Review*, X (1945) pp. 132–39.

and he discusses such matters as the differential status of the business-men and the stigma of the crime attached to the offenders. Not unaware of organizational factors in white-collar crime, it appears that analysis of the crime of the organization, *per se*, was somewhat alien to his approach.

I have said that my main purpose is to argue for the use of a more general theory that encompasses the deviant character of organizations as well as of persons. The remarks that follow are directed toward exploring the more general relations of social organization to deviant behavior leading up to a consideration of the deviant organization.

The social-psychological approach to deviance has generally considered any person as deviant whose behavior departs from normative expectations. This concern with deviance as behavior departing from normative expectations had led social-psychologists into a concern for the comparison of deviants with conformers. Their *bete noire* has been the fact that societal organization has not produced for them the necessary data on *all* deviants of a given kind, e.g., all criminals, or even all homicides. This has led them into the pursuit of the "hidden" deviant—the hidden delinquent, the "white-collar" criminal, the closet sexual offender. Interestingly enough generally this search has been carried out only when social organization makes it fairly easy to detect the "hidden" deviants. There has been little searching for types of deviants that the social organization coerces almost entirely into a hidden or secret position—the subversives, the "closet fags," the members of an "underground," or spys to give a few illustrations.

This search for the "hidden" deviant as well as those who are processed within some organizational context and therefore accessible to investigation has occurred primarily because of an interest in the deviant person, or at most an interest in explaining why deviant persons occur where they do within a structural system. Parenthetically I might say that students of cultural and social structure might find it far more worthwhile to explain differences between "hidden" and "known" delinquents in terms of the organizational system that produces these very differences rather than to try to aggregate all of the delinquents and explain variation in their occurrence in structural locations. But the point I wish to make here is that like Becker and others I find this approach severely limited from a sociological point of view precisely because deviance is defined in purely *cultural and behavioral terms*—that is, it is defined quite apart from social organization. When it is defined in organizational terms, the investigator is almost apologetic—these are only the "official" delinquents, or the "offenders" who were incarcerated. He apologizes because he thinks he "knows" something is missing. But what is missing? For these theorists a norm and behavior is all that is essential to the definition of deviance; there is no social organization related to the definition of deviance in this approach. Social organization, when it is introduced, is introduced as an explanation for the behavior.

Time does not permit me to pursue this point further, but I simply want to suggest that from an organizational point of view, there is no deviant in a purely normative-behavioral sense. This is so for a number of reasons that I shall state briefly before moving on.

First, it is so because the social control systems in societies are differentially organized in relation to deviance. It perhaps is mistaken to posit, as does Parsons, that: "The theory of social control is the obverse of the theory of the genesis of deviant behavior tendencies."[9] Social control—sanctioning systems—are part and parcel of the definition and genesis of deviant behavior.

Second, the definition of deviance, as well noted by Lemert, Kitsuse, Becker and others, is a matter of societal reaction to deviance; it is a matter of organized processing of deviance. A central problem is to explain differences in who is processed as deviant and what difference this makes.

Third, deviant behavior itself bears a complex relationship to organizations. Yet in simple terms, societal processing of deviants is partly a matter of the consequences of deviance for organization and organizations. Some forms of deviance are more clearly related to specific organizational contexts than others and the definition and processing of deviants arises precisely because of their relationship to organizations. To illustrate, check forgery and embezzlement are crimes against businesses. Malicious destruction of property is more often against an organization than an individual property owner so far as the definition and processing of deviants is concerned. Crimes against persons involved a victim and an offender; yet it is the criminal who is most often studied rather than the relational system of victim and offender. A striking sociological fact for example is that a majority of reported rapes are for instances where there was a prior relationship between the victim and the offender. Rape of the person where there is no prior relationship is relatively uncommon.

I might say in this connection that from my point of view the investigation of the organizational relationship of deviants should have a high priority in the study of deviance. This would involve investigations of the relational properties of victims and offenders where victims are broadly defined to include formal organizations as well as persons. It is clear on the one hand that individual deviance may destroy organizations; it is equally clear that societal organization "protects" the victim from the deviant. It is within this context for example, that the

9 Talcott Parsons, *The Social System,* Glencoe: The Free Press, 1951, p. 297.

institution and organization of insurance in modern societies assumes dominant proportions.

My first point then is that from the point of view of social organization (if not altogether by definition of what comprises a social system) *while an individual may deviate from norms without any organization being deviant, there is no individual deviance that does not involve social interaction and organization.* Perhaps this may appear to be saying no more than deviance in the Durkheim sense is a social fact. I am pressing, however, for the consideration of how organization enters into individual deviance as the primary goal of the sociological study of deviance.

My second point is that *much individual deviance is intricately linked to organized systems and organizations that also are defined as deviant.* The illegal acts of persons are facilitated if not altogether engendered by deviant organizational systems.

What I am referring to in this second instance are those cases where persons engage in deviant acts, for example in gambling, in a client system that is defined as deviant—in this example a policy operation. Both the organization—here the policy operation and the client—here someone who buys a number—then are deviant. To distinguish this from the third type, I shall shortly discuss, I want to emphasize that the behavior defined as deviant—in this example gambling—can occur under other organizational circumstances as well—for example, at a licensed track—that is, it can occur apart from a deviant service system.

Quite clearly then what is defined as vice serviced by a criminal organization falls within this category. Though time does not permit me to develop the point, from the standpoint of social control more effort is directed toward control of the organization—for example, policy—than to control the deviance of individuals who are clients, the persons who buy the numbers. This is especially true for forms of vice such as gambling where the deviance of the clients is generally disregarded, or for the illegal sale rather than the consumption of alcohol illegally manufactured, even of the use as against the manufacture or sale of narcotics. Indeed the sanctions at law against the client are considerably less punitive than those against members of the organization, or the organization itself. The bootlegger can loose his entire investment and be individually sanctioned; the purchaser will generally go free.

The third way that organization and persons are related in deviance occurs *when the organization is defined as deviant in such a way as to classify all members or participants in it as deviant.* A most important example of this type of deviance is what Smelser defines as the value-oriented social movement.[10] The value-oriented movement arises under

[10] Neil J. Smelser, *Theory of Collective Behavior,* New York: The Free Press of Glencoe, 1963. Chapter X.

conditions where the means for reconstituting the social order are closed off to persons, thereby turning their attention to a reconstitution of the value-organization of the system. Smelser includes in this class nativistic, messianic, millenerian, sectarian, utopian, and nationalistic movements as well as among others, political revolutions. Though Smelser does not make the point, there is not only an implicit or explicit attack on the value system inherent in these movements but also an attack on the constitutive order that results in their being labeled as deviant and members by inclusion in them are labeled as deviant.

There, of course, is considerable variability in the degree to which a society may formally or legally define such movements and their organizations as deviant. The "subversive" organization is a clear example of such a value-oriented movement and in our own recent past the U.S. Attorney General's list of Subversive Organizations is a case in point. The Wobblies of the early 1900's, the Bolshevik movement of the 20's and the nativist movements of the 30's and 40's are other examples of national concern with political subversion. American history provides ample illustration of national preoccupation with organized subversion of its values, religious, political, and economic, not to extend the list of examples.

Perhaps the best example of a study of this type of organizational deviance is Selznick's study, *The Organizational Weapon*, a study based on a more general theory of organizations. Selznick writes:

"It is a primary function of the constitutional order—whether of a particular organization or of the political community itself—to make power *responsible* by limiting the uses to which it may be put and specifying how it may be won. . . . We shall speak of organizations and organizational practices as weapons when they are used by a power-seeking elite *in a manner unrestrained by the constitutional order of the arena in which the contest takes place.*" In this usage, "weapon" is not meant to denote *any* political tool, but one torn from its normal context and unacceptable to the community as a legitimate mode of action."[11] That is as much a language for the study of deviant organizations perhaps as we have in the literature and it serves as a basis for the study of Bolshevik strategy and tactics—an organizational problem.

The fourth way that persons and organizations are linked in deviance occurs when *the organization is defined as deviant but only those members who can be specifically charged with behavioral participation are defined as deviant.* International law provides some interesting cases in points. Certain of the trials of Nurenberg are of this order and even the Eichmann trial fits in some respects. From a sociological point of view, one should not be misled by the fact that in the specific drama where the individual is tried as deviant, he in all likelihood is accused

11 Philip Selznick, *The Organizational Weapon*, New York: McGraw Hill, 1952, p. 2.

of specific crimes as well. For then drama begins with an indictment of the organizational system as deviant and some are held more responsible than others.

The fifth way that persons and organizations are linked in deviance occurs *when the organization is defined as deviant as a consequence of the behavior of some of its members.* I suppose we all immediately think in this context of the classic cases of corrupt government or organizations—the scandal in a formal organization. Thus the traffic bureau or the police department is defined as corrupt. The organization undergoes some organizational transformation as a consequence and some of its members are removed from their office or position, even indicted and perhaps sentenced. There are other examples that readily come to mind. One of the more recent to come to public attention involved price-fixing among the electrical companies. The major electrical companies were fined and in other ways sanctioned for the behavior of officials; a few officials were indicted, tried and sentenced.

The final way that individuals and organizations are linked in deviance occurs when the *organization is defined and sanctioned as deviant, but the individual participants are not so regarded.* While from a sociological point of view there can be no organization without behavior of individuals, the point here is that none of the individuals in the organization are defined as deviant for the behavior they engaged in, behavior that is related to the organization being defined as deviant. Let me illustrate with several examples from our recent past.

The current civil rights movement provides several cases in point. State commissions against discrimination in employment, housing, and civil rights generally spend the bulk of their time in defining and sanctioning organizations as deviant. An employing establishment will be defined as discriminating against minorities and sanctioned for it. Yet the personnel officer who does the hiring, the officials who set the policy, or the workers who engage in discriminatory practice are under these conditions not defined as deviants and sanctioned for their behavior.

Segregation of public facilities provides other examples. In the case of school desegregation, the charges are brought against a school system through its Board of Education. It is the system that is defined as deviant and sanctioned. The board members, the superintendent, and the teachers may escape specific definition as deviant. The legal system is geared to defining the organized school system as failing to comply and legal and fiscal sanctions are directed against the organization to coerce compliance. In addition, local organizations such as the NAACP and their national Legal Defense Fund exert pressure to comply.

International conflict situations present numerous examples where one or a number of social systems will define others as deviant and impose sanctions without defining any leaders or members as deviant. To be sure, of course, in some cases both nations and leaders are defined as deviant but there are many cases where they are not. The boycott, the blockade, diplomatic recognition, the loan and other forms of aid are important sanctions for deviance in relations among nations.

I cite these examples solely to call attention to the fact that both within and among social systems, organized units can be defined and sanctioned as deviant without any person who is a member of the organization defined as deviant in the processing of deviance.

If time permitted I would like to say something about how the values, norms, and sanctions of social systems are differentially organized so that organizational deviance is more explicitly dealt with in some social systems than in others. It is apparent, for example, that the American social system gives high priority to individual rights in the system. Yet we are constantly engaged in balancing individual against collective interests. In balancing out individual and collective interests, it perhaps becomes more difficult to define and sanction organizational deviance in systems where individual rights occupy the priority they do in our system.

In the American social system, a principal way to sanction organizations is to define the behavior of persons in the organization as deviant, thereby sanctioning the organization by sanctioning its members. Given the importance of leadership in organization, the organization is especially vulnerable to sanctions against its leadership, particularly when those sanctions force a succession in leadership. The decline of the IWW occurred in part because of a coerced succession in leadership.

Yet it would be mistaken to assume that sanctions are not directed against organizations as well as individuals. The strike, the sit-in, the boycott, the blockade, the occupation of a territory, the financial subsidity, second and third class mailing privileges, the court order and police action to coerce are but some of the kinds of sanctions that are generally applied only to organizations when they are deviant.

Conclusion

We are coming to the end of my remarks. Several things I hope have become apparent in this cursory survey of where the action should be in the study of deviance.

I suggest that we have been preoccupied with defining persons as deviant at the expense of examining organizational deviance. Closely related to this is the fact that much of our concern with deviance has focused on violations of the criminal code in western systems, treating deviance under the civil code as nonproblematic in our theory. We have been preoccupied with suicide and homicide but not with deicide or genocide. Indeed I am struck by the fact that there is no sociological writing of consequence on genocide. We have been concerned with hidden deviance of individuals and not the visible deviance of organizations.

In brief the general thrust of my remarks has been to suggest that in the study of deviant behavior the action does not lie primarily in motivation to deviance on the one hand nor in cultural and social structure on the other. The Action rather is in the study of social organization—the organizational matrix that encompasses the deviant behavior of persons and the deviant behavior of organizations. A more general theory can encompass both. Indeed, the theory of organizations is easily adapted to the study of organizational deviance. Perhaps the time has come to remake the scene as well as make it. The action lies not only in a return to actors but to their organization.

6

Shirley S. Angrist

Mental Illness and Deviant Behavior

For over a decade, debate over the nature of mental illness has continued. Titles of articles and books have been suggestive of the various points of view: the myth of mental illness, personality disorder is disease, disease and the patterns of behavior, the social limits of eccentricity.[1] And the debate continues.

In this paper, it will be shown that at least four themes or positions can be culled from the literature and that no single position resolves all the related empirical or theoretical issues. The first approach asserts that mental illness is a type of deviant behavior. A second position takes the basic premise that mental disorders are pathology or disease in the psychological or psychiatric sense and not pertinent to conformity-deviance theory, which is concerned with interactions in a social system. A third approach looks on some types of mental disorder as deviant behavior while other behavioral constellations are defined as illness or medical phenomena. Still a fourth standpoint calls for specifications of the definers of behavior according to their social status and degree of professional training. These four approaches represent some current attempts to answer the question, What is mental illness? In particular, those writings are referred to which tackle some aspect

From *The Sociological Quarterly*, **7** (Fall, 1966) 436–448, by permission of the author and the publishers.

[1] Thomas S. Szasz, *The Myth of Mental Illness* (New York: Hoeber-Harper, 1961); David P. Ausubel, "Personality Disorder is Disease," *American Psychologist*, 16:69–74 (Jan., 1961); Harold Wolff, "Disease and the Patterns of Behavior," in E. Gartly Jaco, *Patients, Physicians and Illness* (Glencoe, Ill.: Free Press, 1958), pp. 54–61; G. Morris Carstairs, "The Social Limits of Eccentricity: An English Study," in Marvin K. Opler, *Culture and Mental Health* (New York: Macmillan, 1959), pp. 373–89.

of the conceptual relationship between mental disorder and deviant behavior.

It is our purpose in this paper, to describe the several prevalent arguments in terms of their major themes. By doing so, we hope to underline the assumptions basic to each approach, to show how the discrepant views articulate with each other, and to specify some unresolved problems in the ongoing debate.

It will be seen that some of the key issues center upon the uncertain state of knowledge about the etiology of illness, the relationship of illness to stress, the difference between organic and functional illness categories, the relationship between role performance, illness, and deviant behavior, the set of concepts central to a theory of conformity and deviance, and their unambiguous meaning. The major conclusion to be drawn is that knowledge in these areas is still tenuous, and that a paucity of tested hypotheses characterizes the sociological levels of analysis. So far we seem to hover in the realm of normative rather than empirical theory.[2]

SCHOOLS OF THOUGHT

MENTAL ILLNESS AS DEVIANT BEHAVIOR: SOCIOLOGICAL APPROACHES

Probably the prototype of this approach is Parson's conception of illness as a type of deviant behavior, i.e., behavior that in some way fails to fulfill the individual's role expectations. Either consciously or unconsciously, illness is motivated deviance which results in disturbed social relations.[3] As a form of deviant behavior, illness is only one of several alternatives open to the individual as a mode of reaction to social pressure or "strains." It is "partly biologically and partly socially defined. Participation in the social system is always potentially relevant to the state of illness, to its etiology and to the conditions of successful therapy. . . ."[4] The individual who is sick is subject to a set of norms governing this category of deviance. According to Parsons, these norms are (1) that the sick person is exempt from normal social obligations; (2) that he is excused from responsibility for his own "condition"; (3) that illness is undesirable and the patient should strive to get well; (4) that the sick person needs to receive help. It then becomes the role of

[2] Don Martindale, "Social Disorganization: The Conflict of Normative and Empirical Approaches," in Howard Becker and Alvin Boskoff (eds.), *Modern Sociological Theory* (New York: Dryden Press, 1957), pp. 340–67.

[3] Talcott, Parsons, *The Social System* (Glencoe, Ill.: Free Press, 1951), chap. 10, "Social Structure and Dynamic Process: The Case of Modern Medical Practice," pp. 428–79; Harry Johnson, *Sociology: A Systematic Introduction* (New York: Harcourt Brace, 1960), chap. 20, "Social Conformity, Social Deviation, and Social Control," pp. 552–86.

[4] Parsons, *op. cit.,* p. 431.

the therapist to provide such help, support and permissiveness, while at the same time he avoids reciprocation of the deviant behavior (e.g., the delusions or fantasies of the mentally ill).

Wolff and Ausubel assert—much as Parsons does—that illness has a fundamentally personal and social basis, and they focus on the deviant act or behavior.[5] Illness, whether the organic, psychosomatic, or mental, is a pattern of response to situational demands which the individual cannot meet appropriately. It is thus an expression of stress, strain, change, or problems of living. The deviant component lies in illness as an available though inappropriate mode of behavior; the individual reacts with maladaptive behavior when he cannot cope with his social situation.[6]

In the classical sociological analysis of deviant behavior, Merton's anomie theory, focus is on the deviant person; here, behavioral manifestations of mental illness are classified as retreatism. Because of their location in the social stratification system, individuals have differential access to societal goals. In this means-end schema, mental illness (along with hoboism, addiction, bohemianism) represents the individual's rejection both of culturally prescribed goals and of institutionally available means for success.[7]

Other characterizations of mental illness as deviant behavior have focused on the set of attitudes America has inherited from its roots in Western Civilization. The mentally ill have always been regarded primarily as deviants.[8] Both the confinement of such persons in jails, workhouses, and almshouses, and their banishment from local communities represented rejection.[9] Today, the Joint Commission for Mental Health reports, this pattern of social rejection is evidenced in the continued existence of primitive custodial hospitals "that seem to have no defenders but endure despite all attacks."[10] The vestiges of stigma and social trouble remain associated with mental disorders; thus, persons with such ailments are legitimately confined in the mental hos-

[5] Wolff, op. cit.

[6] Ausubel, op. cit. For our purposes, Ausubel's title is a misnomer. He really seems to be saying that deviant behavior and mental disorder are essentially the same and not separate phenomena.

[7] Robert K. Merton, Social Theory and Social Structure (rev. ed.; Glencoe, Ill.: Free Press, 1957), pp. 153–55, 187–90.

[8] John A. Clausen, "Mental Disorders," in Robert K. Merton and Robert A. Nisbet (eds.), Contemporary Social Problems (New York: Harcourt, Brace & World, 1961), pp. 127–80. Clausen suggests two reasons for his prevalent attitude. (1) The mentally ill person is often unable to recognize that he is sick and needs help; and (2) mental illness in its various forms tends to disrupt interpersonal relations. See pp. 127–31, especially.

[9] J. Sanbourne Bockoven, "Moral Treatment in American Psychiatry," Journal of Nervous and Mental Diseases, 124:167–94 (Aug., 1956), and 292–321 (Sept., 1956).

[10] Joint Commission on Mental Illness and Health, Action for Mental Health (New York: Basic Books, 1961), p. 190.

pital—a residence for "various categories of socially troublesome people."[11] In one view the institutionalization of the patient emphasizes society's value on conformity and by this token, implies that the mentally ill are primarily to be regarded as deviants who need to learn conforming or socially acceptable behavior.[12]

MENTAL ILLNESS AS PERSONALITY DISTURBANCE: PSYCHOLOGICAL APPROACHES

This school of thought appears simple and clear-cut in the assertion that mental disorders are disease forms or pathology of the personality, it matters not which diagnostic categories are included as mental illness.[13] The gist of this approach is that deviance-conformity theory is basically irrelevant here since its major concern is with social structure in terms of institutionalized expectations and sanctions. The unit of analysis for deviance-conformity theory would therefore be the act, either the "deviant" act or the "conforming" one. By contrast, "Behavior which is psychotic, neurotic, maladjusted, or otherwise pathological from a psychiatric or mental hygiene point of view is defined in terms of its dependence upon or consequences for personality structure. Therefore, the pathology of personality is not, as such, subject matter for the sociology of deviant behavior."[14]

This notion that illness is not simply deviance had to be considered in recent research results on the outcome of mental hospitalization.[15] In order to evaluate outcome, my colleagues and I employed two criteria: the ability of the former patient to avoid rehospitalization and posthospital performance. By posthospital performance we meant instrumental role performance in the basic sociological sense of fulfilling

[11] Ervin Goffman, "The Medical Model and Mental Hospitalization: Some Notes on the Vicissitudes of the Tinkering Trades," Asylums (New York: Anchor Books, 1961), p. 354.

[12] J. Sanbourne Bockoven, "Some Relationships between Cultural Attitudes toward Individuality and Care of the Mentally Ill: An Historical Study," in Milton Greenblatt, et al., The Patient and the Mental Hospital (Glencoe, Ill.: Free Press, 1957), pp. 517–26.

[13] Albert K. Cohen, "The Study of Social Disorganization and Deviant Behavior," in Robert K. Merton, Leonard Broom, and Leonard S. Cottrell, Jr. (eds.), Sociology Today (New York: Basic Books, 1959), pp. 461–84.

[14] Ibid., pp. 462–63.

[15] Shirley Angrist, Simon Dinitz, Mark Lefton, and Benjamin Pasamanick, "Rehospitalization of Female Mental Patients," Archives of General Psychiatry, 4:363–70 (Apr., 1961); Simon Dinitz, et al., "Instrumental Role Expectations and Posthospital Performance of Female Mental Patients," Social Forces, 40:248–54 (Mar., 1962); Shirley Angrist, et al., "Tolerance of Deviant Behavior, Posthospital Performance Levels, and Rehospitalization," Proceedings of the Third World Congress of Psychiatry (Montreal: June, 1961), I: 237–41; Mark Lefton, et al., "Former Mental Patients and Their Neighbors: A Comparison of Performance Levels," J. Health and Human Behavior, 7: 106–113 (Summer, 1966); Howard Freeman and Ozzie Simmons, The Mental Patient Comes Home (New York: Wiley, 1963), especially chap. 12, "Final Considerations and Implications," pp. 196–218.

the expectations of one's roles. Since our patient-subjects were all women, we isolated two role areas: domestic functioning in the household, such as cooking, cleaning, caring for children, and social participation involving leisure activities and interaction with friends, relatives, and neighbors.

Then we developed a measure of "psychological functioning" to indicate which of a series of abnormal symptoms were manifested by the former patient. Since we originally conceived of deficient role performance and abnormal behavior as synonymous (or at least correlative) we were surprised and enlightened by our findings. We found that many patients who showed abnormal behavior in the psychological sense (as appraised both by relatives and by psychiatrists) were adequate role performers socially and domestically. We found also that rehospitalization was explained by relatives not as deviant role behavior but in terms of abnormal or bizarre behavior—i.e., the patient was "sick" rather than unable to perform her role as mother or wife; thus tolerance of deviant behavior by household members and their expectations appeared inappropriate as explanatory of readmission to treatment. Comparison of married former patients with their married neighbors who were never treated for psychiatric difficulties yielded no differences in social participation and domestic role performance, while the patients were significantly lower than controls on the scale of psychological functioning. We concluded therefore that instrumental performance is an unreliable criterion for evaluating total posthospital experience, since it appears to lack concomitance with the patient's psychological condition. It may be inferred that two levels or dimensions of behavior are involved, one with roots in a deviance-conformity framework, the other with meaning in an illness-health framework and the former refers to behavior vis-à-vis the social structure while the latter primarily implicates manifest symptomatology. Thus, our theoretical point of departure had been that the mentally ill are so defined by their deviation from normative behavior. But by the time the data were analyzed we recognized a clear discrepancy between norms governing role performance as compared with those tied to a mental health-mental illness frame of reference.

This leads to conceptual distinction between the abnormal and the deviant. The abnormal person (i.e., one who had a mental disorder) is so defined by reference to "universal indicators" used in psychiatry. In this frame of reference, certain behaviors are viewed as manifestation of anxiety, regression, sensorimotor dysfunctions, reality distortion, depression, excitement; these in turn are taken as evidence of personality abnormality. By contrast, the deviant person underplays, overplays or innovates vis-à-vis socially standardized behavior—that is, he in some way departs from group norms, but he does not necessarily manifest abnormal behavior (although he may theoretically be both deviant and abnormal in his behavior).[16]

NOT ALL TYPES OF MENTAL DISORDER CONSTITUTE ILLNESS

Several discussions of mental illness have provided some modification of the two broader and polar positions. In this third approach, the basic premise held in common (among otherwise disparate dissertations on the subject) is that under *certain conditions* mental illness may be considered deviant behavior, but it cannot so be regarded exclusively— the concept of mental disorder must be qualified. The qualifications can be subsumed into the question of what kind of illness is implied by the term mental illness: psychoneuroses, functional psychoses, organic disorders, bizarre or eccentric behavior.

Writers who concern themselves with this question, point out that the various categories of mental disorders cannot be lumped together because of the wide range of illness types and concomitantly differing degrees of severity involved. Some data bearing on widespread lay conceptions of mental illness are provided by Hollingshead and Redlich. Essentially they modify Parson's approach to mental illness as deviant behavior along two dimensions: by type of illness and in terms of variant social class conceptions of mental disorder. Persons diagnosed as psychoneurotic do not appear to fit the sick role since they retain their social obligations and are, in fact, held responsible for their behavior. Hence, neurotic behavior falls within the scope of conforming behavior. Psychotic patients are more likely to be assigned the sick role especially once they have been institutionalized, but hospitalization itself mitigates the obligation to get well (in deviant behavior terms this would mean the obligation to conform to normal role expectations). The social class factor operates through differing conceptions of mental disorders: patients from higher socioeconomic levels present their symptoms in terms of emotional and interpersonal problems. In the lower classes, the patient's orientation is organic both in the presentation of somatic symptoms and in the request for treatment in the form of drugs or "shots."[17]

Referring to the same issue, Szasz has coined the phrase, "the myth of mental illness." He suggests a basic division of the disease entities usually subsumed under the rubric of mental illness, that is, the separation of brain disease or organic disorders from mental illness or the

[16] John J. Honigmann, "Toward a Distinction between Psychiatric and Social Abnormality," *Social Forces*, 31:274–77 (Mar., 1953). Functional disorders are not distinguished from organic disorders. Honigmann specifies only the symptoms prevented, regardless of origin.

[17] August B. Hollingshead and F. C. Redlich, *Social Class and Mental Illness* (New York: Wiley, 1958), pp. 351–53.

functional and psychoneurotic categories. Although use of these two separate categories is common, the rationale may not be: for Szasz, the functional and neurotic disorders are defined as deviation from psychosocial, ethical, or legal norms. These forms of mental illness are therefore deviant behavior in the basic sociological sense, or in Szasz' terms, these are a medical manifestation of "problems of living," and therefore of central concern to the study of conformity-deviation in a society.[18] The definition of mental illness as deviant behavior is supported in this view, by the negative attitudes toward mentally ill persons who are still often institutionalized involuntarily, and by the fact that in actual practice psychiatrists deal not with a medical phenomenon but with personal, social, and ethical problems.[19] Thus, not only do the diagnostic categories reveal a distinction between actual (organic) disease and basic human problems; both community and professional attitudes toward the mentally ill are thought to reinforce this.

Instead of dichotomizing types of disorders (into functional-organic as does Szasz, or neurotic-psychotic as do Hollingshead and Redlich), the Cummings employ a quasi-dichotomy, if you will.[20] Their distinction is between qualitative deviance, involving bizarre or inappropriate nonnormative behavior which is more likely to be labeled as mental illness by the general public than the second type of quantitative deviance; in quantitative deviance, the concern is mainly with deviation from norms in the sense of falling short of expectations or of overconformity. The distinction between qualitative and quantitative deviance would neatly fit the approach we discussed earlier which conceives of mental illness as a medical entity primarily, were it not for the pains taken by the Cummings to specify that *either* qualitative *or* quantitative deviant behavior may come to be defined as psychological symptomatology. The labeling of behavior as abnormal is governed by the status of the definer, by his impression of the nature of a given act, and by its frequency and duration. For example, they suggest that bizarre (qualitatively nonnormative) behavior of long standing would be thought of as mental illness sooner than the same behavior in intermittent form; quantitatively deviant behavior which is intermittent might be tolerated indefinitely.

THE LABELING OF MENTAL ILLNESS IS A FUNCTION OF
    VARIOUS SETS OF DEFINERS

We look next at a further refinement of the broader conception of mental illness as social deviation. Now we are interested not simply in

[18] Szasz, *op. cit.*
[19] *Ibid.*, pp. 209–11, 296.
[20] Elaine Cumming and John Cumming, "Affective Symbolism, Social Norms and Mental Illness," *Psychiatry*, 19:77–85 (Feb., 1956).

the observed, but also in the observer: Whose judgments are the referents by which to evaluate behavior as deviant or conforming? In other words to which set of definers of behavior do we refer? Some answers to this question have been provided by substantive theoretical analyses of the mental patient's role and by research data from several studies. Recently, Albert Cohen has argued at length for a theory of deviant behavior which accounts for the "interaction between deviance and milieu," for the processual nature of deviance as ongoing interaction between the actor and members of his role set.[21] But so far, we lack precise concepts to handle the variant responses to bizarre behavior. There are varying definitions held by different social classes, ethnic groups, professional and occupational categories, and even family groups.[22]

In one study, it was found that the nature of the help source confers more or less stigma on the seeker—greater stigma attaches to use of psychiatric professional help, less to nonmedical help; the strength of rejection may be a function of visibility of deviance rather than pathology. The mental patient thus is most clearly defined as deviant when he seeks the very category of help which health professionals would consider most appropriate to his difficulty.[23]

In a study of the various definitions wives have of their husbands' mental illness, Charlotte Schwartz shows the contrast in orientation toward behavior between psychiatrist and wife of the hospitalized patient. As might be expected, it is the psychiatrist who tends to see the patient's behavior as abnormal and disturbed, whereas the wife continues to focus on the normality aspects even after her husband is hospitalized. The wife's definition appears to lie in a deviance-conformity framework: "The wife of a patient in a mental hospital almost invariably considers that *something* is wrong with her husband. . . . But although she believes something is wrong with him, she does not necessarily conclude that he is mentally ill."[24]

The very labeling of behavior as sick or deviant may initiate the individual's internalization of the "sick role." The behavior leads to the

[21] Albert K. Cohen, "The Sociology of the Deviant Act," *American Sociological Review*, 30:5–14 (Feb., 1965). Again, Cohen questions the applicability of a deviant behavior theory, such as Parsons' social control approach to illness and therapy.

[22] See Hollingshead and Redlich, *op. cit.*; John P. Spiegel, "Some Cultural Aspects of Transference and Countertransference," in Jules H. Masserman (ed.), *Individual and Family Dynamics* (New York: Grune and Stratton, 1959), pp. 160–82.

[23] Derek L. Phillips, "Rejection of the Mentally Ill," *American Sociological Review*, 29:679–87 (Oct., 1964).

[24] Charlotte C. Schwartz, "Perspectives on Deviance: Wives' Definition of Their Husbands' Mental Illness," *Psychiatry*, 20:275–91 (Aug., 1957); and David Mechanic, "Some Factors in Identifying and Defining Mental Illness," *Mental Hygiene*, 46:66–74 (Jan., 1962). Mechanic suggests not only a difference in attitude between psychiatrists and families of patients, he points out that police may use still other conceptions.

label which again elicits the behavior. Then, deviance generates deviance and halting the process is difficult.[25]

In their study of attitudes toward mental illness, the Cummings report findings to support the hypothesis that psychiatrically trained persons (doctors and nurses) are more likely to define patients' behavior as manifestations of mental illness than are lay persons. But they indicate that such a definition is not an all-or-none matter; rather, the tendency to use psychological-medical criteria rather than deviant behavior criteria increases the more advanced the respondents' professional level. Among the professionally trained, nursing students with each added year of training come increasingly to use medical criteria; but among psychiatric nurses, ward supervisors use such criteria more than nurses at lower levels. In turn, nurses are exceeded in use of psychiatric standards only by hospital psychiatrists.[26]

It has been pointed out that the hospitalized patient usually comes to accept the medical definition while his family retains the lay conception, and this divergence of expectations creates a dilemma for the patient.[27] But as Goffman has indicated, the divergence is not simply between a professional medical orientation and a lay deviancy conception. It is complicated by the ambivalence inherent in the medical attitude towards mental disorder; that is, hospital staff appear to entertain an unofficial negative evaluation of mental illness as shameful (and in this sense as normatively deviant) along with their official assessment of the mental patient as sick. Thus, for all members of the community, psychiatrically-trained persons included, mental illness connotes a "puzzling descriptive phenomenon, a problem whose social aspects are not adequately encompassed within the medical context."[28]

IMPLICATIONS AND UNRESOLVED PROBLEMS

In the foregoing discussion of conceptual approaches to mental disorder, we have attempted to set out major themes or points of view. It must be emphasized that these approaches are often overlapping and rarely mutually exclusive. Our aim has been to stress central themes.

[25] Edwin M. Lemert, "Social Structure, Social Control, and Deviation," in Marshall B. Clinard (ed.), *Anomie and Deviant Behavior* (New York: Free Press, 1964), p. 57–97.

[26] Cumming and Cumming, *op. cit.*

[27] Kai T. Erikson, "Patient Role and Social Uncertainty: A Dilemma of the Mentally Ill," *Psychiatry*, 20:263–74 (Aug., 1957); Goffman, "On Characteristics of Total Institutions," *Asylums*, pp. 3–124.

[28] Clausen, in Merton and Nisbet, *op. cit.*, p. 130. For further hazards in the psychiatric assessment of mental illness, see Benjamin Pasamanick, Simon Dinitz, and Mark Lefton, "Psychiatric Orientation and Its Relation to Diagnosis and Treatment in a Mental Hospital," *The American Journal of Psychiatry*, 116:127–32 (Aug., 1959).

Hopefully, synthesis of the commonalities provides a way to appraise current theory and usage.

To recapitulate the mainstreams of the debate on the nature of mental illness: First, the thesis that mental illness is a type of deviant behavior equates *all* types of illness as manifestations of the individual's inability to conform to institutionalized expectations—illness is one alternative mode of deviant expression open to the individual. Second, the argument for mental disorder as a medical-psychiatric phenomenon regards mental illness as disturbance of the personality system but not of the social system. In this view, no distinction is made among categories of mental illness, such as the common one of functional versus organic disorders; only the overt behavioral manifestations of "underlying" disorder are considered. A third viewpoint holds to the necessary identification of subtypes under the heading of mental illness; this idea is that some types of behavior often labeled mental illness may represent pathology while others fall more properly in the sphere of societal expectations and consequent problems in everyday life. Fourth, there is the argument that nonnormative behavior is defined differentially and an illness rubric may more readily be used by some status occupants than by others in our society.

The loose ends left by any one of the aforementioned approaches are glaring. Even taken together all four schools of thought suffer from sins of omission. Important issues remain unresolved. I want to discuss briefly a few of these issues.

In no field, least of all in sociology, has the etiology of mental illness (or illnesses) been explained. We do not know how the set of behaviors arise which are designated as mentally ill. If indeed the causes are multiple (such as brain damage, or genetic, situational, developmental, or societal factors) what are the relative contributions and conditions characteristic of these causes? How does one sort out the biology, psychology, sociology of mental illnesses?

In Figure 1, I have diagramed a few possible differences in definitions given to mental illness phenomena by the three disciplines. Some distinctions may rely on vocabulary confusion rather than on conceptual discrepancies, and there is obvious overlap across fields. The overlap in explanations of etiology and in definitions would not necessarily be a problem if they did not result in different units for analysis. Furthermore, treatment implications stem most directly from the chosen units for analysis. Do you focus on the symptom, the organ, the act, the person, the group? In other words, what do you study? whom or what do you treat? how do you treat?

Any single approach to defining mental illness makes assumptions about etiology. For example, if mental illness is deviant behavior, the illness behavior appears to be motivated (albeit unconsciously) since the individual has presumably chosen among alternative modes of deviant behavior. From this it follows that a functional-organic dichotomy is irrelevant, and biological bases of illness are probably fictive. Further, this assumes that illness is primarily an expression of life stresses confronting the individual. One might well ask why cannot illness equally represent banal malfunctioning of a fallible machine. The explanation of illness in terms of "deeper" levels of analysis has unfortunately failed to provide guidelines whereby such assumptions might be tested. Whether either stress or motivation is seen as an independent variable, we still have not specified the conditions surrounding the incidence of illness as a dependent variable, nor the category of sick or vulnerable individuals, nor the pattern(s) of illness. A common area of confusion about etiology involves the conceptual relationship between two forms of deviant behavior: crime and mental illness. Illness may be used to explain crime, itself a type of deviance; by this reasoning the crazy, sick person commits crimes!

FIGURE 1.

Approaches of Three Disciplines to Mental Illness

Discipline	Assumptions About Etiology	Definitions of Mental Illness	Units of Analysis
Biology	Organic Genetic	Disease Pathology	Diseased organ Sick person
Psychology	Behavioral Developmental Interpersonal	Personality disturbance Abnormal behavior	Symptom Behavior Abnormal person
Sociology	Behavioral Developmental (socialization) Interpersonal (situational) Social system or group genesis	Deviant behavior Nonconformity Retreatism	Act, behavior Deviant person Category of deviance

A second kind of difficulty might be termed "the sociologistic fallacy." Reference is made here to the attempts to explain both origins of and responses to illness in traditional sociological terms. The impressive materials compiled on juvenile delinquents, criminals, drug addicts, and alcoholics have also been collected on mental patients. So far, however, theories of deviant behavior, such as those based on anomie, illegitimate opportunity structures, differential association, social disorganization, cannot account for mental illness since they assume deviance to be

group-based in genesis and maintenance.[29] At this stage in our knowledge, it is not certain that mental illness either arises through social
interaction or that the mentally ill person is sustained in his unusual or
sick behavior by other sick associates. Nor is it clear that the mentally ill
person need be deficient in role performance. The assumption of role
theories that expectations determine behavior ignores the possible biological independence of the illness.

Conceptually, there has been the blurring of units of analysis. Do
we refer to the deviant person (e.g., "the confirmed alcoholic," "the
hardened criminal"), the deviant act (robbing a bank, seeing ghosts),
or to the category of deviant behavior (crime, addiction, prostitution)?[30] There has also been the difficulty to distinguish clearly among
various categories of mental illness: treated versus untreated disorders,
neuroses, psychoses, brain syndromes, eccentric behavior, disturbed behavior, maladjustment.[31] One interesting and workable solution to the
conceptual problem is to ignore it, as psychologists do now in using behavior modification. They posit no underlying illness; they assume
mainly that behavior can be changed and that there is no difference
between adaptive and maladaptive behavior—any identifiable behaviors
can be reinforced, extinguished, or shaped without assumptions about
the causes or nature of illness.[32]

Although behavior modification may be one answer to treatment
problems, it does not solve the conceptual confusion in deviant behavior
theories. So far the only sociological remedy suggested is Dunham's call
for a clinical sociology to test some hypotheses about social selection;
e.g., drift, differential tolerance of deviance, or voluntary segregation
patterns of schizophrenics.[33]

[29] Edwin H. Sutherland and Donald R. Cressey, *Principles of Criminology* (6th
ed.; New York: Lippincott, 1960) ; and Richard A. Cloward, "Illegitimate Means,
Anomie and Deviant Behavior," *American Sociological Review*, 24:164–76 (Apr., 1959) ;
Marshall B. Clinard, "The Theoretical Implications of Anomie and Deviant Behavior,"
in Clinard (ed.) , *op. cit.*, pp. 1–56.

[30] See, for example, Marshall Clinard, *Sociology of Deviant Behavior* (rev. ed.;
New York: Holt, Rinehart and Winston, 1963).

[31] Cf. Merton's distinction between nonconforming and aberrant behavior, in
Merton and Nesbit, *op. cit.*, chap. 15, "Social Problems and Sociological Theory,"
pp. 697–737. Further, it is pertinent that Merton's retreatism category includes only
a few passive forms of psychoses, thereby omitting the wide range of behavioral manifestations usually subsumed under a mental illness heading. See Social Theory and
Social Structure, pp. 153–55. Cf. Dunham's comment: ". . . It should now be clear that
such an intriguing concept as anomie is hardly sufficient to reveal 'how and why' the
socio-cultural elements of social structures can enter into human experience and produce deviant behavior." H. Warren Dunham, "Anomie and Mental Disorder," in
Clinard (ed.) , *op. cit.*, p. 157.

[32] Leonard P. Ullmann and Leonard Krasner, in *Case Studies in Behavior Modification* (New York: Holt, Rinehart and Winston, 1965) , pp. 1–63.

[33] Dunham, *op. cit.*, pp. 128–57.

7

Thomas S. Szasz

The Myth of Mental Illness

My aim in this essay is to raise the question "Is there such a thing as mental illness?" and to argue that there is not. Since the notion of mental illness is extremely widely used nowadays, inquiry into the ways in which this term is employed would seem to be especially indicated. Mental illness, of course, is not literally a "thing"—or physical object— and hence it can "exist" only the same sort of way in which other theoretical concepts exist. Yet, familiar theories are in the habit of posing, sooner or later—at least to those who come to believe in them—as "objective truths" (or "facts"). During certain historical periods, explanatory conceptions such as deities, witches, and microorganisms appeared not only as theories but as self-evident *causes* of a vast number of events. I submit that today mental illness is widely regarded in a somewhat similar fashion, that is, as the cause of innumerable diverse happenings. As an antidote to the complacent use of the notion of mental illness— whether as a self-evident phenomenon, theory, or cause—let us ask this question: What is meant when it is asserted that someone is mentally ill?

In what follows I shall describe briefly the main uses to which the concept of mental illness has been put. I shall argue that this notion has outlived whatever usefulness it might have had and that it now functions merely as a convenient myth.

MENTAL ILLNESS AS A SIGN OF BRAIN DISEASE

The notion of mental illness derives it main support from such phenomena as syphilis of the brain or delirious conditions—intoxications, for instance—in which persons are known to manifest various peculiarities or disorders of thinking and behavior. Correctly speaking, however, these are diseases of the brain, not of the mind. According to one school of thought, *all* so-called mental illness is of this type. The assumption is made that some neurological defect, perhaps a very subtle one, will ultimately be found for all the disorders of thinking and behavior. Many contemporary psychiatrists, physicians, and other scientists hold this view. This position implies that people *cannot* have troubles—expressed in what are *now called* "mental illnesses"—because of differences in personal needs, opinions, social aspirations, values, and so on. *All problems in living* are attributed to physicochemical processes which in due time will be discovered by medical research.

"Mental illnesses" are thus regarded as basically no different than all other diseases (that is, of the body). The only difference, in this view, between mental and bodily diseases is that the former, affecting the brain, manifest themselves by means of mental symptoms; whereas the latter, affecting other organ systems (for example, the skin, liver, etc.), manifest themselves by means of symptoms referable to those parts of the body. This view rests on and expresses what are, in my opinion, two fundamental errors.

In the first place, what central nervous system symptoms would correspond to a skin eruption or a fracture? It would *not* be some emotion or complex bit of behavior. Rather, it would be blindness or a paralysis of some part of the body. The crux of the matter is that a disease of the brain, analogous to a disease of the skin or bone, is a neurological defect, and not a problem in living. For example, a *defect* in a person's visual field may be satisfactorily explained by correlating it with certain definite lesions in the nervous system. On the other hand, a person's *belief*—whether this be a belief in Christianity, in Communism, or in the idea that his internal organs are "rotting" and that his body is, in fact, already "dead"—cannot be explained by a defect or disease of the nervous system. Explanations of this sort of occurrence—assuming that one is interested in the belief itself and does not regard it simply as a "symptom" or expression of something else that is *more interesting*— must be sought along different lines.

The second error in regarding complex psychosocial behavior, consisting of communications about ourselves and the world about us, as mere symptoms of neurological functioning is *epistemological*. In other words, it is an error pertaining not to any mistakes in observation or reasoning, as such, but rather to the way in which we organize and express our knowledge. In the present case, the error lies in making a symmetrical dualism between mental and physical (or bodily) symptoms, a dualism which is merely a habit of speech and to which no known observations can be found to correspond. Let us see if this is so. In medical practice, when we speak of physical disturbances, we mean either signs (for example, a fever) or symptoms (for example, pain). We speak of mental symptoms, on the other hand, when we refer to a patient's *communications about himself, others, and the world about him.* He might state that he is Napoleon or that he is being persecuted by the Communists. These would be considered mental symptoms *only* if the observer believed that the patient was *not* Napoleon or that he was *not* being persecuted by the Communists. This makes it apparent that the statement that "X is a mental symptom" involves rendering a judgment. The judgment entails, moreover, a covert comparison or matching of the patient's ideas, concepts, or beliefs with those of the observer and the society in which they live. The notion of mental symptom is therefore inextricably tied to the *social* (including *ethical*) *context* in which it is made in much the same way as the notion of bodily symptom is tied to an *anatomical* and *genetic context* (Szasz, 1957a, 1957b).

To sum up what has been said thus far: I have tried to show that for those who regard mental symptoms as signs of brain disease, the concept of mental illness is unnecessary and misleading. For what they mean is that people so labeled suffer from diseases of the brain; and, if that is what they mean, it would seem better for the sake of clarity to say that and not something else.

Mental Illness as a Name for Problems in Living

The term "mental illness" is widely used to describe something which is very different than a disease of the brain. Many people today take it for granted that living is an arduous process. Its hardship for modern man, moreover, derives not so much from a struggle for biological survival as from the stresses and strains inherent in the social intercourse of complex human personalities. In this context, the notion of mental illness is used to identify or describe some feature of an individual's so-called personality. Mental illness—as a deformity of the personality, so to speak—is then regarded as the *cause* of the human disharmony. It is implicit in this view that social intercourse between people is regarded as something *inherently harmonious*, its disturbance being due solely to the presence of "mental illness" in many people. This is obviously fallacious reasoning, for it makes the abstraction "mental illness" into a *cause*, even though this abstraction was created in the first place to serve only as a shorthand expression for certain types of human behavior. It now becomes necessary to ask: "What kinds of behavior are regarded as indicative of mental illness, and by whom?"

The concept of illness, whether bodily or mental, implies *deviation from some clearly defined norm*. In the case of physical illness, the norm is the structural and functional integrity of the human body. Thus, although the desirability of physical health, as such, is an ethical value, what health *is* can be stated in anatomical and physiological terms. What is the norm deviation from which is regarded as mental illness? This question cannot be easily answered. But whatever this norm might be, we can be certain of only one thing: namely, that it is a norm that must be stated in terms of *psychosocial, ethical,* and *legal* concepts. For example, notions such as "excessive repression" or "acting out an un-conscious impulse" illustrate the use of psychological concepts for judging (so-called) mental health and illness. The idea that chronic hostility, vengefulness, or divorce are indicative of mental illness would be illustrations of the use of ethical norms (that is, the desirability of love, kindness, and a stable marriage relationship). Finally, the widespread psychiatric opinion that only a mentally ill person would commit homicide illustrates the use of a legal concept as a norm of mental health. The norm from which deviation is measured whenever one speaks of a mental illness is a *psychosocial and ethical one*. Yet, the remedy is sought in terms of *medical* measures which—it is hoped and assumed—are free from wide differences of ethical value. The definition of the disorder and the terms in which its remedy are sought are therefore at serious odds with one another. The practical significance of this covert conflict between the alleged nature of the defect and the remedy can hardly be exaggerated.

Having identified the norms used to measure deviations in cases of mental illness, we will now turn to the question: "Who defines the norms and hence the deviation?" Two basic answers may be offered: (*a*) It may be the person himself (that is, the patient) who decides that he deviates from a norm. For example, an artist may believe that he suffers from a work inhibition; and he may implement this conclusion by seeking help *for* himself from a psychotherapist. (*b*) It may be some-one other than the patient who decides that the latter is deviant (for example, relatives, physicians, legal authorities, society generally, etc.). In such a case a psychiatrist may be hired by others to do something to the patient in order to correct the deviation.

These considerations underscore the importance of asking the ques-tion "Whose agent is the psychiatrist?" and of giving a candid answer to it (Szasz, 1956, 1958). The psychiatrist (psychologist or nomedical psychotherapist), it now develops, may be the agent of the patient, of the relatives, of the school, of the military services, of a business organization, of a court of law, and so forth. In speaking of the psychiatrist as the agent of these persons or organizations, it is not implied that his values concerning norms, or his ideas and aims concerning the proper nature of remedial action, need to coincide exactly with those of his employer. For example, a patient in individual psychotherapy may believe that his salvation lies in a new marriage; his psychotherapist need not share this hypothesis. As the patient's agent, however, he must abstain from bringing social or legal force to bear on the patient which would prevent him from putting his beliefs into action. If his *contract* is with the patient, the psychiatrist (psychotherapist) may disagree with him or stop his treatment; but he cannot engage others to obstruct the patient's aspirations. Similarly, if a psychiatrist is engaged by a court to determine the sanity of a criminal, he need not fully share the legal authorities' values and intentions in regard to the criminal and the means available for dealing with him. But the psychiatrist is expressly barred from stating, for example, that it is not the criminal who is "insane" but the men who wrote the law on the basis of which the very actions that are being judged are regarded as "criminal." Such an opinion could be voiced, of course, but not in a courtroom, and not by a psychiatrist who makes it his practice to assist the court in performing its daily work.

To recapitulate: In actual contemporary social usage, the finding of a mental illness is made by establishing a deviance in behavior from certain psychosocial, ethical, or legal norms. The judgment may be made, as in medicine, by the patient, the physician (psychiatrist), or others. Remedial action, finally, tends to be sought in a therapeutic—or covertly medical—framework, thus creating a situation in which *psychosocial, ethical,* and/or *legal deviations* are claimed to be correctible by (so-called) *medical action.* Since medical action is designed to correct only medical deviations, it seems logically absurd to expect that it will help solve problems whose very existence had been defined and established on nonmedical grounds. I think that these considerations may be fruitfully applied to the present use of tranquilizers and, more generally, to what might be expected of drugs of whatever type in regard to the amelioration or solution of problems in human living.

The Role of Ethics in Psychiatry

Anything that people *do*—in contrast to things that *happen* to them (Peters, 1958)—takes place in a context of value. In this broad sense, no human activity is devoid of ethical implications. When the values underlying certain activities are widely shared, those who participate in their pursuit may lose sight of them altogether. The discipline of medicine, both as a pure science (for example, research) and as a technology (for example, therapy), contains many ethical considerations and judgments. Unfortunately, these are often denied, minimized, or merely kept out of focus; for the ideal of the medical profession as well as of the people whom it serves seems to be having a system of medicine (allegedly) free of ethical value. This sentimental notion is expressed by such things as the doctor's willingness to treat and help patients irrespective of their religious or political beliefs, whether they are rich or poor, etc. While there may be some grounds for this belief—albeit it is a view that is not impressively true even in these regards—the fact remains that ethical considerations encompass a vast range of human affairs. By making the practice of medicine neutral in regard to some specific issues of value need not, and cannot, mean that it can be kept free from all such values. The practice of medicine is intimately tied to ethics; and the first thing that we must do, it seems to me, is to try to make this clear and explicit. I shall let this matter rest here, for it does not concern us specifically in this essay. Lest there be any vagueness, however, about how or where ethics and medicine meet, let me remind the reader of such issues as birth control, abortion, suicide, and euthanasia as only a few of the major areas of current ethicomedical controversy.

Psychiatry, I submit, is very much more intimately tied to problems of ethics than is medicine. I use the word "psychiatry" here to refer to that contemporary discipline which is concerned with *problems in living* (and not with diseases of the brain, which are problems for neurology). Problems in human relations can be analyzed, interpreted, and given meaning only within given social and ethical contexts. Accordingly, it *does* make a difference—arguments to the contrary notwithstanding— what the psychiatrist's socioethical orientations happen to be; for these will influence his ideas on what is wrong with the patient, what deserves comment or interpretation, in what possible directions change might be desirable, and so forth. Even in medicine proper, these factors play a role, as for instance, in the divergent orientations which physicians, depending on their religious affiliations, have toward such things as birth control and therapeutic abortion. Can anyone really believe that a psychotherapist's ideas concerning religious belief, slavery, or other similar issues play no role in his practical work? If they do make a difference, what are we to infer from it? Does it not seem reasonable that we ought to have different psychiatric therapies—each expressly recognized for the ethical positions which they embody—for, say, Catholics and Jews, religious persons and agnostics, democrats and communists, white supremacists and Negroes, and so on? Indeed, if we look at how psychiatry is actually practiced today (expecially in the United States), we find that people do seek psychiatric help in accordance with their social status and ethical beliefs (Hollingshead & Redlich, 1958). This should really not surprise us more than being told that practicing Catholics rarely frequent birth control clinics.

The foregoing position which holds that contemporary psychotherapists deal with problems in living, rather than with mental illnesses and their cures, stands in opposition to a currently prevalent claim, according to which mental illness is just as "real" and "objective" as bodily illness. This is a confusing claim since it is never known exactly what is meant by such words as "real" and "objective." I suspect, however, that what is intended by the proponents of this view is to create the idea in the popular mind that mental illness is some sort of disease entity, like an infection or a malignancy. If this were true, one could *catch* or *get* a "mental illness," one might *have* or *harbor* it, one might *transmit* it to others, and finally one could get *rid* of it. In my opinion, there is not a shred of evidence to support this idea. To the contrary, all the evidence is the other way and supports the view that what people now call mental illnesses are for the most part *communications* expressing unacceptable ideas, often framed, moreover, in an unusual idiom. The scope of this essay allows me to do no more than mention this alternative theoretical approach to this problem (Szasz, 1957c).

This is not the place to consider in detail the similarities and differences between bodily and mental illnesses. It shall suffice for us here to emphasize only one important difference between them: namely, that whereas bodily disease refers to public, physiochemical occurrences, the notion of mental illness is used to codify relatively more private, sociopsychological happenings of which the observer (diagnostician) forms a part. In other words, the psychiatrist does not stand *apart* from what he observes, but is, in Harry Stack Sullivan's apt words, a "participant observer." This means that he is *committed* to some picture of what he considers reality—and to what he thinks society considers reality—and he observes and judges the patient's behavior in the light of these considerations. This touches on our earlier observation that the notion of mental symptom itself implies a comparison between observer and observed, psychiatrist and patient. This is so obvious that I may be charged with belaboring trivialities. Let me therefore say once more that my aim in presenting this argument was expressly to criticize and counter a prevailing contemporary tendency to deny the moral aspects of psychiatry (and psychotherapy) and to substitute for them allegedly value-free medical considerations. Psychotherapy, for example, is being widely practiced as though it entailed nothing other than restoring the patient from a state of mental sickness to one of mental health. While it is generally accepted that mental illness has something to do with man's social (or interpersonal) relations, it is paradoxically maintained that problems of values (that is, of ethics) do not arise in this process.[1] Yet, in one sense, much of psychotherapy may revolve around nothing other than the elucidation and weighing of goals and values—many of which may be mutually contradictory—and the means whereby they might best be harmonized, realized, or relinquished.

The diversity of human values and the methods by means of which they may be realized is so vast, and many of them remain so unacknowledged, that they cannot fail but lead to conflicts in human relations. Indeed, to say that human relations at all levels—from mother to child, through husband and wife, to nation and nation—are fraught with stress, strain, and disharmony is, once again, making the obvious explicit. Yet, what may be obvious may be also poorly understood. This I think is the case here. For it seems to me that—at least in our scientific theories of behavior—we have failed to *accept* the simple fact that human relations are inherently fraught with difficulties and that to make them even relatively harmonious requires much patience and hard work. I submit that the idea of mental illness is now being put to work to obscure certain difficulties which at present may be inherent—not that they need be unmodifiable—in the social intercourse of persons. If this is true, the concept functions as a disguise; for instead of calling attention to conflicting human needs, aspirations, and values, the notion of mental illness provides an amoral and impersonal "thing" (an "illness") as an explanation for *problems in living* (Szasz, 1959). We may recall in this connection that not so long ago it was devils and witches who were held responsible for men's problems in social living. The belief in mental illness, as something other than man's trouble in getting along with his fellow man, is the proper heir to the belief in demonology and witchcraft. Mental illness exists or is "real" in exactly the same sense in which witches existed or were "real."

CHOICE, RESPONSIBILITY, AND PSYCHIATRY

While I have argued that mental illnesses do not exist, I obviously did not imply that the social and psychological occurrences to which this label is currently being attached also do not exist. Like the personal and social troubles which people had in the Middle Ages, they are real enough. It is the labels we give them that concerns us and, having labelled them, what we do about them. While I cannot go into the

---

[1] Freud went so far as to say that: "I consider ethics to be taken for granted. Actually I have never done a mean thing" (Jones, 1957, p. 247). This surely is a strange thing to say for someone who has studied man as a social being as closely as did Freud. I mention it here to show how the notion of "illness" (in the case of psychoanalysis, "psychopathology," or "mental illness") was used by Freud—and by most of his followers—as a means for classifying certain forms of human behavior as falling within the scope of medicine, and hence (by *fiat*) outside that of ethics!

ramified implications of this problem here, it is worth noting that a demonologic conception of problems in living gave rise to therapy along theological lines. Today, a belief in mental illness implies—nay, requires—therapy along medical or psychotherapeutic lines.

What is implied in the line of thought set forth here is something quite different. I do not intend to offer a new conception of "psychiatric illness" nor a new form of "therapy." My aim is more modest and yet also more ambitious. It is to suggest that the phenomena now called mental illnesses be looked at afresh and more simply, that they be removed from the category of illnesses, and that they be regarded as the expressions of man's struggle with the problem of *how* he should live. The last mentioned problem is obviously a vast one, its enormity reflecting not only man's inability to cope with his environment, but even more his increasing self-reflectiveness.

By problems in living, then, I refer to that truly explosive chain reaction which began with man's fall from divine grace by partaking of the fruit of the tree of knowledge. Man's awareness of himself and of the world about him seems to be a steadily expanding one, bringing in its wake an ever larger *burden of understanding* (an expression borrowed from Susanne Langer, 1953). *This burden, then, is to be expected and must not be misinterpreted.* Our only *rational* means for lightening it is *more understanding*, and appropriate *action* based on such understanding. The main alternative lies in acting as though the burden were not what in fact we perceive it to be and taking refuge in an outmoded theological view of man. In the latter view, man does not fashion his life and much of his world about him, but merely lives out his fate in a world created by superior beings. This may logically lead to pleading nonresponsibility in the face of seemingly unfathomable problems and difficulties. Yet, if man fails to take increasing responsibility for his actions, individually as well as collectively, it seems unlikely that some higher power or being would assume this task and carry this burden for him. Moreover, this seems hardly the proper time in human history for obscuring the issue of man's responsibility for his actions by hiding it behind the skirt of an all-explaining conception of mental illness.

Conclusions

I have tried to show that the notion of mental illness has outlived whatever usefulness it might have had and that it now functions merely as a convenient myth. As such, it is a true heir to religious myths in general, and to the belief in witchcraft in particular; the role of all these belief-systems was to act as *social tranquilizers,* thus encouraging the hope that mastery of certain specific problems may be achieved by means of substitutive (symbolic-magical) operations. The notion of mental illness thus serves mainly to obscure the everyday fact that life for most people is a continuous struggle, not for biological survival, but for a "place in the sun," "peace of mind," or some other human value. For man aware of himself and of the world about him, once the needs for preserving the body (and perhaps the race) are more or less satisfied, the problem arises as to what he should do with himself. Sustained adherence to the myth of mental illness allows people to avoid facing this problem, believing that mental health, conceived as the absence of mental illness, automatically insures the making of right and safe choices in one's conduct of life. But the facts are all the other way. It is the making of good choices in life that others regard, retrospectively, as good mental health!

The myth of mental illness encourages us, moreover, to believe in its logical corollary: that social intercourse would be harmonious, satisfying, and the secure basis of a "good life" were it not for the disrupting influences of mental illness or "psychopathology." The potentiality for universal human happiness, in this form at least, seems to me but another example of the I-wish-it-were-true type of fantasy. I do believe that human happiness or well-being on a hitherto unimaginably large scale, and not just for a select few, is possible. This goal could be achieved, however, only at the cost of many men, and not just a few being willing and able to tackle their personal, social, and ethical conflicts. This means having the courage and integrity to forego waging battles on false fronts, finding solutions for substitute problems—for instance, fighting the battle of stomach acid and chronic fatigue instead of facing up to a marital conflict.

Our adversaries are not demons, witches, fate, or mental illness. We have no enemy whom we can fight, exorcise, or dispel by "cure." What we do have are *problems in living*—whether these be biologic, economic, political, or sociopsychological. In this essay I was concerned only with problems belonging in the last mentioned category, and within this group mainly with those pertaining to moral values. The field to which modern psychiatry addresses itself is vast, and I made no effort to encompass it all. My argument was limited to the proposition that mental illness is a myth, whose function it is to disguise and thus render more palatable the bitter pill of moral conflicts in human relations.

References

Hollingshead, A. B., & Redlich, F. C. *Social class and mental illness.* New York: Wiley, 1958.

Jones, E. *The life and work of Sigmund Freud.* Vol. III. New York: Basic Books, 1957.

Langer, S. K. *Philosophy in a new key*. New York: Mentor Books, 1953.

Peters, R. S. *The concept of motivation*. London: Routledge & Kegan Paul, 1958.

Szasz, T. S. Malingering: "Diagnosis" or social condemnation? *AMA Arch Neurol. Psychiat.*, 1956, **76**, 432–443.

Szasz, T. S. *Pain and pleasure; A study of bodily feelings*. New York: Basic Books, 1957. (*a*)

Szasz, T. S. The problem of psychiatric nosology: A contribution to a situational analysis of psychiatric operations. *Amer. J. Psychiat.*, 1957, **114**, 405–413. (*b*)

Szasz, T. S. On the theory of psychoanalytic treatment. *Int. J. Psycho-Anal.*, 1957, **38**, 166–182. (*c*)

Szasz, T. S. Psychiatry, ethics and the criminal law. *Columbia Law Rev.*, 1958, **58**, 183–198.

Szasz, T. S. Moral conflict and psychiatry, *Yale Rev.*, 1959, June 1960, **49**, 555–566.

Suggested Further Readings

Becker, Howard S., *Outsiders: Studies in the Sociology of Deviance,* New York, Free Press, 1963.

Clinard, Marshall B., *The Sociology of Deviant Behavior,* 2nd ed., New York, Holt, Rinehart and Winston, 1963.

Cohen, Albert K., *Deviance and Control,* Englewood Cliffs, N. J., Prentice-Hall, 1966.

Lemert, Edwin M., *Human Deviance, Social Problems and Social Control,* Englewood Cliffs, N. J., Prentice-Hall, 1967.

Merton, Robert K., and Robert A. Nisbet, eds., *Contemporary Social Problems,* 2nd ed., New York, Harcourt, Brace and World, 1966.

II

The Sociological Approach

Of central importance to the sociological approach to deviance is Durkheim's classic dictum that social facts are to be explained socially. That perspective has two major implications: First, that deviance is understandable in terms of the pattern of social interaction in which it occurs, and second, that deviance is social behavior and as such, can be analyzed in much the same way as other types and forms of social behavior—i.e., as determined by social influences, learned as social roles are generally learned, or as manifestations of subcultural differentials.

The selection by Gibbs and Martin represents one of the major sociological concerns in the field of deviance—to demonstrate that deviant patterns of behavior are a function of various social conditions and circumstances. Their research focuses specifically on the predictive power of measures of status integration as indicators of suicide rates.

Bryan traces the process by which a deviant role is acquired and suggests that the socialization experiences of the prostitute can be generalized—that is, there is much that is common among different persons who manifest different types of deviant behavior.

Nudists, in contrast to criminal deviates, are legally tolerated and openly organized. Martin S. Weinberg's "Sexual Modesty, Social Meanings and the Nudist Camp," explores the means by which this deviant group sets limits for tolerable behavior for its own members.

In an original contribution, Miller and Skipper probe still another facet of concern which further broadens the scope of sociological interest in deviant behavior. Their essay focusses on the strategic importance of the jazz idiom not only as a mode of musical expression but as a barometer of reaction on the part of the American Negro, a deviant by ascription.

While illness in general is not usually thought of in deviation terms, that special form of personal difficulty known as mental illness has traditionally been of major interest to sociological specialists in this field. In contrast to a great deal of early work on the etiology of mental disorders, recent research has attempted to delineate problem foci more amenable to the sociological perspective. The selection by Myers, Bean, and Pepper reports the findings of a study seeking to establish the relationship between social class and particular aspects of the treatment process.

Definitions of deviation often involve the notion of norm violation and equally as often the fact of such violation is taken as the departure point of investigation. In their article, Mizruchi and Perrucci qualify the heuristic value of norm violation *per se* by showing that norms themselves have attributes which differentially contribute to the meaning and significance of deviations from them.

A major preoccupation of sociologists of deviant behavior has been with the causes, nature, and consequences of juvenile delinquency. The complexity of this type of behavior is revealed by the contrasting theories set forth by social scientists. The merit of the selection by Clark and Wenninger is that they propose a series of evaluative guidelines based not on predisposition or allegiance but on empirical findings.

8

Jack P. Gibbs
Walter T. Martin

A Theory of Status Integration and Its
Relationship to Suicide*

This paper explicates a theory that attempts to account for differences in suicide rates of societies and other population categories. While the theory is directly concerned with variability in suicide rates,[1] it has implications of a broad theoretical nature and may prove to be of value in the analysis of behavior other than suicide. In a general sense, the theory represents an attempt to approach the problem of deviant behavior from a point of view that generates specific empirical propositions as opposed to vague ideas that often pass as theory in sociology.

The theory of status integration in its complete form is to be described in full in a much longer report that will also include the derivation of specific hypotheses, the methods of testing these hypotheses, and the results of the actual tests.[2] The present report presents only a brief discussion of the nature and development of the theory of status integration, examples of measures of status integration, and some tests of hypotheses. This restriction means that a number of important theoretical and methodological problems must be treated superficially or ignored for the time being. It is hoped, however, that a preliminary re-

From *American Sociological Review*, 23 (April, 1958), 140–147, by permission of the authors and the American Sociological Association.
* This is an expanded version of a paper presented at the joint session of the American Sociological Society and the Society for the Study of Social Problems in Washington, D. C., August, 1957.
[1] In this connection it should be stressed that the theory does not purport to account for individual cases of suicide.
[2] The larger study was made possible by a grant from the National Science Foundation. At the present time the most complete statement of the theory is to be found in Jack P. Gibbs, "A Sociological Study of Suicide," unpublished Ph.D. dissertation, University of Oregon, 1957.

port may result in evaluations and suggestions that will serve to strengthen the final report.

DURKHEIM'S THEORY

Durkheim's classic monograph on suicide was the first outstanding contribution toward the explanation of variability in suicide rates in terms of social or cultural variables.[3] This contribution took the form of first demonstrating that variables of an extra-social nature that had previously been proposed as explanations of suicide could not account for the differences in suicide rates of European populations. Having demonstrated the inadequacy of extra-social explanations, Durkheim proceeded to formulate what remains today the foremost sociological theory of variability in suicide rates.[4] He wrote: "So we reach the general conclusion: suicide varies inversely with the degree of integration of the social groups. . . ."[5]

While Durkheim's study provides the most promising point of departure for an attempt to formulate a theory of suicide, it must be emphasized that his assertion of an inverse relationship between social integration and the rate of suicide has never been subjected to formal test and is not testable in its present form. At no point in Durkheim's monograph is there an explicit connotative definition of social integration, much less an operational definition. It is not surprising then that there is not a single measure of social integration correlated with suicide rates. Without the specification of the empirical referents for the concept and the operations used in measuring its prevalence, Durkheim's proposition is supported not by its predictive power but by his forceful argument in its defense. Thus, Durkheim's theory is incomplete; and it is to its development that the theory of status integration refers.[6]

INTEGRATION AND SOCIAL RELATIONS

Running throughout Durkheim's comments on the nature of integration is the suggestion that the concept has to do with the strength of the individual's ties to his society. In formal terms, the stronger the ties

[3] Emile Durkheim, *Suicide*. Translated by John A. Spaulding and George Simpson. Glencoe, Illinois: The Free Press, 1951.

[4] Space limitations preclude a discussion of the concepts of anomie and altruism in Durkheim's work.

[5] Durkheim, *op. cit.*, p. 209.

[6] While Henry and Short have done an admirable piece of work that is relevant to the development of Durkheim's theory, their theory leaves unspecified the empirical referents of their key concepts "strength of the relational system" and "strength of external restraint." Andrew F. Henry and James F. Short, Jr., *Suicide and Homicide*, Glencoe, Illinois: The Free Press, 1954, pp. 16–17.

of the individual members to a society the lower the suicide rate of that society.[7] While such a statement has only heuristic value, it is possible to restate it in terms of the stability and durability of social relationships within populations. Thus the fundamental postulate of the present theory reads: The suicide rate of a population varies inversely with the stability and durability of social relationships within that population.[8] While this postulate is potentially testable, the present state of sociological knowledge does not permit a direct measure of the stability and durability of social relationships. Furthermore, the type and amount of data needed for such an endeavor is so far beyond the scope of existing sources that such a measure is not feasible. Because of the difficulties involved in dealing directly with the stability and durability of social relationships, the decision was made to utilize observable conditions that presumably reflect these characteristics.

The predominant type of social relationship in a society is one in which an individual's social identification, his *status*, determines the demands and expectations to which he must conform in order to preserve his social relationships and to maintain his rights—the demands and expectations he can make of others. The rights of persons occupying a certain status and the demands and expectations that can be placed on them by others constitute the *roles* of that status. Conformity to the roles of a status would not be difficult if it were not for the fact that each person occupies several statuses simultaneously. Conformity to the roles of his occupational status alone, for example, will not maintain a man's relationships with his wife and children; the latter relationships can only be maintained by his behavior in conforming to the roles of husband and father.[9]

When conformity to the roles of one status interferes with conformity to others an individual finds it difficult to maintain his social relationships with all the persons who make demands and expectations of him in line with the statuses he occupies. He is faced with a conflict in roles. It would seem likely that the extent of variability in the sta-

[7] It should be noted that Durkheim also suggested that beyond a certain point integration is directly related to the suicide rate. This becomes a testable proposition only when a measure of integration is developed.

[8] A very crucial question is involved in this postulate. It could be argued that the consequences of social relationships lacking stability and durability could be several different forms of deviant behavior and not necessarily suicide alone. The writers can only state that in line with Durkheim it is assumed that a low degree of stability and durability in social relationships has a specific as opposed to a general consequence. In terms of future research, however, it would be desirable to go beyond simply making this assumption to an examination of the relationship between status integration and forms of deviant behavior other than suicide.

[9] For a review of the literature on the role concept see Lionel J. Neiman and James W. Hughes, "The Problem of the Concept Role—A Re-Survey of the Literature," *Social Forces*, 30 (December, 1951), pp. 141–149.

bility and durability in social relationships, as anticipated in the postulate stated above, may be explained by a consideration of the attempts of individuals to conform to conflicting roles.

A considerable amount of theory and research has been devoted to the problem of role conflict. However, the available literature casts no light on a question crucial to the present theory. Under what conditions will a large proportion of a population be confronted with a conflict in roles?[10] Since there appears to be no possibility of answering this question in specific, measurable terms it is necessary to shift from the current emphasis on the psychological dimensions of role to its sociological correlate—the concept of status.

ROLE CONFLICT, STATUS INCOMPATIBILITY, AND STATUS INTEGRATION

One crucial assumption made in the present theory is that, given a collection of statuses and their corresponding roles, the roles of each status tend to conflict more or less with roles of other statuses. The individual is confronted with an incompatibility in statuses if conformity to the roles of one status interferes with his conforming to the roles of another status. While this assumption changes the referent of the present analysis from role to status, two statuses are incompatible only in the sense that their roles are conflicting as described above. Consequently, from the behavioral point of view two statuses with conflicting roles are only incompatible when they are occupied simultaneously.

Having shifted to the concept of status, we can rephrase the question stated above: under what conditions will a large proportion of a population simultaneously occupy incompatible statuses? What is then needed is an observable, mensurable phenomenon that is linked with the extent to which the occupancy of incompatible statuses prevails in a society. As in the case of role conflict, existing theory and research on status do not identify such a phenomenon.

Another assumption of the present theory is that the patterns formed by the actual occupancy of statuses are indicative of the extent

[10] The failure of existing theory and research to provide an answer to this question lies in a psychological orientation to role conflict and the manner in which it is analyzed. For the most part, studies have dealt with real or alleged conflicts among particular roles. The methods employed to identify role conflict, the techniques used to analyze the phenomenon once isolated, and the conclusions reached in these studies do not lend themselves to a theory concerning the conditions that determine or reflect the amount of role conflict that prevails in a population. As examples see: Waldo W. Burchard, "Role Conflicts of Military Chaplains," *American Sociological Review,* 19 (October, 1954) ; Mirra Komarovsky, "Cultural Contradictions and Sex Roles," *American Journal of Sociology,* 52 (November, 1946), and "Functional Analysis of Sex Roles," *American Sociological Review,* 15 (August, 1950) ; Melvin Seeman, "Role Conflict and Ambivalence in Leadership," *American Sociological Review,* 18 (August, 1953) ; J. W. Getzels and E. G. Guba, "Role, Role Conflict, and Effectiveness: An Empirical Study," *American Sociological Review,* 19 (April, 1954) .

to which the occupancy of incompatible statuses prevails in a society. In more specific terms, it is assumed that the actual occupancy of statuses in a society reflects the degree of compatibility among statuses. If two statuses have conflicting roles, thereby making them incompatible statuses when occupied simultaneously, it is assumed that these two statuses would be less frequently occupied simultaneously than would two statuses with roles that do not conflict.[11]

Two statuses with conflicting roles come to be infrequently occupied simultaneously for three reasons. In some cases the incompatibility of the statuses is sufficiently recognized that their occupancy by the same person is socially discouraged. An example of this is the treatment accorded females who aspire to be airline pilots. One cannot assume from this example, however, that universalistic principles of recruitment in the occupancy of a status means that anyone and everyone can occupy the status without facing role conflict. The fact that both men and women are recruited for the army does not mean that males and females in the army are faced with equal amounts of role conflict. In other cases, the person occupying two incompatible statuses will give up one or both because of dissatisfaction arising from attempts to conform to conflicting roles. The large percentage of divorced bartenders illustrates the possibility that the demands of an occupational status may create dissatisfaction with a particular marital status. In still other cases the inability to conform to the roles of one or both of the statuses leads to the person's being deprived of one or both statuses, an example being those persons who are deprived of their occupational status because they are too old to live up to the standards of the job.

Assuming that the actual occupancy of statuses is indicative of the degree of compatibility among statuses, it follows that the degree of compatibility between two statuses is directly proportional to the extent to which the two statuses are occupied simultaneously.[12] As an illustra-

[11] As evidence that this assumption is not without support consider Hughes' observation to the effect that persons who do not conform to the prevailing pattern of status occupancy are confronted with serious problems of adjustment. See Everett C. Hughes, "Dilemmas and Contradictions of Status," *American Journal of Sociology*, 50 (March, 1945). It could be argued, of course, that while status configurations with conflicting rules (i.e. incompatible statuses) may in fact always be infrequently occupied that not all infrequently occupied status configurations involve incompatible statuses. While space limitations preclude a discussion of this question, the writers are well aware that the theory may fail in certain predictive tests and be subject to modification. Once formulated, however, the modification of a theory should be based on its empirical shortcomings rather than on purely *a priori* theoretical objections. The results obtained to date in testing the theory indicate that several objections that could be raised on purely *a priori* theoretical grounds are not valid.

[12] In this connection it should be obvious that the assumption is only valid when one of the statuses is an ascribed status and the other an achieved status or when both are achieved statuses. Differences in the suicide rate of persons occupying two different ascribed status configurations (e.g. white males 60–65 years of age versus Negro males 20–24 years of age in the U. S.) is not a function of absolute numbers but of the

tion of this reasoning, consider a hypothetical population in which 75 percent of the persons in occupation X are married while only 35 percent of those in occupation Y are married. Following our reasoning, these figures constitute a measure of the degree to which being married and occupying the specified occupations are compatible: occupation Y is far less compatible with marriage than is occupation X. Put otherwise, the status configuration "occupation X-married" is one more frequently occupied than the status configuration "occupation Y-married." The relative frequency with which a status configuration is occupied is referred to below as the degree of status integration. Thus, to return to our hypothetical example, if all persons of occupation X were also married, there would be maximum integration between this occupational status and marital status. Since every person in a population occupies a status configuration, the degree to which persons occupy incompatible statuses is a function of the extent to which the occupied status configurations do not conform to a pattern. A pattern of maximum status integration would be found in a society or population in which knowledge of all of an individual's statuses except one would enable an investigator to predict with certainty the remaining undisclosed status of the individual.

STATEMENT OF THE THEORY IN POSTULATE FORM

The line of reasoning in the formulation of this theory of status integration can be summarized in the following series of postulates:

Postulate 1: The suicide rate of a population varies inversely with the stability and durability of the social relationships within the population.

Postulate 2: The stability and durability of social relationships within a population varies directly with the extent to which individuals in that population conform to the patterned and socially sanctioned demands and expectations placed upon them by others.

Postulate 3: The extent to which individuals in a population conform to the patterned and socially sanctioned demands and expectations placed upon them by others varies inversely with the extent to which individuals in that population are confronted with role conflicts.

Postulate 4: The extent to which individuals in a population are confronted with role conflicts varies directly with the extent to which individuals occupy incompatible statuses in that population.

---

extent to which the two populations concentrate in one achieved status within all families of statuses. Thus the differences between the suicide rate of white males and Negro males in the United States is not determined by the number of white males and Negro males but by differential degrees of occupational, marital, parental, and religious integration *within* the two populations.

Postulate 5: The extent to which individuals occupy incompatible statuses in a population varies inversely with the degree of status integration in that population.

From the above postulates there follows the major theorem: *The suicide rate of a population varies inversely with the degree of status integration in that population.*[13]

THE MEASURE OF STATUS INTEGRATION

There are numerous difficulties involved in attempting to develop a measure of the degree of status integration in a population. One major problem is inadequate data. There is no existing source, in fact, for the type of data that would be needed for an ideal test of the major theorem. The dangers of using inadequate data for testing the theorem include the possibility that negative results may stem from inadequacies of the data rather than from a lack of validity in the theory. The availability of data, however, cannot be permitted to determine theory.

Another danger lies in the possibility of over-simplification. For example, a population that shows a high integration measure for marital status, sex, and age conceivably could have a much lower measure for the integration of occupation, age, and race or for marital status, sex, and religion. The tendency to oversimplify is a real one because of the limitations of available data and the labor involved in computing measures of status integration at its more complex levels. On the other hand, it may eventually be shown that status integration is such a general phenomenon that many measures of different dimensions of status integration are highly correlated.

It will be helpful to begin the discussion of measurement by citing a hypothetical society in which status integration is at a maximum. Table 1 represents a society in which measures of integration between a particular family of statuses (in this case, marital statuses) and five status configurations are shown. In this model society letters and numbers indicate families of statuses and particular statuses within families. Thus, for example, R1 is a particular race, O3 a particular occupation, A4 a particular age group, S1 the status of male, Re2 a particular religion, and P2 a particular parental status. The figures in the columns represent the proportion of the persons occupying the status configuration represented by the heading who have a specified marital status. For

[13] An alternative theorem making use of the concept of role conflict can be stated: The suicide rate of a population varies directly with the degree of role conflict in that population. It will be recognized, however, that at this date no quantitative measure of the amount of role conflict in a society or population has been developed. Consequently such a proposition remains untestable.

example, all of the persons occupying the first status configuration are widowed, while all of the persons in the second status configuration are married.

Obviously, many more columns are called for in Table 1 than are actually given. For the table to be complete every status configuration comprised of all major statuses but marital status would be shown provided that the status configuration is actually occupied. Furthermore, only the integration of marital status is shown in this table whereas for a complete measure of status integration there would be as many tables as there are families of statuses, with each family of statuses requiring a different set of occupied status configurations at the head of the columns.

TABLE 1.

The Integration of Marital Statuses with Selected Status Configurations in a Hypothetical Society where Marital Integration Is at a Maximum

Marital Status	All Occupied Status Configurations				
	R1–A1– Re1–O1– S1–P1	R2–A2– Re2–O2– S2–P2	R1–A3– Re3–O3– S1–P1	R1–A4– Re1–O4– S1–P3	R2–A5– Re3–O5– S2–P2
Single	.00	.00	.00	1.00	.00
Married	.00	1.00	.00	.00	1.00
Widowed	1.00	.00	.00	.00	.00
Divorced	.00	.00	1.00	.00	.00
ΣX	1.00	1.00	1.00	1.00	1.00
ΣX^2	1.0000	1.0000	1.0000	1.0000	1.0000
Proportion of population	.0700	.4300	.0300	.1500	.3200

For the model society shown in Table 1 to have heuristic value it must be compared with another society that, while also hypothetical, reflects a pattern of status occupancy more like that of existing societies. Table 2 has been designed for this purpose. For the sake of comparison, the statuses shown in Table 2 are the same as in Table 1; only the cell frequencies are different.

It is apparent that there is far less status integration in the second "society" than in the first. In order to indicate the degree of difference mathematically some formula must be applied. If the figures of each column in Table 1 and Table 2 are simply added, the sum (ΣX) is 1.00 for each column with a total of 5.00 for the five columns combined, results that do not differentiate between the two societies. However, if each cell proportion is squared before the columns are added, the column totals differ for the two tables (see ΣX^2). In a society where status integration is at a maximum the sum of the squares of the proportions in each column will always be 1.0000, and the total status integration measure for the society as a whole will always be 1.0000 multiplied by the number of columns. In Table 1 the total integration measure is 5.0000, while in Table 2 it is only 2.6500. However, this total integration measure does not take into consideration the possibility that a high status integration measure for a column may influence only a small proportion of the total population. For example, the last column of Table 2 has a status integration measure (ΣX^2) of .8150, but only 19 percent of the total population are influenced by this high value. In order to take into account the proportion of the population influenced

TABLE 2.

The Integration of Marital Status with Selected Status Configurations in a Hypothetical Society Where Marital Integration Is less Than Maximum

Marital Status	All Occupied Status Configurations				
	R1–A1– Re1–O1– S1–P1	R2–A2– Re3–O2– S2–P2	R1–A3– Re3–O3– S1–P1	R1–A4– Re1–O4– S1–P3	R2–A5– Re3–O5– S2–P2
Single	.15	.05	.00	.35	.05
Married	.05	.75	.05	.25	.90
Widowed	.60	.15	.25	.20	.05
Divorced	.20	.05	.70	.20	.00
ΣX	1.00	1.00	1.00	1.00	1.00
ΣX^2	.4250	.5900	.5550	.2650	.8150
Proportion of population	.1435	.3825	.0870	.1970	.1900

by the component measures, the status integration measure of each column (ΣX^2) is multiplied by the proportion of the population who occupy the status configurations represented by the column. When this is done the status integration measure for Table 1 is still at the maximum (1.0000), but for Table 2 it is .5420. While the upper limit of the weighted measure is fixed at 1.0000 the lower limit varies with the number of columns.[14] It would be preferable, of course, to have a measure that is unaffected by the number of status configurations being consid-

[14] It will be noted that the procedure described here gives equal weight to all statuses. This may be questioned on the grounds that some statuses are more "important" than others. While this may be true, there is no empirical criterion for distinguishing between important and unimportant statuses. However, in virtually all societies there are major statuses such as age, sex, race, occupation, and marital, parental, and religious statuses; and it is to these statuses that the theory is directed.

ered. Many techniques can be utilized to derive a quantitative measure of status integration as conceived in this theory. It remains to be seen which particular measure will demonstrate the greatest utility.[15]

THE GENERATION OF EMPIRICAL PROPOSITIONS

In the opening paragraph it was specified that a theory should be capable of generating specific empirical propositions. While no attempt will be made here to provide convincing proof that the theory of status integration actually fulfills this requirement, a brief consideration should be suggestive.

It will be recalled that the major theorem of our theory is that the suicide rate of a population varies inversely with the degree of status integration in that population. For any table designed to measure status integration on a societal level there are three types of measures of status integration, each of which provides a test of the major theorem in the form of a hypothesis. For purposes of illustration, the hypothetical society shown in Table 2 will be treated as if it were a real society, with the suicide rate known for any status configuration within the table and for the society as a whole.

One hypothesis derived from the major theorem calls for the comparison of the total weighted status integration measure of the "society" shown in Table 2 with corresponding total weighted status integration measures for other societies. According to this hypothesis any society having a weighted integration measure greater than .5420 would have a lower suicide rate than the society shown in Table 2, while any society with a measure less than .5420 would have a higher suicide rate. In other words, for any given universe of societies there should be an inverse relationship between the suicide rate and the total status integration measure. While it is not yet possible to report tests of this hypothesis involving actual societies, one test was made using the thirty states of the United States for which the necessary data were available for a measure of the integration of occupation with age, sex, and color in 1950. The coefficient of correlation between this measure and the total suicide rate for 1949–1951 was —.57. If one wishes to treat the state as a sample drawn from a hypothetical universe, the coefficient, while

[15] Here, as with the overall theory, the writers are aware of the fact that certain modifications of the method used to measure status integration may have to be made in the future. One possibility is expressing each cell frequency in a status integration table as a ratio to the frequency expected on a purely chance basis. This would make "within column" measures of status integration less dependent upon absolute numbers. Once again, however, modifications in the method of measuring status integration must await an extensive series of tests of the major theorem. Such tests will indicate whether modification is in order and may possibly point to the type of modification that is needed.

only moderately large, is significant beyond the one percent level. The hypothesis is thus supported.

It should be pointed out in connection with this test that these populations are not actual societies and that the measure of integration suffers a serious handicap. The measure is based on employed persons in the labor force while the suicide rate pertains to the total population. Particularly in the case of females, there may be a sizeable discrepancy between these two categories.

Present plans call for testing the theorem on a variety of populations, including nations, through the use of several measures of status integration. Limited comparable data will probably restrict the development, however, of a variety of measures.

A second measure of status integration expresses the degree of integration between a status configuration and a family of statuses. In Table 2 this measure is the sum of the squares of the proportions (ΣX^2) in each column. The hypothesis derived from the major theorem requires an inverse relationship between the ΣX^2 value at the bottom of each column and the suicide rate of all persons occupying the status configuration represented in the column. In Table 2 the status configuration in the fourth column with a ΣX^2 of .2650 would be expected to have the highest suicide rate while the status configuration in the last column with a ΣX^2 of .8150 should have the lowest suicide rate. As an illustration, Table 3 presents occupational integration measures for

TABLE 3.

Mean Annual Suicide Rates per 100,000 Population, 1949–1951, and Measures of Occupational Integration for Six Race-Sex Status Configurations in the U. S., 1950

Race-Sex Status Configuration	Occupational Integration		Suicide	
	Measure	Rank	Rate	Rank
Negro female	.2473	1	1.5	6
White female	.1828	2	5.3	5
Other female	.1416	4	5.9	4
Negro male	.1588	3	6.1	3
White male	.1295	5	18.5	2
Other male	.1243	6	21.3	1

the various race-sex configurations of the United States in 1950. These measures are the ΣX^2 figures appearing at the bottom of the column (in a computational worksheet not shown) which treats the eleven occupational categories employed in census reports as statuses. The hypothesis is definitely supported in this case by a rank-difference correlation of —.94 (P<.01). When the rank orders of the two rates are compared separately by sex, the rank order of the integration measure invariably predicts the rank order of the suicide rate.

The third example of hypotheses generated by the theory concerns the simplest status integration measure, the individual proportions shown in each cell. In the first column of Table 2 the hypothesis would constitute a prediction that widowed persons would have the lowest suicide rate and married persons the highest. Stated more abstractly, the hypothesis calls for an inverse relationship between the status integration measure of each cell and the corresponding suicide rate. As an example, cell frequencies can be pulled from a table not shown here. These frequencies represent the proportion of males 60–64 years of age in the United States in 1950 who occupied each marital status. The marital statuses and proportions ranked by size are married (.793), widowed (.096), single (.086), and divorced (.025). The corresponding average annual suicide rates for 1949–1951 are 36.2, 64.7, 76.4, and 111.1. Thus, without exception, the rank order of the status integration measure representing the integration of marital status and age predicts the rank order of the suicide rate: there is a consistent inverse relationship.[16]

It should be emphasized that the simple measures of status integration used as illustrations here do not invariably relate to suicide rates in the direction anticipated by the major theorem. For example, in the table from which the cell frequencies mentioned above were drawn it would be possible to select an age group in which the rank order of integration measures does not without error predict the rank order of suicide rates. In such cases, however, the predictive power of status integration measures is well beyond chance expectancy; and the errors that are found may be due to the oversimplified measures of status integration that were employed.

The main purpose of this preliminary analysis is to demonstrate that the theory of status integration generates empirical propositions. Evaluation of the theory itself, of course, requires more comprehensive tests.

Analyses now under way involve the testing of a variety of hypotheses by countries and by population categories within certain countries. Judging from the results so far obtained, the tests of the theory demonstrate its predictive power.

[16] In connection with the tests just described it must be recognized that the reliability of suicide rates remains a serious question. It is hard to see, however, how the unreliability of rates can consistently work toward positive results in the test of a theory. It seems much more likely that unreliability of suicide rates would tend to reduce the predictive power of a theory.

9

James H. Bryan

Apprenticeships in Prostitution*

While theoretical conceptions of deviant behavior range from role strain to psychoanalytic theory, orientations to the study of the prostitute have shown considerable homogeneity. Twentieth century theorizing concerning this occupational group has employed, almost exclusively, a Freudian psychiatric model. The prostitute has thus been variously described as masochistic, of infantile mentality, unable to form mature interpersonal relationships, regressed, emotionally dangerous to males and as normal as the average women.[1] The call girl, the specific focus of this paper, has been accused of being anxious, possessing a confused

From *Social Problems,* 12 (Winter, 1965) , 287–297, by permission of the author and the publishers.

* This data was collected when the author was at the Neuropsychiatric Institute, UCLA Center for the Health Sciences. I wish to acknowledge the considerable aid of Mrs. Elizabeth Gordon, Miss Carol Kupers, and Mr. Saul Sherter in the preparation and the analysis of this data. I am greatly indebted to Dr. Evelyn Hooker for both her intellectual and moral support, and to Vivian London for her excellent editorial advice. I particularly wish to express my great gratitude to my wife, Virginia, for her tolerance, encouragement, and understanding.

[1] H. Benjamin, "Prostitution Reassessed," *International Journal of Sexology,* 26 (1951) , pp. 154–160; H. Benjamin & A. Ellis, "An Objective Examination of Prostitution," *International Journal of Sexology,* 29 (1955) , pp. 100–105; E. Glover, "The Abnormality of Prostitution," In A. M. Krich, editor, *Women,* New York: Dell Publishing Company, Inc., 1953; M. H. Hollander, "Prostitution, The Body, and Human Relatedness." *International Journal of Psychoanalysis,* XLII (1961), pp. 404–413; M. Karpf, "Effects of Prostitution on Marital Sex Adjustment," *International Journal of Sexology,* 29 (1953) , pp. 149–154; J. F. Oliven, *Sexual Hygiene and Pathology,* Philadelphia: J. B. Lippencott Co., 1955; W. J. Robinson, *The Oldest Profession in The World,* New York: Eugenics Publishing Co., 1929.

self-image, excessively dependent, demonstrating gender-role confusion, agressive, lacking internal controls and masochistic.[2]

The exclusive use of psychoanalytic models in attempting to predict behavior, and the consequent neglect of situational and cognitive processes, has been steadily lessening in the field of psychology. Their inadequacy as models for understanding deviancy has been specifically explicated by Becker, and implied by London.[3] The new look in the conceptualization and study of deviant behavior has focused on the interpersonal processes which help define the deviant role, the surroundings in which the role is learned, and limits upon the enactment of the role. As Hooker has indicated regarding the study of homosexuals, one must not only consider the personality structure of the participants, but also the structure of their community and the pathways and routes into the learning and enactment of the behavior.[4] Such "training periods" have been alluded to by Mauer in his study of the con man, and by Sutherland in his report on professional thieves. More recently, Lindesmith and Becker have conceptualized the development of drug use as a series of learning sequences necessary for the development of steady use.[5]

This paper provides some detailed, albeit preliminary, information concerning induction and training in a particular type of deviant career: prostitution, at the call girl level. It describes the order of events, and their surrounding structure, which future call girls experience in entering their occupation.

The respondents in this study were 33 prostitutes, all currently or previously working in the Los Angeles area. They ranged in age from 18 to 32, most being in their mid-twenties. None of the interviewees were obtained through official law enforcement agencies, but seven were found within the context of a neuropsychiatric hospital. The remaining respondents were gathered primarily through individual referrals from previous participants in the study. There were no obvious differences

    [2] H. Greenwald, *The Call Girl*, New York: Ballentine Books, 1960.
    [3] H. S. Becker, *Outsiders: Studies in the Sociology of Deviance*, New York: Free Press of Glencoe, 1963. Also see *The Other Side*, H. S. Becker, editor, New York: Free Press of Glencoe, 1964. P. London, *The Modes and Morals of Psychotherapy*, New York: Holt, Rinehart and Winston, Inc. 1964. For recent trends in personality theory, see N. Sanford, "Personality: Its Place in Psychology" and D. R. Miller, "The Study of Social Relationships: Situation, Identity, and Social Interaction." Both papers are presented in S. Koch, editor *Psychology: A study of a Science*, Vol. 5, New York: McGraw-Hill Book Co., Inc. 1963.
    [4] Evelyn Hooker, "The Homosexual Community." *Proceedings of the XIV International Congress of Applied Psychology*, 1961, pp. 40–59. See also A. Reiss, "The Social Integration of Queers and Peers." *Social Problems*, 9 (1961), pp. 102–120.
    [5] D. W. Maurer, *The Big Con*, New York: Signet Books, 1940. H. S. Becker, *Outsiders, op. cit.* E. H. Sutherland, *The Professional Thief*, Chicago: University of Chicago Press, 1937. A. R. Lindesmith, *Opiate Addiction*, Evanston: Principia Press, 1955.

between the "psychiatric sample" and the other interviewees on the data to be reported.

All subjects in the sample were call girls. That is, they typically obtained their clients by individual referrals, primarily by telephone, and enacted the sexual contract in their own or their clients' place of residence or employment. They did not initiate contact with their customers in bars, streets, or houses of prostitution, although they might meet their customers at any number of locations by pre-arrangement. The minimum fee charged per sexual encounter was $20.00. As an adjunct to the call girl interviews, three pimps and two "call boys" were interviewed as well.[6]

Approximately two thirds of the sample were what are sometimes known as "outlaw broads"; that is, they were not under the supervision of a pimp when interviewed. There is evidence that the majority of pimps who were aware of the study prohibited the girls under their direction from participating in it. It should be noted that many members of the sample belonged to one or another clique; their individually expressed opinions may not be independent.

The interviews strongly suggest that there are marked idiosyncrasies from one geographical area to another in such practices as fee-splitting, involvement with peripheral occupations (e.g., cabbies), and so forth. For example, there appears to be little direct involvement of peripheral occupations with call girl activities in the Los Angeles area, while it has been estimated that up to 10 percent of the population of Las Vegas is directly involved in activities of prostitutes.[7] What may be typical for a call girl in the Los Angeles area is not necessarily typical for a girl in New York, Chicago, Las Vegas, or Miami.

Since the professional literature (e.g., Greenwald; Pomeroy) concerning this occupation and its participants is so limited in quantity, and is not concerned with training per se, the present data may have some utility for the social sciences.[8]

All but two interviews were tape recorded. All respondents had prior knowledge that the interview would be tape recorded. The interviewing was, for the most part, done at the girls' place of work and/or residence. Occasional interviews were conducted in the investigator's office, and one in a public park. Interviews were semistructured and

[6] This definition departs somewhat from that offered by Clinard. He defines the call girl as one dependent upon an organization for recruiting patrons and one who typically works in lower-class hotels. The present sample is best described by Clinard's category high-class independent professional prostitute. M. D. Clinard, *Sociology of Deviant Behavior*, New York: Rinehart & Co., Inc., 1957.

[7] E. Reid, and O. Demaris, *The Green Felt Jungle*, New York: Pocket Books, Inc., 1963.

[8] H. Greenwald, *op. cit.* W. Pomeroy, *Some Aspects of Prostitution*, unpublished paper.

employed open-ended questions. One part of the interview concerned the apprenticeship period or "turning out" process.

THE ENTRANCE

I had been thinking about it [becoming a call girl] before a lot. . . . Thinking about wanting to do it, but I had no connections. Had I not had a connection, I probably wouldn't have started working. . . . I thought about starting out . . . . Once I tried it [without a contact] . . . . I met this guy at a bar and I tried to make him pay me, but the thing is, you can't do it that way because they are romantically interested in you, and they don't think that it is on that kind of basis. You can't all of a sudden come up and want money for it, you have to be known beforehand. . . . I think that is what holds a lot of girls back who might work. I think I might have started a year sooner had I had a connection. You seem to make one contact or another . . . if it's another girl or a pimp or just someone who will set you up and get you a client. . . . You can't just, say, get an apartment and get a phone in and everything and say, "Well, I'm gonna start business," because you gotta get clients from somewhere. There has to be a contact.

Immediately prior to entrance into the occupation, all but one girl had personal contact with someone professionally involved in call girl activities (pimps or other call girls). The one exception had contact with a customer of call girls. While various occupational groups (e.g., photographers) seem to be peripherally involved, often unwittingly with the call girl, there was no report of individuals involved in such occupations being contacts for new recruits. The novice's initial contact is someone at the level at which she will eventually enter the occupation: not a street-walker, but a call girl; not a pimp who manages girls out of a house of prostitution, but a pimp who manages call girls.

Approximately half of the girls reported that their initial contact for entrance into the profession was another "working girl." The nature of these relationships is quite variable. In some cases, the girls have been long standing friends. Other initial contacts involved sexual relationships between a Lesbian and the novice. Most, however, had known each other less than a year, and did not appear to have a very close relationship, either in the sense of time spent together or of biographical information exchanged. The relationship may begin with the aspiring call girl soliciting the contact. That is, if a professional is known to others as a call girl, she will be sought out and approached by females who are strangers:[9] "I haven't ever gone out and looked for one. All of these have fell right into my hands. . . . They turned themselfs out. . . . Then come to me for help."

Whatever their relationship, whenever the professional agrees to

[9] A point also made in the autobiographical account of a retired call call. Virginia McManus, *Not For Love,* New York: Dell Publishing Co., Inc., 1960, p. 160.

aid the beginner, she also, it appears, implicitly assumes responsibility for training her. This is evidenced by the fact that only one such female contact referred the aspirant to another girl for any type of help. Data are not available as to the reason for this unusual referral.

If the original contact was not another call girl but a pimp, a much different relationship is developed and the career follows a somewhat different course. The relationship between pimp and girl is typically one of lovers, not friends:

. . . because I love him very much. Obviously, I'm doing this mostly for him. . . . I'd do anything for him. I'm not just saying I will, I am. . . . [After discussing his affair with another woman] I just decided that I knew what he was when I decided to do this for him and I decided I had two choices—either accept it or not, and I have no excuse.

Occasionally, however, a strictly business relationship will be formed:

Right now I am buying properties, and as soon as I can afford it, I am buying stocks. . . . It is strictly a business deal. This man and I are friends, our relationship ends there. He handles all the money, he is making all the investments and I trust him. We have a legal document drawn up which states that half the investments are mine, half of them his, so I am protected.

Whether the relationship is love or business, the pimp solicits the new girl.[10] It is usually agreed that the male will have an important managerial role in the course of the girl's career, and that both will enjoy the gains from the girl's activities for an indefinite period: "Actually a pimp has to have complete control or else its like trouble with him. Because if a pimp doesn't, if she is not madly in love with him or something in some way, a pimp won't keep a girl."

Once the girl agrees to function as a call girl, the male, like his female counterpart, undertakes the training of the girl, or refers the girl to another call girl for training. Either course seems equally probable. Referrals, when employed, are typically to friends and, in some cases, wives or ex-wives.

Although the data are limited, it appears that the pimp retains his dominance over the trainee even when the latter is being trained by a call girl. The girl trainer remains deferential to the pimp's wishes regarding the novice.

APPRENTICESHIP

Once a contact is acquired and the decision to become a call girl made, the recruit moves to the next stage in the career sequence: the

[10] Two of the pimps denied that this was very often so and maintained that the girls will solicit them. The degree to which they are solicited seems to depend upon the nature and extent of their reputations. It is difficult to judge the accuracy of these reports as there appears to be a strong taboo against admitting to such solicitation.

apprenticeship period. The structure of the apprenticeship will be described, followed by a description of the content most frequently communicated during this period.

The apprenticeship is typically served under the direction of another call girl, but may occasionally be supervised by a pimp. Twenty-four girls in the sample initially worked under the supervision of other girls. The classroom is, like the future place of work, an apartment. The apprentice typically serves in the trainer's apartment, either temporarily residing with the trainer or commuting there almost daily. The novice rarely serves her apprenticeship in such places as a house of prostitution, motel, or on the street. It is also infrequent that the girl is transported out of her own city to serve an apprenticeship. Although the data are not extensive, the number of girls being trained simultaneously by a particular trainer has rarely been reported to be greater than three. Girls sometimes report spending up to eight months in training, but the average stay seems to be two or three months. The trainer controls all referrals and appointments, novices seemingly not having much control over the type of sexual contract made or the circumstances surrounding the enactment of the contract.

The structure of training under the direction of a pimp seems similar, though information is more limited. The girls are trained in an apartment in the city they intend to work and for a short period of time. There is some evidence that the pimp and the novice often do not share the same apartment as might the novice and the girl trainer. There appear to be two reasons for the separation of pimp and girl. First, it is not uncommonly thought that cues which suggest the presence of other men displease the girl's customers: "Well, I would never let them know that I had a lover, which is something that you never ever let a john know, because this makes them very reticent to give you money, because they think you are going to go and spend it with your lover, which is what usually happens."

(Interestingly, the work of Winick suggests that such prejudices may not actually be held by many customers.)[11] Secondly, the legal repercussions are much greater, of course, for the pimp who lives with his girl than for two girls rooming together. As one pimp of 19 years experience puts it: "It is because of the law. There is a law that is called the illegal cohabitation that they rarely use unless the man becomes big in stature. If he is a big man in the hustling world, the law then employs any means at their command. . . ."

Because of the convenience in separation of housing, it is quite likely that the pimp is less directly involved with the day-to-day training of the girls than the call girl trainer.

[11] C. Winick, "Prostitutes' Clients' Perception of the Prostitute and Themselves," *International Journal of Social Psychiatry*, 8 (1961–62), pp. 289–297.

The content of the training period seems to consist of two broad, interrelated dimensions one philosophical, the other interpersonal. The former refers to the imparting of a value structure, the latter to "do's" and "don'ts" of relating to customers and, secondarily, to other "working girls" and pimps. The latter teaching is perhaps best described by the concept of a short range perspective. That is, most of the "do's" and "don'ts" pertain to ideas and actions that the call girl uses in problematic situations.[12] Not all girls absorb these teachings, and those who do incorporate them in varying degrees.

Insofar as a value structure is transmitted it is that of maximizing gains while minimizing effort, even if this requires transgressions of either a legal or moral nature. Frequently, it is postulated that people, particularly men, are corrupt or easily corruptible, that all social relationships are but a reflection of a "con," and that prostitution is simply a more honest or at least no more dishonest act than the everyday behavior of "squares." Furthermore, not only are "johns" basically exploitative, but they are easily exploited; hence they are, in some respects, stupid. As explained by a pimp: ". . . [in the hustling world] the trick or the john is known as a fool . . . this is not the truth. . . . He [the younger pimp] would teach his woman that a trick was a fool."

Since the male is corrupt, or honest only because he lacks the opportunity to be corrupt, then it is only appropriate that he be exploited as he exploits. "Girls first start making their 'scores'—say one guy keeps them for a while or maybe she gets, you know, three or four grand out of him, say a car or a coat. These are your scores. . . ." The general assumption that man is corrupt is empirically confirmed when the married male betrays his wife, when the moralist, secular or religious, betrays his publicly stated values, or when the "john" "stiffs" (cheats) the girl. An example of the latter is described by a girl as she reflects upon her disillusionment during her training period.

It is pretty rough when you are starting out. You get stiffed a lot of times. . . . Oh sure. They'll take advantage of you anytime they can. And I'm a trusting soul, I really am. I'll believe anybody till they prove different. I've made a lot of mistakes that way. You get to the point, well, Christ, what the heck can I believe in people, they tell me one thing and here's what they do to me.

Values such as fairness with other working girls, or fidelity to a pimp, may occasionally be taught. To quote a pimp:

So when you ask me if I teach a kind of basic philosophy, I would say that you could say that. Because you try to teach them in an amoral way that there is a right and wrong way as pertains to this game . . . and then you teach them that when working with other girls to try to treat the other girl fairly because a

    [12] H. S. Becker, Blanche Geer, E. C. Hughes, and A. L. Strauss, *Boys In White* Chicago: University of Chicago Press, 1961.

woman's worst enemy in the street [used in both a literal and figurative sense] is the other woman and only by treating the other woman decently can she expect to get along. . . . Therefore the basic philosophy I guess would consist of a form of honesty, a form of sincerity and complete fidelity to her man [pimp].

It should be noted, however, that behavior based on enlightened self-interest with concomitant exploitation is not limited to customer relationships. Interviewees frequently mentioned a pervasive feeling of distrust between trainer and trainee, and such incidents as thefts or betrayal of confidences are occasionally reported and chronically guarded against.

Even though there may be considerable pressure upon the girl to accept this value structure, many of them (perhaps the majority of the sample) reject it.

People have told me that I wasn't turned out, but turned loose instead. . . . Someone who is turned out is turned out to believe in a certain code of behavior, and this involves having a pimp, for one thing. It also involves never experiencing anything but hatred or revulsion for "tricks" for another thing. It involves always getting the money in front [before the sexual act] and a million little things that are very strictly adhered to by those in the "in group," which I am not. . . . Never being nice or pleasant to a trick unless you are doing it for the money, getting more money. [How did you learn that?] It was explained to me over a period of about six months. I learned that you were doing it to make money for yourself so that you could have nice things and security. . . . [Who would teach you this?] [The trainer] would teach me this.[13]

It seems reasonable to assume that the value structure serves, in general, to create in-group solidarity and to alienate the girl from "square" society, and that this structure serves the political advantage of the trainer and the economic gains of the trainee more than it allays the personal anxieties of either. In fact, failure to adopt these values at the outset does not appear to be correlated with much personal distress.[14] As one girl describes her education experiences: "Some moral code. We're taught, as a culture . . . it's there and after awhile you live, breathe, and eat it. Now, what makes you go completely against everything that's inside you, everything that you have been taught, and the whole society, to do things like this?" Good empirical evidence, however, concerning the functions and effectiveness of this value structure with regard to subjective comfort is lacking.

[13] The statements made by prostitutes to previous investigators and mental helpers may have been parroting this particular value structure and perhaps have misled previous investigators into making the assumption that "all whores hate men." While space prohibits a complete presentation of the data, neither our questionnaire nor interview data suggest that this is a predominant attitude among call girls.

[14] There is, from the present study, little support for the hypothesis of Reckless concerning the association of experience trauma and guilt with abruptness of entry into the occupation. W. C. Reckless, *The Crime Problem*, New York: Appleton-Century-Crofts, Inc., 1950.

A series of deductions derived from the premises indicated above serve to provide, in part, the "rules" of interpersonal contact with the customer. Each customer is to be seen as a "mark," and "pitches" are to be made.

[Did you have a standard pitch?] It's sort of amusing. I used to listen to my girl friend [trainer]. She was the greatest at this telephone type of situation. She would call up and cry and say that people had come to her door. . . . She'd cry and she'd complain and she'd say "I have a bad check at the liquor store, and they sent the police over," and really . . . a girl has a story she tells the man. . . . Anything, you know, so he'll help her out. Either it's the rent or she needs a car, or doctor's bills, or, any number of things.

Any unnecessary interaction with the customer is typically frowned upon, and the trainee will receive exhortations to be quick about her business. One girl in her fourth week of work explains: "[What are some of the other don't's that you have learned about?] Don't take so much time. . . . The idea is to get rid of them as quickly as possible." Other content taught concerns specific information about specific customers.

. . . she would go around the bar and say, now look at that man over there, he's this way and that way, and this is what he would like and there are what his problems are. . . .

. . . she would teach me what the men wanted and how much to get, what to say when I got there . . . just a line to hand them.

Training may also include proprieties concerning consuming alcohol and drugs, when and how to obtain the fee, how to converse with the customers and, occasionally, physical and sexual hygiene. As a girl trainer explains:

First of all, impress cleanliness. Because on the whole, the majority of girls, I would say, I don't believe there are any cleaner women walking the streets, because they've got to be aware of any type of body odor. . . . You teach them to French [fellatio] and how to talk to men.

[Do they [pimps] teach you during the turning out period how to make a telephone call?] Oh, usually, yes. They don't teach you, they just tell you how to do it and you do it with your good common sense, but if you have trouble, they tell you more about it.

Interestingly, the specific act of telephoning a client is often distressing to the novice and is of importance in her training. Unfortunately for the girl, it is an act she must perform with regularly as she does considerable soliciting.[15] One suspects that such behavior is embarrasing for her because it is an unaccustomed role for her to play—she has so recently come from a culture where young women do

[15] The topic of solicitation will be dealt with in a forthcoming paper.

not telephone men for dates. Inappropriate sex-role behavior seems to produce greater personal distress than does appropriate sex-role behavior even when it is morally reprehensible. "Well, it is rather difficult to get on the telephone, when you've never worked before, and talk to a man about a subject like that, and it is very new to you."

What is omitted from the training should be noted as well. There seems to be little instruction concerning sexual techniques as such, even though the previous sexual experience of the trainee may have been quite limited. What instruction there is typically revolves around the practice of fellatio. There seems to be some encouragement not to experience sexual orgasms with the client, though this may be quite variable with the trainer. ". . . and sometime, I don't know if it's a set rule or maybe it's an unspoken rule, you don't enjoy your dates." "Yes, he did [teach attitudes]. He taught me to be cold. . . ."

It should be stressed that, if the girls originally accepted such instructions and values, many of them, at least at the time of interviewing, verbalized a rejection of these values and reported behavior which departed considerably from the interpersonal rules stipulated as "correct" by their trainers. Some experience orgasms with the customer, some show considerable affect toward "johns," others remain drunk or "high" throughout the contact.[16] While there seems to be general agreement as to what the rules of interpersonal conduct are, there appears to be considerable variation in the adoption of such rules.

A variety of methods are employed to communicate the content described above. The trainer may arrange to eavesdrop on the interactions of girl and client and then discuss the interaction with her. One trainer, for example, listened through a closed door to the interaction of a new girl with a customer, then immediately after he left, discussed, in a rather heated way, methods by which his exit may have been facilitated. A pimp relates:

The best way to do this [teaching conversation] is, in the beginning, when the phone rings, for instance . . . is to listen to what she says and then check and see how big a trick he is and then correct her from there.

. . . with everyone of them [trainees] I would make it a point to see two guys to see how they [the girls] operate.

In one case a girl reported that her pimp left a written list of rules pertaining to relating to "johns." Direct teaching, however, seems to be uncommon. The bulk of whatever learning takes place seems to take

---

[16] In the unpublished paper referred to above, Pomeroy has indicated that, of 31 call girls interviewed, only 23 percent reported never experiencing orgasms with customers.

place through observation. "It's hard to tell you, because we learn through observations." "But I watched her and listened to what her bit was on the telephone."

To summarize, the structure of the apprenticeship period seems quite standard. The novice receives her training either from a pimp or from another more experienced call girl, more often the latter. She serves her initial two to eight months of work under the trainer's supervision and often serves this period in the trainer's apartment. The trainer assumes responsibility for arranging contacts and negotiating the type and place of the sexual encounter.

The content of the training pertains both to a general philosophical stance and to some specifics (usually not sexual) of interpersonal behavior with customers and colleagues. The philosophy is one of exploiting the exploiters (customers) by whatever means necessary and defining the colleagues of the call girl as being intelligent, self-interested and, in certain important respects, basically honest individuals. The interpersonal techniques addressed during the learning period consist primarily of "pitches," telephone conversations, personal and occasionally sexual hygiene, prohibitions against alcohol and dope while with a "john," how and when to obtain the fee, and specifics concerning the sexual habits of particular customers. Specific sexual techniques are very rarely taught. The current sample included a considerable number of girls who, although capable of articulating this value structure, were not particularly inclined to adopt it.

CONTACTS AND CONTRACTS

While the imparting of ideologies and proprieties to the prospective call girl is emphasized during the apprenticeship period, it appears that the primary function of the apprenticeship, at least for the trainee, is building a clientele. Since this latter function limits the degree of occupational socialization, the process of developing the clientele and the arrangements made between trainer and trainee will be discussed.

Lists ("books") with the names and telephone numbers of customers are available for purchase from other call girls or pimps, but such books are often considered unreliable. While it is also true that an occasional pimp will refer customers to girls, this does not appear to be a frequent practice. The most frequent method of obtaining such names seems to be through contacts developed during the apprenticeship. The trainer refers customers to the apprentice and oversees the latter in terms of her responsibility and adequacy in dealing with the customer. For referring the customer, the trainer receives forty to fifty percent of the total price agreed upon in the contract negotiated by the trainer

and customer.[17] The trainer and trainees further agree, most often explicitly, on the apprentice's "right" to obtain and to use, on further occasions, information necessary for arranging another sexual contract with
the "john" without the obligation of further "kick-back" to the trainer.
That is, if she can obtain the name and telephone number of the customer, she can negotiate another contract without fee-splitting. During
this period, then, the girl is not only introduced to other working colleagues (pimps and girls alike) but also develops a clientele.

There are two obvious advantages for a call girl in assuming the
trainer role. First, since there seems to be an abundant demand for
new girls, and since certain service requirements demand more than
one girl, even the well established call girl chronically confronts the
necessity for making referrals. It is then reasonable to assume that the
extra profit derived from the fee-splitting activities, together with the
added conveniences of having a girl "on call," allows the trainer to
profit considerably from this arrangement. Secondly, contacts with customers are reputedly extremely difficult to maintain if services are not
rendered on demand. Thus, the adoption of the trainer role enables
the girl to maintain contacts with "fickle" customers under circumstances, where she may wish a respite from the sexual encounter without terminating the contacts necessary for re-entry into the call girl
role. It is also possible that the financial gains may conceivably be
much greater for most trainers than for most call girls, but this is a
moot point.

A final aspect of the apprenticeship period that should be noted is
the novice's income. It is possible for the novice, under the supervision
of a competent and efficient trainer, to earn a great deal of money, or
at least to get a favorable glimpse of the great financial possibilities
of the occupation and, in effect, be heavily rewarded for her decision to
enter it. Even though the novice may be inexperienced in both the
sexual and interpersonal techniques of prostitution, her novelty on the
market gives her an immediate advantage over her more experienced
competitors. It seems quite likely that the new girl, irrespective of her
particular physical or mental qualities, has considerable drawing power
because she provides new sexual experience to the customer. Early success and financial reward may well provide considerable incentive to
continue in the occupation.

A final word is needed regarding the position of the pimp vis-à-vis

[17] The fee-splitting arrangement is quite common at all levels of career activity.
For example, cooperative activity between two girls is often required for a particular
type of sexual contract. In these cases, the girl who has contracted with the customer
will contact a colleague, usually a friend, and will obtain 40 per cent–50 per cent of
the latter's earnings. There is suggestive evidence that fee-splitting activities vary according to geographical areas and that Los Angeles is unique for both its fee-splitting patterns and the rigidity of its fee-splitting structure.

the call girl during the apprenticeship period. While some pimps assume the responsibility for training the girl personally, as indicated above, as many send the novice to another girl. The most apparent reason for such referral is that it facilitates the development of the "book." Purposes of training appear to be secondary for two reasons: (1) The pimp often lacks direct contact with the customers, so he personally cannot aid directly in the development of the girl's clientele; (2) When the pimp withdraws his girl from the training context, it is rarely because she has obtained adequate knowledge of the profession. This is not to say that all pimps are totally unconcerned with the type of knowledge being imparted to the girl. Rather, the primary concern of the pimp is the girl's developing a clientele, not learning the techniques of sex or conversation.

The apprenticeship period usually ends abruptly, not smoothly. Its termination may be but a reflection of interpersonal difficulties between trainer and trainee, novice and pimp, or between two novices. Occasionally termination of training is brought about through the novice's discovery and subsequent theft of the trainer's "book." Quite frequently, the termination is due to the novice's developing a sufficient trade or other business opportunities. The point is, however, that no respondent has reported that the final disruption of the apprenticeship was the result of the completion of adequate training. While disruptions of this relationship may be due to personal or impersonal events, termination is not directly due to the development of sufficient skills.

DISCUSSION AND SUMMARY

On the basis of interviews with 33 call girls in the Los Angeles area, information was obtained about entrance into the call girl occupation and the initial training period or apprenticeship therein.

The novice call girl is acclimated to her new job primarily by being thoroughly immersed in the call girl subculture, where she learns the trade through imitation as much as through explicit tutoring. The outstanding concern at this stage is the development of a sizable and lucrative clientele. The specific skills and values which are acquired during this period are rather simple and quickly learned.

In spite of the girl's protests and their extensive folklore, the art of prostitution, at least at this level, seems to be technically a low-level skill. That is, it seems to be an occupation which requires little formal knowledge or practice for its successful pursuit and appears best categorized as an unskilled job. Evidence for this point comes from two separate sources. First, there seems to be little technical training during this period, and the training seems of little importance to the career progress. Length or type of training does not appear correlated with success (i.e., money earned, lack of subjective distress, minimum fee per "trick," etc.). Secondly, the termination of the apprenticeship period is often brought about for reasons unrelated to training. It seems that the need for an apprenticeship period is created more by the secrecy surrounding the rendering or the utilization of the call girl service than by the complexity of the role. In fact, it is reasonable to assume that the complexity of the job confronting a street-walker may be considerably greater than that confronting a call girl. The tasks of avoiding the police, sampling among strangers for potential customers, and arrangements for the completion of the sexual contract not only require different skills on the part of the street-walker, but are performances requiring a higher degree of professional "know-how" than is generally required of the call girl.[18]

As a pimp who manages both call girls and "high class" street-walkers explains:

The girl that goes out into the street is the sharper of the two, because she is capable of handling herself in the street, getting around the law, picking out the trick that is not absolutely psycho . . . and capable of getting along in the street. . . . The street-walker, as you term her, is really a prima donna of the prostitutes . . . her field is unlimited, she goes to all the top places so she meets the top people. . . .

The fact that the enactment of the call girl role requires little training, and the introduction of the girl to clients and colleagues alike is rather rapid, gives little time or incentive for adequate occupational socialization. It is perhaps for this reason rather than, for example, reasons related to personality factors, that occupational instability is great and cultural homogeneity small.

In closing, while it appears that there is a rather well defined apprenticeship period in the career of the call girl, it seems that it is the secrecy rather than the complexity of the occupation which generates such a period. While there is good evidence that initial contacts, primarily with other "working girls," are necessary for entrance into this career, there seems no reason, at this point, to assume that the primary intent of the participants in training is anything but the development of an adequate clientele.

[18] Needless to say, however, all of the sample of call girls who were asked for status hierarchies of prostitution felt that the street-walker had both less status and a less complex job. It *may* well be that the verbal exchange required of the call girl requires greater knowledge than that required of a street-walker, but the nonverbal skills required of the street-walker may be considerably greater than those of the call girl.

10

Martin S. Weinberg

Sexual Modesty, Social Meanings, and the Nudist Camp*

Deviant sub-systems have norms that permit, organize, and control the behavior which defines them as deviant. The nudist camp in an example of such a deviant sub-system, nudists being defined as deviant by their disregard for clothing when in the presence of others, particularly members of the opposite sex. This paper will describe the normative system of the nudist camp, its consequences for sustaining the definition of the situation common to this group, and the way it maintains those interaction patterns this sub-system shares with the outside society.

The general sociological framework to be used emphasizes the study of "social meanings" as a salient subject for understanding the realm of social organization. Such an approach was set forth by Weber:[1] in order to understand social organization it is not sufficient to look at stable and recurrent patterns of social behavior alone; one also must look at the subjective meanings attached to behavior, i.e., those meanings by

From *Social Problems*, 12 (Winter, 1957), 311–318, by permission of the author and the publishers.

* Revision of a paper presented at the annual meeting of the Midwest Sociological Society, Kansas City, 1964. This represents one aspect of a theoretical treatment and study on Sex, Modesty, and Deviants. I am grateful to John I. Kitsuse for his encouragement, suggestions, and criticisms. I would also like to thank Raymond Mack, Scott Greer, Arnold Feldman, Walter Wallace, and Richard Schwartz for their valuable comments.

1 Max Weber, *The Theory of Social and Economic Organization*, Glencoe: The Free Press, 1947, pp. 88ff. Also see: Alfred Schutz, *Collected Papers I: The Problem of Social Reality*, The Hague: Martinus Nijhoff, 1962, p. 59. Schutz insists that in considering these social meanings the sociologist develop "constructs of the second degree" out of the meaning constructs which typically guide the social actor. That is, the sociologist should abstract his more generalized model of social order out of the "order" which channels individual actors in their social behavior.

which social behavior is oriented in its course. The assumption underlying this focus is that stable social meanings are products of a social
standardization process, being controlled by the "molds" which social
organization imposes on patterns of sociation.[2]

The institutionalized patterns of sexual modesty will be viewed as
an aspect of social organization, with attention given to the social meanings linked to normative breaches, i.e., immodesty. A study of the
deviant case of social nudists will then be presented, illustrating how members of this social system are re-socialized in the meaning attributed to
one form of immodesty. It is hoped that this study will contribute to a
better understanding of the nature and essence of sexual modesty, as
well as to the general processes of social organization.

MODESTY AND MEANINGS

Modesty is a form of reserve. Sexual modesty is sexual reserve (or
a communication of non-availability for sexual interaction). This quality
of meaning results from the social actor's following the dictates of sexual
propriety—the common-sense constructs of proper or "decent" behavior.
From the point of view of this paper, sexual modesty is thus defined
as an institutionalized pattern of social interaction.[3] It imposes a pattern of tension management by which social control is maintained over
the sexual interests latent in any heterosexual encounter.

In the sexual realm, acts of immodesty take the following basic
forms, all of them communicating a boldness or lack of inhibition: (1)
verbal communications; and (2) non-verbal communications,[4] which

[2] Cf. Harold Garfinkel, "The Routine Grounds of Everyday Activities," *Social
Problems,* 3 (Winter, 1964), p. 237.

[3] An "institutionalized pattern of social interaction" will be defined as an organized
way of doing something: a formal, legitimized, recognized, established, and stabilized
way in which an aspect of behavior is expected to be performed. (Cf. Robert Bierstedt,
The Social Order, New York: McGraw-Hill Book Co., Inc., pp. 299ff.)

Modesty may additionally be viewed as a pattern of deference, i.e. conducting
oneself with good demeanor is in general a way of showing deference to those present
(Cf. Erving Goffman, "The Nature of Deference and Demeanor," *American Anthropologist,* 58 (June, 1956), p. 492). This could be labeled "deference through non-
initiation" of sexual overtures. This interpretation of modesty leads us to inequalities
in the social structure, since patterns of deference point to the relative positions of the
actor and alter in the social hierarchy. Therefore, as women gain more equality in the
social structure we would expect the "double standard" of modesty to decline—i.e.,
women gain more rights to "initiate" or suspend patterns of deference.

A more extreme degree of deference may, however, lead to immodesty rather than
modesty. This is "deference through subservience." Thus women who dress or act immodestly solely for the benefit of the male may also demonstrate deference. Deference
through both non-initiation and subservience should decrease with equalization of the
social structure.

[4] See Erving Goffman, *The Presentation of Self in Everyday Life,* New York:
Doubleday and Co., Inc., 1959.

typically are differentiated into (a) a display of body or bodily functions, and (b) other forms or erotic overture (e.g., the way one actor
looks at another).

Common-sense definitions assume an interrelationship between verbal and non-verbal expressions of immodesty. Rightly or wrongly, most
men regard a woman who will curse in their presence—that is, use
the proscribed four letter words—as a woman who will suit action to
her language.[5] At one time this imputation went so far that if a woman
talked about the legs of a table or the breast of a chicken, she was immediately typed as being *immodest and unrefined*.[6] The preceding examples illustrate, respectively, two meanings commonly attributed to
immodest acts: (1) the act may be perceived as communicating sexual
availability; and (2) the act may be perceived as a projection of bad
breeding. These types are not mutually exclusive, but they do seem
most typically differentiated by the *blatancy* of display.

TABLE 1.

Typology of Immodest Behavior

Act of:	Display of body	Verbal expression	Erotic overtures
Commission	Shows 1–1	Says 1–2	Does 1–3
Omission	Looks at 2–1	Listens to 2–2	Allows 2–3

Immodest acts may also be analytically differentiated along the
dimension of "commission—omission."[7] That is, acts may be classified as
immodest because of one's *active* performance of an act, or because of
one's *passiveness* or failure to manage effectively an impression of restraint in regard to another's immodest act. Thus, the girl who stares at
a nude man is defined as immodest, as well as the girl who displays
herself nude; the girl who listens to "dirty" jokes (and, if unable to
escape the social gathering, fails to display inattention), as well as the
girl who tells them; the girl who allows herself to be grabbed, as well as
the girl who does the grabbing. Although it may appear contradictory to define *passiveness* as nullifying *reserve*, this may be clarified
by viewing such an omission as invalidating an impression of *sexual* reserve (i.e., non-availability for sexual interaction) .

5 Shailer Upton Lawton and Jules Archer, *Sexual Conduct of the Teen-Ager*, New
York: Spectrolux Corporation, 1951, p. 111.
6 Alexander M. Gow, *Good Morals and Gentle Manners for Schools and Families*,
New York: American Book Co., 1873.
7 Weber, *op. cit.*, p. 88; Schutz, *op. cit.*, pp. 66ff.

HYPOTHESIS AND METHOD

The manifest function of sexual modesty (i.e., those consequences evaluated by common-sense rationality) is maintenance of social control over latent sexual interests. Common-sense conceptions of modesty also put most emphasis on the covering of the body when in the presence of the opposite sex for the performance of this function.[8] Considerations of a breakdown in clothing modesty bring forth images of rampant sexual interest, promiscuity, embarrassment, jealousy, and shame.

Social nudists (i.e., those who practice nudism in a nudist camp) are thus defined as "deviants" by their disregard for body covering, falling in cell 1-1 of our typology of immodesty. The remainder of the paper will discuss an empirical study of this group of systematic deviants.[9] The following general hypothesis provided the foundation for this research:

If nudists effectively change the societal definition of the situation regarding nudity, and are also able to maintain the forms of modesty pertaining to the other cells of our typology, then social control over latent sexual interests will still be maintained.

If we take as given that the nudist camp only changes the definition of one of our cells of immodesty, then when other forms of modesty are not maintained the *indubitableness* or taken-for-grantedness of the changed definition of the situation (regarding nudity) will be called into question.[10]

For an examination of this hypothesis, three nudist camps located near the Chicago metropolitan area were contacted, and readily agreed to be the objects of research. Field work was undertaken in these camps over the course of one summer. During the period of participant observation, nudist members were asked to fill out cards which requested their name and address, so that they could be contacted at a later date for purposes of an interview. These formalized interviews were a supplement to the more exploratory field work, serving as a systematic technique by which to gather the specific data desired. Although nudists tend to be wary of revealing personal data such as last name or address, rapport was high and, when given a promise of confidentiality, very few refused to fill out these sample cards.

After the observational data were organized, an interview sched-

8 See Lawrence Langner, *The Importance of Wearing Clothes*, New York: Hastings House, 1959; René Guyon, *The Ethics of Sexual Acts*, New York: Blue Ribbon Books, 1941; Havelock Ellis, *Studies in the Psychology of Sex*, Vol. 1, Philadelphia: F. A. Davis Co., 1930.

9 For a discussion of the concept "systematic deviant," see Edwin Lemert, *Social Pathology*, New York: McGraw-Hill, 1951.

10 See Schutz, *op. cit.*, pp. 94–95, for a summary discussion of the process by which presuppositions get called into question.

ule was constructed. Selection of respondents was limited to those living within a hundred mile radius of Chicago; a total of one hundred and one interviews were completed.[11]

THE NUDIST CAMP

The ideology of the nudist camp provides a new definition of the situation regarding nudity, which in effect maintains that:

1. nudism and sexuality are unrelated
2. there is nothing shameful about exposing the human body
3. the abandonment of clothes can lead to a feeling of freedom and natural pleasure
4. nude activities, especially full bodily exposure to the sun, leads to a feeling of physical, mental, and spiritual well-being.

These definitions are sustained by nudists to a remarkable degree, illustrating the extent to which adult socialization can function in changing long-maintained meanings; in this case regarding the exposure of one's nude body in heterosexual situations. The tremendous emphasis on covering the sexual areas, and the relation between nudism and sexuality which exists in the outside society, however, suggests that the nudist definition of the situation might, at times, be quite easily called into question. The results of the field work and formal interviews indicate how the social organization of the nudist camp has developed a system of norms that contributes to sustaining the official definition of the situation. Since the major concern of this paper is modesty, we will restrict our discussion to the first two declarations of nudist ideology (i.e., that nudism and sexuality are unrelated, and that there is nothing shameful about exposing the human body). These are also the elements which lead to the classification of nudists as deviant. The normative proscriptions which contribute to the maintenance of this definition of the situation will be described.

ORGANIZATIONAL PRECAUTIONS

Organizational precautions are initially taken in the requirements for admission to a nudist camp. Most camps do not allow unmarried individuals, especially single men, or allow only a small quota of singles. Those camps that do allow male-singles may charge up to thirty-five percent higher rates for the single's membership than is charged for the membership of an entire family. This is intended to discourage single memberships but, since the cost is still relatively low in comparison to

[11] Many of the nudists interviewed had attended or held membership in a number of different camps. Thus, experiences from at least twenty camps provided concurrent data for our conclusions.

other resorts, this measure is not very effective. It seems to do little more than create resentment among the singles. By giving formal organizational backing to the definition that singles are not especially desirable, it also might be related to the social segregation of single and married members that is evident in nudist camps.

An overabundance of single men is recognized by the organization as threatening the definition of nudism that is maintained. The presence of singles at the camp is suspected to be for purposes other than the "nudist way of life" (e.g., to gape at the women). Such a view may call into question the denied relation between nudity and sexuality.

Certification by the camp owner is also required before anyone is admitted on the camp grounds. This is sometimes supplemented by three letters of recommendation in regard to the character of the applicant. This is a precaution against admitting those "social types" which might conceivably discredit the ideology of the movement.

A limit is sometimes set on the number of trial visits which can be made to the camp; that is, visits made without membership in some camp or inter-camp organization. In addition, a limit is usually set on the length of time one is allowed to maintain himself clothed. These rules function to weed out those guests whose sincere acceptance of the "nudist" definition of the situation is questionable.

NORMS REGARDING INTERPERSONAL BEHAVIOR

Norms regarding patterns of interpersonal behavior are also functional for the maintenance of the organization's system of meanings. The existence of these norms, however, should be recognized as formally acknowledging that the nudist definition of the situation could become problematic unless precautions were taken.

No staring. This rule functions to prevent any overt signs of "over-involvement." In the words of a non-nudist who is involved in the publication of a nudist magazine, "They all look up to the heavens and never look below." This pattern of civil inattention[12] is most exaggerated among the females, who manage the impression that there is absolutely no concern or awareness that the male body is in an unclothed state. Women often recount how they expect everyone will look at them when they are nude, only to find that no one communicates any impression of concern when they finally do get up their nerve and undress. One woman told the writer: "I got so mad because my husband wanted me to undress in front of other men that I just pulled my clothes right off thinking everyone would look at me." She was amazed (and somewhat disappointed) when no one did. Thus, even though

12 See Erving Goffman, *Behavior in Public Places,* New York: The Free Press of Glencoe, 1963, p. 84.

nudists are immodest in their behavior by "showing" their bodies, which falls in cell 1-1 of our typology of immodesty, they are not immodest in the sense of cell 2-1 of our table. "Looking at" immodesty is controlled; external constraints prohibit staring.

(Have you ever observed or heard about anyone staring at someone's body while at camp?) [13] I've heard stories—particularly about men that stare. Since I heard these stories, I tried not to, and even done away with my sunglasses after someone said, half joking, that I hide behind sunglasses to stare. Towards the end of the summer I stopped wearing sunglasses. And you know what, it was a child who told me this.

No sex talk. Sex talk, or telling "dirty" jokes, is not common in the nudist camp. The owner of one of the most widely known camps in the Midwest told the writer: "It is usually expected that members of a nudist camp will not talk about sex, politics, or religion." Or in the words of one single-male: "It is taboo to make sexual remarks here." Verbal immodesty was not experienced by the writer during his period of field work. Interview respondents who mentioned that they had discussed or talked about sex qualified this by stating that such talk was restricted to close friends, was of a "scientific" nature or, if a joke, was of a "cute" sort. Verbal immodesty, represented in the second column of our typology of immodesty, is not common to the nudist camp.

When respondents were asked what they would think of someone who breached this norm, they indicated that such behavior would cast doubt on the actor's acceptance of the nudist definition of the situation:

One would expect to hear less of that at camp than at other places. (Why's that?) Because you expect that the members are screened in their *attitude for nudism*—and this isn't one who prefers sexual jokes.

They probably don't belong there. They're there to see what they can find to observe. (What do you men?) Well, their mind isn't on being a nudist, but to see so-and-so nude.

Body contact is taboo. Although the degree to which this rule is enforced varies among camps, there is at least some degree of informal enforcement. Nudists mention that one is particularly careful not to brush against anyone or have any body contact, because of the way it might be interpreted. The following quotation illustrates the interpersonal precautions taken: "I stay clear of the opposite sex. They're so sensitive, they imagine things." One respondent felt that this taboo was simply a common-sense form of modesty: "Suppose one had a desire to knock one off or feel his wife—modesty or a sense of protocol prohibits you from doing this." When asked to conceptualize a break-

---

[13] Interview questions and probes have been placed in parentheses.

down in this form of modesty, a common response was: "They are in the wrong place. (How's that?) That's not part of nudism. (Could you tell me some more about that?) I think they are there for some sort of sex thrill. They are certainly not there to enjoy the sun."

If any photographs are taken for publication in a nudist magazine, the subjects are allowed to have only limited body contact. As one female nudist said: "We don't want anyone to think we're immoral." Outsiders' interpretations of body contact among nudists would cast doubt on the nudist definition of the situation or the characteristics set forth as the "nudist way of life."

A correlate of the body contact taboo is the prohibition of dancing in the nude. This is verbalized by nudist actors as a separate rule, and it is often the object of jest by members. This indication of "organizational strain" can be interpreted as an instance in which the existence of the rule itself brings into question the nudist definition of the situation, i.e., that there is no relationship between nudism and sexuality. The following remark acknowledges this: "This reflects a contradiction in our beliefs. But it's self protection. One incident and we'd be closed." Others define dancing in the nude as an erotic overture which would incite sexual arousal. Such rationalizations are common to the group.

Returning to our typology of immodesty, it can be seen that incitements heightening latent sexual interest that would fall in column three of the typology (i.e., "doing" behavior), are to some extent controlled by prohibiting body contact.

Alcoholic beverages are not allowed in American camps. This rule also functions in controlling any breakdown in inhibitions which could lead to "agressive-erotic" overtures (column three of immodesty). Even those respondents who told the writer that they had "snuck a beer" before going to bed went on to say, however, that they fully favored the rule. The following quotation is representative of nudists' thoughts:

Anyone who drinks in camp is jeopardizing their membership and they shouldn't. Anyone who drinks in camp could get reckless. (How's that?) Well, when guys and girls drink they're a lot bolder—they might get fresh with someone else's girl. That's why it isn't permitted, I guess.

Rules regarding photography. Taking photographs in a nudist camp is a sensitive matter. Unless the individual is an official photographer (i.e., one photographing for the nudist magazines), the photographer's definition of the situation is sometimes suspect, especially when one hears such remarks as the following: "Do you think you could open your legs a little more?"

There may be a general restriction on the use of cameras and, when cameras are allowed, it is expected that no pictures will be taken without the subject's permission. Members especially tend to blame the misuse of cameras on single men. As one nudist said: "You always see the singles poppin' around out of nowhere snappin' pictures." In general, however, control is maintained, and any infractions which might exist are not blatant or obvious. Any overindulgence in taking photographs would communicate an over-involvement in the nude state of the alters and bring doubt on the denied connection between nudism and sexuality. This, like staring, would fall in cell 2-1 of our topology of immodesty; like staring, it is controlled by the norms of the nudist camp.

The official photographers who are taking pictures for nudist magazines recognize the impression communicated by forms of immodesty other than nudity, i.e., for the communication of sexuality. In regard to the erotic overtures of column three of our typology, the following statement of an official photographer is relevant: "I never let a girl look straight at the camera. It looks too suggestive. I always have her look off to the side."

Accentuation of the body is suspect as being incongruent with the ideology of nudism. The internalization of the previously discussed principles of nudist ideology would be called into question by such accentuation. Thus, one woman who had shaved her pubic area was labeled as disgusting by those members who talked to the writer about it. Women who blatantly sit in an "unladylike" manner are similarly typed. In the words of one female nudist:

It's no more nice to do than when you are dressed. I would assume they have a purpose. (What's that?) Maybe to draw someone's attention sexually. I'd think its bad behavior and it's one thing that shouldn't be done, especially in a nudist camp. (Why's that?) Because it could lead to trouble or some misfortune. (Could you tell me some more about that?) It could bring up some trouble or disturbance among those who noticed it. It would not be appreciated by "true nudists."

Unnatural attempts at covering any area of the body are similarly ridiculed, since they call into question the actor's acceptance of the definition that there is no shame in exposing any area of the human body. If such behavior occurs early in one's nudist career, however, it is responded to mostly with smiles. The actor is viewed as not yet able to get over the initial difficulty of disposing of "outsiders'" definitions.

Communal toilets are also related to the ideological view that there is nothing shameful about the human body or its bodily functions. Although all camps do not have communal toilets, the large camp at which the writer spent the majority of his time did have such a facility, which was labeled "Little Girls Room and Little Boys Too." The stalls were provided with three-quarter length doors. The existence of this combined facility helped, however, to sustain the nudist definition of

the situation by the element of consistency: if you are not ashamed of
any part of your body, or of any of its natural body functions, why do
you need separate toilets? Thus, even the physical ecology of the
nudist camp is designed in a way that will be consistent with the organization's definition of modesty.

CONSEQUENCES OF A BREAKDOWN IN CLOTHING MODESTY

In the introductory section of this paper it was stated that common-
sense actors anticipate breakdowns in clothing modesty to result in
rampant sexual interest, promiscuity, embarrassment, jealousy, and
shame. The field work and interview data from this study, however, indicate that such occurrences are not common to the nudist camp. The
social organization of the nudist camp provides a system of meanings
and norms that negate these consequences.

CONCLUSIONS

Our results make possible some general conclusions regarding modesty: (1) Covering the body through the use of clothes is not a necessary
condition for a pattern of modesty to exist, nor is it required for tension
management and social control of latent sexual interests. Sexual interests are very adequately controlled in nudist camps; in fact, those who
have visited nudist camps agree that sexual interests are controlled to
a much greater extent than they are on the outside. Clothes are also
not a sufficient condition for a pattern of modesty; the manipulation of
clothes and fashion in stimulating sexual interest is widely recognized.
(2) Except for clothing immodesty, which represents one cell of our
typology of immodesty, all other forms of modesty are maintained in a
nudist camp (e.g., not looking, not saying, not communicating erotic
overtures). This suggests that the latter proscriptions are entirely adequate in achieving the functions of modesty when definitions regarding
the exposure of the body are changed. (3) When deviance from the
institutionalized patterns of modesty is limited to one cell of our typology, (i.e., clothing is dispensed with), and the definition of the
situation is changed, the typically expected consequence of such a
breakdown in this normative pattern does not occur. Rampant sexual
interest, promiscuity, embarrassment, jealousy, and shame were not
found to be typical of the nudist camp.

11

Lloyd Miller
James K. Skipper, Jr.

Sounds of Protest: Jazz and the Militant Avant-Garde

Historians of the future may well view the 1960's as the decade of social protest. Marches, strikes, boycotts, stand-outs, sit-ins, riots have become commonplace. One is surprised if a day passes without the reporting of yet another demonstration by: some group protesting for or against segregation in schools, housing or the labor market; housewives boycotting a grocery chain because of high prices; dairy farmers pouring milk in the street in protest against the low prices they receive for their product; nurses, teachers, and other public servants striking for higher wages; college professors marching in protest against American foreign policy; young men burning their draft cards; college students rioting for more freedom and power. The list could go on and on. Much has been written and will continue to be written about these obvious and conspicuous forms of social protest and what they symbolize.

However, there are other forms of protest which are not so visible or obvious but are nonetheless powerful in their influence and worthy of attention. One of these is the protest represented in the art form of instrumentalized music (instrumentalized in the sociological sense). Music has always been an effective device for the release of cathectic responses relating to controversy, conflict, alienation, and even revolution. As such it often symbolizes the thoughts, feelings, and mood of the times. When we think of protest music today, we usually associate it with the category referred to generically as "Folk." The civil rights song "We Shall Overcome" is a popular and perhaps representative example of this type of social protest music.

However, there is a far less commercial area of contemporary Amer-

This selection, written especially for this book, is published here for the first time.

ican music which is also producing the sounds of protest. This is the jazz idiom. Jazz music is one of America's unique contributions to world culture, and it is this unique identity which makes jazz of importance in terms of social protest. The roots of jazz are undoubtedly in the rural milieu of the southern Negro, having origins in the field songs and chants of plantation days. Significant as this historical rural setting was vis-à-vis the chant and the blues, the maturity of jazz expression today is a characteristically urban phenomenon. It is an expression of the view from the ghetto, urban tension, alienation, and anomic response. Its bold, lean, and sometimes shocking cacophony lends itself to this purpose. Jazz has never been committed to the preservation of the past, or for that matter to passive acceptance of the present. Its very essence is dedication to outdating itself daily. This does not mean that the projection into the future occurs in limbo but that it represents both functional and dysfunctional values of the present, and at the same time is a reaction to these values as well as a prediction of values to come.

Jazz has always been a disturbing element on the American scene. To the uninitiated ear, its sounds are often strange, exotic, and unpredictable. It commits the sin of noncomformity to the norms of traditional music. In addition, to a large portion of the white community jazz has been stereotyped as "race music." As such it has been discriminated against in much the same way that the American Negro has himself. For example, the circular that appears on the next page appeared recently in, of all places, New Orleans, Louisiana.

Finally, the jazz musician is somewhat of a deviant. He is completely dedicated to the small world of his type of music: a "true believer" "with the zeal of a fanatic." He is unconcerned with the demands of those outside his own perspective.[1] His image has been tarnished by an association with drink, drugs, and dives. Many of the early artists grew up around and played in the brothels of New Orleans' infamous red light district—"Storyville." This was the initial association of jazz with sin and sex. The urban working environment of the musician was never very conducive to the middle class standards of the good life. Working almost exclusively at night in smoke-filled clubs in the more seamy sections of major metropolitan areas, surrounded by liquor, and in constant association with underworld elements often made overindulgence in alcohol and narcotics both feasible and enticing. So great has been the jazz musician's association with drugs that at one time the federal hospital at Lexington, Kentucky was able to field an entire all-star band of addict inmates.[2] Primarily for

[1] For a discussion of this point see Howard S. Becker, "The Professional Dance Musician and His Audience," *American Journal of Sociology*, 58 (1951), 136–142; and Alan P. Merriam and Raymond Mack, "The Jazz Community," *Social Forces*, 38 (1960), 211–222.

[2] Leonard Feather, *Encyclopedia of Jazz*, New York, Bonanza Books, 1962, p. 85.

NOTICE!

STOP

Help Save the Youth of America

DON'T BUY NEGRO RECORDS

(If you don't want to serve
negroes in *your* place of business,
then do not have negro records on
your juke box or listen to negro
records on the radio.)

The screaming, idiotic words, and
savage music of these records are
undermining the morals of our white
youth *in America*.

Call the advertisers of the radio
stations that play this type of
music and complain to them!

Don't Let Your Children Buy, or
Listen To These Negro Records

For additional copies of this
circular, write

CITIZEN'S COUNCIL OF GREATER NEW
ORLEANS, INC.

509 Delta Building, New Orleans,
Lousiana 70112

these reasons the Negro jazz musician and his ever changing and
evolving music have never been well accepted by the vast majority
of the general society.

A GLANCE AT THE PAST

Most Americans are ignorant of African prehistory and history. There
is little realization that the American Negro was brought to this country

from societies whose culture placed great emphasis on social change, especially in the verbal arts. Topical songs, for example, are common in African cultures. Although they may be based on old rhythms and melodies, their texts are composed for specific occasions and are essentially creative commentaries on the present social scene. When an African dons a mask and performs certain dances or sings about people and events, he is no longer acting as a person but as a being or spirit. In this role, he often has freedom for comments on social relations and for actions that, if unmasked, would produce social friction or hostility.

It may not be an exaggeration to observe that when the African Negro came to America he brought this cultural trait with him. In the work songs and chants of the plantation fields, when he cried out to his brothers, "Ahm tired a dis mess/Oh, yes, Ahm tired a dis mess," he was commenting on society, but now as an American. This tradition has remained with him. While he no longer hides behind a tribal mask, to commune with spirits, he may symbolically take refuge behind a horn, a drum, a piano, or a voice to give expression to his deepest thoughts and feelings. These expressions take many different forms. Examples are the "shout" (to utter a sudden loud cry), the "shout song" (a rhythmic religious song characterized by responsive singing between leader and congregation), and the "moan" (to make a low, prolonged sound of grief or pain). These utterances represent the beginnings of Negro protest under the bonds of slavery. However "the cry" (an inarticulate utterance of distress, rage, or pain; to cry out for help or to proclaim publicly) is unique, because it is the quintessence of the new sound of protest in avant-garde jazz today.

The bondage of slavery evoked the cry, as represented in the work songs, and the shouts and moans were strident laments. They were also chronicles, but of such a mean kind of existence that they could not assume the universality any lasting musical form must have. The work songs and later blues forms differ profoundly, not only in their form but in their lyrics and intent. Since most Negroes before and after slavery were agricultural laborers, the corn songs, the shouts, and hollers issued from this kind of milieu. Some of the work songs used as their measure the grunt of a man pushing a heavy weight or the blow of a hammer against rock to provide the metrical precision and rhythmical impetus behind the singer. Probably one of the best known examples, is the traditional "Take This Hammer."

> Take this hammer, uh;
> Take it to the captain, uh;
> Take it to the captain, uh;
> Tell him I'm gone.

Because of his status as a slave, there were lyrics to some of the songs that the Negro could not sing in front of his master. The protest was there, nonetheless, and while it could not be given free and strong expression, its importance as a mechanism for cathectic release cannot be underestimated. As the slaves were introduced to Christianity, gospel singing also served the same purpose. The Negro's religious music and spirituals were possibly the first completely native American music.

The church was an important part of the slave's life. For the white masters who had "given Christianity to the heathens," it was seen as a socializing influence and a means of social control. For the Negro, it was to become the 'one institution where he could escape, momentarily, from a subhuman existence.

It was not until well after Emancipation that the Negro experienced any real secular life. Often the churches considered "fiddle songs," "devil songs," and "jig tunes" of the period sinful. Certain musical instruments such as the violin and banjo were also thought to be "the devil's invention."

As the Negro church became institutionalized in the image of the white model, a definite social hierarchy developed. Ministers, deacons, elders, trustees, and even the ushers of the Baptist and Methodist churches formed a definite social hierarchy which dominated the whole of Negro society. In the new theocracy, the "backslider" (the sinning churchgoer) and the "heathen" became the lowest rung of the social ladder.

With the end of slavery there was less dependency on the church as arbiter of the Negro's life style. As the alternatives of secular life began to take shape, there were more and more "backsliders" and, consequently, more and more of the devil music was heard. With emancipation came increasing mobility. The Negro began to leave the plantation for the city in hopes of finding work and a better way of life. In many respects his rural background left the Negro ill-prepared to adjust and adapt to the more complex patterns of urban living. The frustrations, tension, and anxieties encountered in these new settings were symbolized in a new style of music—"the classic blues."

Louis Wirth classified minorities into four basic types: (1) pluralistic—live and let live, (2) assimilationist—desire to join the dominant group, (3) secessionist—rejection of the values and norms of the dominant group, and (4) militant—desire to dominate. It is our contention that jazz today, in its most progressive form, is rapidly becoming instrumentalized as protest and that its evolution as such conforms to the Wirth paradigm with a surprising "goodness of fit."[3]

[3] Louis Wirth, "The Problems of Minority Groups," in *The Science of Man in the World Crisis*, Ralph Linton, ed., New York, Columbia University Press, 1945, pp. 347–372.

PLURALISTIC STAGE

Classic blues is called "classic" because it was the music that seemed to contain all the diverse and conflicting elements of Negro music, plus the smoother emotion of the performance. It was the first Negro music that appeared in a formal context as entertainment. It is probably the end product of more diverse sociological, as well as musical, influences than any other music with the exception of jazz. In contrast to primitive blues, which emerged from the work song era and was characterized by the mastery of simple musical instruments such as the banjo and guitar, classic blues became more stylized and reflected many changes that were taking place in the life of the Negro. It also reflected the urban way of life, in contrast to the rural environment of the past. The blues communicated the pluralistic desire to be accepted, of a people free, but still in economic bondage. Blues are simple and elemental, but they express the profound depths of suffering, sense of defeat, and down-heartedness of the Negro. Yet they are not intrinsically pessimistic. In many of the blues, there is a steady, throbbing undertone of hope. "Times is bad, but they won't be bad always" is the lyric carried in a score of blues songs. For example, in the classic "Trouble In Mind," regardless of the specific troubles the performer may be singing about (women, money, liquor, unemployment, etc.), the last lyric always centers on the theme that someday the sun will shine on the individual again.

Blues are also characterized by lusty vulgarity, sensuality, and exuberance for life, love, and sex. The suggestive titles of many popular blues songs hint at these themes: "She Can Love So Good," "Drive Me Daddy," "Don't Come Too Soon," "Cherry Red," "Feather Bed Mama," "Let Me Play With Your Poodle," "Mother Fuyer." From "barrel-houses" and "honky-tonks" came many of the descriptive words which were applied to the music played there. Included were such graphic terms as "gulley-low," meaning, as its name implies, low as a ditch or gulley; hence, "low-down" and "gut-bucket." This was in reference to the bucket which caught drippings or "gutterings" from the barrels. Invariably, a pastiche for all this was provided by a small band, notable for their lack of restraint.

ASSIMILATIONIST STAGE

The emergence of classic blues and the popularization of jazz occurred at approximately the same time. Both were the results of social and psychological changes within the Negro community as it moved toward the mainstream of American society. By 1914 masses of Negroes began to move toward the northern industrial centers such as Chicago, Detroit, and New York in hopes of high paying jobs and a better way of life. But the urban milieu proved harsh, and invariably Negroes received the lowest wages and the most debasing jobs. For many it was simply a new form of slavery. World War I played an important role in the assimilation of the Negro into secular life. It tended to broaden his horizons to the world beyond America and the realization that the inequalities he experienced were not necessarily the inevitable lot of the Negro.

It was during this period that jazz began to develop in New Orleans and other sections of the South.[4] As the Negro migrated north, the influence of this new music spread to the major metropolitan areas, but especially Chicago, Kansas City, and New York. Jazz was not so much a successor to the blues as it was a seminal music that developed out of, but independent of, the blues. It was an artistic form of expression, a type of communication between those experiencing the plight of existence in big city slums.

During the late 1920's and 1930's the white community came in contact with jazz and a number of white musicians began to learn and imitate this music.[5] White bands were formed and gained a high degree of proficiency, popularity, and financial success during the "Swing era." However, inevitably, the feeling of rejection the Negro was experiencing in the urban milieu and society at large began to manifest itself in his music. At about the time white musicians began to understand and master the new type of music, the form of jazz changed radically. It turned its back on the past.[6] The new sounds of the 1940's began to evoke strange, sympathetic, and to many, mystifying vibrations. The incipient pitch of protest, a musical harbinger of things to come, had begun.

SECESSIONIST STAGE

The emergence of identifiable alienation in jazz began in the middle 1940's. It was known generically as "bop" and became a movement of major proportions. Charlie Parker and Dizzy Gillespie were the major innovators of the period and usually receive the lion's share of credit for its development.

The two main alienating factors in the bop era were the growing complexity of the music which many musicians did not understand, let

---

4 Barry Ulanov, *Handbook of Jazz*, New York, Viking Press, 1959, pp. 5–6.

5 However, a few white musicians were playing a *type* of jazz almost from the beginning. See Joachim Berendt, *The New Jazz Book*, New York, Hill and Wang, 1962, pp. 10–12.

6 John S. Wilson, *Jazz: The Transition Years 1940–1960*, New York, Appleton-Century-Crofts, 1966, p. 26.

alone the general public, and the bop artist's quest to individualize his own identity. Acceptance per se was no longer a goal. He began to "deminstralize" himself. Gillespie launched a broadside against Negro stereotypes. He began wearing sneakers, baseball cap, goatee, and heavy horn-rimmed glasses. Between trumpet excursions into regions of startling technical brilliance, he quoted Shakespeare extensively and accurately, both on and off the bandstand.[7]

Parker in his own way was even more deviant than Gillespie. Musically he was a genius. He attempted to translate everything he saw and heard into music. He set new standards on every level: harmonic, rhythmic, tonal, and melodic. His ability to improvise influenced almost all musicians who heard him. Parker's haunting solos with their plaintive cry established him as the reigning jazz musician of the era. His recordings have been rereleased and his stature continues to grow. Like many of the bop artists, Parker's life was plagued by alcoholism, drug addiction, and mental illness. He died in 1955 at the age of 35 of a complex of illnesses including ulcers and cirrhosis of the liver. However, to many jazz men the cause of Parker's death was simply "too much Soul."

Along with the development of bop emerged another music termed "cool." It was characterized by restraint, depersonalized and introverted sound, suppressed cathexis, and sociologically speaking, incipient alienation. Vestiges of the cool school are still part of the jazz colloquy today. In the 1950's a new musical current began to flow from "cool" musicians located on the West Coast. It formed a direct link between earlier, more traditional jazz forms and what in the 1960's became the violent protesting of avant-garde jazz.

Representing a major stream in jazz today, it is sometimes referred to by such patois as "hard bop," "roots," and "funky," which means hard-driving, blues-infected jazz. The term which enjoys the most currency today and subsumes all of the above designations is "soul," a word rapidly becoming semantically overloaded. In today's racial disturbances its mere presence on a store window—it connotes black ownership—may save an establishment from destruction. In nonmusical terms, the chief quality of "soul" music is ingenuousness, or honesty, both in its musical content and its rubric and dialogue. In reverting to earlier jazz forms, spirituals, and blues, soul music symbolizes a growing disenchantment and rejection of contemporary values.

The rejection may take many forms. Trumpeter Miles Davis often

[7] Wilson comments: "The only aspect of bop that had real appeal to the public was its decor—the beret, dark, heavy-rimmed glasses and goatee that were publicized as the standard bop garb. Bop kits, consisting of a real beret, empty glasses frames and false goatees enjoyed a brisk sale. (More than a decade later the same equipment was being peddled around San Francisco as a 'Beatnik Kit.')" *Ibid.*, pp. 22–23.

shows his contempt and disdain for an audience by not facing them while playing. Saxophone Virtuoso John "Soultrane" Coltrane sometimes left the bandstand before his group was through playing so that he did not have to accept applause from the audience. Drummer Max Roach composed the "We Insist: Freedom Now Suite," one part of which, "The Protest," consists of several minutes of unaccompanied screaming by vocalist Abbey Lincoln.[8] Nina Simone's hostility to both audiences and co-artists is legendary. She has been known to leave the stage during her own numbers, and upon returning, deliver a tirade against the audience, whose attention had waned. The title of her own composition, "Mississippi God Damn!"[9] symbolizes her uncontained rage about racial conditions existing in the South.

Finally, Archie Shepp, a complete avant-garde saxophonist, is also a merciless parodist. He has been known to make appearances in a World War I officer's jacket, tan glen plaid pants, knitted cap, and tinted Ben Franklin spectacles. Thus a bit of American culture becomes instrumentalized. But the protest is by no means confined to the instrumentalization of jazz as parody. Parody is muted protest, but the new jazz is being used as a forum for protest of the strongest kind— complete secession. In addition, avant-garde jazz is proving to be a fountainhead of secessionist jargon, a jargon which is the essence of the "black power" concept. Rarely in history has a relatively small metronymic compound evoked so much hue and cry.

MILITANT MINORITY

At the far end of the continuum lies Wirth's fourth type of minority, which he designates the militant:

Its goal reaches far beyond toleration, assimilation, and even cultural and political autonomy. The militant minority has set domination over others as its goal. Far from suffering from feelings of inferiority, it is convinced of its own superiority and inspired by the lust for conquest. While the initial claims of minority movements are generally modest, like all accessions of power, they feed upon their own success and culminate in delusions of grandeur.[10]

The new music indeed reaches far beyond toleration and assimilation, and certainly it suffers from no apparent inferiority complex. Aggressive tendencies are already manifest in its willingness to offend most tastes and obliterate old musical norms.

On February 23, 1965, playwright-critic-author LeRoi Jones announced the opening of the Black Arts Repertory Theatre-School in

8 Max Roach, *We Insist: Freedom Now Suite,* Candid Records, 8002, 1960.
9 Nina Simone, *Mississippi God Damn!* Phillips Records, 200–135, 1965.
10 Wirth, *op. cit.,* p. 363.

Harlem. This marked Mr. Jones' emergence as one of the chief spokesmen for Black Power through the mediums of jazz criticism and the theater. Mr. Jones has been warming to his assignation for some time. Although his primary concern has been with jazz, he has enjoyed considerable notoriety, as well as artistic and commercial success with his plays, *The Dutchman, The Slave*, and most recently, *The Toilet*. Jones writes for several influential publications including *Downbeat* which is circulated in 142 foreign countries. Like other advocates of black power, Jones' commitment is to black culture only; he rejects all white culture. Among his favorite artists are: Ornette Coleman, John Coltrane, Archie Shepp, the Ayler brothers, and Sun Ra.

Ornette Coleman was one of the original innovators focusing on his new styles as early as 1954. His music is completely atonal and lacks the conventional patterns of improvisation based on chord patterns. He plays a *plastic* alto saxophone which in itself is deviant. Of his music Coleman states he can "groove myself by finally saying something since nothing says nothing to me."[11] In an attempt to expose their own personality, each member of Coleman's group at times appears to go his own way paying little attention to what the others are playing. A critic was once reported to have inquired as to whether listening to Ornette Coleman was covered by Blue Cross.

John Coltrane died at the age of forty in July of 1967. He was probably the best known, most influential, and most financially successful avant-garde musician. Originally a "hard-bopist," before his death Coltrane had moved into a musical realm quite unconnected and almost antithetical to the work of other bop artists. Coltrane was accused of playing "strings of meaningless notes," and playing his tenor saxophone as if he were trying to "blow it apart." Yet LeRoi Jones said of Coltrane that "when he speaks (plays) of God, you realize it is an Eastern God, Allah perhaps."[12]

Archie Shepp's saxophone screams and rants in imitation of the human voice. LeRoi Jones calls him "the age of cities, an urbane traveler with good senses (heart and ear)."[13] Shepp is an outspoken advocate of black culture and black power.

Jazz is the product of the whites—the ofays—too often my enemy. It is the progeny of the blacks—my kinsmen. By this I mean, you own the music and we make it. By definition, then, you own the people who make the music. You own us in whole chunks of flesh—I play about the death of me by you. I exult in the life of me in spite of you—That's what the avant-garde is about.

[11] A. B. Spellman (liner notes), *Ornette Coleman On Tenor*, Atlantic Records, 1394, 1963.
[12] LeRoi Jones (liner notes), *The New Wave in Jazz*, Impulse Records, A = 90, 1965.
[13] *Ibid.*

We're not simply angry young men—we are enraged, and I think it's damn well time.[14]

The Ayler brothers, Donald on trumpet and Albert on tenor saxophone are second only to the fabled Sun Ra in their jazz extremities. Often their music sounds like squawks, screeches, moans, and human cries. They emphasize the feeling, the sound, and not the musical notes. Albert insists that their music comes from the black ghetto: "Why should I hold back the feeling of my life, of being raised in the ghetto of America?"[15] Both men attempt to emphasize their own consciousness, strength, and pride in being black.

Sun Ra is fervently anti-white. His music reflects the ultimate militancy in jazz. He calls his group of ten to twelve musicians a Solar Arkestra, and even denies that they play jazz. Supposedly the music is other-worldly, played on a plane beyond everyday consciousness. When performing the men dress in shining tunics and gold cloth or velvet headbands or hats. On some tunes the only lights are those flashing off the costumes of the musicians and especially Sun Ra's headband. On others, the group marches in a long line playing and chanting as the lights flash on and off. Although Sun Ra plays regularly on the south side of Chicago, the actual time and place of his gigs are not publicized, and only a small circle of his followers are allowed to hear him. Even his recordings are almost impossible to obtain through conventional channels. He records on the most esoteric label in the United States—E.S.P. with liner notes in Esperanto!

These men and their music are deviant; not only in the general society, but also to the mainstream of jazz. Undoubtedly they have been caught up in the civil rights movement and the thrust for black power. They form a perfect example of Wirth's militant minority. The musical sounds of protest by this new breed of musicians are many and varied. They range from the protest against an obsequious self-image to the vigorous protest which perceives the white man as the devil. To what extent they represent and symbolize the feeling, thought, and mood of the new generation of American Negroes is still problematic. But the avant-garde jazz musician just may be the revolutionary intellectual communicating to all who have ears to hear. Steve Young, Music-Art co-ordinator of the Black Arts Repertory Theatre School has said: "These men are dangerous and someday they may murder, send the weaker hearts and corrupt consciences leaping through windows or screaming through their destroyed dream world."[16]

Without a "critical mass" of social protest of some form, few basic

[14] Nat Hentoff, "The New Jazz—Black, Angry and Hard to Understand," *New York Times Magazine*, December 25, 1966, p. 10.
[15] *Ibid.*, p. 38.
[16] Steve Young (liner notes), *The New Wave in Jazz, op. cit.*

structural changes take place in society. The radical, yeasty element in the "new music" may be one manifestation of this "critical mass." At what point do the elements of social fermentation reach the proper proportions for fusion? It appears that the threshold was approached in the recent riots in the Negro ghettoes of New York, Cleveland, Chicago, Los Angeles, Newark, Detroit, and a host of other metropolitan areas.

This, then, is protest. Protest with a sound. A sound with a semantic thrust which demands to be heard, will not be silenced, and should not be overlooked.

12

Jerome K. Myers

Lee L. Bean

Max P. Pepper

Social Class and Psychiatric Disorders:
A Ten Year Follow-Up[*]

This article reports on part of an extensive follow-up study of persons enumerated in the 1950 New Haven Psychiatric Census.[1] In the original study, significant relationships were found between social class and the prevalence, treatment and development of diagnosed mental illness.[2] The present study focuses upon what has happened to the patients in the ten years following the original study. Specifically, significant relationships were hypothesized between social class and (1) 1960 treatment status, (2) relapse rates for patients discharged from treatment during the 10 year period, and (3) community adjustment for discharged patients.[3]

Previous follow-up research on psychiatric illness has been fragmentary.[4] It has focused primarily upon either etiological factors,

From *Journal of Health and Social Behavior*, Summer, 1965, pp. 74–79, by permission of the author and the American Sociological Association.

[*] The research reported in this paper is supported by USPHS, NIMH Grant HM-03569.

[1] For other reports on the study, see J. K. Myers, L. L. Bean and M. P. Pepper, "Social Class and Mental Illness: A Ten Year Follow-Up of Psychiatric Patients," *Connecticut Medicine*, 28:355–59, 1964; and L. L. Bean, J. K. Myers and M. P. Pepper, "Social Class and Schizophrenia: A Ten Year Follow-Up," in A. B. Shostak and W. Gomberg (eds.), *Blue-Collar World*, Englewood Cliffs, N. J., Prentice-Hall, 1964.

[2] See A. B. Hollingshead and F. C. Redlich, *Social Class and Mental Illness*, New York, John Wiley, 1958; and J. K. Myers and B. H. Roberts, *Family and Class Dynamics in Mental Illness*, New York, John Wiley, 1959.

[3] The patients' 1950 social class status is used in all analyses in this paper.

[4] For example, see: L. M. Adler, J. W. Coddington, and D. D. Stewart, *Mental Illness in Washington County, Arkansas: Incidence, Recovery and Posthospital Adjustment*, Fayetteville, Univ. of Arkansas, Institute of Science and Technology, Research Series, No. 23, July, 1952; E. D. Bond and F. J. Braceland, "Prognosis in Mental Disease," *Amer. J. Psychiatry*, **94**: 263–74, 1937; T. Braatoy, "The Prognosis in Schizo-

discharge and relapse rates, or upon the effectiveness of various types of treatment. A few studies have followed patients into the community, but little attention has been given to the effects of social factors upon patient readjustment.[5] Most research has focused upon specific problems relating to the former mental patient and thus has been limited in scope. For example, follow-up studies generally include only a small number of cases, patients from one treatment agency or diagnostic category, persons of one sex or age grouping, or some other relatively homogeneous group of patients. Most investigators have restudied their subjects at relatively short periods after discharge from treatment or after the original study—a few months to a few years at most.[6] All such studies have been limited to a patient population. Without a control group, however, it is impossible to determine whether adjustment variations are unique or are reflections of differences to be found within any population.

The present research differs from most previous studies at a number of points. All New Haven psychiatric patients in hospital or out-patient clinic treatment in 1950 were followed for ten years. A number of indices of treatment outcome were investigated, and a control group of non-patients was employed in evaluating community adjustment. Finally, it was the first follow-up research to study social class extensively.[7]

---

phrenia with Some Remarks Regarding Diagnosis and Therapy," *Acta Psychiat. et Neurol.*, 11: 63–102, 1936; N. Q. Brill and G. W. Beebe, *A Follow-Up Study of War Neuroses*, V. A. Medical Monograph, Government Printing Office, Washington, D. C., 1955; G. W. Brown, "Experiences of Discharged Chronic Schizophrenic Patients in Various Types of Living Group," *Milbank Memorial Fund Quart.* **XXXVII**: 105–31, 1959; G. W. Brown, G. M. Carstairs, and G. Topping, "Post-Hospital Adjustment of Chronic Mental Patients," *Lancet*, Sept. 27, 1958, 685–89; S. Dinitz, S. Angrist, M. Lefton and B. Pasamanick, "Instrumental Role Expectations and Posthospital Performance of Female Mental Patients," *Social Forces*, **40**: 248–54, 1962; H. E. Freeman and O. G. Simmons, *The Mental Patient Comes Home*, New York, John Wiley, 1963; R. G. Fuller, "What Happens to Mental Patients After Discharge from Hospital," *Psychiatric Quart.* **9**: 95–104, 1935; L. B. Hohman, "A Review of 144 Cases of Affective Disorders After Seven Years," *Amer. J. Psychiatry*, **94**: 303–08, 1937; M. Kramer *et al.*, *A Historical Study of the Disposition of First Admissions to a State Mental Hospital: Experience of Warren State Hospital During the Period 1916–1950*, Public Health Monograph No. 32, Government Printing Office, Washington, D. C., 1955; V. Norris, *Mental Illness in London*, London, Chapman and Hall, 1956; T. A. C. Rennie, "Prognosis in Manic-Depressive Psychoses," *Amer. J. Psychiatry*, **98**: 801–14, 1942.

[5] The major exceptions are the following recent studies which have dealt with the effect of social factors. However, the follow-up period and patient population have been limited in each case. See Brown, "Experiences of Discharged Chronic Schizophrenic Patients in Various Types of Living Group," *op. cit.*; A. Harris, I. Linker, V. Norris and M. Sheperd, "Schizophrenia, a Prognostic and Social Study," *British J. Social and Prev. Med.*, **10**: 107–14, 1956; and Freeman and Simmons, *op. cit.*

[6] Most medical and psychiatric follow-up studies are limited to a period of five years or less.

[7] Generally, previous studies have been limited to an analysis of hospital discharge rates. See for example, R. H. Hardt and S. J. Feinhandler, "Social Class and Mental Hospitalization Prognosis," *Amer. Sociological Rev.*, **24**: 815–21, 1959.

The findings reported in this article deal with the study's first major hypothesis, i.e., *there is a significant relationship between social class and 1960 treatment status.*

METHODS

The status of all individuals from greater New Haven, 1565 in number, who were in psychiatric treatment between May 31 and December 1, 1950 in psychiatric out-patient clinics or psychiatric hospitals, was re-examined on June 1, 1960.[8] Patients treated by private practitioners in 1950 were not restudied because of commitments the research group made to these physicians at the time of the original psychiatric census.

The research consisted of two phases: (1) a study of records at the 1950 and subsequent treatment agencies, and (2) interviews with patients discharged from treatment and their families to determine their mental status and social adjustment in the community. A control group of individuals who were never treated for mental illness was also interviewed in the second phase of the research. These persons were individually matched with the discharged patients on the basis of the following six variables: sex, race, social class, religion, age and marital status. This group was selected from a list of names drawn systematically from the city directories of the greater New Haven area.

In the first phase, a 43-item schedule was employed to abstract social, psychiatric and medical data from hospital and clinical records covering the patients' histories during the ten years studied. The original records collected in the 1950 New Haven Census were also re-examined in this phase of the research. Materials collected for patients who are still in hospital treatment or who died in treatment were limited to these two sources. In the second phase, extensive additional information was gathered through interviews for those persons who were not hospitalized in 1960.

Of the 1,565 patients studied in 1950, 1,547 (99 percent) were located in 1960. Only the cases located will be included in the analysis in this paper. Two additional cases whose class was unknown in both 1950 and 1960 are excluded. These were long-term patients who were continuously hospitalized from 1950 until their death.

The independent variable in this study, social class, was measured by Hollingshead's Two Factor Index of Social Position which utilizes occupation and education to rank the study population into five classes

---

[8] The towns included in greater New Haven are as follows: New Haven, West Haven, East Haven, North Haven, Hamden, and Woodbridge, Connecticut.

where I is the highest and V the lowest.[9] A brief descriptive characterization of these social classes follows: Class I (the highest socio-economic position) comprises families of wealth, high education and occupation, and top-rank social prestige. Class II consists of families in which the adults for the most part hold college or advanced degrees and are in professional or high-level managerial positions. Class III includes the bulk of small business and white-collar workers together with a sizeable number of skilled workers. This group consists predominantly of high school graduates. Class IV consists largely of semi-skilled workers with some secondary education. Class V includes unskilled and semiskilled workers who have an elementary education or less and who live in the poorest slum areas of the community.

SELECTED FINDINGS

This paper presents selected findings relevant to the first hypothesis that there is a significant relationship between social class and the patients' follow-up treatment status.[10] Data for patients hospitalized and for those in clinic treatment in 1950 were analyzed separately for a number of reasons. First, clinic patients were generally less severely disturbed than hospitalized patients. For example, 71 percent of patients in clinic treatment in 1950 were diagnosed as neurotic, 20 percent as alcoholic and only 9 percent as some type of psychotic. The corresponding percentages for hospitalized cases were 4, 4 and 92. Next, the experience of being hospitalized and isolated from normal community and family living is also markedly different from that of being treated in an out-patient clinic. Undoubtedly, differences in pathways to the treatment process itself, in precipitating events related to entering treatment, and in attitudes toward treatment are present between the two groups. Finally, hospitalized patients so greatly outnumbered clinic cases, 1412 to 133, that any analysis of total cases would reflect to a large extent the obviously distinctive experience of the former.

1950 HOSPITALIZED PATIENTS

Of the 1,420 patients who were in state, private and veterans hospitals at the time of the original study, 1,412 were located in 1960. Of this number, 54 percent were still hospitalized in 1960, 31 percent had died, 14 percent were no longer hospitalized or under any psychiatric

[9] See A. B. Hollingshead, *Two Factor Index of Social Position*, mimeographed publication, copyright, 1957; and Myers and Roberts, *op. cit.*, 130. For a detailed description of the five social classes, see Hollingshead and Redlich, *op. cit.*, 69–135.

[10] The chi-square test was used in all computations to determine whether significant differences existed between frequency distributions.

treatment, and 2 percent were discharged from the hospital but under out-patient care.

The data in Table 1 demonstrate a strong relationship between social class and follow-up treatment status. Significantly more persons in the lower classes were still hospitalized ten years after the original 1950 study. Whereas 39 percent of class I and II individuals were in hospitals in 1960, the percentage increased steadily to 49 in class III, 52 in class IV and 57 in class V.[11] The proportion of persons who had died differed neither greatly nor in any consistent manner among the classes. However, the percentage living in the community and no longer hospitalized declined steadily from 30 in classes I and II, to 27 in class

TABLE 1.

1960 Treatment Status by Social Class of Hospitalized Patients

1960 Treatment Status:	Social Class:				
	I-II Pct.	III Pct.	IV Pct.	V Pct.	Total Pct.
Hospitalized	39	49	52	57	54
Dead	30	24	30	33	31
Discharged from hospital	30	27	18	10	16
a. Not under treatment*	(21)	(23)	(16)	(9)	(14)
b. Out-patient treatment*	(9)	(4)	(2)	(1)	(2)
N =	46	121	559	686	1412

$x^2 = 39.80; P < .001, 6$ df.
*Subcategory of "Discharged from Hospital."

III, 18 in class IV, and 10 in class V. Thus, the proportion of persons discharged from hospital treatment in the two highest classes was three times as great as in the lowest. Most persons discharged from the hospital were no longer under any type of psychiatric therapy. However, those receiving out-patient care were concentrated in the middle and upper classes. Only one percent of former class V patients were being treated in a clinic or by a private practitioner, whereas the percentage rose to nine in classes I and II.

The percentages in Table 1 are based upon the total cohort of 1950 hospitalized patients, and thus include persons who had died by

[11] Classes I and II are combined in this report because of the small number of cases in Class I.

1960 as well as those still alive. If only those persons still living in 1960 are considered, the same class differential is found. The percentage of patients no longer in hospital declined from 44 in classes I and II, to 36 in class III, 26 in class IV, and 15 in class V.

Since factors other than social class are related to discharge from hospital treatment the data were analyzed further. We determined whether follow-up treatment status was related to variables presumably related to discharge from hospital treatment such as sex, religion, marital status, age, diagnosis, length of hospitalization at the time of the original study, previous psychiatric treatment history, major type of treatment, and type of hospital by sponsorship.[12]

Two factors—sex and religion—were unrelated to current therapy status when these analyses were made.[13] The other seven variables were related to treatment outcome in the following manner:

1. *Marital status*—The proportion of patients no longer hospitalized in 1960 was greater for the married than for the unmarried, separated, divorced or widowed.

2. *Age*—As would be expected, more persons age 60 and over than below 60 had died by 1960, and fewer had been discharged from the hospital.

3. *Diagnosis*—Significantly fewer neurotics than psychotics were hospitalized in 1960. Within the psychotic group, the lowest discharge rate was found among the senile psychoses, followed in order by schizophrenic and paranoid psychoses, and all others.[14]

4. *Length of hospitalization at time of original study*—Significantly more persons whose hospital treatment began in 1949 or 1950 than in 1948 or earlier were out of hospital by 1960.[15]

5. *Previous psychiatric treatment history*—Persons who were in their first course of psychiatric treatment at the time of the original study were more likely to have died by 1960 or to be still hospitalized than individuals with previous treatment records.

6. *Major type of treatment*—The highest percentage of patients still hospitalized and the lowest percentage discharged and living in the community were found among those receiving custodial care only in 1950, followed in descending order by patients orig-

[12] Patients are classified according to their 1950 status on each of these variables. See Hollingshead and Redlich, *op. cit.*, 28–29 and 253–57 for a description of the diagnostic scheme employed and the classification of types of psychiatric treatment and treatment facilities.

[13] The chi-square test was used to determine whether significant differences existed between frequency distributions. P was greater than .30 for sex and religion.

[14] Because of the relatively small numbers involved, affective and organic psychoses were combined.

[15] Persons hospitalized for more than two years are generally considered as chronic patients.

inally designated as receiving organic treatment, and those receiving psychotherapy.

7. *Type hospital by sponsorship*—The highest percentage of patients no longer in hospital care was found among those originally in private hospitals, followed in order by those in veterans hospitals and finally state hospitals.

Although the above variables are related to follow-up treatment status, our interest is in determining whether any of them account for the significant social class differences in outcome already noted. Therefore, detailed analyses were made to determine whether there were social class differences in treatment outcome within each of the specific groupings into which the seven controls were divided. These specific breakdowns were:

1. *Marital status*—(a) married, (b) single, (c) separated, widowed and divorced.
2. *Age*—(a) 60 and above, (b) below 60.
3. *Diagnosis*—(a) neuroses, (b) schizophrenic and paranoid psychoses, (c) senile psychoses, (d) other psychoses.
4. *Length of hospitalization at time of original study*—(a) hospitalized in 1949 or 1950, (b) hospitalized in 1948 or earlier.
5. *Previous psychiatric treatment history*—(a) no psychiatric treatment previous to 1950 course of treatment, (b) previous psychiatric treatment.
6. *Major type of treatment*—(a) custodial care, (b) psychotherapy, (c) organic therapy.
7. *Type hospital by sponsorship*—(a) private, (b) veterans administration, (c) state.

The introduction of these controls did not negate any of the class differences found for 1960 treatment status. Analyses were made for each of the above 19 categories, and a chi-square test was applied to determine whether significant relationships existed between social class and follow-up treatment status. In each case, we discovered the same relationship within each grouping: the higher the social class, the greater the percentage of patients discharged from hospital care.[16]

1950 CLINIC PATIENTS

The experience since 1950 of persons treated in clinics at the time of the original study was markedly different from that of hospitalized patients. At the time of the follow-up research 80 percent of the 133 for-

---

[16] The distribution of significance levels found was: p less than .05 — fourteen tests; p less than .10 — two tests; and p less than .20 — three tests.

mer clinic patients studied were living in the community and no longer under psychiatric care, whereas the corresponding percentage for hospitalized cases was 14. Only six percent of clinic patients had died and another six percent were hospitalized. The low proportions of dead and hospitalized reflect the younger average age of the former clinic patients and the small number of psychotics among them. These factors also probably help to account for the larger percentage of former clinic than hospital patients who were under out-patient care in 1960, eight compared to two.

Despite these differences in the experience of clinic and hospitalized patients, the same pattern of social class variations in treatment outcome was found among the former as among the latter. Examining the status of former clinic patients in 1960 or at the time of their death, we find that the percentages hospitalized were six in classes I—III, five in class IV and 15 in class V.[17] The opposite relationship was found between social class and out-patient care at follow-up for these patients: the percentage decreased from 14 in classes I—III to seven in class V.

Because of the small number of former clinic patients who were dead or in treatment in 1960, it was not possible to control for other variables possibly related to treatment outcome as was done for patients hospitalized in 1950.

SUMMARY AND DISCUSSION

The findings reported in this article support the hypothesis that there is a significant relationship between social class and patients' treatment status at follow-up in 1960. As the social class of patients becomes higher, the proportion not under hospital care increases.

The follow-up status of patients in hospital and out-patient clinic treatment in 1950 differed significantly. Whereas most of the former were still hospitalized ten years later, most of the latter were no longer under any type of psychiatric therapy. This difference is not unexpected due to differences between the two groups in the types and severity of psychiatric illnesses, age distribution and other factors at the time of the original study. However, in both groups the same pattern of class differences were found: the lower the social class position of patients, the greater the proportion under hospital care in 1960 or at the time of their death.

Among patients living in the community the opposite relationship

[17] Classes I, II and III were combined in this analysis because of the small number of cases. In the chi-square test, classes I through IV were combined because of the small number of hospitalized cases. P was less than .10.

was found between social class and psychiatric treatment: the lower the social class, the smaller the proportion of patients in out-patient care, either in clinics or private practice. Thus, of the 1545 patients in hospital and clinic treatment in 1950 considered in this analysis, the percentage in out-patient therapy in 1960 declined from 13 in classes I and II to five in class III, three in class IV, and two in class V. These percentages are based upon the total cohort of 1950 cases, and thus include persons who had died by 1960 and those who were still hospitalized as well as those no longer under in-patient care. Therefore, a more realistic way of viewing the extent of out-patient treatment is to base percentages upon only those persons who could utilize such services, i.e., those living in 1960 who were no longer hospitalized. Although class differences decline on this basis, they remain striking, the percentages by class being 33 in I and II, 12 in III, 10 in IV and 10 in V.

These striking class variations in treatment outcome indicate the influence of social, as well as medical and psychiatric factors upon follow-up treatment status. They probably reflect to some degree the class differences in therapy found at the time of the original study.[18] They may also reflect class differences in the community's reaction to the ex-mental patient. For example, there may be social class differences in the ability and willingness of the family to accept a patient back into the community. Although a lower class patient may be functioning adequately under supervision and care, his family may be unable to undertake the required supervision of the patient at home, no matter how minimal, because of limited resources, restricted living quarters, or the community services now available. Furthermore, lower class families have little interest in accepting the burden of caring for the patient even if they are able.[19] Middle and upper class families, on the other hand, are not only more willing to have the patient home, but they have available a greater range of resources to provide for his care and supervision.

Important among the resources available to higher class families are out-patient therapy facilities. Although these are ostensibly available to all, previous research has shown their greater use in general by higher class persons as well as the preferential treatment accorded them.[20] Since most out-patient agencies are day clinics, their differential use by social class may be a function of the time an individual has available during the day to attend them. Class differences in occupational demands would seem to provide higher class individuals with

18 See Hollingshead and Redlich, *op. cit.*, 253–303.
19 Myers and Roberts, *op. cit.*, 217 and Appendix Table 22, 285.
20 Myers, J. K., and L. Schaffer, "Social Stratification and Psychiatric Practice: A Study of an Outpatient Clinic," *Amer. Sociological Rev.*, 19: 307–10, 1954; D. Rosenthal and J. D. Frank, "The Fate of the Psychiatric Clinic Outpatients Assigned to Psychotherapy," *J. Nervous and Mental Dis.*, 127: 330–43, 1958.

an advantage in this respect. Private psychiatric treatment is also made available to upper and middle class persons because of their obviously superior financial resources.

Exploration of these and other factors in greater depth will be possible through the analysis of interview materials collected in the second phase of the research. Differential utilization patterns of not only psychiatric resources but also of the entire spectrum of community services need to be examined. The results should be important not only for the evaluation of existing facilities and for planning future services, but also for better understanding of the etiology and life history of psychiatric disorders.

13

Ephraim H. Mizruchi
Robert Perrucci

Prescription, Proscription and Permissiveness: Aspects of Norms and Deviant Drinking Behavior

INTRODUCTION

A major problem for contemporary sociologists revolves about the issue of long range vs. short range goals in the solution of perceived social problems. Should the sociologist concern himself primarily with abstract theory which is of a level of generality capable of application to many social settings, once developed and refined? Or, should he apply himself to a particular question yielding more immediate rewards for the process of solving seemingly urgent societal problems? In reality we find only a small number who clearly espouse either one position or the other. More typical of contemporary research is an effort to study the particular in order to cast light on the general.

The present paper attempts to illustrate how the study of normative and deviant drinking behavior yields hypotheses which are explicitly tied to more abstract generalizations which are applicable to a variety of social settings. Thus, research in the sphere of alcohol and society can make simultaneous contributions to the solution of immediate social problems and to the development of general theories of social processes.

Our data in this paper are analyzed within a broad framework which embodies questions about the nature of normative integration, deviance, group reactions to deviance and social change.

From "Norm Qualities and Deviant Behavior" in *The Substance of Sociology: Codes, Conduct and Consequences*, Ephraim H. Mizruchi, ed., New York, Appleton-Century-Crofts, 1967. An extension and revision of an earlier paper, "Norm Qualities and Differential Effects of Deviant Behavior," *American Sociological Review*, 27 (June, 1962), 391–399, by permission of the authors and Appleton-Century-Crofts.

The organizing concepts emerged both from a study of the data on cultural factors in drinking behavior and further induction into an appropriate theoretical model. The process includes the establishment of ideal type aspects of norms; providing data illustrating the significance of distinguishing these aspects from other norm qualities; and deriving *explicit* empirically testable hypotheses for the assessment of the original typology. Thus what is being attempted, in addition, is a study of how ideal-type method can be directly integrated with more formal empirical analysis.

NORMS AND NORMATIVE INTEGRATION

A fundamental notion embodied in the functional approach to social systems is that certain tasks must be performed in order that a given system may persist. Among the various tasks, or functional prerequisites, is the maintenance of a system of order. Many of the traditional dichotomies associated with the names of eminent forerunners of contemporary sociology reflect explicit and implicit concern with order. Durkheim's mechanical and organic solidarity (12), Tönnies' Gemeinshaft-Gesellschaft (33) Redfield's Folk-Urban (25) and Becker's Sacred-Secular (3) to name only a few, indicate a concern with the fundamental question of how society is organized and changed.

Though there are great divergences of viewpoint among contemporary sociologists regarding which factors are most significant in contrasting relatively simple and complex social organizations, few would disagree that the process of group adherence to shared norms represents an important dimension of order. Thus Durkheim (12) and Freedman *et al.* (13) have focused their attention on the contrast between normative and functional integration. These two dimensions as conceived by these writers are to be found in all group structures and represent ideal-typical states of systems. Thus contemporary urban communities, for example, would be expected to be integrated not only in terms of functional integration, i.e., integration based on the interrelated activities of heterogeneous groups, but normatively as well. The norms, consequently, represent crucial factors in the process of maintaining order.

Relatively little attention has been paid to the qualitative nature of the norms themselves as contrasted with the great concern associated with the direct effect of norms in controlling the activities of individuals in groups.[1] This is particularly the case with regard to the role played by the qualitative characteristics of norms in the process of normative integration and the utility of this dimension in empirical analysis.

---

[1] The most conspicuous exceptions are to be found in the work of William Graham Sumner (32), Talcott Parsons (22), Pitirim Sorokin (30), and Robin M. Williams, Jr. (36).

In terms of the sociocultural system, the problem of order may be analyzed with respect to the particular characteristics of the norms themselves, in addition to the control processes associated with the norms. In other words, the stability or integration of a system is not insured simply because the normative system is effectively transmitted (socialization) or collectively controlled (sanctions). The qualities of the norms themselves provide an inherent potential for system maintenance and system mal-integration.

PROSCRIPTIVE AND PRESCRIPTIVE DIMENSIONS OF NORMS

Richard T. Morris (19), in a paper published a decade ago, suggested a classification of norms which focused on four significant aspects: their distribution; the mode of enforcement associated with a given norm; the transmission of norms; and the process of conformity to given norms. Robin M. Williams, Jr., has also incorporated this scheme in his systematic study of American society (36, pp. 26–27). Though there is no shortage of classificatory schemes in this important area of sociological theory, it would seem to the present writers that still another dimension is worthy of consideration as a possible addition to Morris' classification.

Indeed, Morris himself has suggested that "probably the most striking omission . . . [in his typology of norms] . . . is the content of the norms" (19, p. 612). "Content" is used here in two senses: classification of norms according to the area of behavior regulated . . . , or classification of norms according to the nature of action called for by the norms . . ." (19). It is the latter to which we are addressing ourselves in this paper.

Our specific objective will be to present an additional typology, to illustrate its potential value by making reference to several sets of data related to the typology, and to suggest how greater attention to this dimension may prove fruitful in assessing the functional significance of certain aspects of norms in social systems.

In discussing norms in general, Williams points out that ". . . norms always carry some prescriptive or proscriptive *quality* . . ." (36, p. 26).[2] Talcott Parsons, in discussing the integration of social systems, has also directed attention to the significance of the proscriptive-prescriptive dimension. He states,

It is this integration by common values, manifested in the action of solidary groups or collectivities, which characterizes the partial or total integrations of social systems.

[2] It should be noted that we are not concerned here with *types* of norms as such, but only with specific *aspects* of norms. It should also be kept in mind that the proscriptive-prescriptive notions have existed in the anthropological literature for some time.

Social integration, however much it depends on internalized norms, cannot be achieved by these alone. It requires also some supplementary coordination provided by explicit *prescriptive* or *prohibitory* role-expectations (e.g., laws) (23, pp. 202–203) .[3]

This particular dimension appears worthy of further exploration on the level of system-maintenance analysis. A preliminary ideal-typical description should prove sufficient for the first step in our analysis.

Norms in which the *proscriptive* element is most predominant are those which direct participants in the social structure to avoid, abstain, desist, and reject all forms of behavior associated with a particular potential type of activity. Examples of this dimension are the "thou shalt not" directives of the Ten Commandments and abstention from the pleasures of the flesh as directed by ascetic Protestantism.

The *prescriptive* dimension, on the other hand, directs participants to act in a particular way, spelling out the forms of behavior to which group members must conform. Typical of prescriptive directives are the norms requiring periodical church attendance and confession among Roman Catholics and the elaborate directives associated with the consumption of alcoholic beverages among the Orthodox Jews.

Thus the mandate of the predominantly proscriptive norm is "do not" while the mandate of the predominantly prescriptive norm is "do this" or "do that." The former provides only a goal viewed negatively; the latter provides a goal viewed positively, as well as a set of means for its attainment.

Whether this scheme is worthy of serious attention as a possible addition to the body of theory on norms would seem to depend upon its usefulness as an analytical tool, particularly as a means of organizing empirical findings. We have, with this in mind, selected some studies which help illustrate the possible utility of these notions in the process of relating theory to concrete data.

At least one area of patterned activity which particularly lends itself to analysis in this context has undergone extensive investigation.[4] The several sociological studies of the relationship between sociocultural factors and the consumption of alcoholic beverages should provide us with a "goodness of fit" criterion for our conceptual analysis.[5] The specific studies to which we refer are those of Straus and Bacon (31),

[3] It should be noted also that the present writers do not view the significance of the prescriptive and proscriptive dimensions as operative on the external level alone, i.e., external to the internalized norms, as Parsons implies here, but on both the internalized and externalized levels of social control. Note also Robert K. Merton's awareness of the significance of these dimensions (17, p. 133).

[4] Note the similarity between our independently conceived approach and the earlier approach of Edwin M. Lemert (15, p. 33).

[5] For a discussion of the "goodness of fit" concept in the verification of typologies, see, for example, James M. Beshers (5).

Snyder (28), Skolnick (27), Mulford and Miller (21), Allardt, *et al.* (1), and more recently, Bruen and Hauge (6). All represent a high order of methodological procedure in terms of sampling, question design and data analysis. All of these studies focus on variations in drinking behavior among various social strata and ethnic groups, and provide a broad range of data on norms, beliefs, and sentiments concerning the uses of alcohol. Thus they are particularly valuable for codification. Our first problem, then, is to demonstrate whether the differences between prescriptive and proscriptive dimensions of norms are of significance in the analysis of concrete data.

The above studies report significant differences among the various groups with regard to pathological reactions resulting from differential patterns of alcohol consumption. By "pathological" we mean the extent to which these behaviors represent deviations which are threats to the personal well-being of group members, e.g., problem drinking or psychosis: We are suggesting that the extent to which these levels of pathology are present in a given system is directly related to problems of system maintenance although as we suggest below, these threats may also play a role in attaining greater short-run integration.

Cultural Norms and Drinking Pathology

Three sets of data have been selected to demonstrate the existence of a relationship between types of normative system and drinking pathology. Snyder's study shows that intoxication is related to religio-ethnic group affiliation for college students.[6] As contrasted with the rates for the Jewish students, whose behavior is presumably directed by prescriptive norms, for example, the intoxication rate is much higher for the ascetic Protestant and Mormon groups, for whom the drinking of alcoholic beverages is proscribed. Snyder holds that,

These data should not be construed as representing the comparative overall effectiveness of the norms of these groups in minimizing intoxication. The percentages . . . are based on the numbers of students in each group who have had some experience in using alcoholic beverages. They, therefore, do not reflect the large numbers of abstainers, especially in the Protestant group, who have never been intoxicated (29, p. 189).

We would hold that Snyder's interpretation is most meaningful within the context of the relationship between group affiliation and overall drinking behavior. However, it is precisely the question of the "overall effectiveness of the norms" for those who drink which concerns us here; this is the sphere in which the fundamental difference between

---

[6] Snyder's data were derived from original data gathered by Straus and Bacon for the college drinking study. See Snyder (29, p. 190).

our concern and that of the various analysts of drinking behavior manifests itself. While their focus is on the relationship between norms and specified features of the social structure, ours is on the qualitative nature of the norms themselves.

Skolnick's data[7] reveal even more sharply some of the consequences of normative deviation. When one compares the degree of social complications associated with religio-ethnic group affiliation, one finds that social complications tend to increase for selected groups of students. While social complications for the Jewish students are minimal, there is a marked increase for the ascetic Protestant groups. Thus, the data again reflect a relationship between ascetic Protestant affiliation and drinking pathology with respect to the extremities of deviant reactions for these groups.

Still other results that are significant in the context of the present study are the findings of Mulford and Miller in one of the most elaborate and extensive studies of the drinking behavior of an adult population. They approach questions similar to those posed by the other researchers from a social psychological viewpoint. Differentiating between drinking behavior that is directed by normative systems and that which involves idiosyncratic decisions regarding alcohol consumption, they developed a scale of "personal-effects definitions," which makes a distinction between relatively normative and non-normative drinking behavior (20,2).

Mulford and Miller's interpretation of their findings is consistent with those of Straus and Bacon and Snyder with regard to the non-existence of group norms which characterizes the drinking behavior of respondents with abstinence backgrounds. From their results, it seems clear that the focus on "personal-effects" on the part of the drinker as contrasted with a more normative orientation is associated with problem drinking. An extensive statement by Mulford and Miller with regard to their findings reflects some points of convergence between their viewpoint and our own.

The heavier consumption by the personal-effects drinker may also be a reflection of the *relative absence of social norms* in the situations where he does much of his drinking. Persons who drink primarily for social effects may be presumed to do most of their drinking in more intimate group situations, involving family and friends, where restrictive norms are relatively effective;

---

[7] Skolnick's data were derived from original data gathered by Straus and Bacon for the college drinking study. The reader should note a possible objection associated with the groups on which *problem drinking* rates are based. For example, it has been pointed out that comparisons of alcoholism rates can be variously interpreted, depending upon whether the *base* of the comparison is the *total* membership of the two groups, or solely on the *drinkers* in the two groups. It should be clear, however, that (1) we are not speaking of *alcoholism* rates, but *problem drinking* rates; and (2) that we are primarily concerned with comparing alcohol pathology rates in different groups *for those who do drink*. For a discussion of these points, see Skolnick (27, p. 460).

although, of course, the party norms may permit considerable latitude. The personal-effects drinker who attends parties probably is the one most likely to exceed the party norms, but as he does so repeatedly, he may find that he is not welcome and is then 'forced' to do more of his drinking alone and in public places where there is relative freedom from intimate group-norm restrictions.

Finally, the heavy drinking of the individual who is drinking mainly for the personal effects of alcohol may also reflect the likelihood that he does not carry in his mind a conception of *how many drinks* it takes to attain the desired effect, especially since such *prescriptions* are presumably not general in our culture. . . . (21, pp. 276–277) .[8]

We can conclude from the above studies that normative systems play a role in the consumption of alcoholic beverages, and that pathological reactions to drinking tend to be greater for certain ascetic Protestant and Mormon groups, as compared with other religious groups. We would hold, in general, that pathological drinking behavior is associated with a relative absence of directives for the act of drinking alcoholic beverages itself. The important question then is: What is there about the nature of the normative systems of the ascetic Protestant and Mormon groups that predisposes their deviants to greater pathological reactions and, consequently, their structure to greater strain?

Significance of Prescriptive and Proscriptive Dimension

We have indicated above that there is an absence of directives regarding drinking behavior among the ascetic Protestant and Mormon groups. In contrast to the prescriptive norms associated with drinking by Jews, for example, the ascetic Protestant and Mormon norms may be characterized as primarily *proscriptive*. Total abstinence, is the norm for these groups. Hence, deviation from the abstinence pattern, even in what is ordinarily recognized as socially approved drinking in the larger society, e.g., before dinner, at parties, and like occasions, is associated with an almost complete absence of directives. As Straus and Bacon have pointed out in discussing the drinking behavior of Mormons, "If drinking behavior is adopted, variation must be the rule since there is no norm. Extremes are likely since the behavior itself represents rejection of social rules." (31, p. 144) .[9]

[8] See also, Allardt (1), which provides additional data to support the hypothesis about the conditions associated with relative lack of drinking norms and our discussion below.

[9] Skolnick (27, p. 265), makes the point that extreme drinking behavior of those exposed to abstinence teachings is a result of another norm derived from descriptions of the behavior of extreme drinkers, i.e., "the horrible example." Although we see the virtue of his notion of a "negative" role model, we would hold that theoretically, at least, a distinction must be made between role models—both positive and negative— role expectations, and norms. Thus, unless the expected behavior of the role model becomes generalized to the larger group, i.e., becomes an explicit, shared norm, it

Jewish drinking, as Snyder has shown, is patterned by an elaborate system of explicit directives as to what, when, where, with whom, how much, and why one is expected to consume alcoholic beverages. The norm is predominantly *prescriptive* in nature, and deviation from the drinking norms is associated with gradual and predictable patterns of deviant behavior. Thus Snyder's statistics show that tendencies to alcohol pathology increase in "step like" fashion from Orthodox Jewish drinking, which is associated with the relative absence of signs of pathology, to the Reform and Secular drinking pattern in which pathology is relatively high. Nevertheless, the highest rate still tends to remain lower than rates for the Protestant group (29, p. 197).

We would hold that it is inherent in the nature of the two sets of norms, the ascetic Protestant and Mormon norms, on the one hand, and the Jewish norms, on the other, that they predispose group members to different kinds of deviant reactions. The consequence of the differential deviant reactions is differential strain for the two sub-systems. Alcohol pathology represents not only personal problems, but problems for the group as well. The various efforts to cope with problems of alcohol on the part of different groups—governmental agencies, private welfare organizations, and religious groups, to name only a few—suggest that strain exists not only for the sub-systems in which they occur, but for larger social systems as well. In general, it can be noted that at least four types of group reactions to system strain can be isolated as indices of the extent of perceived threat to the system or its members. Group reactions may take the form of: (1) *Retrenchment*, in which all deviants are cast out of the group, leaving only a small hard core of adherents; (2) *Regeneration*, in which there is an attempt to revitalize the norm through a cultural renaissance; (3) *Rational-Scientific Innovation*, which includes efforts on the part of persons outside of the group as well as enlightened group participants to adapt new normative patterns to the pre-existing cultural system; and (4) *Permissiveness*, which involves individual determination of limits.[10] Examples of these types of

---

remains external to a given social system. In the case of drinking norms, Skolnick's observations need not lead to a rejection of our own explanation, since the negative role model, as we see it, may represent an *additional* factor rather than an exclusive causal factor. However, the reader should keep in mind the fact that these notions—both Skolnick's and our own—represent hypotheses rather than conclusive generalizations.

[10] Merton and Parsons, it should be noted, have focused on deviant reactions to structured strain. Merton's typology is concerned with structured individual reactions to a disjunction between norms and success goals in American society. Parsons also deals with individual deviant reactions in terms of motivational analysis. The typology presented here differs from both Merton and Parsons in the following respects: (1) Our focus is on *collective* reactions rather than *individual* reactions; (2) This typology is concerned with *normative* reactions to strain rather than *deviant* reactions to strain; and (3) Whereas Merton's focus is on *chronic* strain, i.e., a persistent element in the

reactions may be found reflected in behavior associated with deviant drinking activities. *Retrenchment* has manifested itself in the strong reactions to public intoxication on the part of the Chinese in the United States, who in the past, forced alcoholics and problem drinkers to return to the Chinese mainland if they failed to mend their ways, at the same time reinforcing the norms of individual responsibility to the group (14).[11] *Regeneration* is reflected in the abstinence movement in the United States. The *Rational-Scientific Innovation* reaction is exemplified in Mulford and Miller's suggestion that prescriptive drinking norms should replace proscriptive drinking norms for the ascetic Protestant groups in the United States (21, p. 498). And the persistence of patternless drinking in a good many American social contexts is a manifestation of *Permissiveness*.[12]

A Typology of Norms

We have suggested above that the proscriptive and prescriptive dimensions of norms do make it possible for us to attain greater understanding of the dynamics of social pathology. We have, up to this point, discussed the two dimensions in very broad terms. To what extent can we specify the nature of these dimensions and place them in a context of social system analysis? With this perspective in view, norms may be classified ideal-typically in terms of the following descriptive characteristics which have emerged from our view of the various studies cited

---

system, the above typology, at least in this context, is concerned with *acute* strain. Adding to the above approaches Williams' concept of "patterned norm evasion," we may derive the following classification of approaches to reactions to strain:

Deviant-Individual[a]
Normative-Individual[b]
Deviant-Group[c]
Normative-Group[d]

[a] See, for example, Robert K. Merton (17), Talcott Parsons (23, Ch. 7), Albert E. Cohen (11).

[b] This category is perhaps the most prevalent in the sociological literature. It is characterized by the following sequence: deviant act—group reaction—individual conformity. One of many examples may be found in Fritz J. Roethlisberger and William J. Dickson's description of "binging" as a negative sanction for nonconformity (26).

[c] See, for example, Robin M. Williams, Jr. (36). Chapter 10 is devoted in its entirety to norm evasion.

[d] In addition to our independently conceived notions concerning normative group reactions to strain, Howard Becker's posthumously published paper deals with similar types of problems (4).

[11] In the general context of group reactions to system strain, see Anthony F. C. Wallace (34).

[12] Our usage of "permissiveness," or individual determination of limits, represents what might otherwise be called unresolved *anomie*. However, since the group reactions described above are in effect reactions to an anomic condition, we have attempted to avoid using *anomie* for purposes of clarity. The significance of *permissiveness* as both a norm and as a type of *laissez faire* reaction is dealt with below.

above: (1) the degree of elasticity; (2) the degree of elaboration; (3) the degree of pervasiveness; and (4) the degree of functional interrelatedness.

Table 1 describes those aspects of norms which make them classifiable as either proscriptive or prescriptive.[13] Table 2 shows how these

TABLE 1.

Qualitative Characteristics of Prescriptive and Proscriptive Norms

Characteristic of Norm	Proscriptive	Prescriptive
Elasticity	Inflexible: Behavior is defined as either compliant or deviant and there are no directives for action.	Flexible: Behavior is defined in degree of conformity and directives for how to act are explicit
Elaboration	No ritual, no embellishment associated with act	Great deal of embellishment in ritualized and symbolic acts
Pervasiveness	Focus on a specific act applying to any and all contexts	Focus on a variety of similar acts in specified contexts
Functional interrelatedness	Norm tends to have few or no convergences with other norms in the larger system	Norm tends to converge with other norms in the larger system

TABLE 2.

Drinking Norms for Selected Groups by Qualitative Characteristics and Prescriptive-Proscriptive Dimension

	Elasticity	Elaboration	Pervasiveness	Functional Interrelatedness	
Prescriptive					
	++	++	++	++	Jews[1]
	+	++	+	++	Italians[2]
	-	-	-	+	Mormons[3]
Proscriptive					

[1] For an elaborate description of Orthodox Jewish drinking patterns, see Charles R. Snyder (28).

[2] Wine is viewed by Italians as both a food and as a beverage. It does not, however, embody the sacred element associated with Orthodox Jewish drinking. Italians do not recite blessing over the wine. See, for example, Phyllis Williams and Robert Straus (35); and Giorgio Lolli, et al. (16).

[3] References to Mormon drinking may be found in Robert Straus and Selden Bacon (31).

[13] In an initial classification of norms for general purposes, for example, norms may be classified as being predominantly proscriptive or prescriptive according to whether they enjoin or prohibit behavior. For a more complete understanding of the dynamics of normative behavior, especially with reference to problems of social control, a more intensive analysis of the norms themselves is necessary. Our hypothetical scheme, it should be noted, is derived from: (1) inspection of the various monographs cited in Table 2; (2) inspection of unpublished data on the Chinese; and (3) participant observation in various subcultural contexts.

factors are related, by way of illustration, to drinking behavior. The extent to which these factors, in varying degree, manifest themselves in given normative systems represents, in our judgment, a measure of the relative degree of predisposition to normative mal-integration with respect to a given norm.

THE NORMATIVE AND THE FACTUAL

As we have suggested above, the overall effectiveness of norms in the process of system maintenance can be attributed to at least two characteristics: (1) the extent to which both internal and external sanctions effectively direct the behavior of group members; and (2) the nature of the norms themselves. It is the latter to which we have addressed ourselves in this paper. Although the two are undoubtedly related, we would hold that the qualitative nature of the norm is analytically distinct from the strength of sanctions attached to the norm. Thus, whether controls are internalized or externalized, or whether the sanctioning agents are informally or formally designated does not concern us here. The above data are consistent with our hypothesis that predominantly proscriptive norms are more likely than predominantly prescriptive norms to lead to extreme degrees of pathological reactions when deviation occurs.

It is possible to treat the whole matter of the relationship between norms and social pathology in terms of the relationship between the normative and factual orders. While we have indicated that our focus is on the qualitative nature of the norms themselves, our ultimate concern is with social control and group integration. The normative-factual orders lend themselves to analysis within the framework of the prescriptive-proscriptive dimension. Thus, one could interpret our discussion as an attempt to explore the consequences of situations in which the normative order and the factual order are more or less convergent or divergent. Rather than assume that it is simply the divergence between these two orders which is primarily productive of strain, we would hold that it is the quality of the normative order which determines the extent of strain in this context. The following suggestive scheme provides an illustration of a possible systematic approach to these dimensions. Thus, the following table describes a factual order, given a certain prescriptive-proscriptive normative order. The examples represent approximate empirical referents with regard to drinking norms.

As this preliminary scheme suggests, the following propositions can be formulated with respect to the aspects of norms referred to above:

1. Given a situation in which there is either *prescription* on the *normative* level and *deviation* on the factual level, pathology will be *high*.

2. Given a situation in which there is *prescription* on the *normative* level and *deviation* on the factual level, pathology will be *low*.

The above discussion implies that under certain normative conditions behavior which deviated from the norm does not threaten the system of order, while under other conditions it does. It should be added that the present analysis does not include a discussion of the relative effec-

Norms

	Jewish Italian	Mormon Methodist
Normative order	Highly prescriptive	Highly proscriptive
Factual order	Deviation	Deviation
Level of pathology	Low level of pathology	High level of pathology (anomie)

tiveness of each type of norm under conditions of normative integration without strain. Presumably, pathology is minimized as a result of conformity to both the predominantly proscriptive and prescriptive norms referred to above. Stated as a third proposition:

3. Given a situation in which there is *either* prescription or proscription on the *normative* level and *conformity* on the *factual* level, pathology will be low.

Thus, this approach is systematic and directly lends itself to empirical analysis.

PERMISSIVENESS AND ANOMIE

A third general aspect, to which we referred only briefly, is permissiveness. Although the evidence with respect to this pattern or lack of pattern is scanty, permissiveness appears to be characteristic of periods of normative transformation. Thus, in the United States the shift from proscription among Protestant abstentionist groups *without the provision of a corresponding set of clear directives* for drinking behavior appears to represent a period of *anomic* behavior which will, in time, become organized into a new pattern. In this context directives tend to be vague injunctions to avoid immoderate drinking and to "stay out of trouble." That this condition may persist over very long periods of time without becoming organized, thus enhancing the anomic condition and consequent deviant behavior, is illustrated by studies of Finnish drinking.

In Finland, where religious groups preach proscription and where the sale and distribution of alcohol is carefully controlled, the arrests for drunkenness rate in 1959 was 72.0 per 1000 inhabitants compared with 26.0 for Norway, 17.2 for Sweden and 6.3 for Denmark. Finland and Norway, it should be noted, are countries which had prohibition laws following World War I in contrast to Sweden which rejected prohibition as a solution to drinking problems and Denmark which did not even entertain the question of prohibition (6). Assuming that the behaviors associated with efforts to solve problems reflects underlying differences in normative orientations, it seems clear that arrests for drunkenness as a reflection of deviant behavior are higher where a background of proscription is greater.

Straus and Bacon (31), and Mulford and Miller (21), as we noted above, held that when those who were reared as abstainers drink there are no directives for how, when, how much and with whom to drink. Allardt (1) explored the intensity of attitude toward drinking in his Finnish sample and found what he described as an intensive negative attitude toward drinking (proscriptive) as contrasted with "an ambivalent one."

The finding agrees very well with the intuitive picture one gets of the attitudes toward drinking in Finnish society. There are certain people with a strong negative attitude towards drinking, while most other people may show a very positive verbal attitude towards drinking and towards the functions of drinking, but this attitude is not consistent, and it is often expressed in a jocular way (1, p. 26).

Permissive attitudes toward drinking in Finland are also associated with acceptance of the value of occasional unrestrained drinking, suggesting still another link between permissiveness and deviance (1, p. 28). Thus the study of drinking in Finnish culture lends support to our original assumption regarding permissiveness and deviance.

We suggested above that permissiveness represents a condition of unresolved anomie. Recent research in the area of deviant behavior has focused on Merton's hypothesis that strains in social systems lead to deviant behavior and consequent anomie (17; 18; 29). More specifically, in American society the discrepancy between the American desire for success and differential opportunity for the attainment of success goals leads to deviant reactions and, ultimately, to anomie.

Although a thorough discussion of Merton's approach to anomie is beyond our primary concern here, it is well to comment briefly at this point since permissiveness and anomie represent aspects of the same phenomenon.

Our usage of anomie suggests that the source of the weakening of social controls on drinking is a reflection of general societal transformation related to industrialization and urbanization which were the foci of attention of the sociologists to whom we referred at the outset—Durkheim, Tönnies, Redfield, and Becker. Given the kind of rapid transformation which characterizes the responses of subsystems to increase in population, change in type of production, and modification of family functions, to suggest only a few consequences of industrialization and urbanization, there is a simultaneous change in group attitudes toward the normative order. Thus, although there still tends to be an awareness of the rules limiting and directing man's desires, there is somewhat less certainty regarding whether or not adherence to these norms should be enforced. As social structures undergo change, so do normative systems. During periods of uncertainty a wider range of deviance is tolerated in the form of permissiveness, which, as we suggested above, allows the person rather than the group to determine the range of appropriate conduct. While all societies and groups must provide for flexibility in order to persist, periods during which permissiveness predominates do not always result in a reinforcement of the original normative system, as we noted above. Thus the uncertainty, i.e., associated with some of these periods is often the prelude to the emergence of new *normative patterns*.

With respect to drinking behavior in particular, however, the flexibility associated with change, if we are correct in our analysis of deviance, has more profound effects in systems undergoing change from proscription to other normative forms.

Similar to Merton's approach which deals directly with the group's response to deviance is our concern with what we have called permissiveness.

Recently several analysts of deviant drinking behavior, following Merton, have suggested that problem drinking represents a *retreatist* reaction to the strain associated with the discrepancy between success goals and opportunity to attain them. Thus the retreatist, having failed to reach his goal, withdraws from the race and turns to excessive drinking and, finally to problem drinking (29, pp. 202–205). This in turn leads to more deviant drinking on the part of others who observe the toleration of deviance. Given the paucity of empirical data on this aspect of anomie it is not possible to draw any conclusions at this time. If, however, patterns of deviant drinking can be linked to more general societal processes and their impact on normative systems then our objectives in this paper will have been served.

We have suggested that proscriptive and prescriptive dimensions are to be found in the analysis of other normative systems and data other than those dealing with alcohol pathology alone. We would suggest that sex behavior may be a fruitful area of investigation.[14] Some specific examples of other problems that would seem to lend themselves to this type of analysis would be studies of norms proscribing aggression among Jews; norms proscribing female pre-marital intercourse among Italians; and norms proscribing the acquisition of material luxuries among the Old Order Amish.

Finally, although we have abstracted norm qualities as our focus of attention and hold that they are an essential aspect of the processes enhancing and inhibiting deviance and pathology we do not feel that this approach is alone sufficient to understand these phenomena. Thus the subsequent experiences of persons reared in proscriptive cultures and subcultures play an important role in decisions to conform or deviate. Ernest Campbell (7, pp. 406–407) in a recent study, for example, presents data which indicate that college students who have internalized proscriptive drinking norms are more likely to form peer group associations that encourage personal abstinence and non-drinkers are less likely to pledge fraternities and sororities than drinkers. The study of the effects of drinking norms on behavior, then, also provides entree into the sphere of group formation studies. In short, the study of drinking behavior is not only significant because it contributes directly to the solution of social problems but also for its contribution to the understanding of basic societal processes.

REFERENCES

1. Allardt, E., T. Markanen, and M. Takala, *Drinking and Drinkers,* Helsinki, The Finnish Foundation for Alcohol Studies, 1963.
2. Bales, Robert F., "Cultural Differences in Rates of Alcoholism," *Quarterly Journal of Studies on Alcohol,* 6:400–499, 1946.
3. Becker, Howard, "Ionia and Athens: Studies in Secularization," Unpublished Ph.D. dissertation, University of Chicago, 1930.
4. Becker, Howard, "Normative Reactions to Normlessness," *American Sociological Review,* 25:803–810, 1960.
5. Beshers, James M., "Pragmatic Criteria in Typology Construction," paper read at the annual meeting of the American Sociological Association, New York City, August, 1960.
6. Bruen, K. and R. Hauge, *Drinking of Northern Youth: A Cross-Cultural Survey,* Helsinki, The Finnish Foundation for Alcohol Studies, 1963.
7. Campbell, Ernest, "The Internalization of Moral Norms," *Sociometry,* 27:391–412, 1964.
8. Christensen, Harold T., "Cultural Relativism and Premarital Sex Norms," *ASR,* 25:31–39, 1960.

[14] Christensen has noted the possible connection between proscription and extreme reactions, and has suggested that sex behavior and drinking behavior may be analogous in this respect. See Harold T. Christensen (8; 9).

9. Christensen, Harold T., "Child Spacing Analysis Via Record Linkage," *Marriage and Family Living*, 25:272–280, 1963.

10. Clinard, Marshall, ed., *Deviant Behavior and Anomie*, New York, The Free Press, 1964.

11. Cohen, Albert K., "The Study of Social Disorganization and Deviant Behavior," in Robert K. Merton, *et al.*, eds., *Sociology Today*, New York, Basic Books, 1959.

12. Durkheim, Emile, *The Division of Labor in Society*, (1893), translated by George Simpson, New York, Macmillan, 1933.

13. Freedman, Ronald, *et al.*, *Principles of Sociology*, New York, Henry Holt, 1952.

14. Lee, Rose Hum and Ephraim H. Mizruchi, "A Study of Drinking Behavior and Attitudes Toward Alcohol of the Chinese in the United States," unpublished manuscript.

15. Lemert, Edwin M., *Social Pathology*, New York, McGraw-Hill, 1951.

16. Lolli, Giorgio, *Alcohol in Italian Culture*, Glencoe, Illinois, The Free Press, 1958.

17. Merton, Robert K., "Social Structure and Anomie," In *Social Theory and Social Structure*, Glencoe, Illinois, The Free Press, 1957.

18. Mizruchi, Ephraim H., *Success and Opportunity*, New York, The Free Press, 1964.

19. Morris, Richard T., "A Typology of Norms," *American Sociological Review*, 21:610–613, 1956.

20. Mulford, Harold A. and Donald A. Miller, "Drinking Behavior Related to Definitions of Alcohol: A Report of Research in Progress," *American Sociological Review*, 24:385–389, 1959.

21. Mulford, Harold A. and Donald A. Miller, "Drinking in Iowa," five articles appearing in separate numbers of Volume 21 (1960), *Quarterly Journal of Studies on Alcohol*.

22. Parsons, Talcott, *The Structure of Social Action*, New York, McGraw-Hill, 1937.

23. Parsons, Talcott, *The Social System*, Glencoe, Illinois, The Free Press, 1951.

24. Parsons, Talcott, "The Social System," in Talcott Parsons and Edward A. Shils, eds., *Toward a General Theory of Action*, Cambridge, Harvard University Press, 1951.

25. Redfield, Robert, *The Folk Culture of Yucatan*, Chicago, University of Chicago Press, 1941.

26. Roethlisberger, Fritz J. and William J. Dickson, *Management and the Worker*, Cambridge, Harvard University Press, 1939.

27. Skolnick, Jerome H., "Religious Affiliation and Drinking Behavior," *Quarterly Journal of Studies on Alcohol*, 19:452–470, 1958.

28. Snyder, Charles R., *Alcohol and the Jews*, Glencoe, Illinois, The Free Press, 1958.

29. Snyder, Charles R., "Inebriety, Alcoholism and Anomie," in Marshall Clinard, ed., *Deviant Behavior and Anomie*, New York, The Free Press, 1964.

30. Sorokin, Pitirim, *Society, Culture and Personality*, New York, Harper, 1947.

31. Straus, Robert and Seldon D. Bacon, *Drinking in College,* New Haven, Yale University Press, 1954.

32. Sumner, William Graham, *Folkways,* Boston, Ginn, 1906.

33. Tönnies, Ferdinand, *Gemeinschaft und Gesellschaft,* (1887), translated by Charles P. Loomis as *Community and Society,* East Lansing, Michigan, Michigan State University Press, 1957.

34. Wallace, Anthony F. C., "Revitalization Movements," in Seymour M. Lipset and Neil J. Smelzer, eds., *Sociology, The Progress of a Decade,* Englewood, New Jersey, Prentice-Hall, 1961.

35. Williams, Phyllis and Robert Straus, "Drinking Patterns of Italians in New Haven," *Quarterly Journal of Studies on Alcohol,* 11 (1950), 4 papers.

36. Williams, Jr., Robin M., *American Society,* New York, Knopf, 1960 revision.

14

John P. Clark
Eugene P. Wenninger

Goal Orientation and Illegal Behavior Among Juveniles*

During recent years a basic conflict has arisen in the literature concerning the role of goals or values in the etiology of illegal behavior among juveniles. Whereas some authors have attributed a large part of the involvement in misconduct to the pursuit of goals peculiar to certain segments of the population, other authors have suggested that desired goals are essentially similar for everyone, but that the means of attaining these goals are unequally distributed. The latter condition requires illegal behavior on the part of the disadvantaged in the attempt to overcome or compensate for their handicap.

An example of the first explanation is the position taken by Miller in which he states that the behaviors associated with the "focal concerns" of certain segments of our population are directly or indirectly related to acts of official delinquency. The commitment to such "focal concerns" as trouble, toughness, smartness, excitement, fate, and autonomy, *which characterizes lower class culture*, is said to account for the great over-representation of lower class youngsters in official delinquency statistics.[1]

Lower-class culture refers specifically to a way of life which is followed by a large segment of the present-day population of this country, whose concerns, values, and characteristic patterns of behavior are the product of a well-formed

From *Social Forces*, October, 1963, pp. 49–59, by permission of the author and the publishers.
* The total project, of which this paper is a part, was sponsored by the Ford Foundation and the University of Illinois Graduate Research Board. Professor Daniel Glaser was very helpful throughout the project and in the preparation of this paper.
[1] Walter B. Miller, "Lower Class Culture as a Generating Milieu of Gang Delinquency," *Journal of Social Issues*, Vol. 14, No. 3, 1958, pp. 5–19.

168

cultural system. . . . In its most representative form, it reveals a distinctive patterning which differs significantly from that of middle-class culture.

Much of the delinquency of the lower-class youngsters may be seen as an attempt of the acting individual to adhere to forms of behavior and to achieve standards of value as they are defined within this type of community. (Italics added) [2]

Whereas a significant difference in goals between the lower-class and other classes is central to Miller's formulations, other authors suggest that there is essential agreement on the goals or values among the social classes. To these latter authors differences in misconduct rates occur because illegal behavior patterns are thought to be the most appropriate or only available paths to the realization of these goals by certain segments of the population. Sutherland specifically dealt with the pervasiveness of values in the ninth item of his "theory of criminal behavior": "While criminal behavior is an expression of general needs and values, it is not explained by those general needs and values since non-criminal behavior is an expression of the same needs and values."[3] Matza and Sykes come to somewhat similar conclusions in their article concerning the similarity of delinquent values and those of the leisure class: "In short, we are arguing that the delinquent may not stand as an alien in the body of society but may represent instead a disturbing reflection or a caricature. His vocabulary is different, to be sure, but kicks, big-time spending, and rep have immediate counterparts in the value system of the law-abiding."[4] In his discussion of the emergence of deviant behavior, Merton implies great pervasiveness of certain goals (especially "success") even though the chances of reaching these goals via legitimate means may vary by social class and/or ethnic grouping:

A high frequency of deviant behavior is not generated merely by lack of opportunity or by this exaggerated pecuniary emphasis. . . . It is only when a system of cultural values extols, virtually above all else, certain *common* success-goals *for the population at large* while the social structure rigorously restricts or completely closes access to approved modes of reaching these goals *for a considerable part of the same population,* that deviant behavior ensues on a large scale. . . . Goals are held to transcend class lines, not to be bounded by them, yet the actual social organization is such that there exist class differentials in accessibility of the goals.[5]

[2] William C. Kvaraceus and Walter B. Miller, *Delinquent Behavior* (National Education Association of the United States, 1959), p. 63.

[3] Edwin H. Sutherland and Donald R. Cressey, *Principles of Criminology* (Chicago: Lippincott, 1955), p. 79.

[4] David Matza and Gresham M. Sykes, "Juvenile Delinquency and Subterranean Values," *American Sociological Review*, Vol. 26, No. 3, p. 715.

[5] Robert K. Merton, *Social Theory and Social Structure* (Glencoe, Illinois: The Free Press, 1957), p. 146.

Within this same orientation Cloward and Ohlin have hypothesized that:

The disparity between what lower-class youth are led to want and what is actually available to them is the source of a major problem of adjustment. Adolescents who form delinquent subcultures, we suggest, have internalized an emphasis upon conventional goals. Faced with limitations on legitimate avenues of access to these goals, and unable to revise their aspirations downward, they experience intense frustration; the explorations of nonconformist alternatives may be the result.[6]

Differences between the point of view taken by Miller and that of Sutherland, Matza and Sykes, Merton, and Cloward and Ohlin, cannot be dismissed as stemming entirely from "frantic semantics." The basic issue of the pervasiveness of certain goal orientations or concerns throughout the population[7] and the relationship between commitment to these goal orientations and illegal behavior requires considerable *more* investigation.

Several tentative relationships, stated below as working hypotheses, suggest themselves from the above brief discussion.

1. Socio-economic classes are significantly different in their general life goals.
2. Adherence to lower class goal orientations is directly related to illegal behavior rates.

These two hypotheses are designed to test the Miller thesis of unique social class concerns and their relationship to illegal behavior. The following two hypotheses should provide data which tend to refute or support the "all-pervasive goals, but differential access" theories.

3. Socio-economic status is directly related to perceived chances of achieving goals without employing illegal means.
4. The perceived chances of achieving desired goals without employing illegal means is inversely related to illegal behavior rates.

The Study

These hypotheses were tested on a large selected sample of public school students from the sixth through the twelfth grades in four widely-different types of community. The data were collected via an anony-

[6] Richard A. Cloward and Lloyd E. Ohlin, *Delinquency and Opportunity* (Glencoe, Illinois: The Free Press, 1960), p. 86.

[7] See the classic study of Herbert H. Hyman, "The Value Systems of Different Classes: A Social Psychological Contribution to the Analysis of Stratification," in the reader by Reinhard Bendix and Seymour M. Lipset, *Class, Status and Power* (Glencoe, Illinois: The Free Press, 1953), pp. 426–442.

mous questionnaire which was administered to groups of from 20 to 40 students by the senior author. Considerable precaution was taken to insure reliability and validity of the responses. For example, assurances were given that the study was not being monitored by the school administration; questions were pre-tested to eliminate ambiguity; and the interview situation was made as threat-free as possible.

The four communities represented in the study were chosen for the unique social class structure represented by each. The Duncan "Socio-Economic Index for All Occupations"[8] was used to determine the occupational profile of each community by assigning index scores to the occupations of the respondents' fathers. The results are summarized in Table 1.

TABLE 1.

Duncan Socio-Economic Index Scores Based on Occupation of Father

Score	Type of Community			
	Percent Rural Farm	Percent Lower Urban	Percent Industrial City	Percent Upper Urban
(1) 0–23	75.9	40.4	36.4	5.7
(2) 24–47	9.9	15.5	19.3	4.8
(3) 48–71	4.7	12.5	22.9	43.9
(4) 72–96	1.5	4.2	10.0	34.6
(5) Unclassifiable*	8.0	27.4	11.4	11.0
Total	100 (N–274)	100 (N–265)	100 (N–280)	100 (N–335)

*This category includes those respondents from homes with no father and those respondents who did not furnish adequate information for reliable classification. The 27.4 percent figure in the lower urban community reflects a higher proportion of "fatherless" homes rather than greater numbers of responses which were incomplete or vague in other ways.

The overwhelming majority of the respondents comprising the *rural farm* population live on farms, farming being by far the most common occupation of their fathers. Even of those fathers not listed as farmers, many are "part-time" farmers. Therefore, though the Duncan Index would classify most of the residents in the lower class, most of these public school children live on farms in a prosperous section of the Midwest. The sixth, seventh, and eighth graders were drawn from schools located in very small villages. Grades 9–12 were drawn from the high school which was located in open-farm land.

The *lower urban* sample is primarily composed of children of those with occupations of near-equal ranking but certainly far different in nature from those of the rural farm community. The lower urban sample

[8] Albert J. Reiss, *Occupations and Social Status* (New York: The Free Press of Glencoe, 1961), especially pp. 109–161 prepared by Otis D. Duncan.

was drawn from a school system located in a very crowded and largely-Negro area of Chicago. The fathers (or male head of the family) of these youngsters are laborers in construction, waiters, janitors, clean-up men, etc. Even among those who place relatively high on the Duncan Scale are many who in spite of their occupational title reside, work, and socialize almost exclusively in the lower class community.

As Table 1 demonstrates, the occupational structure of the *industrial city* is somewhat more diffuse than the other communities, though consisting primarily of lower class occupation. This city of about 35,000 is largely autonomous, although a small portion of the population commutes daily to Chicago. However, about two-thirds of these students have fathers who work as blue-collar laborers in local industries and services. The median years of formal education of all males age 25 or over is 10.3.[9] The median annual family income is $7,255.[10] The population of this small city contains substantial numbers of Polish and Italian Americans and about fifteen percent Negroes.

Those in the *upper urban* sample live in a very wealthy suburb of Chicago. Nearly three-fourths of the fathers in these families are high-level executives or professionals. The median level of education for all males age 25 or over is 16 plus.[11] The median annual family income is slightly over $20,000—80 percent of the families make $10,000 or more annually.[12]

With two exceptions, representative sampling of the public school children was followed within each of these communities: (1) those who could not read at a fourth-grade level were removed in all cases, which resulted in the loss of less than one-half of one percent of the total sample, and (2) the sixth-grade sample in the industrial city community was drawn from a predominantly Negro, working class area and was, therefore, non-representative of the total community for that grade-level only. All the students from grades six through twelve were used in the rural farm community "sample."

INSTRUMENTS

Three instruments and several individual questions were used to gather the required data with which to submit the four hypotheses to test. An inventory of goal orientations was constructed consisting of 30 items, each representing a "value," "goal," "standard," or "focal concern" suggested in the literature. The first 15 items, as shown in Table 2,

9 *U.S. Census of Population: 1960,* Final Report PF (1)-15C, pp. 15–295.
10 *Ibid.,* pp. 15–335.
11 *Ibid.,* pp. 15–305.
12 *Ibid.,* pp. 15–344.

stem from the same number of major value orientations identified by Williams as characterizing American society as a whole.[13] The next six items portray the focal concerns said by Miller to predominate only in the lower class culture.[14] The last nine items are representations of the middle class standards as seen by Cohen.[15] Respondents were asked to indicate the degree of importance each particular item held for them at the time of the study—"great importance," "some importance," or "little or no importance." For purposes of analysis, the last two choices were combined. The percentage of the sample in the four individual communities for which each goal is of "great importance" is shown in the first four columns of Table 2.

The second instrument contained identical items to the above. However, on this part of the questionnaire the respondents were asked to register what they believe their chances to be of achieving each of the goals without breaking the law—"good," "fair," or "poor." The last two responses were combined for purposes of analysis. The percentage of the sample in each community that believed they have "good" chances of achieving each goal without breaking the law ranged from 30 to 89 percent.

The third instrument, described in detail elsewhere, was constructed to measure the extent and nature of illegal behavior. The sample was asked to respond to an inventory of 38 widely-varied offenses. All respondents indicated if they had committed each of these offenses *within the past year*, thus furnishing data amenable to age-level analysis.[16] If the respondents admitted commission of an offense, they so indicated by disclosing the number of times they had done so. The rate of admission, of course, varied widely by offense, ranging from roughly 90 percent on such items as disobeying parents, and minor theft[17] to one or three percent for arson, use of narcotics, and attacking someone with the intent to kill.

13 Robin M. Williams, Jr., *American Society: A Sociological Interpretation* (New York: Knopf, 2nd ed., 1960), especially pp. 395–470.

14 Miller, *op. cit.*, pp. 6–13.

15 Albert K. Cohen, *Delinquent Boys: The Culture of the Gang* (Glencoe, Illinois: The Free Press, 1955), pp. 84–94.

16 One of the most frequent and damaging criticisms of "admitted delinquency studies" has been their lack of sensitivity to when in the juvenile's life his misbehavior occurred. See John P. Clark and Eugene P. Wenninger, "Socio-Economic Class and Area as Correlates of Illegal Behavior Among Juveniles," *American Sociological Review*, Vol. 27, No. 6 (December 1962), pp. 826–834.

17 Ordinarily, not receiving 100 percent admission to the least serious offenses included would have raised doubt as to the validity of those questionnaires on which these extremely common offenses were not admitted. However, since the respondents were asked in this study to admit their offenses during the past year only, it was thought that less than 100 percent admission would be highly possible when one considers the entire age range.

TABLE 2.

Percentage of Respondents Indicating Goal Orientation of "Great Importance," and Differences Among Communities

Goal	Community				Significance of Differences*					
	(1) Percent Industrial City N-280	(2) Percent Lower Urban N-265	(3) Percent Upper Urban N-335	(4) Percent Rural Farm N-274	(1-2)	(2-3)	(3-4)	(1-3)	(1-4)	(2-4)
Williams Items- "Major Value Orientations" of America										
1. Being a success at what I do.	83	89	81	89	2	2	4	x	4	x
2. Keeping busy at something most of the time.	27	27	33	41	x	x	4	x	4	4
3. Doing the things that are right for me to do.	61	75	67	82	2	2	4	x	4	4
4. Helping others when they need it.	54	65	65	68	2	x	x	3	4	x
5. Not wasting time in getting things done.	36	48	45	51	2	x	4	3	4	x
6. Having the latest things and looking ahead to better things.	38	54	26	39	2	2	4	1	x	2
7. Being able to have nice things.	47	63	37	44	2	2	x	1	x	2
8. Being equal to other people.	60	71	51	58	2	2	x	1	x	2
9. Having enough freedom to do things.	79	74	76	78	x	x	x	x	x	x
10. Fitting in with those around me.	62	53	66	74	1	3	x	x	4	4
11. Making up my mind about things only after I've thought for awhile about it.	42	59	40	44	2	2	x	x	x	2
12. Standing up for the United States.	76	63	73	84	1	3	4	x	4	4
13. Going along with what most of my friends decide to do.	9	8	11	20	x	x	4	x	4	4
14. Not let people run over me or push me around.	70	78	69	65	2	2	x	x	x	2
15. Sticking up for my own kind of people.	59	68	59	72	2	2	4	x	4	x

Note: N = 1154.

*Significance of Difference determined by chi-squares. The "x" indicates no significant differences, while a number indicates a significant difference and identifies the community of the comparison in which the greater proportion of

TABLE 2. Continued

Goal	Community				Significance of Differences					
	(1) Percent Indus- trial City N-280	(2) Percent Lower Urban N-265	(3) Percent Upper Urban N-335	(4) Percent Rural Farm N-274	(1-2)	(2-3)	(3-4)	(1-3)	(1-4)	(2-4)
Miller Items-Lower Class "Focal Concerns"										
16. Being able to stay out of trouble and handle any that comes my way.	3	2	3	2	x	x	x	x	x	x
17. Getting my share of fun and excitement.	10	5	5	2	1	x	3	1	1	2
18. Being able to handle myself, being tough.	44	42	43	29	x	x	3	x	1	2
19. Being smart enough to stay one jump ahead of others.	33	19	32	26	1	3	x	x	1	x
20. Playing my luck or breaks to get the most out of them.	52	44	35	42	1	2	x	1	1	x
21. Being my own boss.	24	32	12	19	2	2	4	1	x	2
Cohen Items-Middle Class "Standards"										
22. Working hard at trying to get ahead.	67	82	66	74	2	2	4	x	x	2
23. Showing I'm good enough to be on my own sometimes.	60	72	67	72	2	x	x	x	4	2
24. Learning how to do the things I will need to know when I grow up.	78	87	72	88	2	2	4	x	4	x
25. Being able to pass up things now, can have things later.	34	50	30	45	2	2	4	x	4	2
26. Planning what lies ahead for me as much as possible.	67	67	50	71	x	2	4	1	x	x
27. Having good manners and getting along well with others.	81	86	83	86	x	x	x	x	x	x
28. Keeping out of fights and rough stuff.	59	71	55	73	2	2	4	x	4	x
29. Make good use of my free time.	49	60	55	63	2	2	4	x	4	x
30. Being very careful with things that belong to others.	82	83	80	86	x	x	x	x	x	x

the respondents attaches "great importance" to the goal.

FINDINGS

SOCIO-ECONOMIC CLASS AND GOAL ORIENTATIONS

Though admittedly crude, the first hypothesis was initially tested by comparing total communities on their goal orientations, since each community represented a predominant social class. Considerable difference was found between the various communities on the Williams, Miller, and the Cohen items. However, not only were significant differences found between the upper urban community and the three lower class communities, but also among the three lower class communities as well. This is in keeping with the differences found among these same four communities in admitted illegal behavior rates and attitude toward the legal institution reported elsewhere.[18]

The examination of the last column of Table 2 reveals two other interesting relationships. When compared to other communities, the rural farm sample consistently places highest importance on the Williams items, lowest importance on the Miller lower class culture items, and highest value on the Cohen middle class items, while the industrial city places roughly at the opposite extreme. Somewhat more surprising is the relative lack of difference in goal orientations between the rural farm and the Negro lower urban and between the upper urban and industrial city samples. Therefore, the first hypothesis—that there are significant differences among socio-economic classes in their goal orientations—received qualified support by these data when whole communities are compared.

Further comparisons were made between social class categories both *among* and *within* these communities. Although it was determined that neither age nor sex was significantly related to the goal orientations of these in-school samples, the following comparisons were made by using only those age 15 and younger in order to minimize any effect that might occur due to differential school drop-out rates of the various social classes.

First, comparisons were made among the available social classes *within* each community by using the chi-square technique on individual items to determine if goal orientations were strictly social class qualities, per se, or more generally a community or "status area"[19] characteristic. Since the number of differences did not exceed chance within any of the four communities, we conclude that goal orientations are equally distributed within "status areas" consisting of a predominant social class.

18 Clark and Wenninger, *op. cit.,* and John P. Clark and Eugene P. Wenninger, "The Attitude of Juveniles Toward the Legal Institution" (Submitted).
19 Albert J. Reiss and Albert L. Rhodes, "The Distribution of Juvenile Delinquency in the Social Class Structure," *American Sociological Review,* Vol. 24, No. 5, pp. 720–732.

Comparisons were also made among similar social class categories *across* the different communities. These differences were highly significant on all three sets of items in the lowest social class category (index scores 0–23). Here again the rural farm sample consistently held "high values" followed by the Negro lower class urban and the industrial city. (There were too few in the lowest social class category in the upper urban community for comparison.) Differences among the second category (index scores 24–47) or socio-economic class were barely significant on the Miller items. Likewise, the differences among the third social class category (index scores 48–71) when compared across communities were just barely significant on the Williams items, but not on the Cohen nor Miller items. No significant difference was found in goal orientation between the fourth socio-economic category (index numbers 72–96) in the industrial city and upper urban communities where there were sufficient numbers for testing.

In summary, communities or "status areas" appear to vary widely in their goal orientations although the various social classes within these communities do not. However, when comparisons are made among similar social strata in different communities, significant differences are found at the lowest levels but these differences diminish to nonsignificance at the highest levels.

GOAL ORIENTATIONS AND ILLEGAL CONDUCT RATES

As reported above these four communities were found to differ significantly in their illegal behavior rates. In order of decreasing admitted misconduct rates across all offenses, the communities rank: industrial city, lower urban, upper urban and rural farm. Again using inter-community comparisons as crude measures, and examination of the relative rankings of the communities on the Miller lower class culture items shown in the last column of Table 2 reveals a direct relationship between the degree of importance assigned to these goal orientations (or focal concerns) and admitted rates of misconduct, i.e., the communities fall in identical order. Therefore, when community rates are considered, hypothesis #2 is accepted, though the reader is reminded that significant differences are found among the various "types of lower social classes" both in their goal orientations and illegal behavior rates.

The hypothesized relationship is not as clearly supported when the Williams and Cohen items are considered. With both of these sets of statements the samples arrange themselves into pairs (rural farm–lower urban and upper urban–industrial city) with the latter pair of communities having a smaller proportion of respondents who consider these goals of "great importance." Therefore, the alignment of the communities by illegal conduct rates (i.e., rural farm, upper urban, lower urban, and industrial city) is only roughly opposite to the alignment on the Cohen middle class items as well as the Williams items. The manner in which the Williams items are related to those of Cohen and those of Miller, coupled with their relationship to illegal conduct rates, suggests that the "major value orientations" identified by Williams are more highly associated with the middle classes than with the lower classes.

The relationship between goal orientations and illegal behavior was tested in another manner. A "total misconduct score" was calculated by summing the number of offenses individuals admitted of the 35 most frequently admitted offense items. Those with a score less than five were considered "non-delinquent" (N = 321 for the entire sample) and those with a score of 15 or higher (N = 279 for the entire sample) were considered "delinquent." The distribution of non-delinquent and delinquent was examined against their goal orientations on each of the 30 value items using the Yule's Q technique. As shown in Table 3, 23 of the 30

TABLE 3.

Degree of Association* of Goal Importance and Involvement in Illegal Behavior

Williams Items		Miller Items		Cohen Items	
Item:	Yule's Q	Item:	Yule's Q	Item:	Yule's Q
1.	−.01†	16.	−.44	22.	−.02
2.	−.41	17.	.24	23.	.13
3.	−.61	18.	.33	24.	-.26
4.	−.47	19.	.24	25.	−.26
5.	−.20	20.	.31	26.	−.20
6.	.26	21.	.33	27.	.39
7.	.26			28.	−.63
8.	.14			29.	−.32
9.	.15			30.	−.57
10.	−.03				
11.	−.28				
12.	−.01				
13.	−.19				
14.	.25				
15.	−.10				

*Degree of Association was determined by employing the Yule's Q Technique. See Moris Zelditch, Jr., *Sociological Statistics* (New York: Holt-Dryden, 1959), pp. 168–171.

†Negative values indicate an inverse relationship.

relationships fall in the hypothesized direction, i.e., those individuals who place high importance on middle class goals (Williams and Cohen items) are less likely to be "delinquent" than those who do not or those who assign high importance to lower class goals (Miller items). In addition to some of these relationships being of low order, a few fall opposite of the hypothesized direction. However, a close examination of the items in the latter instance reveals the "delinquents" to be concerned with gaining material goods and personal autonomy—both logically related to illegal behavior.

GOAL ORIENTATIONS AND PERCEIVED CHANCES OF ACHIEVING THEM VIA LEGAL MEANS

As in the above comparisons, communities as a whole varied considerably in the perception juveniles have of their chances of obtaining goals by legal means. Those boys and girls in the upper urban sample believe they have the best chances of avoiding illegal behavior in their pursuit of goals. The three remaining communities were considerably more pessimistic in their predicted avoidance of illegal behavior. The industrial city community had the highest proportion of boys and girls who expected to utilize illegal means to legitimate goals, followed closely by the Negro lower urban and rural farm communities which were surprisingly similar in their perceived chances of non-participation in illegal behavior.

Therefore, when the ranking of communities by perceived chances of not indulging in illegal behavior (i.e., industrial city, lower urban, rural farm, and upper urban) is compared to their ranking by goal orientation on the Miller lower class culture items (i.e., industrial city, lower urban, upper urban, and rural farm) either the upper urban or rural farm is "out of order" in one of the rankings. Perhaps a greater percentage of the urban boys and girls have lower class goals than the rural farm sample but because of the relatively advantageous economic position of the upper urban social strata, fewer juveniles in this community feel the "necessity" to resort to illegal means in order to attain their goals. It may also be that relatively fewer of the illegitimate means to which upper urban juveniles may eventually employ are actually conceived as illegal by this social strata, e.g., drinking and gambling.

Inter-class comparisons *within* communities by individual items again revealed no significant differences in perceived chances for illegal behavior related to goal orientations. As with the goal orientations themselves, similar expectations apparently pervade the total class structure within each "status area." However, unlike the cross-community social class comparisons on goal orientations wherein differences were found among the various lower classes, practically no such differences were found in regard to chances of achieving goals legally.

One might conclude that although highly significant differences exist between upper urban "status areas" and a variety of lower class areas as to the perceived chances of attaining goals legally, there are no great significant differences among the lower class communities and no differences among the social class categories within the communities.[20]

PERCEIVED CHANCES OF ACHIEVING GOALS VIA LEGAL MEANS AND ILLEGAL CONDUCT RATES

A comparison of the rank order of communities on their perceived chances of achieving goals legally and their illegal conduct rates resulted in qualified support of the hypothesis that these two phenomena are related. Whereas the communities rank (from highest chances of employing illegal means to least) industrial city, lower urban or rural farm, and upper urban, the communities rank industrial city, lower urban, upper urban and rural farm in order of decreasing illegal conduct rates. Apparently, the expectations of either or both the upper urban or rural farm respondents are not accurately reflected in their relative rates of admitted misconduct. Either the rural farm youngsters are participating in relatively less illegal behavior than they predict will be required in the pursuit of goals, or (as was suggested previously) upper urban juveniles underestimate their future involvement in misconduct. Or per-

FIGURE 1.

Goal Importance

		Great	Some, Little or None
Chances of attaining goals by legal means	Good	(1) High goals—high chances	(3) Low goals—high chances
	Fair	(2)	(4)
	Poor	High goals—low chances	Low goals—low chances

haps the discrepancy lies in the relative degree to which illegal behavior is a function of the pursuit of goals in these two communities. That is, upper urban children may be quite accurate in their prediction of misconduct associated with goal realization, but this category of illegal acts may represent disproportionally less of the total illegal behavior rate for that community than it does for the rural farm area. A greater proportion of the misconduct of upper urban boys and girls may stem from "non-goal-oriented" behavior as Miller has suggested.[21]

Hypothesis #4 was also submitted to test in the following manner in order to more adequately test the theory that the blockage to *desired* goals results in deviant behavior: Four categories were established by

[20] Although these relationships were not affected by age, boys indicated their chances to be significantly poorer (on all three sets of items) than did the girls. This, of course, is in line with their differential delinquency rates.

[21] Kvaraceus and Miller, *op. cit.*, p. 86.

combining goal importance with perceived chances of reaching these goals legally.

The total misconduct score described above was employed again to divide the sample into "delinquent" and "non-delinquent" populations. The distribution of those in these two populations among the four possible categories was determined for each of the 30 goals. Guided by our hypothesis, we expected the categories to rank #3, #1, #4, #2 on the Williams and the Cohen items in order of increasing involvement in illegal behavior. Due to the demonstrated relationship between the Miller items and involvement in illegal behavior, we predicted that the categories would fall in #2, #4, #1, #3 order in regard to these items. As can be seen in the data below, the actual rank orders were somewhat as predicted on the Williams and the Cohen items, but very different on the Miller items.

FIGURE 2.

Rank of Categories*

	Low Illegal Behavior Rate	High Illegal Behavior Rate
Major value orientations	1–3	4–2
Miller lower class culture	1–3	2–4
Cohen middle class standards	1–3	2–4

*These rankings were derived by assigning ranks to the four categories on each item and then applying the sign test to determine significant difference between categories within the three sets of items. These categories connected by a dash are not statistically significantly different in the proportion of "delinquents" that fall within them. The percentage of "delinquents" in the categories ranged from 21 percent to 90 percent, the average range being 34.7 percent on each item.

These data suggest that *regardless of the goals juveniles desire to reach and the importance attached to them,* the extent of illegal behavior is more highly related to the chances they perceive themselves having of reaching these goals without resorting to illegal means. Thus the fourth hypothesis is supported in the sense that an inverse relationship exists between perceived chances of achieving goals without employing illegal means and illegal behavior rates but the extent to which these goals are "desired" is apparently not a very significant feature in the relationship.

CONCLUSIONS

From the results of this study we draw the following tentative conclusions:

1. The goal orientations (standards, values, or concerns) with which this study has dealt pervade general society, but various segments of the population are characterized by somewhat different proportions of their members being committed to these goals. The conclusion appears to apply as much to the goal of "success," to which Merton has specifically addressed himself, as it does to other goals. Therefore, Miller's theory has received support in that significant differences can be found between the focal concerns of the lower and middle classes. However, these differences are not great, which also tends to support the position of Merton and others, that values are essentially similar throughout the social strata. Both theoretical statements seem, then, to have merit, i.e., major goal orientations are rather similar in nature throughout society, but significant differences in this distribution are found among various communities.

2. Differential goal orientations are related to socio-economic class only when the individual classes are present in large, concentrated areas (communities or "status areas"), the goal orientation of all other social classes found *within* these areas being the same as those of the predominant socio-economic class of that community. This study has not identified the size a community or "status area" must attain before it can achieve relative autonomy from the surrounding area in its goal orientations. However, the social class concentrations in our industrial city of 40,000 are apparently not large enough nor those numbers in the individual social classes of our fashionable suburb of 25,000. Obviously, however, other considerations such as ethnic composition, proportional representation of social classes, and the specific goal in question may play important roles in determining the presence or absence of differential goal orientations.

3. The findings suggest that the differences of goal orientations among communities is largely a result of differences in the goal orientations among various lower classes and less to differences among the middle and upper classes. Apparently, middle and upper social class members are more alike in their goal orientations regardless of where they are found. This may result from the security they derive from their adherence to goals, standards, or values that are more closely attuned to the "official goals" of the American society. By "official goals" we mean the goals that are most often mouthed by school, church, police, community officials, and that underlie the success stories in the major communication media. Contrariwise, unless those in the lower socio-economic classes occur in sufficient quantity to develop a "culture" of their own which will provide them relative "immunity" from the middle and upper social classes, they appear to adopt the goal orientations of higher classes—at least to the extent that they are measured on questionnaires.

These findings aid the establishment of limits of Miller's "lower class culture."

4. Goal orientations do not change appreciably from age 10 through age 18 for both boys and girls *that remain in school*. Apparently girls are not more "idealistic" or "middle-class oriented" than boys and younger juveniles are not more "traditional" nor less "realistic" than older juveniles.

5. Our data support the Miller findings that the pursuit of lower class cultural goals raises the chances of indulgence in illegal behavior. We emphasize that this apparently is true in the behavioral sense, per se, and that the overrepresentation of lower class juveniles in official statistics is not only a result of differential law enforcement, for the measure of illegal behavior employed here is not thought to be much contaminated by the legal process. This conclusion raises the very interesting question of why those of the lower classes residing in communities that are not predominantly of this class composition are more likely to become involved with the law even though their goals, their prediction of their probable reliance on illegal behavior in order to reach these goals, and their actual admitted misconduct rates are similar to those of the predominant class. These data would suggest that other factors are at work—perhaps differentials in law enforcement, visibility of offenders, and reporting of offenders.[22]

6. Our results support the findings of the Reckless "good boy-bad boy" studies[23] in the sense that juveniles apparently are able to predict to some degree whether they will employ illegal means in order to achieve their desired goals. Youngsters are sensitive to the behaviors required of them in the pursuit of cherished goals. We point out that the youngsters in this study were predicting actual illegal behavior and not whether they would become entangled with law enforcement agencies as was the case in the Reckless studies.

7. Not only do these data support the Miller thesis of a relationship between lower class "focal concerns" and illegal behavior, but they also confirm the position that misconduct results from the frustration of legal means of achieveing desired goals. Again, both points of view appear to account for illegal behaviors.

8. The combined findings of the relationships between commitment to lower class cultural norms and the incidence of illegal behavior, and the prediction of the probable use of illegal behavior in the pursuit of goals and the incidence of illegal behavior, both suggest considerable

[22] This study included some data pertinent to this point and will be reported later.
[23] For a summary statement of these studies see Simon Dinitz, Frank R. Scarpitti, and Walter C. Reckless, "Delinquency Vulnerability," *American Sociological Review*, Vol. 27, No. 4, pp. 515–517.

rationality on the part of the juvenile offender. Apparently their acts are utilitarian and goal oriented and are not just immediately negativistic and malicious. Neither do they appear to be impulsive acts unless we have inadvertently measured impulsivity.

RESEARCH SUGGESTIONS

1. The results of this study and others have suggested that the factor of proportional representation of socio-economic classes in a given area is influential in the determination of differential behavior patterns. The sheer quantity of social class members seems, also, to be related to the development of certain unique behavior patterns. A general research question in this area would be: What is the nature of the relationship between the size, concentration, and proportional composition of various socio-economic class populations and the presence or absence of unique behavior patterns, particularly those that may be declared illegal?

2. A limiting aspect of this study, and of numerous others of this nature, has been the inclusion of only in-school juveniles. Approximately one of every four youngsters drops out of school prior to completion of the twelfth grade and these boys and girls are often ignored. The research question in a very general way is: What are the relationships between dropping out of school and goal orientations, prediction of the necessity of resorting to illegal behavior, and the extent of misconduct?

3. The results of this study have suggested an interesting insight into lower class behavior that has not been investigated to any great degree. Where not found in areas of considerable size and concentration, lower class juveniles apparently subscribe to the same goals in similar proportions as other social classes. Furthermore, they manage to conform to legal standards as well as do other classes. Extensive research on the specific processes by which this is accomplished or by which illegal behavior is avoided should provide valuable knowledge in the general areas of social control and social change. Perhaps such research would provide an indication of ways through which much larger numbers of lower class juveniles could be motivated to modify some of their behaviors to more closely conform to legal standards. The same studies may even provide insights into the control and prevention of illegal behaviors in the other social classes.

Suggested Further Readings

Clinard, Marshall B., ed., *Anomie and Deviant Behavior*, New York, Free Press, 1964.

Cloward, Richard A., and Lloyd E. Ohlin, *Delinquency and Opportunity: A Theory of Delinquent Gangs*, New York, Free Press, 1960.

Durkheim, Emile, *Suicide*, trans. by John A. Spaulding and George Simpson, New York, Free Press, 1951.

Hollingshead, August B., and Frederick C. Redlich, *Social Class and Mental Illness*, New York, Wiley, 1958.

Lemert, Edwin M., *Social Pathology*, New York, McGraw-Hill, 1951.

Lindesmith, *Opiate Addiction*, Bloomington, Indiana University Press, 1947.

McCaghy, Charles H., James K. Skipper, Jr., and Mark Lefton, *In Their Own Behalf: Voices from the Margin*, New York, Appleton-Century-Crofts, 1968.

Suggested Further Readings

III

The Social Psychological Approach

Whereas the sociology of deviance is largely concerned with understanding deviance in terms of behavioral patterns influenced and/or determined by social factors and conditions, the social psychological approach pointedly contends that explanatory models must make provision for the role of the individual as well. An examination of the relevant works subscribing to that perspective shows that the individual is considered to be of critical importance in one of two ways—*first*, as the source for locating specific causal mechanisms for the behavior at issue, and *second*, as a principal psychological reactor to social pressures.

The article by Davidman and Preble, "Schizophrenia Among Adolescent Street Gang Leaders," while not strictly representative of the social psychological approach, forcefully takes issue with what is sometimes referred to as sociological determinism. Their position, based on a series of intensive case analyses, is that individual personality structure is a vital causative factor in producing deviant behavior.

In his article on right-wing extremism, Rush is similarly concerned with the consequences of the psychological states of individuals but views such states as reactions to particular social pressures rather than as deeply rooted and independent psychic manifestations.

Edwin Lemert acknowledges the relevance of both the psychological and sociological levels of analysis and details the interaction of both types of variables in terms of a specific form of criminal behavior— check forgery.

The deviant behavior which is at issue in Jessor's article is excessive alcohol use. The selection represents a major research effort to test the efficacy of integrating sociological and psychological theories of deviance. The author identifies specific mechanisms on both levels of analysis and argues that these converge to produce deviant behavior patterns.

The final two selections are concerned specifically with juvenile delinquency, and each attempts to trace the relationship between the delinquent and his behavior. In the first of these articles, Richard Ball empirically examines the efficacy of "neutralization," a process by which violations of norms are judged by the violator as permissible in certain

187

situations. The findings presented have clear implications for questioning the cogency and empirical value of subcultural theories of delinquency. Peter M. Hall, on the other hand, regards delinquent subcultures as critical factors in accounting for juvenile delinquency but suggests that psychological preparedness is as important a condition as is the availability of the subculture itself.

15

Howard Davidman
Edward Preble

Schizophrenia Among Adolescent Street Gang Leaders*

Juvenile delinquency research during the past 30 years has been conducted under two distinct theoretical disciplines: sociology and psychology. Sociologists investigate the social conditions that promote delinquent behavior in the individual; psychologists investigate the psychic phenomena in the individual which predispose him toward delinquency as an attempted solution of his emotional problems.

The early sociological studies of Shaw and McKay,[1] and Sutherland[2] included accounts of the individual processes involved in delinquent behavior, but argued that these processes were the same as those operating in nondelinquent individuals. The delinquent behavior of the individual was seen by them as a normal adaptation to the conditions and cultural traditions of urban slum areas. Healy and Bronner,[3] early representatives of the psychological approach to delinquency, paid attention to the social conditions related to delinquent behavior, but explained the individual's delinquent behavior as an abnormal attempt to solve the frustrations which derive from a given family and social context. The main difference between these early sociological and psychological approaches was that the sociologist viewed the individual as the constant factor, and the psychologist viewed the social context as the constant factor. In other words, the sociologist considered society to be

From *Psychopathology of Schizophrenia*, ed. Paul H. Hoch and Joseph Zubin, New York, Grune and Stratton, 1966, pp. 372–383. Paper presented at the meetings of the American Psychopathological Association in 1964. Reprinted by permission of the authors and the publishers.

* This investigation was supported in part by Public Health Service Grant #1-R11-MH 728-A-1, from the National Institute of Mental Health.

the patient and the psychologist identified the individual as the patient
—an understandable professional bias in both bases.

With a few notable exceptions, the interaction between social and
individual factors has received little serious attention by students of
delinquency. Albert Cohen,[4] a sociology student of Sutherland, has
proposed that the "delinquent subculture" provides for the delinquent
a cultural solution to the psychological stresses suffered by a working-
class boy who has integrated middle-class values and goals, but who is
socially restricted to lower-class achievements. On the other side, Fritz
Redl,[5] for example, has made a serious effort to study and treat the
"genuine delinquent" within the group psychological context of his effective social environment.

The recent, influential sociological study of Cloward and Ohlin[6]
reasserts the sociological determinism of the early sociological work in
delinquency, invoking a revised version of Durkheim's theory of
anomie.[7] Their conclusion is that delinquency "is not, in the final analysis, a property of individuals or even of subcultures; it is a property of
the social systems in which individuals and groups are enmeshed."
Cloward and Ohlin recognize "problems of adjustment" within the delinquent, but assert that these problems "are engendered by acts of
social conformity performed under adverse circumstances."

Walter Miller,[8] an anthropologist, goes even further than Shaw,
McKay, and Sutherland in imputing a normal, healthy psychological
life to the delinquent. He states that members of street-corner gangs
"are not psychopaths, nor physically or mentally defective; in fact, since
the corner group supports and enforces a vigorous set of standards, it
tends to recruit from the most 'able' members of the community."

The polemic between sociologists and psychologists regarding the
presence or absence of pathology within the street delinquent is still
a basic one today, in spite of the verbal efforts of representatives from
both disciplines toward theoretical convergence. The state of this polemic has important consequences for practical measures instituted in
the interest of delinquency prevention, control, and treatment. At the
present time, the tide seems to be favoring the sociologists—a consequence, perhaps, of the somewhat justified disappointment with programs of action based on the psychological approach to delinquency.

It is the opinion of the authors of this paper that the reaction
against the psychological approach to delinquency has gone too far
and has approached the early sociological view that the street delinquent exhibits a psychologically healthy adaptation to his social environment. Our study, over a 7-year period, of the members of high status,
fighting street gangs in New York City reveals a high degree of individual

pathology among the members, with schizotypal[9] problems frequent, especially among those in leadership positions. Degrees of emotional problems of adaptation are evident in all gang members studied, with the seriousness of the problems being roughly correlated with the extent of delinquent behavior.

METHODOLOGY

The data on which the conclusions of this paper are based were secured by the anthropologist over a 7-year period as a "participant observer" in three lower-class urban communities in New York City.

In the initial stage of each inquiry—a period of at least one year—the anthropologist established an identity in a neighborhood both as a research worker interested in delinquency and as a professional person who could sometimes help individuals and families with social and emotional problems. After having established himself as a trusted and friendly participant in the life of the community, he secured the voluntary participation of youths from high status, adolescent street gangs who related their "life histories" in individual interview sessions of one hour in length. A minimum of 25 interviews with each of 20 subjects was recorded for the present study. The interviews were designed to obtain both developmental and environmental material. The relatively unstructured nature of the interview and the close relationship between the interviewer and the subject made it possible to elicit unconscious as well as conscious, learned responses. Dreams and other projective material were obtained.

The psychiatrist did a psychodynamic analysis of each subject based on the verbatim records of the interviews. He also studied the daily field journal records regarding the communities and the gangs which were kept during the 7-year period.

A psychologist, Dr. Murray Bilmes, interviewed the subjects and administered psychological tests (Rorschach, Thematic Apperception Test, Figure Drawings, Wechsler Adult Intelligence Scale). A summary of five typical cases are reported here.

CASE #1

This 22-year-old man was, at the age of 15, the leader of the most feared street gang in the community. He achieved this position as a result of the admiration and awe which his intrepid and extravagant rageful outbursts of violence elicited. He fought often, used all types of weapons, and was known as a "sneaky" and "dirty" fighter who could attack viciously without provocation of warning. He was arrested for one homicide and probably committed one more. He began using heroin at the age of 17 and immediately became less violent. Many of his followers began using heroin, as a result of both indoctrination and emulation, and the gang changed from a fighting group to a coterie of drug addicts which soon split up into groups of two and three.

The subject has never worked, having maintained himself and his drug addiction by armed robbery, burglary, selling drugs, and "scheming" on his family, friends, and street associates. In addition to homicide, he has been arrested and served prison sentences for assault, robbery, larceny, and narcotics.

The subject fought throughout his childhood. His father became concerned about his fighting only when he was apprehended by the police. As a child he performed sadistic acts on animals and engaged in petty thefts. He did not get along well with other children. He began to have sexual intercourse at the age of thirteen and associates sexual desire with evil and dirt. In later years he suffered from ejaculatio praecox and retardata.

In recent years he has had feelings of desperation, tantrums, crying fits, and rageful, uncontrollable violent outbursts which frighten him. He expects to die young and fears for his sanity. In his last incarceration, where he was deprived of heroin, he got in so many fights that he was isolated as a security risk. Thereafter he became grandiosely delusional and planned litigious actions against the prison personnel. He regarded himself as infallible and distorted reality in a way that he had never done before. He became convinced that his wild exaggerations were true. At this time he also feared for his sanity and developed psuedohomosexual panic. After release from prison on the last occasion he went through a period of extreme agitation and quickly reverted to heroin. This time, however, the heroin did not allay his fears.

The psychodynamic report as well as the psychological report stress his chronic, pervasive fear and his explosive, unpredictable rage which endanger his life and freedom. Heroin provided a partial way out of this dilemma as well as an escape from sex, work, and normal competition, for all of which he is incapacitated and impotent. He fears for his sanity and worries lest he will kill friends or bystanders as a result of minor annoyances. There is no capacity for empathic resonance with people except in terms of violence, hero doings, vengeance for the sexual misdeeds of others, desire for huge power, and effortlessly gained money.

The family is intact. The mother and father have emotional problems, as do two older siblings, but the family has stuck together and, with the exception of the subject, avoided serious trouble. The family environment does not seem especially unfavorable.

The diagnostic impression separately arrived at by both the psychiatrist and the psychologist is of *paranoid schizophrenia*.

CASE #2

This 23-year-old man has been arrested several times for felonious assaults and burglary. He is unstable in mood—at one time very dependent and jovial and at another time utterly resistive and defiant. He is prone to outbursts of rage and violence over small frustrations. The intensity and lack of control over those outbursts frighten him. He does not carry weapons, but does not hesitate to use any weapon that comes to hand in an emergency. An excellent athlete and fighter, he was well liked by the boys with whom he associated as an adolescent and became the "war counselor" for his gang.

He left school at the age of 16, worked for a short period as a mechanic's helper, and has since showed no particular ambition. He has taken money from homosexuals in exchange for their use of him. He drinks heavily and is apt to be violent, especially when drunk.

The picture is of a chronically frightened, aimless, and mistrustful youth, incapacitated for long-range, goal-directed activity. His fear of loss of inner control, which he sees as his craziness and stupidity, is matched by his desire for release of rage through combat. Drinking offers this freedom, as well as an opportunity for freer communication with other people. When sober, he is ashamed, frightened, amazed, and panic-stricken about his criminal acts—an unworthy sinner who needs to be punished.

He has been in a state of excessive fear and rage since early childhood. The mother seems to have been unavailable to him when he was a child. He ran the streets and could make contact with his mother only if he were physically hurt or in serious trouble. His memories are loaded with details of physical injury and fears of illness. He has a persistent, insatiable, dependent craving and no realistic way to obtain the money and success by which he might win his mother's attention.

He is profoundly mistrustful of the sexual aspect of girls, whom he regards as inciters of trouble who induce men into dangerous battle out of their desire for flattery. On the other hand, he is protective and warm to the desexualized and helpless image of the female. He has grave doubts about his virility and has suffered a major loss of conscious heterosexual interest. His masculinity must be proved through violence and aggressive homosexual acts. He has a pervasive feeling of helplessness and a yearning for magical success. His dreams allude to rage, violence, impotence, fears of mutilation, lack of sexual and assertive equipment, overdependence, and despair.

The diagnosis is *schizotypal organization*.

CASE #3

This 23-year-old man was a leader of boys of his street group because of his explosive violence, daring, inventiveness, and superiority at
scheming and planning group raids and thefts. His history of violence,
cruelty, and incorrigibility goes back to the age of five, with accounts
of battle, mayhem, truancy, sexual activities, fire-setting, smoking, and
drinking. There is a repeated desire to kill, dating back to the age of
five; several attempts to kill animals and people were actually made.
Despite opportunities, he has never been able to make a satisfactory
human relationship, but could only be defiant, violent, and desperate.
At the age of 16 he started using heroin and is a confirmed heroin
addict today.

His parents' marriage dissolved when he was six, after the mother
threw the father out of the house because of his drinking and extra-
marital sex relations. Over the years, the mother has alternately rejected the subject and fostered extreme dependency on her.

The subject has served several prison sentences for assault, burglary, and narcotics. In prison he suffered from a continued feeling of
tension and a need to be away from his fellow inmates for fear that
they would irritate him and cause him to explode. At his own request,
he was isolated in jail, where there were few troublesome stimuli. He
fears contact with people because he becomes suspicious and resent-
ful, and eventually convinced that someone has injured him. Later he
realizes that the injury he resented was imaginary, and he becomes
frightened about his sanity.

He has no friends now nor does he attempt to make any. He lost
a girlfriend to a resented rival and feels too hurt to approach any other
woman seriously. Once he dares trust someone he becomes inordinately dependent, then hostile to that person, whom he expects to force
him to do the things he should despite his huge resistance. He does
nothing to sustain a relationship, and people abandon him. He yearns
for a normal, conventional, responsible life but can see no realistic paths
open that he can follow. Whenever stress or anxiety arises, he uses
magical escape routes, notably heroin.

The picture is that of a paranoid schizophrenic defended first by
violent street activities, then by heroin, and eventually by self-institu-
tionalization within prison. Psychological tests reveal pervasive mistrust, hatred, shame, and a tendency to isolate himself in situations
demanding social interaction. There is no sense of strength or virility,
but rather a feeling of vulnerability to attack and injury. The tests cor-
roborate the uncertain integration and unpredictable violent outbursts.

He is self-destructive, punitive and is filled with fears and guilt. The psychologist agrees that he is a disturbed person with a poor prognosis who possesses a *schizotypal organization*.

CASE #4

This 23-year-old man has never worked; for the last five years he has supported himself by burglaries. He has served jail sentences for assult and burglary. He is a habitual drinker and when drunk is given to blind violence. When younger he was popular with his fellow gang members and had a few close friends. He had prestige in the gang and was a dependable fighter; however, he would assert his independence rather than exercise leadership. He would not follow anyone blindly. Violent when drunk, he is placid when sober. His blind rage is murderous when it is released: On one occasion, when sober, he "blanked out" while assaulting someone uncontrollably.

This subject trained himself to suppress and conceal his feelings, and he often acts in opposition to his emotions. This is particularly true of his pleasurable emotions and his desire for recognition, praise, and achievement. His pride depends on not being a "sucker" and precludes any revelation of his yearning for approval. As a result he keeps rigid control and maintains a flat, disinterested behavior. He expects to be robbed and frustrated if anyone perceives his tender or pleasurable feelings; he is particularly afraid of women in this connection. He ragefully defends a "good" woman's honor and is especially sensitive about any slurs on his mother. His rage is chronic, and constantly threatens to boil over, which frightens him. He welcomes incarceration and gets himself jailed by transparently ineffectual crimes when he is ready to go to jail. There he gains external control and avoids the company of females.

The childhood history shows fear of mutilating injuries, injury being expected as a punishment for his defiant anger at his mother. There is fear of new situations, repeated failures in learning and socialization, and a history of fainting and febrile hallucinosis. The life history data shows lively shame and guilt feelings about his mother and about masculine sexual desires. He sees the area of sexuality in terms of violence, exploitation, and degradation. Both parents were prone to violence in their own behavior.

He feels that he is a hopeless failure and believes that smaller, less-promising looking males will surpass and outdo him. There is a strong need to escape from those with whom he has emotional ties, despite his yearning for magical, dependent fulfillments.

He is diagnosed as a *schizotype*.

CASE #5

This 23-year-old man was known as the "best fighter on the block" from the ages of ten to fifteen. During that time he was respected and feared by the other youths over whom he exercised an inconspicious leadership. He fought frequently, with minor provocation, and in a state of rage. He was aware of extreme fear of mutilation and loss of prestige, and hid this fear from others under his anger and "courageous" behavior. He dates the end of his success in life from the onset of heroin use when he was fifteen. He soon was heavily addicted, supporting his habit through daily thievery. He gradually gave up his social relations and adopted the addicted way of life with its concomitant of non-violence. There developed an increasing feeling of loss of identity, of intellect, of personal controls, and "decent" habits, and an increasing sense of hopelessness. He felt he was slowly dying inside, losing his humanity, and losing "shape." His only dependent gratification now comes from the drug.

As a small child he was considered sickly, without any major disease. He could not sleep with the light out and suffered from nightmares of being crushed by huge animals.

His father was a dapper man and a barroom fighter who was belligerent when drunk. He beat the mother and they were divorced after four years of marriage. As a father he had a friendly interest in his son and served as a figure for identification.

The mother is described as a persistent, pseudoreasonable nagger. She remarried when he was ten. The mother seems to have provoked and encouraged her son to get into trouble so that she could then upbraid him. Their relationship became one in which they could only reach each other through anger. He developed a sullen, passive, hostile withdrawal from her anger and nagging because he knew it frustrated her. If he became openly angry, he felt that she had won the struggle.

He has no capacity for love and trust in the sexual area, having the conventional "street" attitude of the good and faithful woman being asexual. His sexual relationships have been restricted to experiences with female heroin addicts.

This man shows evidence of deficits in welfare emotions and emotional resonance. His inordinate fear and rage and awareness of failure and impotence is partly solved through heroin; nevertheless, there is gradually increasing decompensation. Feelings of depersonalization are present, and there is extreme overdependence. He shows evidence of schizotypal organization which was first masked by violent behavior and later by the effects of heroin.

DISCUSSION

Our long-range study, based on intimate associations in the community with the subjects and their families over a 7-year period, reveals that most of the delinquent street gang members who enjoyed status and prestige on the street have emotional disorders. They are definitely not psychologically healthy members of a delinquent subculture.

Five histories were singled out for this report because they show evidence of schizophrenia. The schizophrenic disorders are of types frequently seen in adolescent offenders. They are easily misdiagnosed at hospital admission or at jail classification as psychopathic or sociopathic in etiology. Dunaif and Hoch[10] have already described these conditions in their paper, "Pseudo-psychopathic Schizophrenia." All the cases cited in their paper happen to have been sexual offenders. Their recognition of a schizophrenia masked by acting-out behavior applied to a much wider variety of offenders seen in jail and among street gang members. In current psychodiagnostic practice in the city prisons, only the most severe and obvious schizophrenias in full decompensation are diagnosed as schizophrenic. The others are termed sociopaths or passive-aggressive personalities. However, on careful examination, these individuals show signs that are consistent with Rado's criteria for schizotypal organization.[9] Rado stresses in his analysis of schizotypal organization the presence of two fundamental forms of damage of the integrative apparatus of the psychodynamic cerebral system. These are (1) an integrative pleasure deficiency, and (2) a proprioceptive disorder. Our cases show the deficiency in pleasure yield, the resultant unbalanced rage and fear, and the deficiency in pleasurably motivated behavior. At various times in their lives they show signs of decompensation under stress. There is evidence, as Dunaif and Hoch found in their cases, of overwhelming guilt.

In addition to guilt feelings, intense feelings of shame, depression, pervasive anxiety, and great uncertainty about ego-identity are observed. Perceptiveness of the emotions of other people is very poor in most cases, with a special inability to respond to the pleasurable emotions of others. There is considerable chaos and fear in sexual attitudes and behavior, a common feature of which is the experience with homosexual prostitution, always in the aggressive role.

Evidence for pathology among the street gang delinquents in this study is also found in the high percentage of converts among them to heroin addiction. Three of the five gang members whose histories are abstracted here are now confirmed heroin addicts. The ratio is approximately the same for another sixty gang members about whom we have direct knowledge.

This observation that high status fighting gang members are especially vulnerable to heroin addiction contradicts a widely held belief. Chein and his associates[11] have maintained that organized street gangs in New York City in the early 1950's were, on the whole, resistant to drug use and even provided help for those who did become addicted. They held that only a minority of addicts belonged to organized gangs and that those who did were likely to have been "anxious, inadequately functioning boys" who were peripheral or rank and file members. Cloward and Ohlin[6] adopted the same thesis in describing adolescent street addicts as "retreatists" and "double failures," who could not qualify for membership in conflict and criminal gangs.

It is our contention that large-scale heroin experimentation by street youths of New York City during the years from about 1955 to 1958 originated among high status conflict gang members and spread to other boys through indocrination and emulation. The pacific effects of heroin and aggressive behavior are well known, and we believe that the observed decrease in street gang conflict during the past five years and the increase in heroin use among street adolescents—an observation that can be verified in conversation with any candid police official, if not by statistical reports—are related phenomena.[12-15]

The evolution of behavior patterns among more than half of our subjects—street gang violence, heroin addiction, decompensation—has been a common one for street gang members of the mid-fifties in New York City, and it contradicts the "healthy street delinquent" thesis of some social scientists that is gaining popularity again today. This is not to deny that social factors may be largely responsible for the individual pathology found in street delinquents and that social conditions constitute a legitimate, even primary, target for delinquency prevention programs.

It is a mistake, however, to maintain that the street delinquent in his individual economy is an emotionally healthy person. One implication of that position is that the so-called delinquent subculture is founded upon psychodynamic imperatives independent of, or in opposition to, those that exist in society at large. Ironically, it was Durkheim, one of the great influences in modern sociology, who argued strongly against such a view. The final version of his sociology stressed the conviction that social constraints, in the form of a "conscience collective," were integrated in the psychic life of every individual in a given society.[7]

SUMMARY

Social scientists who study the problem of street gang delinquency
tend to view the individual delinquent as psychologically healthy on the
presumption that his behavior represents a positive adaption to the
social conditions and cultural traditions of the urban slum community.
Some go further and maintain that the street gang draws its membership from among the healthiest adolescent personalities in the community.

A 7-year psychosocial study of 20 high status street gang members
in New York City refutes these contentions. Psychodynamic and sociological analyses of the life history and cultural data reveal a high degree
of individual pathology, with the schizophrenic process apparent, especially among those in positions of leadership.

REFERENCES

1. Shaw, C. R., and McKay, H. D.: *Juvenile Delinquency and Urban Areas.*
   Chicago, The University of Chicago Press, 1942.
2. Sutherland, E. H.: *Principles of Criminology* (4th ed.). New York, J. B.
   Lippincott and Company, 1947.
3. Healy, W., and Bronner, A. F.: *New Light on Delinquency and Its Treatment.* New Haven, Yale University Press, 1936.
4. Cohen, A. K.: *Delinquent Boys.* Glencoe, Ill. The Free Press, 1955.
5. Redl, F.: "The Psychology of Gang Formation and the Treatment of Juvenile Delinquents." In *The Psychoanalytic Study of the Child.* New York,
   The International Universities Press, 1945, Vol. I, pp. 367–377.
6. Cloward, R. A., and Ohlin, L. E.: *Delinquency and Opportunity.* New York,
   The Free Press, 1960.
7. Durkheim, E.: *Suicide: A Study of Sociology* (trans. J. A. Spaulding and G.
   Simpson; ed. G. Simpson). Glencoe, Ill. The Free Press, 1951.
8. Miller, W. B.: "Lower Class Culture as a Generating Milieu of Gang Delinquency." *J. Social Issues,* Vol. 14, 3:5–19, 1958.
9. Rado, S.: "Theory and Therapy: The Theory of Schizotypal Organization
   and its Application to the Treatment of Decompensated Schizotypal Behavior." In *Psychoanalysis of Behavior: Collected Papers* (ed. S. Rado).
   New York, Grune & Stratton, 1962, Vol. II.
10. Dunaif, S. L., and Hoch, P. H.: "Pseudopsychopathic Schizophrenia." In
    Psychiatry and the Law (eds. P. H. Hoch and J. Zubin). New York, Grune
    & Stratton, 1955.
11. Wilner, D. M., Rosenfeld, E., Lee, R. S., Gerard, D. L., and Chein, I.:
    "Heroin Use and Street Gangs." *J. Criminal Law, Criminology and Police
    Science,* Vol. 48, No. 4, November-December, 1957.
12. Preble, E.: "Heroin Addiction Among Street Gang Adolescents in New York

City." Paper read at the Sixth International Congress, World Federation for Mental Health, Paris, France, 1961. Mimeographed, The New York School of Psychiatry, Wards Island, New York City.

13. ————: "Making and Maintaining Contact with the Adolescent Street Addict." Paper read at the American Orthopsychiatric Association Annual Meeting, Los Angeles, California, 1962. Mimeographed, The New York School of Psychiatry, Wards Island, New York City.

14. ————: "The Community's Role in Reinforcing Drug Use in New York City." *Internat. J. Addict.* Accepted for publication.

15. ————: "Narcotic Use, Delinquency and Social Policy." *Bull. New York State District Branches.* Amer. Psychiat. Assoc., Vol. 7, No. 5, January 1965.

16

Gary B. Rush

Status Consistency and Right-Wing Extremism*

Since its first formal specification approximately two decades ago,[1] the status crystallization hypothesis has generated an increasing number of studies analyzing the effect of status inconsistency on human behavior. Status crystallization, or status consistency, may be defined as the extent to which an individual's rank positions on given status hierarchies are at a comparable level. Lack of such crystallization, i.e., status inconsistency, is said to create a number of social and psychological problems for the individual, the underlying nature of which Elton Jackson sees as conflicting status expectations.[2] That is, holding out-of-line status positions creates ambiguous, unclear and inconsistent "normative expectations" not only for the incumbent of these statuses but also for those with whom he must interact. Jackson proposes that the main consequences stemming from a situation of normative conflict are frustration and uncertainty, which in turn create a condition of psychological stress. Individual responses to this stress which have been reported in the lit-

From *American Sociological Review,* 32 (February, 1967), 86–92, expanded version, by permission of the author and the American Sociological Association.

* The investigation of which this paper is a part was supported by a Public Health Service Fellowship(#MPM 17-207 C1) from the National Institute of Mental Health. The author also wishes to express appreciation to the Institute for Community Studies, University of Oregon, and particularly to Professor Robert E. Agger for permission to use the data on which this study is based.

[1] See Emile Benoit-Smullyan, "Status, Status Types, and Interrelations," *American Sociological Review,* 9 (April, 1944), pp. 151–161; and Pitirim A. Sorokin, *Society, Culture, and Personality: Their Structure and Dynamics,* New York: Harper, 1947, pp. 289–294.

[2] Elton F. Jackson, "Status Consistency and Symptoms of Stress," *American Sociological Review,* 27 (August, 1962), pp. 469–480.

erature on status crystallization include social isolation,[3] desire for change,[4] motivation to action,[5] conservatism,[6] upward mobility,[7] and political liberalism.[8]

The present study will attempt to show that right-wing extremism is another possible political response to status inconsistency. A number of assertions have been made linking right-wing extremism to status discrepancies. In his discussion of the tendency toward a liberal political bias found in persons with uncrystallized status, Lenski made the following note:

In connection with this finding, Gordon has commented that this may be but part of a still more general tendency for persons with poorly crystallized status to adopt *extreme* political positions, whether on the extreme left or the extreme right. In the present data, there was no clear evidence of such a tendency, but no fully satisfactory test was possible because of the very small number of persons adopting an extremely conservative position on the three controversial issues.[9]

Lipset and Bendix have observed that class discrepancies seem to predispose groups or individuals to accept extremist views.[10] Elsewhere, Lipset has noted that five national right-wing movements (McCarthyism, Poujadism, Italian Fascism, and German and Austrian Nazism) appealed mainly to the self-employed urban and rural middle classes.[11] Lipset observes that individuals in these classes, whose status and influence within the larger community is declining, tend to feel cut off from the main trends of modern society. This observation is entirely consistent with those regarding social isolation as a consequence of un-

[3] Gerhard E. Lenski, "Social Participation and Status Crystallization," *American Sociological Review*, 21 (August, 1956), pp. 458–464.

[4] Irwin W. Goffman, "Status Consistency and Preference for Change in Power Distribution," *American Sociological Review*, 22 (June, 1957), pp. 275–281.

[5] Stuart Adams, "Status Congruency as a Variable in Small Group Performance," *Social Forces*, 32 (October, 1953), pp. 16–22.

[6] Melvin Seeman, *Social Status and Leadership: The Case of the School Executive*, Columbus, Ohio: Bureau of Educational Research and Service, The Ohio State University, Monograph No. 35, 1960.

[7] Elton F. Jackson, *op. cit.;* Gerd H. Fenchel, Jack H. Monderer and Eugene L. Hartley, "Subjective Status and the Equilibration Hypothesis," *Journal of Abnormal and Social Psychology*, 46 (October, 1951), pp. 476–479; George C. Homans, "The Cash Posters: A Study of a Group of Working Girls," *American Sociological Review*, 19 (December, 1954), pp. 724–733.

[8] Gerhard E. Lenski, "Status Crystallization: A Non-Vertical Dimension of Social Status," *American Sociological Review*, 19 (August, 1954), pp. 405–413; Elton F. Jackson, *op. cit.*

[9] Lenski, "Social Participation and Status Crystallization," *op. cit.*, footnote 3, p. 459.

[10] Seymour Martin Lipset and Reinhard Bendix, *Social Mobility in Industrial Society*, Berkeley and Los Angeles: University of California Press, 1960, pp. 64 ff.

[11] Seymour Martin Lipset, "Social Stratification and 'Right-Wing Extremism,'" *British Journal of Sociology*, 10 (December, 1959), pp. 1–38.

crystallized status. Finally, the concept of "status politics," which re-fers essentially to the projection of status anxieties and frustrations into the political sphere, has been advanced by a number of analysts as a possible cause of extreme right-wing political tendencies.[12] When we consider that status anxieties and frustrations seem to be consequences of poorly crystallized status "status politics" and "status inconsistency" appear to be nearly synonymous as variables predisposing to right-wing extremism.

The foregoing evidence strongly suggests that an empirical relation-ship may exist between status consistency and right-wing extremism. Before proceeding to test this relationship, certain theoretical assump-tions regarding the nature of these two phenomena must be brought to-gether. A basic assumption of the status crystallization model is that status inconsistencies result in frustration and uncertainty for the indi-vidual. Numerous studies of collective behavior and the processes in the development of social norms have established the fact that a basic reaction to such uncertainty is the attempt to restructure the situation and to find meaning.[13] It has been demonstrated that upward mobility, expression of a desire for change, activism and political liberalism are some of the social expressions resulting from such attempts to restruc-ture the situation on the part of status inconsistents. With respect to political extremism, the author has argued in an earlier paper that the American two-party system precludes the development of institutional-ized channels of extremist expression within the existing political frame-work, and that the militant and millenarian aspects of the extreme right reflect the "crises of legitimacy" to which this element in the American political system is exposed.[14] In this paper, it was suggested that the extreme right provides an activistic political philosophy of "individu-alism" in a society characterized by "collectivism." Activism also appears to be a primary response to status inconsistency. As has been noted in the literature, individuals who suffer status inconsistencies, although they may be socially "detached," are likely to be "activistic," particularly where political issues are concerned.[15]

[12] See, for example, Daniel Bell, "Interpretations of American Politics—1955," in Daniel Bell (ed.), *The Radical Right (The New American Right* expanded and up-dated), Garden City, New York: Doubleday and Company, Inc., 1963, pp. 39–61; Richard Hofstadter, "The Pseudo-Conservative Revolt—1955," in Bell, *ibid.*, pp. 63–80; Seymour Martin Lipset, "The Sources of the 'Radical Right'—1955," in Bell, *ibid.*, pp. 259–312.

[13] See, for example, the studies reported in Ralph H. Turner and Lewis M. Killian, *Collective Behavior*, Englewood Cliffs, New Jersey: Prentice-Hall, 1957; Muzafer Sherif, *The Psychology of Social Norms*, New York: Harper, 1936.

[14] Gary B. Rush, "Toward a Definition of the Extreme Right," *Pacific Sociological Review*, 6 (Fall, 1963), pp. 64–73.

[15] See Lenski, "Status Crystallization: A Non-Vertical Dimension of Social Status," *op. cit.*, and Goffman, *op. cit.*

In light of this summary, the assumption of the present study is that right-wing extremism is a form of political expression offering simplistic, highly structured solutions to the frustrations arising from status inconsistency, and that persons suffering from status inconsistencies will be more likely to maintain this political ideology than those whose statuses are crystallized.[16] The basic hypothesis to be tested in this study is therefore: *Individuals characterized by status inconsistency are more likely to be right-wing extremist in their political attitudes than individuals who are characterized by status consistency.*

METHOD

This research consists of a secondary analysis of data collected for the purpose of studying local political attitudes, opinions and behavior.[17] Available data frequently contain shortcomings of which the researcher should be aware. Perhaps the greatest shortcoming of the data used in the present study is the attrition of the sample due to non-response to a mail-back part of the schedule. The original probability sample consisted of 1231 respondents. Of these, 741 (60 percent) returned the mail-back part containing items related to right-wing extremist attitudes. Fortunately, occupation, income and education data for non-respondents were available from the main interview schedule. As might be expected, the non-response group was characterized by lower education, occupation and income status than the response group. However, the main concern of the present study is with the multivariate distribution of these variables in the status crystallization model. If the non-response and response groups varied significantly with respect to the independent variable of status crystallization, then any findings regarding the relationship of this variable to right-wing extremism would be suspect. With this consideration in mind, the standard error of the difference between status crystallization means of the two sub-samples was computed. This calculation revealed no significant difference between response and non-response groups with respect to crystalliza-

---

[16] The concept, "simplistic," as it is used in this context, refers to the extreme right tendency to reduce complex factors and issues to a single element, e.g., the right-wing extremist blaming the failure of the United States to "win" the "Cold War" on an internal "conspiracy." This tendency has also been suggested by a number of the contributors to Daniel Bell (ed.), The Radical Right, *op. cit.* For example, Talcott Parsons refers to right-wing "individualism" as the "idealization of pristine simplicity as against organizational and other complexity" ("Social Strains in America: A Postscript—1962," p. 195), and Alan F. Westin discusses the "fundamentalistic" characteristics of the extreme right, such as the belief that there are always solutions for social problems and the advocacy of "direct action" ("The John Birch Society: 'Radical Right' and 'Extreme Left' in the Political Context of Post World War II—1962," p. 203).

[17] The "Eugene-Springfield Metropolitan Area Study" conducted by the Institute for Community Studies, University of Oregon, 1959.

tion. In fact, the distribution of crystallization scores within the two groups was remarkably similar.

Lenski's method of measuring status crystallization was utilized in the present study.[18] The variables chosen for this measure were occupation, income and education, since they are germane to most measures of social status and because the data with which they are concerned are readily quantified. Following Lenski's lead, the family was treated as the basic status unit for the variables of occupation and income. That is, for married and other attached individuals in this study, i.e., separated or divorced persons supported by the former spouse, income is defined as that of the total family, and occupation is taken as that of the family head, with the exception that in the case of single and other unattached individuals, i.e., widowed or separated or divorced, and self-supporting, the respondent's own income and occupation have been used. On the other hand, education is regarded in our society as a distinctive and personal status attribute of the individual rather than one accruing to a family as such. Therefore education has been defined in this study as that of the respondent.

The first procedure in obtaining a measure of status consistency was to establish common vertical scales for these three variables so that the relative position of respondents on each of them might be compared. To this end, ten class intervals, ranked on a superiority-inferiority continuum, were established for each variable. Next, a frequency distribution of respondents over these ten ranked intervals was made for each variable. From these, cumulative percentile ranges for each hierarchy were computed. A score for each class interval was then assigned on the basis of the mid-point of the percentile range for that interval. The last step was to arrive at a quantitative measure of status consistency. Lenski describes his quantification of status crystallization as follows: "This was accomplished by taking the square root of the sum of the squared deviations from the mean of the four hierarchy scores of the individual and subtracting the resulting figure from one hundred."[19] In algebraic terms, this may be expressed by the formula,

$$\text{Status Crystallization Score} = 100 - \sqrt{\Sigma d^2}$$

where d represents deviations from the mean and 100 is a score inversion factor intended to lend semantic clarity to the scores obtained. Using a frequency distribution of scores obtained in this way, the sample of 673 respondents was divided into two categories, "low consistency" (N=176) and "high consistency" (N=497), on the basis of what appeared to be a "natural break" in the distribution. The propor-

[18] Lenski, "Status Crystallization: A Non-Vertical Dimension of Social Status," op. cit.

[19] Ibid., pp. 407–408.

tions are similar to those found by Lenski when he divided his sample on the same basis.[20]

In a previous article, the findings of a survey of the literature on extreme right characteristics was reported.[21] This investigation took the form of a content analysis to determine what the extreme right advocated or supported and what they opposed or rejected. As might be expected, a considerable overlapping of the attitudes expressed by different groups and individuals occurred. However, some twenty-eight relatively distinct attitudes, mostly negativistic, appeared manifest. A preliminary inspection of these attitudes suggested that they fell under four general headings. These hypothesized categories and the attitudes constituting them are as follows:

I. *Attitudes regarding government:*
   opposition to strong central government.[22]
   belief in strong government and leaders, but at the local level.
   dissatisfaction with the United States Supreme Court.
   opposition to the Federal Reserve System.
   conviction that there is corruption in government.
   general distrust of the federal government.
   opposition to increased government spending, higher taxes.
   opposition to metropolitan government.
   opposition to urban renewal.

II. *Attitudes regarding international relations:*
   opposition to foreign entanglements.
   dedication to an "America First" approach.
   opposition to the United Nations.
   opposition to foreign aid, Point Four Programs, NATO, etc.

III. *Attitudes regarding modern social principles:*
   opposition to modern education.

[20] *Ibid.*, p. 408. See also William F. Kenkel, "The Relationship Between Status Consistency and Politico-Economic Attitudes," *American Sociological Review*, 21 (June, 1956), pp. 365–368, and Gerhard E. Lenski, "Comment on Kenkel's Communication," *American Sociological Review*, 21 (June, 1956), pp. 368–369.

[21] Gary B. Rush, "Toward a Definition of the Extreme Right," *Pacific Sociological Review*, 6 (Fall, 1963), pp. 64–73.

[22] It must be borne in mind that this opposition is selective. The Right-Wing Extremist's conception of the function of the state is not unlike that of the classical liberal who saw the state as a protector of property and a preserver of order, much like a night watchman, rather than as an entity which imposed positive obligations upon individuals. Thus, the extremist's major opposition to the federal government is in those areas where he is told what he *should do* (e.g., desegregation). On the other hand, Right-Wing support is given to strong government in matters pertaining to security (e.g., congressional investigating committees). For an interesting discussion of this conception of the state, see Harry K. Girvetz, *From Wealth to Welfare: The Evolution of Liberalism*, Stanford, California: Stanford University Press, 1950, pp. 68–78.

opposition to racial integration.

suspicion of international collectivism (e.g., the Common Market.)

militant anti-Communism.

political cynicism.[23]

opposition to "social gospel" Protestantism.

IV. *Attitudes regarding modern social structure and operation:*[24]

opposition to socialized medicine.

opposition to collective bargaining.

support of "right to work."

support of "free enterprise."

opposition to "full employment."

opposition to the "welfare state."

opposition to federal aid to health and education.

suspicion of modern "progressive" innovations.[25]

On the strength of this analysis, the extreme right was defined as a militant and millenarian political ideology, espoused by numerous Right-Wing groups and individuals, which maintains as an ideal the principle of "limited individualism"; this principle being articulated as opposition to "collectivism" in government, international relations, modern social principles, and modern social structure and operation.

The attitude data used for the empirical part of this research contained no items related to the category of "international relations." However, thirty available attitudinal items appeared to be manifestly related to the remaining three hypothesized clusters of extreme right attitudes, under the following sub-headings:

I. Attitudes Regarding Government

Opposition to increased government spending, higher taxes:

20. What do you feel about increasing taxes to provide improved city services? (Disapprove taxes city services.)

25. What do you feel about spending more money on special education? (Disapprove money special education.)

27. What do you feel about increasing taxes to provide public kindergartens? (Disapprove taxes public kindergartens.)

---

[23] This attitude refers primarily to the attitudes and motivations of politicians and to the operation of the political system in general rather than to any specific political issue.

[24] A distinction should be drawn between this category and the preceding one regarding "modern social principles." The latter refers primarily to a generalized attitudinal framework through which the right-wing extremist regards his society. "Modern social structure and operation," on the other hand, refers more to specific programmatic policies, particularly those of the contemporary liberal state.

[25] E.g., fluoridation, psychiatry, pastoral counseling, mental health programs, mental hospitals, etc.

Opposition to metropolitan government:

21. What do you feel about annexation to the city of suburban areas? (Disapprove annexation suburban areas.)

51. It would be a good thing for the residents of both cities if Eugene and Springfield merged and became one city. (Disagree Eugene and Springfield merge.)

Opposition to urban renewal:

18. What do you feel about urban renewal? (Disapprove urban renewal.)

36. The urban renewal program is one of the worst "tax and spend" enterprises yet devised by government planners. (Agree urban renewal worst "tax and spend.")

37. The urban renewal program represents interference and regimentation by government. (Agree urban renewal government interference.)

38. In urban renewal programs, the federal government helps the local community. (Disagree urban renewal helps community.)

39. Urban renewal is a much needed program for community betterment and development. (Disagree urban renewal needed program.)

40. The urban renewal program will make the community a better place in which to live. (Disagree urban renewal improve community.)

II. Attitudes Regarding Modern Social Principles

Opposition to modern education:

29. The public schools are not teaching the fundamentals as well today as they used to. (Agree schools not teaching fundamentals.)

30. Nowadays children get pampered too much in the public schools. (Agree children pampered in school.)

31. There is too much emphasis on cooperation in our public schools and not enough emphasis on competition. (Agree too much emphasis cooperation in school.)

32. Public schools change too many children away from their parents' ideas. (Agree schools change children's ideas.)

Opposition to racial integration:

45. The government in Washington should stay out of the question of whether white and colored children go to the same school. (Agree federal government out of school desegregation.)

47. If Negroes are not getting fair treatment in jobs and housing,

the government in Washington should see to it that they do. (Disagree federal government role Negro fair treatment.)

Political cynicism:[26]

48. Politicians spend most of their time getting re-elected or re-appointed. (Agree politicians spend time re-election.)
49. People are very frequently manipulated by politicians. (Agree politicians manipulate people.)
50. Most politicians in the community are probably more interested in getting known than in serving the needs of their constituents. (Agree politicians' interest get known.)

III. Attitudes Regarding Modern Social Structure and Operation

Opposition to socialized medicine and/or health insurance:[27]

44. The government ought to help people get doctors and hospital care at low cost. (Disagree government doctors and hospital.)

Opposition to collective bargaining:

22. What do you feel about labor unions in Eugene? (Disapprove labor unions.) [28]

Support of "free enterprise":

23. What do you feel about public housing? (Disapprove public housing.)
26. What do you feel about city-owned parking lots? (Disapprove city-owned parking lots.)
33. A municipal power system is a form of socialism. (Agree municipal power socialism.)
34. The federal power program in the Pacific Northwest is one of the best possible solutions to the region's economic problems. (Disagree federal power economic solution.)
46. The government should leave things like electric power and housing for private businessmen to handle. (Agree power and housing private business.)

Opposition to "full employment":

43.. The government in Washington ought to see to it that everybody who wants to work can find a job. (Disagree federal government find jobs.)

[26] I.e., cynicism about politicians' self-interest.

[27] Since the indicator available here would not tend to discriminate between related attitudes surrounding "socialized medicine" and federal "health insurance," this attitudinal component was expanded from the original one of "opposition to socialized medicine."

[28] Since a primary aspect of organized labor is the principle of collective bargaining, it was felt that an item regarding labor unions is a valid indicator of the attitude towards collective bargaining.

Opposition to federal aid to health and education:

41. If cities and towns around the country need help to build more schools, the government in Washington ought to give them the money they need. (Disagree federal government finance schools.)

Opposition to modern "progressive" innovations:

24. What do you feel about fluoridation of the community's water supply? (Disapprove fluoridation.)

The identifying numbers for these items refer to IBM card columns, and indicate the order in which the questions were asked on the interview schedule. The parenthetical short form of each item, which will be used for subsequent reference, indicates the direction of extremist response. All items were coded on a Likert-type scale of responses.[29] Items 18, 20, 21, 22, 23, 24, 25, 26, and 27 were coded as follows: "Approve Strongly," "Approve," "Undecided," "Disapprove" and "Strongly Disapprove." In addition, these items contained three residual response categories of "Don't Care," "Don't Know" and "No Answer." The remaining items were coded as follows: "Agree Strongly," "Agree Somewhat," "Agree Slightly," "Disagree Slightly," "Disagree Somewhat," and "Disagree Strongly," as well as residual categories of "Don't Know" and "No Answer."

In order to compute the inter-item correlation matrix for the cluster analysis, responses to these items were dichotomized by placing the "Strongly Agree (Approve)" or the "Strongly Disagree (Disapprove)" response (whichever was applicable to the sense of the question) in the "extremist" category, and the remaining responses (with the exception of "No Answer") in the "non-extremist" category. Thus, only those respondents with a "strong" attitude toward the item in question were regarded as having given an extremist response. It should be noted that responding "strongly" to any one item *does not* classify the respondent as being an extreme rightist. This is merely considered as being the response an extremist would make to the item in question.

The limitations of secondary analysis become apparent in the above assignment of attitudinal indicators to clusters. What has been attempted in this procedure is to assign each item to the attitudinal component to which it *most closely* corresponds. Thus, urban renewal items were assigned to "government," since this program is most closely associated with the federal government. Items 20 (Disapprove taxes city services), 25 (Disapprove money special education) and 27 (Disapprove taxes

---

[29] See Rensis Likert, "A Technique for the Measurement of Attitudes," *Archives of Psychology*, No. 140 (June, 1932), and Allen L. Edwards, *Techniques of Attitude Scale Construction*, New York: Appleton-Century-Crofts, Inc., 1957.

public kindergartens), although they are concerned with different aspects of local politics, all involve the element of increasing local government expenditures and consequently of increasing taxes. Therefore, they have been assigned to the cluster on "government," under the specific component of "opposition to increased government spending, higher taxes." Item 47 (Disagree federal government role Negro fair treatment), while not directly related to racial intergration, does deal with racial discrimination, and is thus included under the former heading.

To test our hypothesized clustering of attitude items the method of "correlation profile analysis," developed by Tyron, was used.[30] This method involves the plotting of intercorrelations between related variables as pictorial "profiles." On the basis of these profiles, the dimensions or "operation unities" underlying certain clusters (comprised of variables with congruent profiles) can be inferred. Tryon discusses these "operational unities" as follows:

These are defined as those components which result in two or more variables showing the same pattern of correlation coefficients with all the other variables in an investigation. Two variables, A and B, are said to be wholly or partially determined by an operational unity if both correlate high with variable M, low with N, intermediate with O, and so on throughout the other variables. In such a case, clearly what is general in A and B is behaving in an identical and unitary fashion. Correlation profile analysis is a simple method for discovering and grouping together variables which have identical patterns or profiles of correlations.[31]

During the course of the cluster analysis, four items were eliminated because of their low correlation with the other variables. These were items 23 (Disapprove public housing), 46 (Agree power and housing private business), 47 (Disagree federal government role Negro fair treatment), and 51 (Disagree Eugene and Springfield merge). For the most part, the originally hypothesized clustering of attitudes was borne out. The major exception to this was the appearance of a distinct fourth cluster of attitudes related to "urban renewal." Otherwise, most of the variables under analysis clustered together as initially posited. Although some variations in the profiles of the variables constituting each cluster were evident, the overall patterns of consistency between the clustered variables seemed tangible enough to warrant the conclusion that the four clusters discerned by this analysis constitute four distinct attitudinal components of the extreme right. A brief discussion of each of these clusters follows.

[30] Robert Choate Tryon, *Cluster Analysis: Correlation Profile and Orthometric (Factor) Analysis for the Isolation of Unities in Mind and Personality*, Ann Arbor, Michigan: Edwards Brothers, Inc., 1939.
[31] *Ibid.*, p. 2.

CLUSTER   I. Attitudes Regarding Urban Renewal
                18. disapprove urban renewal.
                36. agree urban renewal worst "tax and spend."
                37. agree urban renewal government interference.
                38. disagree urban renewal helps community.
                39. disagree urban renewal needs program.
                40. disagree urban renewal improves community.

This cluster is comprised of several items which were initially hypothesized to belong to the cluster related to the factor of "government." Although the profiles for these urban renewal items were similar, in many respects, to those in the cluster regarding government, the extremely high intercorrelation between these items warranted their inclusion as a separate cluster. At least two reasons may be adduced to explain this high intercorrelation. First, these items are undoubtedly Guttman scale items, included in the metropolitan area study because they yield a high coefficient of reproducibility. Second, urban renewal is a *specific* issue which unlike many of the more general "ideological" issues raised in the other clusters, can evoke a definitive and consistent response. This fact is probably intensified for the Eugene-Springfield area, where a strong public opinion was polarized on a local urban renewal project at the time the metropolitan survey was made.

CLUSTER   II. Attitudes Regarding Modern Social Structure
                    and Operation
                22. disapprove labor unions.
                33. agree municipal power socialism.
                34. disagree federal power economic solution.
                41. disagree federal government finance schools.
                43. disagree federal government find jobs.
                44. disagree government doctors and hospitals.

The above items were initially hypothesized to be in this cluster. Four hypothesized items, however, failed to cluster in this group. Variables 24 (Disapprove fluoridation) and 26 (Disapprove city-owned parking lots) fell into the cluster on "government," and will be discussed under that heading. Variable 23 (Disapprove public housing) and 46 (Agree power and housing private business) failed to cluster, and were eliminated from the analysis. Regarding item 23, it may be that the meaning of "public housing" was not understood by, or was not made clear to, the respondents interviewed. The failure of item 46 to cluster raises two points. First, if "public housing" is not opposed by right-wing extremists in the Eugene-Springfield area (a possible interpretation of the finding regarding item 23), then the extremist who opposed government operation of electric power—as suggested be the clustering of items 33 (Agree municipal power socialism) and 34 (Disagree federal power economic solution)—would have been "cross-pressured" by item 46, which is a "double-barreled" question concerning both electric power and housing. The second point has reference to the unique situation regarding public power in the Eugene area. Although the right-wing extremist may be ideologically opposed to municipal power in general, the Eugene extremist faces the fact that the electric rates charged by the Eugene Water and Electric Board (a municipal power enterprise) are among the lowest in the nation. Thus, the failure of this item to cluster may reflect a conflict between the right-wing extremist's ideology and his pocketbook.

CLUSTER III. Attitudes Regarding Government
        20. disapprove taxes city services.
        21. disapprove annexation suburban areas.
        24. disapprove fluoridation.
        25. disapprove money special education.
        26. disapprove city-owned parking lots.
        27. disapprove taxes public kindergartens.

Items 20, 21, 25 and 27 were initially hypothesized to be in this cluster. Items 24 and 26 (from "modern social structure and operation") undoubtedly fell into this cluster on government because they concern local political issues. It is not unlikely that extreme right opposition to local political issues is primarily tactical—the greatest opportunity for extremist elements to gain access to political power being at the local level. Therefore, it may be expected that the right-wing extremist will attack the kinds of issues represented by items 24 and 26 on what is basically a political level.

CLUSTER IV. Attitudes Regarding Modern Social Principles
        29. agree schools not teaching fundamentals.
        30. agree children pampered in school.
        31. agree too much emphasis cooperation in school.
        32. agree schools change children's ideas.
        45. agree federal government out of school desegregation.
        48. agree politicians spend time re-election.
        49. agree politicians manipulate people.
        50. agree politicians' interest to get known.

All of the above items were originally hypothesized to be in this cluster. Item 47 (Disagree federal government role Negro fair treatment) was hypothesized as belonging to this cluster, but was eliminated during the analysis. The failure of this item to cluster is probably due to the fact that racial tensions are less evident in the Pacific Northwest than in other areas of the nation. Thus, racism is not a central concern of right-wing extremists in this area.

The limitations of secondary analysis notwithstanding, the empirical investigation of attitudes undertaken through the cluster analysis appeared to justify defining the extreme right in terms of an ideology opposing "collectivistic" tendencies in distinct areas of the social system. The existence of separate extremist attitudinal "sets" related to "government," "modern social principles" and "modern social structure and operation" was, to a large extent, verified.

The "right-wing extremism" scale used in this study was constructed by first coding the responses to the twenty-six Likert-type attitude items selected by the cluster analysis as "right-wing extremist" (with an assigned score value of one) and "non-extremist" (with an assigned score value of zero.) As discussed earlier, the former consisted of only the contextually most "extremist" response of the alternatives given for each item. A total score for each respondent was obtained by computing the sum of his scores for the twenty-six items. When scaled, these scores ranged from 0 to 22, higher scores indicating a more consistently "extremist" set of responses.

TABLE 1.

Frequency Distribution of Scores on the
Right-Wing Extremism Scale

Score	Number	Score	Number
0	157	12	1
1	125	13	5
2	95	14	3
3	90	15	1
4	63	16	2
5	36	17	0
6	32	18	0
7	20	19	1
8	20	20	0
9	7	21	1
10	4	22	1
11	9		
		Total:	673

Although no definitive estimation is available of the proportion in the general population of extreme right *supporters*, i.e., not only members of extreme right groups but also persons who hold attitudes consistent with the extreme right ideology, a certain amount of evidence exists to suggest a cutting-point that will divide extremists from non-extremists in the proportion of about one to four.[32] An examination of the frequency distribution of right-wing extremism scale-scores in Table 1 suggests that the rather significant break between scores 4 and 5 is the best cutting point between "extremist" and "non-extremist." For the purposes of this study, therefore, those individuals receiving scores of 5 or higher on the extremism scale will be classified as "right-wing extremist." This category represents twenty-one percent of the sample under study, a proportion which is consistent with the findings of other studies.

FINDINGS

As a test of the hypothesis that status inconsistents are more likely to be right-wing extremist in their attitudes than status consistents are, a difference of 4 percent in the predicted direction was found between the two consistency groups. Although this difference is not statistically significant, it serves as a reference point for a more elaborate test which will hold status dimensions constant. This is necessary since status consistency is a function of given status variables—in this case, occupation, income and education. Controlling for the effects of status is one of the major problems faced in using the status-crystallization model. Lenski has used a matched, distribution technique, and both he and Jackson have made comparisons of paired status patterns in the low consistency category.[33] From the author's point of view, however, neither of these techniques provide a satisfactory control for the effect of status.[34] Lazarsfeld's technique of elaborating a relationship by stratifying on antecedent test variables provides a procedure, based on the logic of the controlled experiment, which permits the researcher to "control" for the invalidating effects of given factors. In the present study, the effects of status in the relationship between status consistency and right-wing extremism will be controlled by "explaining" the relationship found between these variables in terms of the status factors of occupation, income and education. If a relationship between consistency and extremism as great as or greater than that already observed

[32] For example, see Martin Trow, "Small Businessmen, Political Tolerance, and Support for McCarthy," *American Journal of Sociology*, 64 (November, 1958), pp. 270–281; Charles H. Stember, "Anti-Democratic Attitudes in America: A Review of Public Opinion Research," *Bureau of Applied Social Research*, New York: Columbia University, 1954 (mimeographed), p. 52 (cited in Trow, *ibid.*, p. 271); Hanan C. Selvin and Warren O. Hagstrom, "Determinants of Support for Civil Liberties," *British Journal of Sociology*, 11 (March, 1960), pp. 51–73; Fred J. Cook, "The Ultras: Aims, Affiliations and Finances of the Radical Right," *The Nation*, June 30, 1962, p. 571.

[33] Lenski, "Status Crystallization: A Non-Vertical Dimension of Social Status," *op. cit.*, and Jackson, *op. cit.*

[34] Lenski's application of the former involves an ecological fallacy; the latter controls for only two variables at a time and only within the low consistency group. These observations will be discussed fully in a forthcoming research report.

still remains in the partials after stratifying simultaneously on these status variables, then it will be assumed that this relationship is a "true" casual one, i.e., that it is not attributable to either occupation, income or educational differences.

In light of the foregoing discussion, the basic hypothesis to be tested in this study may now be expressed as follows:

Individuals characterized by status inconsistency are more likely to be right-wing extremist in their political attitudes than individuals who are characterized by status consistency, when the invalidating effects of status differences in occupation, income and education are controlled.

The data for the test of this hypothesis are presented in Table 2.

In this table, right-wing extremists for low and high consistency categories are stratified by occupation, income and education. Thus, column (a) contains data for respondents with white collar occupations, high income and high education, column (b) contains data for respondents with white collar occupations, high income and low education, and so forth.[35] The widely disparate cell frequencies between low and high consistency groups at the extremes of Table 2, i.e., columns

TABLE 2.

Right-Wing Extremism by Low and High Status Consistency, Controlled for Status Differences in Occupation, Income and Education (in percentages)

Occupation:	White Collar				Blue Collar			
Income:	High		Low		High		Low	
Education:	High	Low	High	Low	High	Low	High	Low
	(a)	(b)	(c)	(d)	(e)	(f)	(g)	(h)
Low consistency	−(−)	40 (15)	15 (46)	38 (32)	29 (14)	21 (38)	12 (26)	40 (5)
High consistency	20 (111)	24 (33)	21 (34)	19 (26)	0 (10)	9 (45)	8 (45)	25 (213)
Percentage difference	−	16	−6	19	29	12	4	15

(a) and (h), may seem incongruous when compared to the more or less equal distributions in the remaining six columns. However, when one considers the meaning of status consistency, it becomes apparent that the particular combination of status variables characterizing columns (a) and (h) are the only two of the eight combinations that will yield "pure" crystallized status. Unfortunately, this fact also determines that few cases if any will be recorded in the low consistency group for

[35] The cutting points for the dichotomizations of income, occupation and education used in this study correspond roughly to the medians of the frequency distributions of respondents on these variables used to measure status consistency.

columns (a) and (h). The complete loss of cases for the low consistency category of column (a) caused by this feature reduces to seven the number of comparisons that can be made in this table. In six of these, percentage differences in the predicted direction as large as or larger than the original relationship between the two consistency groups are observed. A Sign Test shows these results to be significant at the 0.06 level.

With respect to the effect of individual status variables on the distribution of right-wing extremists in the status consistency categories, little in the way of pattern can be discerned. The data of Table 3 suggest that low educational status might be more closely related to right-wing extremism than differences in either occupational or income status. Comparison of the percentage differences between columns (c) and (d), and (g) and (h) of Table 2 indicates that this relationship may remain when other status variables are controlled. The evidence is not complete, however, since this relationship is reversed between columns (e) and (f) and no comparison is possible for columns (a) and (b).

TABLE 3.

Right-Wing Extremism by Occupation, Income and Education (in percentages)

	Occupation		Income		Education	
	White Collar	Blue Collar	High	Low	High	Low
Percent	23	30	20	22	17	24
N	297	376	266	407	266	407

Nevertheless, one patterned relationship for combinations of status variables may be discerned in Table 2. The two lowest percentage differences—6 percent and 4 percent for columns (c) and (g) respectively—are observed for the "low income, high education" combination. A possible explanation for this finding is that people in this circumstance, regardless of their occupation level, feel the need for some redistribution of economic opportunities, and have a sufficient level of educational sophistication to believe that contemporary American liberalism can bring this about. Therefore status inconsistency as a result of low income and high education does not seem to result in a highly disproportionate incidence of right-wing extremism. This finding is significant in comparison with the findings of the status-crystallization studies conducted by Lenski and Jackson.[36] Both of these researchers found that high occupation or education combined with low racial-ethnic status

[36] Lenski, "Status Crystallization: A Non-Vertical Dimension of Social Status," *op. cit.*, and Jackson, *op. cit.*

predisposed respondents with status inconsistencies to a "left" or liberal
political response. It may be that, under given conditions, a combination of high income and low education may predispose right-wing attitudes, whereas a combination of low income and high education may
predispose left-wing attitudes.

The conclusion which may be drawn from the foregoing analysis
of the relationship between status crystallization and right-wing extremism is that individuals whose statuses are inconsistent are more
likely to be right-wing extremist in their political attitudes than individuals whose statuses are consistent. The implications and significance
of this finding are considered in the final section of this paper.

Discussion

One contribution which the present research has sought to make
concerns the problem of controlling for the effects of status variables
in the status-crystallization model. In the present investigation, relevant
status variables have been controlled simultaneously. However, the
method by which this has been achieved requires exceptionally large
sample sizes; it is not likely that controlling can be done for more
than three or four status variables at one time. In fact, the author is
willing to concede that the low frequencies recorded in some of the
cells of Table 2 produced by this method of controlling may cast doubt
on the significance of the findings of this study. Nevertheless, the present
findings seem to point to a definite relationship between inconsistent
status and right-wing political extremism.

Another point concerns the relationship between the present findings and those of Lenski. In his 1954 study, he found low status-
crystallization to be related to political liberalism.[37] On the surface, the
apparent relationship of uncrystallized status to both right-wing extremism and political liberalism may seem inconsistent. However it is
possible that this inconsistency can be explained in terms of certain
evidence of similarities between left-wing and right-wing extremism.
Westin has discussed similarities in ideologies, programs, strategies and
tactics between the right wing of today and the left wing of 1945–1948;[38]
Ringer and Sills have discerned a number of similarities in social
characteristics between right-wing and left-wing extremists in Iran. [39] Al-

[37] Lenski, "Status Crystallization: A Non-Vertical Dimension of Social Status,"
op. cit.

[38] Alan F. Westin, "The John Birch Society: 'Radical Right' and 'Extreme Left'
in the Political Context of Post World War II—1962" in Daniel Bell (ed.), The Radical
Right, op. cit., pp. 201–226.

[39] Benjamin B. Ringer and David L. Sills, "Political Extremists in Iran: A
Secondary Analysis of Communications Data," Public Opinion Quarterly, 16 (Winter,
1952–1953), pp. 689–701.

though the extreme left is virtually nonexistent in contemporary American society, it is possible that Lenski's indicators of liberalism did not discriminate between the moderate "liberal" left and what vestiges of the extreme left may have been in the population. If this is the case, and since there is reason to believe that Lenski's Detroit Area data may have contained a large number of working-class respondents, much of what Lenski measured as "liberalism" may actually be Lipset's "working-class authoritarianism."[40]

In the present study, observations have been made regarding the relationship of status consistency to both left-wing and right-wing political extremism. It would appear that a significant contribution to our knowledge of these forms of political behavior could be made by studying both of them simultaneously, using the status-crystallization model. A major question to which such a study might be directed would be what elements, working in conjunction with status inconsistency, predispose to a "left" or a "right" political response. It is possible that the crucial factor may be certain configurations of inconsistent statuses as opposed to others. Both Lenski and Jackson found that high occupation or education combined with low racial-ethnic status predisposed status inconsistents to a "left" or liberal political response. The present study indicates that low educational status may be a salient factor in predisposing to a "right" political response. As discussed earlier, it is possible that the combination of high education and low income is responsible for the low percentage difference between high and low consistency groups in column (g) and the reversal of predicted percentage difference in column (c) of Table 2.

These observations regarding education also point to its implications for social change, especially with reference to vertical mobility. Education may be regarded as an irreversible achieved status. That is, it is possible to gain an education, but it is not possible to lose it. With educational opportunities becoming available to an increasingly large segment of the population, it is possible that upward educational mobility may be a more significant indicator of social change than occupational mobility, since the former often precedes upward occupational changes. It would appear, therefore, that the role of educational status is an important one in determining the possible reaction to status inconsistency.

In conclusion, despite the relatively small amount of research that has been done using the status-crystallization of status-consistency model, it appears to be an important and useful predictive tool for the social sciences. Considering the variables to which this predictive model has been applied (psychosomatic symptoms of stress, social isolation,

[40] Seymour Martin Lipset, "Democracy and Working-Class Authoritarianism," *American Sociological Review*, 24 (August, 1959), pp. 482–501.

conservatism, desire for change, upward social mobility, motivation to action, political liberalism, and right-wing extremism), the implications of the crystallization hypothesis for the study of a wide range of social and psychological behaviors are considerable.

17

Edwin M. Lemert

An Isolation and Closure Theory of Naive Check Forgery

The research on forgery we report here is inspired by the methodological dissent from older formulations in criminology—formulations which incorporated generalizations covering all crime and all criminals. At the same time our report is a part of that dissent. As such it seeks to build in a cumulative way upon the work of Hall and Sutherland, who have insisted that criminological research will best advance through the study of sociologically defined units of criminal behavior.[1] Over and beyond this, ready justification for the inquiry rests in the paucity of descriptive data available on the crime of forgery itself and the almost complete absence of efforts at its systematic analysis.[2]

In the process of collecting and analyzing our data it soon became apparent that the invocation of many of our more generalized theories of crime provided only minimal insight into the cases which came under our purview. Culture conflict, delinquency area background, emotional conflict and others proved either to be completely irrelevant or non-discriminating theories so far as causation was concerned. While Suther-

Reprinted from the *Journal of Criminal Law, Criminology and Police Science* Copyright © 1953 by the Northwestern University School of Law, Vol. 44, No. 3, by permission of the author and the publishers.

[1] Jerome Hall, *Theft Law and Society*, 1935, Introduction; E. H. Sutherland, *Principles of Criminology*, Revised, 1947, Chapter 13.

[2] While there are incidental data on forgery scattered through the literature on crime we note only two descriptive articles exclusively devoted to forgery: I. A. Berg, "A Comparative Study of Forgery," *Journal of Applied Psychology*, 28, 1944; David Mauer, "The Argot of Forgery," *American Speech*, December 1941, pp. 243–250: some attempt at the analysis of the forger's behavior will be found in John Gillin, *The Wisconsin Prisoner*, 1949, p. 167; an informal historical treatment of the subject is at hand in Henry T. F. Rhodes, *The Craft of Forgery*, 1934.

land's concept of differential association appeared as a necessary factor in the explanation of professional forgery it was found to be unrelated in any important way to the class of forgery cases we chose to consider, namely, naive check forgeries. Hence, a considerable amount of innovating became necessary in order to explain and interpret our research findings. A preliminary of our theoretical formulation was the definition of the behavior unit subsumed under naive check forgery.

In terms of generic or common law, forgery is thought of as the false signing of a legal instrument which creates a liability. This holds even if or when the entire legal instrument is false and only gives the appearance of legality. Thus defined, forgery covers a wide variety of acts, such as forging wills, public documents, sales slips and prescriptions for narcotic drugs. It is not our purpose to propound a theory subsuming all such acts but rather one for check forgeries only. This includes all acts commonly charged as forgery, fictitious checks, issuing checks without sufficient funds, and uttering and passing falsified checks. The theory cannot without further research be applied to forgeries arising out of mail thefts or out of the theft and the raising of money orders.

The concept of naive forgery was devised to indicate forgeries committed by persons who have had no previous criminal record and no previous contact and interaction with delinquents and criminals. It is designed to exclude forgeries which are incidental to the commission of other crimes, and forgeries which are retrogressive or progressive phases of an already established criminal career. Common examples of the types of forgeries eliminated would be those of burglars who come onto a drawer full of checks in burglarizing a business office and often —not too wisely—cash them. We also exclude the forgeries committed by embezzlers, as well as the occasional forgeries of con men, chiefly because they are incidental or alternative techniques by which their crimes are committed. The embezzler is further distinguished from the forger by reason of his being in a position of trust.

The validity of our delimitation of the class of forgeries about which we seek to generalize may be questioned on the grounds that it narrows excessively the universe of crimes and correspondingly decreases the usefulness of our generalizations. The answer to any such question we hold will be found in the nature of the prior records of those convicted of forgery. From the following tabulation we can make several important observations on this point. First we see that almost one-third of the forgers had no prior record whatsoever and almost one-half were either in this class or had committed only prior forgeries. In the other two categories there are included substantial numbers of persons convicted on petty theft or grand theft charges which in actuality were forgeries but which for legal reasons were prosecuted otherwise. Also there was a sizeable number of persons whose records involved forgeries plus drunkenness or drunkenness only, which cases we may regard as involving persons essentially without criminal sophistication. Finally there was a fair number of cases such as those of sex offenders, offenders against family laws, desertions from the armed forces and certain Federal offenses (illegal entry, impersonating an officer) which do not presume criminal associations or learning. Altogether we would be inclined to add another 27 percent of the cases to our general category of naive forgeries, thus raising the total to 75 percent for which our theory is pertinent.

TABLE I.

Prior Records of 1023 Persons Convicted for Forgery in Los Angeles County 1938 and 1939.

Nature of Prior Record	Number	Percent
No prior record	306	99.9
Prior forgery only	189	18.5
Prior forgery plus other crimes	211	20.6
Other crimes only	317	30.9
Total	1023	99.9

Our theory of naive check forgery as delimited above can be stated in terms of (*a*) the characteristics of the crime (*b*) the person (*c*) the situation (*d*) the sociopsychological process. The hypothesis in general is that naive check forgery arises at a critical point in a process of social isolation, out of certain types of social situations, and is made possible by the closure or constriction of behavior alternatives subjectively held as available to the forger. We will attempt to show how the four enumerated factors operate both directly and in interaction with one another to produce the crime.

The Characteristics of Crime

A number of crimes such as robbery, assault, rape, certain forms of theft and burglary are high visibility crimes in that they are either objectively apparent to others or subjectively perceived by their perpetrators as crimes prior to or at the time they are committed. In contrast to these, check forgeries, especially those committed by first offenders, have low visibility. There is little in the criminal act or in the interaction between the check passer and the person cashing the check to identify it as a crime. Closely related to this special quality of the forgery crime is the fact that while it is formally defined and treated as a felonious or "infamous" crime it is informally held (by the legally untrained public) to be a relatively benign form of crime.[3] The combined effect of these two factors, we will show, facilitate the subjective acceptance of a particular criminal solution to the crisis situation.

THE PERSON

The concept of person is used here simply as a way of delimiting the class of people most likely to commit forgery when situational and sociopsychological factors are present and operate in certain sequence. Generally speaking, forgers tend to be native white in origin, male, and much older than other criminals when they commit their crimes—somewhere in their very late twenties and early thirties. Their intelligence is much higher than that of other criminals and they equal or surpass the general population in the number of years of education they have completed. The occupational classes contributing disproportionately to the population of forgers are clerical, professional, and skilled or craft workers. More particularly, salesmen within the clerical group have a greater-than-expected representation among persons convicted of this crime. Many forgers come from prestigeful, wealthy families in which siblings have achieved considerable social eminence. A large percentage of forgers for many years have been residents of the community in which their crimes are committed. According to comparisons we have made between the past records of forgers and those of burglars and robbers the former are less likely to have a record of juvenile delinquency. From this and the data of our interview sample we are convinced that very few forgers have originated from the so-called "delinquency areas" of their communities.[4]

The description of forgers in terms of temperament and personality tendencies is a much more hazardous academic task than their demographic characterization. Nevertheless, we will suggest certain differentials of this sort, chiefly because of their rather uniform occurrence in the interview data. The most obtrusive of these appeared as a distaste or sense of repugnance towards forms of crime other than forgery. In case after case come the unsolicited "I could never hurt anyone," or "I wouldn't have the nerve (or guts) to rob anyone or to steal." While all criminals tend to rationalize their crimes somewhat in the prison

[3] This inconsistency has a long history. See Henry Rhodes, *op. cit.*, p. 22.

[4] The data for this paper consist of statistical materials compiled on 1023 cases of forgery in Los Angeles County for 1938 and 1939 and a sample of 29 forgers interviewed by the writer at the Los Angeles County Wayside Honor Rancho. Interviews lasted from 45 minutes to two hours. We are indebted to the Los Angeles County Sheriff's department and especially to Captain Harold Stallings for making available facilities and permission to conduct the interviews. In general what we have said thus far about the population of forgers is corroborated by the findings of I. Berg, *op. cit.*

situation evidence that we were confronted with real differentials came from other sources, namely, the experience of detectives, who say they seldom if ever have trouble arresting a forger; often they are waiting for the police to come, or they voluntarily give themselves up. Guns are very rarely found in the possession of persons arrested on forgery charges and when they are it is usually a case of some other type of criminal casually turned to check passing. It is also true that inmates of prisons recognize a temperamental difference of forgers, sharply distinguishing them from men in the so-called "heavy rackets."[5]

Detectives who have dealt many years with forgers depict them generally as people who are personally likeable and attractive, who easily ingratiate themselves and who have a facile grasp of the arts of convincing others. They are people who like to live well and fast, being able to con a merchant or "snow a dame under" with equal dispatch. As one burglar (non-forger) put it: "Forgers are guys who like to pretend to be someone they ain't." In addition it has been observed that an element of impulsiveness seems to thread through the behavior of forgers, being detectable even among professionals, who, for example, have expressed to the writer their dislike for con games because of the slow "build-up" involved.

Because the observations we record above refer to sophisticated forgers as well as to naive forgers it is difficult to say to what extent such personal tendencies exist in nascent form in the previous histories of forgers and how far they have been the function of the life a forger must necessarily pursue once committed to his check passing. However, it is hard to escape the idea that some sort of precriminal personal differentiae are present in the winsomeness and tempo of behavior shown by persons who resort to check forgery.

In summary at this point it can at least be stated that forgers come from a class of persons we would ordinarily not expect to yield recruits to the criminal population. By definition, of course, naive forgery is a crime of persons who are unacquainted with criminal techniques; but aside from this the persons involved would appear to have acquired normal attitudes and habits of law observance. It follows that naive forgery emerges as behavior which it out of character or "other than usual" for the persons involved. In the act of forging an ephemeral personal reorganization occurs in response to situational interactors which may be recognized as a special symbolic process conceived to cover aspects of motivation, feeling, emotion and the choice of adjustment alternatives. The personal differentiae we have set down here are the original broad limits within which a certain class of situations can impinge upon the person with the possibility of emergent forgery.

5 I. Berg, *op. cit.*

THE SOCIAL SITUATION

That the social situation is a dynamic factor in naive check forgery is obvious from even the most cursory reading of case history materials, and it has been commented upon widely by probation officers, judges, social workers and others who have come into contact with forgers. Such contingencies as unemployment, business failure, gambling losses, dishonorable discharge and desertion from the armed forces, alcoholic sprees, family and marital conflict, and separation and divorce all figure prominently in the case histories of naive check forgers. Yet to set down such critical experiences as "causes" of forgery is only indicative and not discriminating, because many people similar in background to naive forgers confronted by similar crises do not seek a solution by forgery. A more discriminating factor was suggested by the unusually high rate of divorce and separation among married forgers and the high incidence of family alienation and repudiation among single forgers. The very high rates of marital disruption for our cases can be seen in Table II. Even when allowances are made for the somewhat higher divorce rate to be expected in a middle class group such as our forgers it will be appreciated that the rate remains inordinately high.

TABLE II

Marital Status of 473 Persons Convicted of Forgery and 53 Persons Convicted of Grand Theft in Los Angeles County 1938.

| | Forgery | | Grand Theft | | Los Angeles City |
	No.	Percent	No.	Percent	Population, Percent
Single	118	24.9	16	30.1	30.8
Married	172	36.3	25	47.1	54.9
Divorced, Widowed or Separated	183	38.6	12	22.6	15.3*
Totals	473	99.8	53	99.8	100

*Includes divorced, widowed and "wives not present in home." *United States Census*, 1940, pp. 182, 190, tables 8 and 11.

Examination of case history documents and our interview materials revealed that the marital breakups of the persons who later became forgers often were exceptionally rough, and usually grossly traumatic experiences, particularly from the view of their subjective impact. The marital ruptures quite frequently were followed by continuous drunkenness, job inefficiency, occupational detachment, and occupational mobility, often in decided contrast to the pre-divorce history. This, of course, is not to say that the marital breakups always initiated the social isolation, for in some cases it was a non-marital crisis which led to exces-

sive drinking, sexual promiscuity or loss of
sulted in separation and divorce. Howev
isolating experiences tended to be progressiv

Among the forgers with no marital ex
ceived as alienation from the parental fa
"black sheep" being fairly expressive of the
also noted among both the single and marri
sons who had begun their adult lives with so
isolation could be inferred; here we refer to
caps, members of ethnic minorities, orpha
the occasional homosexual. In all 29 of our interview cases we were
able to find at least one measure of social isolation and in most of them,
multiple measures.[6] This may be seen in the accompanying table.

Assuming we have established situational isolation as the more
general prerequisite for the commission of naive check forgery it is
still necessary to factor out more specific situational factors conducive
to the crime. These we believe are found in certain dialectical forms
of social behavior, dialectical in the sense that the person becomes
progressively involved in them. These behaviors are further distinguished in that they make imperative the possession of money or money
substitutes for their continuance or fulfillment. They are objective and
identifiable and once a person is committed to them the impetus to
"follow through" with them is implicit. A quick example is that of a
man away from home who falls in with a small group of persons who
have embarked upon a two or three-day or even a week's period of
drinking and carousing. The impetus to continue the pattern gets mutually reinforced by interaction of the participants, and tends to have
an accelerated beginning, a climax and a terminus. If midway through
such a spree a participant runs out of money the pressures immediately
become critical to take such measures as are necessary to preserve the
behavior sequence. A similar behavior sequence is perceived in that
of the alcoholic in a bar who reaches a "high point" in his drinking and
runs out of money. He might go home and get clothes to pawn or go
and borrow money from a friend or even apply for public relief, but

---

[6] Specifically: *occupational isolation* was taken as unemployment, job instability
(some cases had as many as 20 or 30 different jobs per year) or conditions of work
separating the person from his customary association; *marital isolation* was taken as
divorce, separation or alienation of spouses; *family isolation* was taken as an invidious
position in the parental family due to educational, occupational or economic inadequacy; *ethnic isolation* was taken as isolation due to race or national status, i.e., a
rural Negro migrant, a second generation Portuguese in conflict with parents and his
neighborhood, a Jew who due to bankruptcy and sexual immorality was alienated
from other Jews as well as gentiles; physical and "other" isolation was that of physically handicapped persons, homosexuals in conflict and the deviants we mention in the
text above; *subjectively felt isolation* was taken as a sense of isolation expressed in
response to direct questions on the subject.

tives become irrelevant because of the immediacy of his
lcohol. Another example, fairly common during the late war,
of the individual who impersonates a high-ranking army officer
blic official and get increasingly involved in a whole set of recipro-

TABLE III

The Frequency of Occurrence of Measures of Social Isolation in 29 Cases of Naive Check Forgery, Los Angeles County 1951.

Case No.	Measures of Isolation			Ethnic, Physical, "other"	Subjectively Felt Isolation	Case Frequency
	Occupational	Marital	Family			
1	X		X	X		3
2			X	X		2
3	X		X	X		3
4	X			X	X	3
5	X	X				2
6	X	X		X	X	4
7	X			X		2
8	X	X	X			3
9	X			X		2
10		X		X		2
11	X		X		X	3
12	X	X		X	X	4
13			X	X	X	3
14	X	X				2
15	X		X	X		3
16		X	X	X		3
17	X	X			X	3
18	X		X	X	X	4
19		X			X	2
20			X		X	2
21	X	X			X	3
22	X					1
23			X			1
24	X	X	X		X	4
25		X			X	2
26	X	X				2
27	X		X	X	X	4
28			X	X		2
29	X	X		X		3
Totals	20	14	14	16	13	77

cal obligations, which, when his money is exhausted he must implement
with false credit or worthless checks. Otherwise he must expose himself
or put an end to the whole fraudulent business by leaving town,
as he often does.

We encountered several cases in which forgeries occurred around

Christmas time, and the evidence seems strong that the institutionalized, cumulative social pressures to engage in buying behavior at this time (symbolized in newspaper box-scores of the "number of shopping days left before Christmas" and "getting the Christmas spirit") were real factors in building up a sense of crisis leading to forgeries. The sense of social isolation among the forgers detached from their families also was intensified during this holiday period. It was our further impression that many of the type situations more specifically leading to forgeries— gambling, borrowing and "kiting" to meet debts and business obligations, desertion and escaping authorities, and being the *bon vivant* tended to be dialectical, self-enclosed systems of behavior in the sense that the initial behaviors called for "more of the same." While making the possession of money critically necessary they also reinforced or increased the social isolation of the indulgee; many forgers admitted that at the time such behavior was perceived as having a "false structure" to it.

THE SOCIOPSYCHOLOGICAL PROCESS—CLOSURE

Thus far we have spoken of the election of check forgery as a behavior alternative in relation to the general social isolation of the person and in relation to his involvement in collective or institutionalized behavior dialectics directly dependent upon the use of money or symbolic substitutes for money. It is also necessary to note the way in which the sociopsychological processes in the person interact with them to produce check forgeries. The special process is one of closure. This we take to mean a process whereby the tension initiated by a situation is resolved and the configuration (whether of behavior or of mental process) tends to as complete or "closed" a condition as the circumstances permit. The concept denotes a "demand for meaning" as well as a fitting or selection from alternative modes of behavior to resolve a critical situation.[7] As it operates in check forgery it is a total behavioral response, more frequently impulsive and unverbalized than deliberative or narrowly perceptual.

The significant fact to account for in our data was the apparent contradiction of well educated, often gifted, and certainly otherwise law-abiding persons electing a criminal alternative as a solution in this closure process. A second fact to explain is why they selected the particular crime of check forgery. Beginning with the second fact we can say rather simply that the class of persons committing naive check forgery do not have the skills nor are they in a position to carry

[7] See J. F. Brown and D. W. Orr, "The Field Theoretical Approach to Criminology," *Jour. of Crim. Psychopathol.*, 3, 1941, pp. 236–252; Cesar Castillo, "Una Teoria gestalgica del delito," *Archivo de medicina legal*, Buenos Aires, 1948, 18, pp. 387–396.

out or "close on" most other forms of crime. Furthermore, in contrast to many other types of crime no special skills or knowledge are needed in order to manufacture and pass worthless or even forged checks. In thus commenting upon what may be an obvious fact we digress somewhat to discuss the importance of prior learned behavior in commission of this crime.

The first thing to be said in this connection is that forgery (excluding actually imitating other people's signatures) is very simple to perform; it is probably the easiest major crime to commit that we have. Most people in their everyday transactions have occasions to cash personal or payroll checks and hence encounter all the precautions business uses to prevent the making and uttering of bad checks. From this it is arguable that the criminal defense measures adopted by business become in effect an inverted education in the simple essentials of forgery. We can also hold with good reason that in a competitive society which modally creates aggressive temperament they become a challenge to contrive workable evasions of the protective devices. We see this in the resentment shown by "honest" customers at having their checks questioned and in the gamelike characteristics of many of the techniques invented and employed by forgers.

The point we dwell upon here was demonstrated by asking a college class of 25 students to write brief accounts of how they would obtain and pass a bad check if circumstances forced them to do so. The results showed that while the range of ingenuity was wide, nevertheless about the same class of techniques were described as those actually employed by the forgers in our sample. Only one female student was unable to devise a workable scheme. Sources of the ideas in a few cases were listed as radio programs and crime fiction, but most students simply put down "experience with checking account," "experience in retail stores," or "just imagination." Quizzing of the naive forgers in our interview group revealed few or none who could trace in retrospect the sources of their specific forgery behavior.

Another reason for the congeniality of the check forgery alternative lies in the previously mentioned facts that while it is formally treated as a serious crime, informally it is held to be a relatively minor offense and indeed in some forms not a legal offense at all. Thus when the situation or special variations in the subjective reactions of the person dissociate the more formal business and legal control symbols from the act it becomes a more attractive or acceptable choice for the crisis-bound individual. It is in this connection that the low social visibility of the crime excludes social clues which otherwise would weight the forgery choice with unpleasant connotations for the self and person considering it.

Even more important than the low social visibility of check forgery in suspending the formal control symbols of this crime is the social isolation of the person. In general we believe from our data that this isolation brings about a real, albeit ephemeral, suspension, abeyance or distortion of the internal aspects of social communication. It led in our forgery cases to an attenuation of what Mead called the "inner forum of thought," and lowered sensitivity to the "generalized others" which might otherwise have produced a rejection or inhibition of the criminal alternative of forgery. The evidence for this came out in strong feelings of unpleasantness immediately following first forgeries, in the tendency for naive check forgers to give themselves up to the police, in great feelings of relief on being arrested, in desires to "pay their debts to society," in extreme puzzlement as to how they "ever could have done it," and in personality dissociations attributing the behavior to "another me," or to a "Dr. Jekyll-Mr. Hyde" complex.

A high degree of tension appeared in practically all of our cases, being manifested as a sense of urgency which also contributed greatly to the disturbance of the subjective aspects of the communication process.[8] In some cases this sense of urgency, as we have shown, arose from commitments to certain types of dialectical social behaviors. In other cases the sense of urgency seemed to arise from special definitions of the social situation. In such cases there appeared to be a heavy discharge of socially unshared or private meanings into the circumstances of the crime. The insurgency of these private meanings into the thought processes seemed clearly to be a function of the social isolation of the person.

Some of these private meanings proved to be specialized extensions of common cultural meanings. Thus, for some of the check forgers ordinary expenditure behavior in our society took on a desperate kind of meaning. Indulgence in clothes, automobiles, housing, and expensive leisure time pursuits seemed to fulfill intricate, specialized sociopsychological functions over and beyond the satisfactions people ordinarily or "modally" receive from buying such things. These people "get the bug," as one detective put it; they become fixated upon some object and spend most if not all of their waking moments scheming how to obtain it. Such fixating, in part a response to high pressure advertising and selling methods, is, we urge, more commonly the reaction of the socially isolated person.

In other cases the tension or sense of urgency felt by the person who resorted to check forgery emerged out of definitions of the situation which were more intimately personal or perhaps interpersonal. In

[8] It is to be noted that Lottier found a high degree of tension to be a significant factor in embezzlement, which bears many similarities to forgery. Stuart Lottier, "A Tension Theory of Criminal Behavior," *Amer. Sociol. Rev.*, 7, December 1942, pp. 840–848.

such instances checks or money came to have a special symbolic value apart from any which the culture assigns to them. Thus in a number of cases strong elements of aggression figured in the forgery act, often aggressions against a particular person. In one such case a youthful epileptic man with a well-defined sense of isolation passed an illegal check immediately after quarreling with his father and preparing to leave for another city. While his need for money to travel was urgent, still it is significant that he wrote the check in such a way as to embarrass his father in the local community.

In many cases the impression is strong that forgery of checks becomes a way of punishing "others" or the "self," with banks, department stores, loan companies and material objects taking on very private meanings for the check criminal. While it is not always clear just what these meanings are nevertheless they constrict the choices of behavior in the situation. In order to satisfy the immediate special subjective needs of the individual, such as aggression against a particular person or organization he must exploit the situation as it arises, or, in more familiar terminology, "strike while the iron is hot." The several or many legal alternatives which might serve the same function as a bogus check are "out of place" to him, or else the time required to use them causes them to lose their value to him.

The importance of the sense of urgency in narrowing the range of subjectively acceptable means of meeting the forger's crisis was supported in our data by the fact that as a group our forgers were not without resources. They possessed good clothes, jewelry, sporting equipment and other things which could have been pawned or sold; some had families and relatives from whom they might have borrowed money. Some actually had money in the bank at the time the bad check was passed, and some had bonds which could have been cashed to obtain money. Indeed, one of our forgers was a wealthy landowner with large amounts of money on deposit in England and Australia.

18

Richard Jessor

Toward a Social Psychology of Excessive Alcohol Use: A Preliminary Report from the Tri-Ethnic Project

A principal concern of the Tri-Ethnic Project[1] has been to provide an understanding of deviance and drinking behavior as it occurs in a natural social setting. The research community—a small town and its rural surrounds in southwestern Colorado—is comprised of three ethnic groups which maintain fairly distinct social networks despite geographic intermingling. Out of a population of roughly 3,000, there are about 350 Anglo-American, 200 Spanish-American, and 80 Indian households in the community.

One of the salient characteristics of the community is the obvious difference among ethnic groups in rate of occurrence of a variety of

From *Proceedings Research Sociologists' Conference on Alcohol Problems*, ed. Charles R. Snyder and David R. Schweitzer, Southern Illinois University, April 30–May 1, 1964, by permission of the author, the editors, and the publishers.

[1] The material presented here is a condensation and extension of the Tri-Ethnic Project Research Report No. 25, University of Colorado, mimeo., November, 1963. The report contains the following sections: R. Jessor, "Theory and Method in the Study of Deviance in a Tri-Ethnic Community"; R. C. Hanson, "The Sociocultural Context of Deviance"; T. D. Graves, "Social-Psychological Processes in Differential Patterns of Deviance"; L. Jessor, "Cultural Factors and Socialization Into Deviance." The four authors of that report share responsibility for formulating these ideas and carrying out the research and analyses. Our indebtedness to a large number of graduate student research assistants is acknowledged with pleasure; special appreciation is gratefully extended to Mr. Peter Grossman who has contributed in a major way to the measurement and analysis of drinking behavior.

The segment of the Tri-Ethnic Project reported on in this paper has been under the direction of the writer and was carried out under the aegis of the Institute of Behavioral Science at the University of Colorado. This paper is Publication No. 46 of the Institute.

Financial support has been provided by National Institute of Mental Health Grant No. 3M-9156, O. C. Stewart and R. Jessor, co-principal investigators.

social problem behaviors, especially those involving excessive alcohol use. As in similar communities in or near an Indian reservation, the relatively high rate of deviance and alcohol use among the Indian segment of the population is readily noted. So also is the fact that, as a group, the Anglos have the lowest rate, with the Spanish being intermediate. Wide individual variation within ethnic groups and overlap between groups are also notable. Observations such as these presented us our problem: how to account for both group and individual differences in deviance and alcohol-use in the community. It was this task to which the research was addressed.

This paper will include some general remarks about theoretical orientation of the research, brief discussion of the major social and psychological concepts employed and their interrelations, description of the methodology and the several empirical foci of the investigation, and the presentation of some preliminary analyses of data related to alcohol use.

Two qualifications should be made at this point. The first is that a number of other variables, in addition to those which will be mentioned in this paper, have been investigated during the course of the research. For example, a major effort was made to study, among teenagers, the relationship between patterns of alcohol use and the tendency to delay gratification. Another example is the analysis of the acculturation process in relation to drinking. Neither these nor certain other facets will be discussed here. The point of this first qualification is that the Tri-Ethnic Project is considerably broader and more complex than will emerge from this presentation. The second qualification is a reminder that the primary focus of the research has been on deviance. While certain forms or amounts of alcohol use can readily be considered examples of deviant behavior, this is, of course, not true of the use of alcohol in general. It has been our thesis that the category of deviant behavior can usefully be defined to include a large number of different behavior patterns with similar adaptive functions; excessive alcohol use is treated, from that viewpoint, as an instance of the category of deviance. This second qualification, then, refers to the fact that the theoretical scheme to be presented is not specific to excessive alcohol use but is an effort to comprehend a larger focus—that of deviance—within which certain aspects of alcohol use reasonably be seen to fall.

THEORETICAL ORIENTATION OF THE RESEARCH

In their pursuit of understanding of significant areas of social behavior, anthropologists and sociologists have traditionally maintained a different conceptual focus and made use of a different explanatory paradigm than that employed by psychologists, even when the behavior under investigation has been identical. Focusing upon the sociocultural system, their traditional paradigm involves the establishment of a relationship between some attribute or condition of that system and the prevalence or rate of occurrence of some category of behavior. The psychologists' traditional paradigm, on the other hand, focusing upon the individual, involves the establishment of a relationship between some aspect of the personality system and behavior. For each of these divergent paradigms, explanation resides in the demonstrated relationship.

Useful as such "division of labor" has been, the limitations of the separate paradigms become immediately obvious whenever more exhaustive explanation is sought. The sociocultural approach provides little or no understanding of *the processes which mediate between the state of society and the occurrence of behavior,* nor does it account in the variance, i.e., the individual differences that inevitably obtain in the relationship between society and behavior. The psychological approach fails, in its turn, to provide an account for the *distribution in society of certain kinds of personality systems,* and for the fact that similar constellations of personality attributes may result in different behavior at different times or under different circumstances. An analysis of these respective limitations makes clear that the two traditional paradigms are, in fact, logically complementary, the boundary conditions or the "givens" of each being the conceptual focus of the other. The outcome of such an analysis therefore suggests a *third,* more inclusive, paradigm which, encompassing the separate conceptual foci of the sociocultural and psychological approaches, can organize them into a single and logically coherent system. What I have just described is, of course, what is increasingly understood by the term "field theory," an approach which would seem logically capable of yielding more comprehensive explanation of a domain of behavior than either of its traditional elements.[2]

Despite the appeal of such an orientation it is obvious that most social science work retains the traditional stamp of each discipline. The most important reason for this would seem to be the absence of theoretically and empirically established coordinations between the concepts or theories of the different disciplines. Considerations such as these influenced us from the outset. The research problem—the explanation of deviance in a setting with *both* group and individual differences— seemed to be a suitable vehicle for an effort to develop and test a synthetic theoretical framework which might draw together the conceptual foci of both the sociocultural and the psychological approaches.

[2] For an excellent recent statement of the research implications of the field theoretical viewpoint, see J. M. Yinger, "Research Implications of a Field View of Personality," *American Journal of Sociology,* 68:580–592, 1963.

The Development of a Social Psychological Theory
of Deviance and Excessive Alcohol Use

A useful linkage between personality concepts and sociocultural concepts is unlikely to be accomplished arbitrarily or by the haphazard aggregation of variables. Certain properties are necessary in the concepts if a unified, coherent and systematic framework is to be achieved. Constraints are imposed on the selection of concepts by the requirement that they ultimately contribute to a workable social psychological theory.

With respect to the selection of personality concepts, at least three constraints may be mentioned. First the personality concept must be the type of abstraction which is likely to be relevant to social variations, i.e., which has obvious possibilities for coordination to sociocultural variables.[3] Second, the personality concept must have some clear-cut implication for *behavior*, since it is only through its own linkage with behavior that it illuminates the process by which sociocultural conditions can in turn be related to behavior. Finally, the concept should be amenable to measurement in ongoing social settings without requiring elaborate laboratory apparatus and experimental controls.

Parallel constraints are imposed, of course, upon the selection of sociocultural concepts—they must be readily measurable, have clear-cut implications for behavior, and, especially important, must be capable of logical or sociological coordination with personality concepts.

With these considerations in mind, we drew upon Merton's theory of anomie[4] and the Cloward-Ohlin extension of Sutherland's theory of differential association[5] for our concepts and formulation at the sociocultural level; Rotter's social learning theory of personality[6] was the

[3] In discussing some relationships between the fields of personality, sociology, and anthropology, Child states: ". . . relevance to social variations may usefully serve as one criterion for the importance of any dimension of personality . . . for limited purposes, it might be the most significant one." See I. L. Child, "Problems of Personality and Some Relations to Anthropology and Sociology," in S. Koch, ed., *Psychology: a Study of a Science*, Vol. 5, New York: McGraw-Hill, 1963, pp. 593–638; quotation from p. 628. Also, in this connection, see A. Inkeles, "Some Sociological Observations On Culture and Personality Studies," in C. Kluckhohn and H. A. Murray, eds., *Personality in Nature, Society, and Culture*, New York: Knopf, 1953, pp. 577–592; and "Personality and Social Structure," in R. K. Merton, L. Broom and L. S. Cottrell, Jr., eds., *Sociology Today: Problems and Prospects*, New York: Basic Books, 1959, pp. 249–276.

[4] R. K. Merton, *Social Theory and Social Structure*, Glencoe, Illinois: The Free Press, 1957, Chapters 4 and 5.

[5] E. H. Sutherland, *Principles of Criminology*, (4th ed.), Philadelphia: Lippincott, 1947.

[6] J. B. Rotter, *Social Learning and Clinical Psychology*, New York: Prentice-Hall, 1954.

source of our concepts and formulation at the individual level. The appropriateness of these sources to our aim of developing a *synthetic* explanatory framework will be seen shortly in the analogous relationships which obtain between the concepts at two different levels and in the exact consonance between the resulting explanatory models at each level.

Merton's theory of anomie is an effort to account for the differential distribution of deviance rates at different locations in American society. Deviant behavior is elaborated as a *socially-induced phenomenon*, the extent and distribution of which follows the topography of value-access disjunctions and anomie in society.

Merton assumes that there is in American society, differentiated though it is, a pervasive and heavy emphasis upon achievement or success values or goals—especially occupational, monetary, and material; but also interpersonal, e.g., leadership; and personal, e.g., independence. Merton asserts, further, that the institutionalized channels of access or the availability of legitimate means for achieving these pervasively emphasized culture goals are not uniformly distributed throughout the social structure; the lower social strata and certain subgroups, notably racial and ethnic, represent disadvantaged social locations. The malintegration between the cultural values and socially-structured access to these values (value-access disjunctions) generates strain or pressure toward a breakdown or attenuation of normative consensus (anomie) and toward engaging in alternative, even if illegitimate, means to achieve success or to cope with failure. The pressure is greatest where access to legitimate means to success, e.g., via education, occupation, or income, is most limited, and this is largely what accounts for the higher rates of deviance generally found in the lower socio-economic strata and among marginal ethnic and racial groups.

The primary emphasis of Merton's formulation is, thus, upon *instigation* to the use of illegitimate means as a way of adapting to value-access disjunction. Beyond instigation to deviance, value-access disjunction, when chronic or pervasive results in the attenuation of regulatory norms or in the withdrawal of legitimacy from normative controls—a state of *anomie*. The distribution of anomie in society should follow the distribution of value-access disjunctions. As far as it goes, this formulation is useful in describing a sociocultural source of instigation or pressure toward deviance and a sociocultural source of control against deviance. Such a formulation, however, remains generally applicable to *all* forms of deviance and does not specify the conditions under which delinquency or excessive alcohol use will occur, for example, rather than mental illness. It is to this latter concern that the Sutherland theory of differential association, as extended by Cloward and Ohlin,[7] is directly relevant. These authors have pointed out that access to *illegitimate* means is also differentially distributed in the social structure and that the actual adoption of certain *specific* alternatives to legitimate means is dependent, not only upon value-access pressure and normative attenuation, but also upon access to *specific kinds* of illegitimate means.

Access to illegitimate means, as a concept, can be seen to have several component dimensions. One has to do with access to the *learning* of or about illegitimate means. This stress upon learning is a salutory one which serves to encompass the effects upon behavior of differential exposure to role models of deviance, a variable obviously differentially distributed in the social structure. A second component has to do with access in the sense of differential *opportunity to perform* or engage in deviant behavior, e.g., the greater opportunity to spend time drinking when unemployed than when employed. The third component focuses upon the *differential operation of sanctioning systems* to forestall deviance or to punish it when it occurs. Social controls of this sort are relatively absent when a person is not mapped into a solidary social network as evidenced by membership in groups, church attendance, and the like. These three components of access to illegitimate means should operate to influence the *kind* of deviance occurring under value-access pressure and the degree to which such deviance tends to persist or be maintained. And access to illegitimate means, defined in these terms, should vary with location in the social structure.

Our formulation at the sociocultural level has led us, therefore, to abstract aspects of three substructures relevant to deviance and to posit the mode of their interaction in generating deviance rates.

The linkage with deviance can be expressed in the following proposition: deviance rates should be higher, other things equal, where value-access disjunction in the opportunity structure is greater, where anomie is more severe, and where access to illegitimate means is greater.

At the level of the individual, Rotter's theory provides an account for the way in which personality variables contribute to the occurrence of deviant behavior. In this theory, the occurrence of any behavior is a function of subjectively-held *expectations* that it will lead to a goal, and the subjectively-held *value* of that goal. Systems of expectations and of values build up into higher-order cognitive orientations which influence the perceived world (the life-space), and thereby affect the decision or behavior process. These systems are an outcome of experience, i.e., they are socially learned and socially patterned. They reflect not

[7] R. A. Cloward, "Illegitimate Means, Anomie, and Deviant Behavior," *American Sociological Review,* 24:164–176, 1959; and R. A. Cloward and L. E. Ohlin, *Delinquency and Opportunity: A Theory of Delinquent Gangs,* Glencoe, Illinois: The Free Press, 1960.

only the past history of experience, both success and failure, but also the present set of options perceived by the individual to be available to him, and the consequences perceived to be likely upon each option.

Three major variables derived from or elaborated within Rotter's theory will be discussed in this report. Of central significance is the concept of *personal disjunction*, a variable referring to the perceived disparity or gap between the *value* an individual places on the potential gratifications he confronts in a variety of life-areas and his *expectations* of attaining those gratifications. The concept of personal disjunction (value-expectation disjunction) is actually an analogue at the individual level of Merton's value-access disjunction at the societal level. Personal disjunctions, when high and pervasive, create intra-personal pressure toward adopting technically effective alternative behaviors, even if il-

FIGURE 1.

Sociocultural Substructures and Deviance Rates

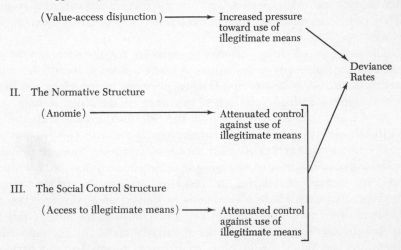

I. The Opportunity Structure

    (Value-access disjunction) ⟶ Increased pressure toward use of illegitimate means

                                          Deviance Rates

II. The Normative Structure

    (Anomie) ⟶ Attenuated control against use of illegitimate means

III. The Social Control Structure

    (Access to illegitimate means) ⟶ Attenuated control against use of illegitimate means

legitimate, to reach value goals. They also, when chronic and pervasive, influence the second major personality variable to be dealt with in this report, namely *alienation*, a concept referring to a generalized sense of meaninglessness, helplessness, hopelessness, and social isolation. Alienation also is constituted from specific expectations and reflects previous socialization and social interaction experiences. In referring to a sense of disorganization of society and a personal loss of identity with larger social units or other persons, alienation should also reflect or parallel the degree of anomie in the social milieu. Alienation should conduce to deviance since personal concern about group monitoring and the personal influence of normative controls have been attenuated. The third major personality system variable is *tolerance of deviance,* an attitudinal variable reflecting the degree of personal acceptance or tolerance of transgression. Tolerance of transgression is interpreted as an indirect measure of expectancy, i.e., of the degree to which a person expects that such behavior will be followed by punishment or negative sanctions or the degree to which he expects that deviant behavior is required in order to achieve given goals. Since attitudes are also a consequence of experience and exposure, holding a highly accepting attitude toward deviance may reflect learning conditions in which deviant behavior was widely present, was not "defined" as wrong or, more critical, was not systematically followed by punishment or the application of social controls. Since expectations of punishment or negative sanctions would, in Rotter's theory, operate to inhibit behavior, tolerance of deviance can be seen to be a crucial part of the personality process generating or inhibiting deviant behavior.

Our formulation at the individual level has led us, therefore, to abstract aspects of three personality substructures relevant to deviance and to posit the mode of their interaction in generating deviant behavior.

The relation of these personality variables to deviance can be expressed in the following proposition: deviant behavior should be more likely to occur, other things equal, when personal disjunctions are high, when alienation is high, and when tolerance of deviance is high.

At this point it is possible to see the relationships between the sociocultural and the personality formulations. First, the two models are formally identical. Each proposes a source of strain or pressure or instigation—a dynamic—toward engaging in illegitimate behavior. Each proposes two sources of control or restraint against the instigation to illegitimacy. In each model deviance is conceived of as the resultant or balance of the interaction of pressure and controls. Second, it can be seen that the elements in each model are analogues of the corresponding elements in the other model, thus enabling a logical linkage between the two models. The straightforward and direct relationship between value-access disjunction and personal disjunction, between anomie and alienation, and between access to illegitimate means and tolerance of deviance—each pair of concepts a social psychological linkage—provides the systematic basis for assessing the mediational role of personality between society and behavior.

The calculus connecting our theory to behavior is no more elegant than the usual in social science. We expect that the more variables—and the more of each variable—present, the greater the rate or likelihood of occurrence of deviance. Conversely, the fewer variables—and the less of each variable—present, the lower the rate of occurrence of deviance or the greater the rate of occurrence of likelihood of conforming behavior. This is true within the subset of sociocultural variables and within the subset of personality variables, as well as within a set which combines variables from both subsets, i.e., the "field" set or pattern.

FIGURE 2.

Personality Substructures and Deviant Behavior

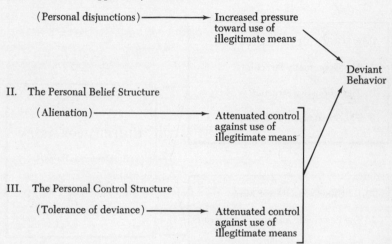

I.   The Perceived Opportunity Structure

(Personal disjunctions)⟶ Increased pressure toward use of illegitimate means

Deviant Behavior

II.   The Personal Belief Structure

(Alienation)⟶ Attenuated control against use of illegitimate means

III.   The Personal Control Structure

(Tolerance of deviance)⟶ Attenuated control against use of illegitimate means

The test of our theory then requires the establishment of the following kinds of relations:

1.   Relation between sociocultural variables and deviance.
2.   Relation between sociocultural variables and personality variables.
3.   Relation between personality variables and deviance.
4.   *Joint* relation between sociocultural and personality variables and deviance.

These relations are all diagrammed as arrows in Figure 3.

Before turning to the empirical implementation of this approach it may be useful, in forestalling misunderstanding, to make the following comments. First, the scheme as presented is not considered to constitute an exhaustive explanation of deviance. Rather it is an effort to gain a degree of conceptual control over some portion of the social and personal variance in deviance in the kind of community in which the research was carried out. Second, our use of the term "deviance" carries

with it no moral implications. Neither is it seen as necessarily dysfunctional, either socially or personally. Although a full analysis of the concept of deviance cannot be undertaken here, the term is used to refer
to a category of behaviors covering a variety of specific acts or sequences of acts departing from institutional prescription, varying at
different ages, and ranging through much of the behavior considered as
a "problem" by the norms of middle-class American society. Deviant
behaviors, like all other learned behavior, are considered to be goal-

FIGURE 3.

Theoretical Schema

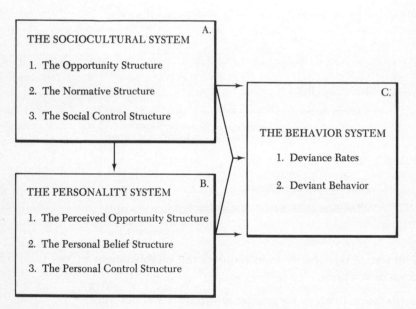

directed or functional for the actor and require no unique explanatory
principles. In short, a theory of deviance is considered to be at once a
theory of conformity.[8] Third, while the scheme has been presented with
respect to the general term, "deviance," the intent of this paper is to
apply it to certain aspects of drinking behavior which may be considered
deviant, or excessive, or social problem behavior. In the application of
the theory, excessive alcohol use is viewed as an instance of the cate-

[8] Further elaboration of this point of view may be found in A. K. Cohen, "The
Study of Social Disorganization and Deviant Behavior," R. K. Merton, L. Broom and
L. S. Cottrell, Jr., eds., *Sociology Today: Problems and Prospects,* New York: Basic
Books, 1959, pp. 461–484; and R. Jessor, "A Social Learning Approach to Culture and
Behavior," in T. Gladwin and W. C. Sturtevant, eds., *Anthropology and Human Be-
havior,* Washington, D. C.: The Anthropological Society of Washington, 1962, pp.
96–114.

gory of deviant behavior reflecting, in its occurrence, therefore, the pressure of limited access to valued goals and the relative absence of social and personal control systems.

METHODOLOGY AND RESEARCH DESIGN

In general, the research has been guided by what may be termed a "convergent validity" orientation to methodology. Convergent validity is based on the idea that the meaning of any concept is not exhausted by any particular measure and that, in order to increase the conviction that a given concept is actually accounting for a set of observations, it is necessary to "triangulate" or converge upon the concept by multiple, independent operations or procedures. To the extent that the influence of a given concept can be demonstrated in different contexts or with different phenomena, to that extent is the likelihood lessened that alternative explanations would prove adequate. This methodological orientation had several implications for the research. First, it meant that all the tests and measuring procedures had to derive from the theory and that, with almost no recourse to available standard testing procedures, an extensive program of theory-derived test and interview development had to be undertaken. Second, it required that central concepts have multiple procedures developed for their measurement. Third, it suggested the use of different kinds of measures of a concept, such as interviews, questionnaires, semi-projective measures, behavioral measures, and documentary record measures. Finally, and most fundamental, it required the carrying out of multiple and independent *studies*, each dealing with similar concepts and providing tests of the same propositions, but involving different subjects, different measures, and different kinds of deviance.

Three such separate studies were carried out in the community. Study I, the Community Survey Study, was a survey interview of a random sample of adults between the ages of 20 and 65, stratified by sex and ethnic group. The sampling ratio used for drawing names from an alphabetized census list of the community population was 1 in 6 for the Anglo and Spanish and, because of their small proportion in the community, 1 in 3 for the Indians. Interviewing was done by a team of a dozen trained interviewers over a period of three weeks. Respondents were interviewed individually by a member of the same sex and, where language seemed to be a problem among the Spanish, Spanish-speaking interviewers and a Spanish version of the interview were used. Cooperation was excellent and 96 percent of the designated respondents available in or near the community were interviewed. Only 4 percent refused after repeated contacts. Final sample size is 221, comprised of 45 Anglo males and 48 Anglo females; 30 Spanish males and 30 Spanish females; 35 Indian males and 33 Indian females. Though small in absolute numbers, the sample has the advantage of being selected randomly, of not being biased by a large refusal rate, and of being based on unusually large sampling ratios.

Study II, the High School Study, was a comprehensive and intensive investigation of the entire student population of the local senior High School which has an enrollment of 129, and involves an age range just below that studied in the Community Survey. After two successive years of development, pre-testing, and revision of procedures, a large battery of diverse measures was administered to all students and data were also collected from school records and from interviews with teachers. The measures ranged from questionnaires dealing with expectations for achievement and perceived life-chances in the opportunity structure, to sociometric schedules for nominating "trouble-makers," to the writing, supposedly as part of regular class assignments, of structured essays codable on several variables, to self-reports of drinking and deviance, to measures of ability to delay gratification.

The Community Survey Study and the High School Study each yield data on the major concerns of the theory and enable entirely independent but parallel tests of the basic propositions.

Study III, the Socialization Study, was focused on the process of preadolescent socialization and consisted of a detailed interview of nearly all the mothers and a sample of fathers of the high school students who live in the community. The concern of this study was to trace out the kinds of socialization practices and family variables likely to influence those adolescent personality attributes and behavior patterns which were measured directly in the High School Study. The Socialization Study, beyond its convergence with the other two studies, has, by virtue of its historical depth, the further advantage of making possible a stronger causal or directional inference than can legitimately be made in the two other studies which are essentially cross-sectional in nature.

Before concluding this section, a word should be said about the *sources* of data on deviance and alcohol use. In this Community Survey, the data were provided by self-report during the interview and by a comprehensive search of court records in the local, county, and district courts. In the High School Study, deviance data came from four separate and independent sources: self-reports, peer-nominations, teacher-ratings, and school records. The Socialization Study supplemented the High School data with mother-reports on their child's deviance. While there are variations depending on source of data and reflecting the usual problems with self-report, our analyses indicate that all sources are positively intercorrelated and that each source has some degree of validity.

THE CONFRONTING PROBLEM:
THE ETHNIC TOPOGRAPHY OF DEVIANCE

With this general discussion of theory, methodology and research design in mind, a return to a brief discussion of the domain of behavior which provided the impetus for and the focus of the research is in order. The primary empirical fact with which the data from the community confront us is *the relative position of the three ethnic groups with respect to deviance rates*. In Table 1, seven separate criteria or indexes relevant to ethnic rates of alcohol use are presented. Although not all independent of each other, and although only a selected set of available criteria, these indexes are fair representatives of the total situation.

TABLE 1.

Ethnic Group Percentages on Various Measures of Alcohol Use (Community Survey Data)

	Anglo (N=64)+	Spanish (N=46)+	Indian (N=53)+
1. Percentage whose drinking is usually in bars or cars	16	17	46
2. Percentage who sometimes or often drink in the morning	9	22	33
3. Percentage who were drunk 3 or more times last year	3	15	38
4. Percentage who report 5 or more occurrences of drinking-related deviance (e.g., fights while drinking, etc.)	14	15	53
5. Percentage whose overall alcohol consumption pattern is describable as "usually heavy"	2	9	26
6. Percentage whose Quantity-Frequency index is above the total group median Q-F	34	50	74
7. Percentage who report problem and/or heavy drinking in home of orientation	19	29	45

+All the drinking measures are based on *present drinkers only*. 64 out of 92 Anglos are present drinkers (70%); 46 out of 60 Spanish are present drinkers (77%); and 53 out of 66 Indians are present drinkers (80%). Note that the percentage which drinks in each ethnic group is not very different.

The fact of the relatively high position of the Indians on every criterion is the most striking. The measures take on greater meaning if it is kept in mind that the *proportion* of persons who represent drinkers in each ethnic group is quite similar (Cf. footnote to Table 1). The measures show, without exception, the higher rate of excessive or deviance-prone use of alcohol by the Indians. The Indians do more of their drinking outside the home, i.e., in bars or cars; they more often drink in the mornings; they were drunk more often during the previous year; they have more drinking-related incidents of deviance (such as getting into fights or trouble with the law because of drinking); their drinking pattern is more often heavy; and their Quantity-Frequency intake index is higher. That this is not just a recent problem may be seen in the fact that the Indians report more often coming from families of orientation where heavy- or problem-drinking was present (Measure 7). Although these measures vary in degree of refinement, their overall import cannot be doubted. Furthermore, a fairly complex and refined index—Quantity-Frequency—does yield compatible findings. The Anglo mean Q.F. is .27 ounces of absolute alcohol per day, or an average of about 3–4 drinks per week; the Spanish mean Q.F. is .60 ounces of absolute alcohol per day, or 8–9 drinks per week; and the Indian mean Q.F. is 1.86, or about 26 drinks per week. The Spanish, on the average, then, drink twice as much per unit of time as the Anglos, and the Indians drink three times as much as the Spanish.

The second most striking fact about these data is the consistently intermediate position of the Spanish. Worth noting also, in this regard, is the closer proximity of the Spanish to the Anglos rather than to the Indians on most of the alcohol use measures.

Finally, it should be emphasized that there are strong within-group differences and extremely wide ranges on nearly every measure. Sex differences on the measures are ubiquitous, with males showing higher rates than females within all three ethnic groups.

This paper has thus far presented a theoretical framework and a methodological orientation to the study of deviance and excessive alcohol use. It has also described an empirical situation in which three ethnic groups living together in a small rural community generate very different rates of deviance and excessive alcohol use.

SOME PRELIMINARY FINDINGS

It is only possible, within the scope of this paper, to take the first step in evaluating the adequacy of the formulation presented. This first step takes as its focus the relative positions of the three ethnic groups with respect to rates of excessive alcohol use. *It will attempt to show that the relative positions of the three ethnic groups on the sociocultural variables and on the personality variables are entirely consonant with their contributions to excessive alcohol use.* This kind of evidence, consonance between group rates of deviance and group averages on predictor variables, has the advantage of retaining the focus on the ethnic groups which are the salient divisions in the community. It provides descriptive data, in terms of the theoretical variables, about the main social units in the community and, in that sense, is like a theoretical ethnography. It cannot, of course, serve as a direct test of the theory in that it does not show the *necessity* of the relationship between the theoretical variables and the occurrence or non-occurrence of deviant behavior. Such a direct test of the theory, involving correlational and multi-variable pattern analyses and relying on the data from all three studies, is the concern of a book which is currently in preparation.

The first part of this section will describe the measurement of the sociocultural variables and their relation to ethnic group status. The second part will then deal with the personality variables and their ethnic group distributions. The data to be presented are taken from the Community Survey Study only.

The measurement of *access in the opportunity structure* (value-access disjunctions) relies upon two indices. The first, Socio-Economic Status (SES), is a single score based on the occupation of the breadwinner and the respondent's level of education. The higher the score the lower one's socio-economic status. The second, Objective Access (OA), is a more elaborate index of position in the opportunity structure and was influenced by the work of Meier and Bell.[9] The OA score is based upon eight dichotomized indicators of access, including age and marital status, language spoken at home, present occupation of breadwinner, education, between-generation mobility of breadwinner, religion, and social participation. The higher the score the higher one's access to opportunity. The correlation between SES and OA for the total group in the Community Survey Study (N=221) is —.73, indicating the similarity but lack of identity between the two measures. (The negative sign merely reflects that the two indices are scored in opposite directions.)

The measurement of *anomie* followed a differentiation of the concept into three types of anomie: dominant culture anomie, sub-cultural anomie, and community anomie[10] Only the first two types will be discussed here. Dominant culture anomie refers to a relative lack of censensus with the normative emphases of the dominant American culture on appropriate behavior for achieving success goals. Since the dominant culture ideally prescribes only legitimate means, any departure from the ideal—indicated by the acceptance of illegitimate means—is evidence of the lack of an authoritative normative regulatory structure and, therefore, an indication of some degree of anomie.

9 Dorothy L. Meier and W. Bell, "Anomia and Differential Access to the Achievement of Life Goals," *American Sociological Review,* 24:189–202, 1959.

10 For further details on the operationalization of the anomie concept, see P. Chassey and R. C. Hanson, "Measuring Anomie—An Analysis of the Group Norms Items on the Community Survey," Tri-Ethnic Project Research Report No. 12, University of Colorado, mimeo., March, 1963; C. Frank, "Acceptance of Illegitimate Means—A Measure of Dominant Culture Anomie," Tri-Ethnic Project Research Report No. 15, University of Colorado, mimeo., April, 1963; and R. C. Hanson and P. Chassey, "Three Types of Anomie: Theory and Measurement," Tri-Ethnic Project Research Report No. 8, University of Colorado, mimeo., March, 1962.

Dominant culture anomie was operationally defined by group averages obtained from a 16-item scale measuring acceptance of the use of illegitimate means. Each item described a situation in which a protagonist uses illegitimate means to obtain a culturally valued success goal. Respondents were asked to evaluate how wrong the behavior was on a scale from 0, "not wrong at all," through 9, the extreme of "very wrong." Items were balanced in terms of high and low status protagonists, and balanced for content concerned with violations of legal norms involving formal control sanctions versus violations of moral norms involving informal control sanctions. A sample item classified as a case of a high status protagonist violating a legal norm is: "A big rancher grazes his stock on other people's property without their permission." The more a person accepts the use of illegitimate means, the lower his score will be. The state of dominant culture anomie in the group is defined as the group average, and a lower average indicates more anomie.

Sub-cultural anomie refers to the relative lack of consensus around an ethnic group's *own* empirically-defined norms. The measure of sub-cultural anomie is derived from responses to a 21-item scale, where each item describes a common family, sex, or occupational role behavior. An example is: "A father teaches his children to have a special respect for the eldest son." For each item, respondents were asked to state whether the person holding the position "absolutely should," "should," "may or may not," "should not," "absolutely should not" engage in that behavior.[11] *Sub-cultural anomie* is operationally defined, then, as the sum of item variances exhibited by each ethnic group around its own group-defined norms, i.e., around the statistical modes of the items for each ethnic group. In addition the *strength* of a norm is defined operationally as the percentage of an ethnic group selecting the modal response category on an item. The *certainty* or predictability of a group norm was measured by an information theory statistic, relative entropy.[12]

The measurement of *access to illegitimate means* was concerned with the three previously mentioned components: Exposure to deviant role models (whether the respondent, in his family of orientation, was exposed to heavy problem drinking, to family fights, to family members in trouble with the law, etc.); opportunity to engage in deviance (unemployed status, living in town, etc.); and absence of social controls (no formal group membership, no informal visiting, low church attendance,

---

[11] The procedure used for defining group norms follows the work of N. Gross, W. S. Mason, and A. W. McEachern, in *Explorations in Role Analysis,* New York: Wiley and Sons, 1958.

[12] F. Attneave, *Applications of Information Theory to Psychology,* New York: Holt, 1959, p. 9.

living unattached to a spouse or a family of orientation, etc.). These items can be combined to a single score, the higher the score the greater the access to illegitimate means.

It is now possible to examine the relative positions of the three ethnic groups on these sociocultural variables. Means and t-tests are presented in Table 2.

Part A of Table 2 shows clearly that the Anglo group has, as expected, significantly greater access in the opportunity structure than either of the non-Anglo groups. This is true for both the SES and the

TABLE 2.

Ethnic Group Means on Major Sociocultural Variables (Community Survey Study)

	Anglo	Spanish	Indian	A vs S	A vs I	S vs I
A. *Value-Access Disjunction*						
1. Socioeconomic status[+]	33.9	52.0	45.5	+++	+++	++
2. Objective access	6.0	3.4	3.8	++++	++++	NS
B. *Anomie*						
1. Dominant culture anomie[+]	105.9	100.5	88.1	NS	+++	+++
2. Sub-cultural anomie						
a. Variance around mode	10.57	17.73	17.66	++	+++	NS
b. Number of modes with greatest certainty (relative entropy)	8	11	2			
C. *Access to Illegitimate Means*	3.2	4.1	5.3	++++	++++	++++

+ = The lower the score, the *higher* the amount of the variable. For all other variables the lower the score, the *lower* the amount of the variable.
  ++ = mean differences are significant at $\leqslant$ .05 level
  +++ = $\leqslant$ .01 level
  ++++ = $\leqslant$ .001 level

OA measures. Among the non-Anglos, the Indian group, contrary to what might be expected from their relative rates of excessive alcohol use, have somewhat greater access to opportunity than the Spanish on one of the two measures, SES.

Part B shows that both the Anglo group and the Spanish group have significantly less dominant culture anomie than the Indians. With respect to sub-cultural anomie, the Anglo group has significantly less anomie than either the Spanish or the Indian group. While there is no difference between the two non-Anglo groups when the variance measure (*a*) is used, a clear difference emerges when number of modes with greatest certainty (*b*) is considered, with the Spanish showing more frequent consensus around its own norms than the Indians.

Part C of Table 2 indicates that the three ethnic groups are significantly different from each other, in the order expected, with respect to access to illegitimate means.

To summarize these findings, the Anglos have the greatest access in the opportunity structure, the least anomie, and the least access to illegitimate means. This is consonant with their least contribution to the rates of excessive alcohol use. Of the two non-Anglo groups, the Spanish have somewhat less access to opportunity than the Indians (as measured by SES, but not by OA), but significantly less dominant culture anomie, less sub-cultural anomie (as measured by number of modes with greatest certainty), and significantly less access to illegitimate means than the Indians. The Spanish, then, despite their somewhat lower socio-economic position, appear to be located in a more solidary community with greater repudiation of deviance and controls against its occurrence. They are, therefore, subject to less *total* pressure toward deviance than the Indians. This is consonant with their lesser contribution to rates of excessive alcohol use than that of the Indians. In summary, the sociocultural variables successfully order the three ethnic groups in the same way as they are ordered by their contributions to rates of deviance or excessive alcohol use. The findings are clearest with respect to the Anglos versus the non-Anglos. Within the non-Anglos, the data suggest that the Spanish occupy the more favorable sociocultural position with respect to the *overall* balance of factors conducing to deviance.

The same kind of analysis just completed with respect to sociocultural variables can now be undertaken with respect to the major personality variables. The measurement of psychological *disjunction* in the community was a derived score, based on how much *value* subjects placed on twenty-four general goals varying across different need and life-areas, and how strongly they *expected* to achieve these goals. A disjunction was counted for each goal considered "very important" or "important" by the subject which he was "not too sure" or "not sure at all" of attaining. The greater the number of disjunctions, the higher the score.

The measurement of *alienation* used was based on a series of thirteen statements expressing either a sense of helplessness, normlessness and hopelessness, or the opposite, a feeling of personal efficacy and optimism.[13] For example, the first item states: "I often feel that people around here are not too friendly." For each item subjects were asked whether they "strongly agree," "agree," "disagree," or "strongly disagree" with the statement. These responses were then scored from zero to three, with a high score indicating a high degree of alienation.

[13] The content of this scale has some similarity to the content of the Srole anomia scale. See L. Srole, "Social Integration and Certain Corollaries: An Exploratory Study," *American Sociological Review*, 21:709–716, 1956.

For the measurement of *tolerance of deviance* subjects were asked to rate along a ten-point scale how wrong they felt it was to engage in each of twelve deviant acts with regard to work, alcohol use, sex, child-care, etc. Zero indicates that the subject felt "no wrong" attached to the act, nine indicated "very wrong." A high score, therefore, represents a high repudiation of deviance.

The relative positions of the three ethnic groups on these three personality variables can be examined in Table 3.

These results are very much in accord with the findings in Table 2 on the sociocultural variables. Both the Spanish and Indians in our community occupy a relatively disfavored position in the opportunity structure, and as can be seen, this is consonant with the relatively high personal disjunctions found among these two groups. Similarly, both minority groups display a relatively high lack of normative consensus within their own groups, and again this is consonant with significantly

TABLE 3.

Ethnic Group Means on Major Personality Variables (Community Survey Study)

	Anglo	Spanish	Indian	A vs S	A vs I	S vs I
A. Total personal disjunctions	2.8	5.7	5.7	++++	++++	NS
B. Alienation	15.7	19.3	18.7	++++	++++	NS
C. Tolerance of deviance+	79.8	86.5	72.6	++	++	++++

+ = On this variable, the lower the score the *greater* the amount of the variable. On the other two variables, the lower the score the *lower* the amount of the variable.
++ = mean differences are significant at ≤ .05 level
+++ = ≤ .01 level
++++ = ≤ .001 level

stronger individual feelings of alienation than are found among the Anglos. Finally, both Anglos and Spanish are lodged within a stronger social control system than the Indians. This social fact is in accord with the greater individual repudiation of deviant behavior among members of these two groups, though the Spanish subjects actually repudiate deviance more strongly than their relative access to illegitimate means score would lead one to expect. In general, it can be said that a rough concurrence appears to exist between the magnitude of various sociocultural variables impinging differentially upon these three ethnic groups and the magnitude of psychological variables characterizing these groups. Having demonstrated this concurrence, it becomes possible to consider the personality variables as *mediating* between the sociocultural variables and deviant behavior.

Further, there is an observable consonance between the ordering of the ethnic groups on these personality variables and their contribution to rates of excessive alcohol-use. The Anglos again appear to be in the theoretically most benign position (least disjunctions and least alienation), the Spanish next (greater repudiation of deviance than either the Anglos or the Indians), and the Indians in the least benign position (high disjunctions, high alienation, and highest tolerance of deviance). This accords completely with the fact of their relative contribution to deviance rates, the Indians being the highest of the three ethnic groups. This section may be concluded by summarizing what has been shown. Given our knowledge of the different ethnic group rates of deviance and excessive alcohol use, we undertook to see whether the ethnic groups varied in a similar fashion with respect to the sociocultural and personality variables in our theory. Following their relative contribution to deviance rates, the Anglos should occupy the theoretically more benign position, the Indians the theoretically more malignant position, and the Spanish an intermediate position on the variables. An examination of mean scores provided strong confirmation of this expectation for both the sociocultural and personality variables.

These results, as remarked earlier, do not constitute a direct test of the explanatory role of our theoretical formulation. They do make clear, however, that the variables dealt with have relevance to the empirical phenomena—they vary as expected with measured rates of drinking behavior and they characterize the ethnic groups relative to each other in accord with our expectations. The results are of further interest in that they show that the distribution of the personality variables is consonant with the distribution of the sociocultural variables. There is, in short, empirical evidence for the previously posited social-psychological linkages and there is provided a logical basis for treating the personality variables as mediating between society and behavior. Finally, the results make clear that it is possible to operationalize and to measure each of the major variables in the theoretical scheme: value-access disjunction, anomie, and access to illegitimate means at the sociocultural level and personal disjunctions, alienation, and tolerance of deviance at the personality level. Beyond the initial encouragement yielded by the results presented, their most exciting implication is the possibility now at hand for a direct test of a social psychology of excessive alcohol-use.*

* A full report of the findings of the Tri-Ethnic Research Project has since appeared. See: R. Jessor, T. D. Graves, R. C. Hanson, and Shirley Jessor, *Society, Personality, and Deviant Behavior: a Study of a Tri-Ethnic Community,* New York, Holt, Rinehart and Winston, 1968.

SUMMARY

This paper has taken as its focus a selected aspect of a larger community study of deviant behavior. The present concern with drinking behavior, or, more particularly, excessive alcohol use, has been approached from the point of view of the larger study, i.e., the general formulation about deviance has been applied to the specific analysis of drinking. The explanatory formulation emphasizes that excessive alcohol use, like other forms of deviant behavior, may be viewed as an adaptation to strain or pressure in both the social and the personality systems. Such pressure is generated by deprivation or limited access to the achievement of valued goals. The extent to which and the kind of deviance engaged in as an adaptation to such pressure depends upon certain social and personal controls reflecting past socialization and the present social condition.

With full recognition that this can only be a partial account of deviance or excessive alcohol use, an effort was made to test the theory by initiating a research project in a small tri-ethnic community in southwestern Colorado. Theory-derived measures were applied in three separate studies, each serving as an independent test of the theory. Data from one of the studies, a community survey of the adult population, were considered in this paper.

The findings, although still preliminary, have given strong initial support to our conceptualizations. Taking ethnic group differences as the analytical focus, we have been able to show a clear consonance between ethnic group rates of excessive alcohol use, on the one hand, and the ethnic group distributions on our major explanatory variables. Thus the Anglo ethnic group, which makes the least contribution to drinking rates, has the highest access in the opportunity structure, the lowest sub-cultural anomie, the lowest dominant culture anomie, and is located within the strongest social control system. The Indian group, which makes the greatest contribution to rates of excessive alcohol use, clearly demonstrates the opposite pattern. And the Spanish group, intermediate in drinking, tends to occupy an intermediate position on these variables; despite somewhat lower access to the opportunity structure than the Indians, the Spanish are located in a much stronger social control structure. This is best evidenced by their dominant culture anomie scores which are not significantly different from those of the Anglo group. Distributions on the personality variables, reflecting the sociocultural influences, evidence a similar consonance.

While such evidence as presented is encouraging in its own right, its major import lies in the fact that we are now at the point where a

comprehensive and direct assessment of the explanatory value of our
formulations can be made. If the promise thus far can be fulfilled, we
may be in possession of the initial outlines of a social psychology of
excessive alcohol use.

19

Richard A. Ball

An Empirical Exploration of Neutralization
Theory

Sociological theories of crime and delinquency, emphasizing the etiological importance of social factors, have been characterized by one
major deficiency: these theories do not satisfactorily explain why one
individual does and another does not succumb to various pressures
toward delinquency. This problem suggests that more adequate formulations must somehow take cognizance of personal factors. The persistent failure of sociological theories to deal with a "readiness" or "self"
factor was explicitly recognized years ago. At that time, Reckless called
for a reformulation of theories to take account of "differential response"
to similar social pressures.[1]

A recent formulation which appears to incorporate the recognition of a self factor in delinquent behavior is the "neutralization theory" advanced by Sykes and Matza.[2] According to their statement,
norms are not to be conceived as categorical imperatives but rather
as qualified guidelines for a *zone* of acceptable behavior. The particular
norms embodied in law have undergone considerable specification, and
these specifications include completely or partially extenuating circumstances as, for example, in the principle of *mens rea*. Thus, the legal
code itself supplies potential rationalization for violation.

Sykes and Matza maintain that much delinquency is based upon

From *Criminologica*, 4 (August, 1966), by permission of the author and the
publishers.
[1] Walter C. Reckless, *The Etiology of Delinquent and Criminal Behavior* (New
York: Social Science Research Council, Bulletin 50, 1943), 51–52.
[2] Gresham M. Sykes and David Matza, "Techniques of Neutralization: A Theory
of Delinquency," *American Sociological Review*, 22, 6, (December 1957), 664–673.

such justifications.[3] They contend that, while excuses are usually considered to be rationalizations following violation, they might also be viewed as neutralizations which occur prior to deviant behavior. That is, the actor learns certain excuses or justifications for violation and is therefore able to violate the very norms to which he is at least partially committed. The following major "techniques of neutralization" were specified: (1) the denial of responsibility, (2) the denial of injury, (3) the denial of the victim, (4) the condemnation of the condemners, and (5) the appeal to higher loyalties.

The research reported here was designed as a preliminary exploration of the neutralization theory, and it must be emphasized that the study provides no complete test. The theory asserts that (a) delinquents accept the techniques of neutralization and (b) this acceptance facilitates violation by neutralizing the norms. The present study explores the first assertion. Assessment of the second will require a longitudinal design beyond the limitations of this study. The essential hypothesis was that delinquent boys would accept more justifications for violation of law than would nondelinquent boys. Since there is apparently no single conception of delinquency which satisfies all students of the problem, three of the more common definitions were employed. The use of such definitions seemed most suitable at this stage of research.

CONSTRUCTION OF A NEUTRALIZATION INVENTORY

Since Sykes and Matza describe the techniques of neutralization as ". . . a system of beliefs and attitudes . . .,"[4] it seemed most desirable to attempt to measure neutralization by means of an attitude inventory. Such inventories are frequently criticized on grounds that (1) they elicit responses to highly generalized items which respondents may interpret differently, and (2) that such general responses have too little relationship to the overt behavior of respondents. The present study adopts the view of attitude which insists upon closer specification of the subject-object referents. Thus, Sherif and Cantril have argued that "attitudes are always related to definite stimuli or stimulus situations."[5] The neutralization inventory was therefore constructed so as to present the respondent with fairly specific stimulus situations.

Ten specific situations were developed, each describing the commission of some offense by a sixteen-year-old boy. Both personal and

[3] A more recent exposition of Matza's thinking is presented in David Matza, *Delinquency and Drift,* (New York: John Wiley and Sons, 1964). Certain valuable leads are contained there, but the present study is based explicitly on the original article.
[4] *Ibid.,* 670.
[5] Mazafer Sherif and Hadley Cantril, *The Psychology of Ego-Involvements: Social Attitudes and Identification,* (New York: John Wiley and Sons, 1947), 19.

property offenses were represented, and the offenses were intended to reflect a rough continuum of severity. These variations were considered especially desirable as a means of increasing sensitivity (discrimination). The situations were written for sixth grade reading level and checked against published reading lists. In order to locate these situations along the assumed continuum of severity, the schedule of 10 situations was administered to a sample of 203 college students. The students were asked to rank the 10 situations, in terms of "seriousness" *as they felt their mothers would rank them.* Perceived ranking by the mother was obtained because her opinion seemed more likely to reflect conventional morality.

An exhaustive set of 790 items was prepared, an average of approximately 80 items for each of the 10 situations. Each item presented an excuse (neutralization) for the infractious behavior specified in the particular situation to which it pertained.[6]

The 790 items were then submitted to five judges for a "jury opinion" as to validity.[7] Judges were requested to rate each item as follows: "VD" (very definitely indicates a neutralization technique), "D" (definitely indicates a neutralization technique), "F" (fair indication of a neutralization technique), "N" (does not indicate a neutralization technique), and "DN" (definitely does not indicate a neutralization technique). In addition, the judges were instructed to edit or eliminate any item considered "ambiguous, incomplete, verbose, irrelevant, inconsistent, or in any other way unsatisfactory." General comments and suggestions were solicited. An item was retained only if all judges agreed that it "definitely" or "very definitely" represented neutralization.

The final inventory was reduced to 4 situations representing different points along the continuum of offense "seriousness" as defined by the 203 students' perceptions of mothers' rankings. The 4 situations included an equal number of personal and property offenses. Ten items (with the highest "neutralization ratings" given by the judges) were listed under each of the behavior situations. The inventory was intensively pretested with 5 fifteen and sixteen-year-old boys in detention at the Juvenile Center, Columbus, Ohio, in order to determine their com-

6 No attempt was made to identify an item specifically with one of the five techniques of neutralization. It was feared that such a method might result in arbitrary rejection of potentially powerful items which fit the theory but overlapped two or more of the techniques.

7 Judges came from the Department of Sociology and Anthropology, The Ohio State University. They included two professors with specialities in criminology and deviant behavior, two professors with special competencies in research methods, and one advanced graduate student specializing in criminology. Each judge was given a reproduction of Sykes and Matza's original article, the set of 790 items subsumed under the 10 situations, and a set of instructions requesting him to rate each item according to how well it indicated neutralization as defined by Sykes and Matza.

prehension of the verbal statements and any reluctance to respond or to disguise attitudes.[8]

ADMINISTRATION

The completed neutralization inventory formed the first part of a schedule which also included a set of items from the M.M.P.I., the Srole Scale (anomia), an "Index of Incipient Alienation," an inventory of self reported delinquency, and a background information section.[9]

After completion of the neutralization inventory, and subsequent to its administration to the high school boys, the author learned that another attempt was being made to devise an index of neutralization, for administration to the institutionalized delinquents only. This instrument was attached to the original schedule.[10] It was felt that some additional evidence of validity might be gained from the correlation of scores on the two independently prepared measures.

Data were obtained for two separate groups of adolescent boys. One group consisted of 197 boys from Central High School, Columbus, Ohio. The second group included 200 boys enrolled in the academic program at the Fairfield School for Boys, Lancaster, Ohio. (The latter is a state institution for male juvenile delinquents.) It was felt that a more meaningful comparison could be made by sampling from this particular segment of the institutionalized population. The two groups, with age ranges from fifteen to eighteen, were virtually identical in age

[8] The five boys were randomly selected. An intensive pretest with a careful probing of each boy's understanding of every item was considered more desirable than a cursory survey of responses from a large number of boys.

[9] Hathaway and Monachesi have reported the specific M.M.P.I. items as those discovered to be most closely associated with delinquency. See Starke R. Hathaway and Elio D. Monachesi, *Adolescent Personality and Behavior*, (Minneapolis: The University of Minnesota Press, 1963), 89–90.

The Srole Scale (anomia) is widely used to determine the degree to which the individual feels that (1) social leaders are indifferent to his problems, (2) there is little chance for accomplishment in what is an unpredictable society, (3) goals are receding from him, (4) no one can really be counted on to support him, and (5) life itself is meaningless and futile. See Leo Srole, "Social Integration and Certain Corollaries: An Exploratory Study," *American Sociological Review*, Vol. 21, No. 6 (December 1956), 709–716.

The "Index of Incipient Alienation" is designed to indicate early developmental stages of alienation in which the adolescent becomes estranged from proximate social systems. See William H. Jarrett and Archibald O. Haller, "Situational and Personal Antecedents of Incipient Alienation: An Exploratory Study," *Genetic Psychology Monographs*, Vol. 69 (1964), 670–677.

The inventory of self-reported delinquency was based on a 7-item scale developed by Nye and Short. One item of the 7-item scale had to be deleted to insure that the instrument could be used with the intended respondents. The abridged inventory was used as one operational measure of delinquency. See F. Ivan Nye and James F. Short, Jr., "Scaling Delinquent Behavior," *American Sociological Review*, Vol. 22, No. 3 (June 1957), 326–331.

[10] This instrument was prepared by Terry Nesbit, Ohio University, Athens, Ohio.

distribution. All respondents were working class boys; the North-Hatt Score distributions were nearly identical for the two groups.[11]

Since even an initial exploration of hypotheses regarding neutralization would be of little value without a reasonably reliable and valid measure of neutralization, an analysis of the neutralization inventory was undertaken prior to testing of hypotheses. Reliability was established by use of the Kuder Richardson Formula.[12]

Although, according to the consensus of the judges, the inventory appeared to possess face validity, additional evidence was sought. Correlations, obtained between the neutralization inventory and the various measures discussed above, tended to substantiate the claim for reasonable validity of the former.[13]

FINDINGS

The essence of Sykes and Matza's theory lies in the hypothesized connection between two variables—neutralization and delinquency. Neutralization was operationally defined in terms of scores on the neutralization inventory; for purposes of this study three different definitions of delinquency were employed, each of which represents an admittedly oversimplified dichotomy of "delinquents" and "nondelinquents." Again, it seemed advisable to employ these gross distinctions during an initial exploration. For similar reasons, two-tailed t-tests were used throughout as difference tests.

Following a simple dichotomy between boys committed to an institution (delinquents) and those not in such an institution (nonde-

[11] For purposes of the study, working class was defined as a score of 70 or below on an interpolated North-Hatt Scale. See "The North-Hatt Scale" (mimeographed report, The Ohio State University, Columbus, n.d.).

[12] See G. F. Kuder and M. W. Richardson, "The Theory of Estimation of Test Reliability," *Psychometrika*, 1937, 151–160. Reliability coefficients were computed for the total neutralization inventory and for each of the four sub-scales (individual situations with a set of ten items respectively). The reliability coefficient for the entire inventory was .98; reliability coefficients for the subscales were .91, .95, .92, and .94 respectively.

[13] Since neutralization is theoretically associated with other variables, scores on a valid neutralization inventory should be positively correlated with scores on inventories designed to measure these other variables (assuming their validity). On the other hand, extremely high correlations might suggest that the inventories were measuring essentially the same variable. To provide some modest supplementary evidence regarding validity, Pearsonian correlation coefficients were computed for the two samples separately. For the high school boys correlation between the neutralization inventory and the M.M.P.I. items, Index of Incipient Alienation, and the Srole Scale were .46, .17, and .33 respectively. For the institutionalized delinquents correlation between the neutralization inventory and the other measures were .36, .28, and .41 respectively. The coefficients are statistically significant (P < .05). It appears that these instruments do measure variables related to, but different from, that measured by the neutralization inventory, although correlations between the latter and the Index of Incipient Alienation were lower than expected.

linquents) comparisons were made between the Central High School group and the Fairfield School group. The institutionalized delinquents scored significantly higher (P<.001) on the neutralization inventory, and on each of its four subscales, than did the high school boys. There was no significant difference between the scores of older (17–18 years old) and younger (15–16 years old) boys within each group. Negro boys tended to score somewhat higher than did the white boys in the same group, but the difference was statistically significant (P<.05) on two subscales only. Since the computation of so many difference tests increases the probability of obtaining one or more which will be statistically significant, these findings were regarded as highly tentative.

While they do not establish any clear connection between neutralization and race, the findings do suggest that race should be controlled in the analysis of neutralization scores. Taking white boys only, the results showed that the institutionalized delinquents scored significantly higher (P<.01) on the neutralization inventory, and each of its four subscales, than did the high school boys. Similarly, the Negro institutionalized delinquents scored significantly higher (P<.01) on the neutralization inventory, and on each subscale, than did the Negro high school boys. The differences apparently hold regardless of race.

Fifty of the 197 high school boys, while not meeting the criterion of institutionalization, did themselves report juvenile court appearances. Since delinquency has frequently been defined in terms of juvenile court appearances, a second definition was employed. The second definition of delinquency was based not only upon institutionalization, but also upon self reported court appearances.

The neutralization theory would lead one to hypothesize significant differences between the high school boys reporting court appearances and those reporting none. This hypothesis was substantiated; the high school boys reporting juvenile court appearances scored significantly higher (P<.001) on the neutralization inventory, and on each of its subscales, than did the high school boys reporting no appearances. The Negro high school boys reporting court appearances scored significantly higher (P<.01) than those Negro boys reporting no appearances; the white high school boys reporting appearances scored significantly higher (P<.01) than those white boys reporting no such appearances. The differences, then, hold within each racial category.

In an effort to explore further than relation of court appearances to neutralization, the institutionalized delinquents were subdivided into two groups, by dichotomizing at the median number of reported juvenile court appearances. No significant differences appeared, either on the neutralization inventory or any of its four subscales, between the institutionalized boys reporting "many" and those reporting "few" juvenile court appearances. There were no significant differences between the Negro institutionalized delinquents with "few" and those with "many" appearances, and there were no significant differences between the white institutionalized delinquents with "few" and those with "many" court appearances.

To probe still further, comparisons were made between the scores of all high school boys reporting some juvenile court appearances and the institutionalized delinquents reporting few (below the median number for all the institutionalized boys) such appearances. Again, no significant differences appeared. The findings were essentially the same when the two racial categories were kept separate. There were no significant differences, either on the total neutralization inventory or on any of its four subscales, between the Negro high school boys reporting some appearances and Negro institutionalized delinquents reporting few appearances. No significant difference appeared between the two groups of white boys, with one exception. A significant difference ($P<.05$) appeared on one subscale only. This single exception offers no substantial support for a hypothesis of neutralization differences, especially in view of the increased probability resulting from so many computations.

Since both institutional commitment and self reported court involvements fail to take account of intervening variables such as detection, willingness to report, and willingness to hold for court action, a third definition of delinquency was also employed. The third definition of delinquency was based on self reported involvement in delinquent behavior. The problem of the delinquent-nondelinquent dichotomy becomes especially obvious here, since few of the boys were expected to be so "good" as to report no violations at all.

To provide for direct comparison with the findings previously discussed, all 397 boys were placed in one of two categories by dichotomizing at the median of scores on the abridged Nye-Short scale of self reported delinquency. These two categories were referred to as "more seriously delinquent" boys and "less seriously delinquent" boys, respectively.

The neutralization theory would lead one to expect a significant difference in neutralization scores for the two groups of boys. This hypothesis is supported by the findings. The boys with many self reported delinquent acts scored significantly higher ($P<.001$) on the neutralization inventory, and on each of its four subscales, than did the boys with few self reported violations.

Since it seemed conceivable that these differences might hold for one racial category but not another, separate tests were again made for white and Negro boys. All white boys in the study were divided into two categories, by dichotomizing the white respondents at the median scores on the abridged Nye-Short scale. The findings indicated that the more seriously delinquent white boys (above the median for whites) scored significantly higher (P<.001) on the neutralization inventory and on each of the four subscales, than did the less seriously delinquent (below the median for whites) white boys. The more seriously delinquent Negro boys (above the median Negro score on the abridged Nye-Short scale) scored significantly higher (P<.001) on the neutralization inventory and on each of its four subscales than did their less seriously delinquent (below the median) counterparts. The differences, then, hold within each racial category.

CONCLUSIONS

Summarized in terms of an admittedly oversimplified dichotomy, the results of this study reinforce the general argument that "delinquents" tend to accept more excuses for a variety of offenses than do "non-delinquents." Specifically, the differences appear for both personal and property offenses, and along a continuum of severity, no matter whether the "delinquent" is defined as a boy who has been committed to an institution or one who has reported a high incidence of delinquent behavior. If juvenile court appearances are used to define delinquency the findings suggest greater acceptance of these excuses for boys with such appearances, but no significant differences with the occurrence of institutionalization or between institutionalized boys with "few" and those with "many" appearances.[14] It may be that acceptance of excuses facilitates initial stages of delinquency, while other factors more adequately explain the persistence and severity of delinquency.

These findings, then, support Sykes and Matza's assertion that delinquents will accept the techniques of neutralization more than will nondelinquents. The data do not allow us to specify whether the excuses are accepted before, during, or after delinquency. The next logical step would be to investigate the assertion that acceptance of these excuses precedes delinquency and makes it possible.

Sykes and Matza's statement is not only a theory of neutralization: it is also an explicit denial of Cohen's "delinquency subculture" thesis. The neutralization theory maintains that most delinquents do not adhere to a different (subcultural) set of norms, but rather that they basically adhere to the conventional norms while accepting many justifications

---

[14] Although the distribution of self-reported appearances did reflect what was known from the records of the boys, the requirement of respondent anonymity made it impossible to verify the self reports individually. No attempt was made to identify the nature of the offense which led to a specific court appearance. It is, of course, possible to argue that a boy reporting one appearance for a serious offense is "more delinquent" than another boy reporting five appearances for minor offenses (who may have actually been innocent of one or more charges). The reported court appearance is thus a very gross index of delinquency, but one suitable for exploration.

for deviance. In this sense, the norms have been "eroded" but not substantially replaced. The findings tend to support this position. Possible scores on the neutralization inventory range from 40 to 200, yet the mean score for all institutionalized delinquents was only 111. While these findings cannot be generalized to the entire population of institutionalized delinquents, they indicate that the attitudes of boys in the specific sample were not as deviant as the "delinquent subculture" thesis suggests. In fact, if adherence to a set of norms is viewed as a continuum extending from total commitment to rejection and substitution, the boys' attitudes were not even as far into "neutralization" as might have been expected.[15]

While referring to techniques of neutralization as a "theory" of delinquency, Sykes and Matza clearly recognized that neutralization could be considered as one component of some more general "theory." Differential association theory was mentioned in the original article, but Matza has come to view this and other sociological theories as overly deterministic.[16] Actually, certain theoretical clarifications make it *possible* to incorporate neutralization into at least one more general theory of delinquency, and to use the above data as an indirect test of this more general theory.

The support for Sykes and Matza's neutralization theory may be interpreted as support for Reckless' and Shoham's "norm erosion" thesis, and at a more general level, as support for Reckless' "containment theory."[17] The containment theory stresses the chances of becoming involved in delinquency or crime. The basic contribution of this approach lies in its blending of self factors (inner containment) with social factors (outer containment). The theory is regarded as noncausal; "good" inner and "good" outer containments minimize the chance of delinquency involvement, while "poor" inner and "poor" outer containments produce the highest expectancy for delinquency. Containment theory applies only to the broad "middle range" of delinquency: "extreme personal disorders and extreme identification with a delinquent subculture" are specifically excluded.[18]

Containment theory has been cast at a very general level. The

---

[15] Matza has recently suggested that the individual delinquent may not be as committed to delinquency as he appears, but may rather be responding to misunderstandings which have led him to believe that his companions are highly committed. (See Matza, *op. cit.*, pp. 50–59.)

[16] *Ibid.*, pp. 1–32.

[17] See Walter C. Reckless, *The Crime Problem* (New York: Appleton-Century-Crofts, 1961), 332–333; Walter C. Reckless, "A Non-causal Explanation: Containment Theory," *Excerpta Criminologica*, Vol. 2, No. 2, 1962, 131–134; Walter C. Reckless and Shlomo Shoham, "Norm Containment Theory as Applied to Delinquency and Crime," *Excerpta Criminologica*, Vol. 3, No. 6, 1963, 1–9.

[18] Some confusion may be resolved by emphasizing that containment theory is built on the concept of "risk" rather than pure determinism.

subsuming nature of the approach is an asset: it attempts to pull together previously separate and ostensibly discordant explanations. Yet such efforts at generalization often end in deceptive generality. The "theory" which purports to explain so much may explain nothing. Any explanation should be divisible into connected propositions which may be posed as researchable hypotheses. Thus, attempts have been made to identify, measure, and relate the various self factors which together form "inner containment."[19] The theory has never been considered as complete and "closed."

Reckless and Shoham have recently suggested that "norm erosion" (the sloughing off of the moral significance of norms, the neutralization of the oughtness, the emancipation from internalized norms, etc.) is one important factor operating to reduce the holding power of inner containment. A variety of processes (e.g. incipient alienation, alienation, anomia, neutralization, etc.) might be expected to contribute to any such erosion, and the major source of this erosion might vary with different categories of actors.

Rather than indicating that neutralization is the single factor leading to delinquency, the findings may be interpreted as suggesting that *neutralization is one self factor which, in contributing to norm erosion, weakens inner containment and increases the risk of delinquency.*[20] This conclusion seems preferable. Delinquency consists of many different kinds of behavior, and it seems probably that different combinations of self factors, along with outer containments, will be associated with these different forms of delinquency. It is possible that neutralization is the most significant of these self factors for certain forms of gang delinquency (where the excuses may be learned and accepted) but less important as an explanation of lone delinquency. It is possible that neutralization will characterize some gang members, while a few may actually have inverted the norms in the manner suggested by Cohen's delinquent subculture hypothesis.

[19] See Walter C. Reckless, Simon Dinitz, and Ellen Murray, "Self Concept as an Insulator Against Delinquency," *American Sociological Review,* 21, 6 (December 1956), 744–746; Simon Dinitz, Frank R. Scarpitti, and Walter C. Reckless, "Delinquency Vulnerability: A Cross Group and Longitudinal Analysis," *American Sociological Review,* 27, 4 (August 1962), 515–517; Frank R. Scarpitti, "Differential Socialization: The Delinquent Versus the Nondelinquent" (unpublished doctoral thesis, The Ohio State University, 1962); Judson R. Landis, "Social Class Differentials in Self, Value, and Opportunity Orientation as Related to Delinquency Potential" (unpublished doctoral thesis, The Ohio State University, 1962).

[20] This conclusion is supported by the findings, which show that the M.M.P.I. items, the Srole Scale, and the Index of Incipient Alienation also distinguished between the high school boys and the institutionalized delinquents. Other studies have discovered still different self factors which seem to be associated with delinquency, and some investigations have indicated that self factors may actually vary among types of delinquents. See, for example, John W. Kinch, "Self Conceptions of Types of Delinquents," *Sociological Inquiry,* 32 (Spring 1962), 228–234.

This study is considered only a rough preliminary step to further investigation of neutralization. Such research will probably require improved measures of neutralization, more sophisticated definitions of delinquency, and statistical techniques beyond simple difference tests. Above all, further research must specify whether acceptance of various justifications does in fact precede and effectively facilitate delinquency.

20

Peter M. Hall

Identification with Delinquent Subculture and Level of Self-Evaluation*

Two theoretical approaches which have been useful in the study of juvenile delinquency are a psychological one emphasizing the consequences of inadequate family relationships, and a sociological one emphasizing deviant subcultural resolutions of social structural strains. Inasmuch as these approaches appear to be divergent, or at least to view the same object from different perspectives, they have sometimes been thought to be mutually exclusive. A resolution of these supposed differences can be accomplished by utilizing the process of identification to examine the career of the juvenile delinquent.

It is often argued that juvenile delinquents possess low estimations of themselves due to parental rejection and deprivation. For example, from Healy and Bronner's finding that 92 percent of a sample of delinquents felt rejected and unloved by their parents, as compared to only 13 percent of their non-delinquent siblings, it was concluded that these feelings led to a general sense of inadequacy and a low level of self-evaluation, which in turn were important in producing delin-

From *Sociometry*, **29** (June 1966), 146–158, by permission of the author and the American Sociological Association.

* This paper is based on a dissertation submitted in partial fulfillment of the requirements for the Ph.D. degree at the University of Minnesota (December 1963), entitled *The Self-Conception of Juvenile Delinquents: A Symbolic Interactionist Approach.* The study was supported in part by a fellowship from the Ford Foundation and a NIMH traineeship grant. The writer wishes to acknowledge the support and advice of Arnold M. Rose, Roy G. Francis and Gregory P. Stone of the University of Minnesota. The critical comments of Donald Cressey and David Gold, University of California, Santa Barbara, and of William Erbe, the State University of Iowa, were extremely helpful. I am also indebted to Hugh F. Cline, University of California, Santa Barbara, for his methodological advice.

quency.[1] Those individuals who became delinquent were seeking emotional satisfactions that they could not find in their home environment. This psychological view of the delinquent has been supported by the Gluecks, Aichhorn, Redl and Wineman, among others.[2]

Recent sociological views, by contrast, suggest that the delinquent has joined a delinquent subculture as a solution to the problem of adjustment often arising because of the disadvantaged position of the working class vis-à-vis the dominant middle class.[3] This perspective places the delinquent in a special world which has its own anti-social set of meanings and values to guide perceptions, motivate actions, and provide statuses and identities. Participation in this delinquent subculture allows the delinquent to gain a high estimation of himself by engaging in behavior which is rewarded, even if delinquent.

From the psychological and sociological approach, one can observe the centrality of two concepts, self-evaluation and subculture. What is of concern in this paper is the manner in which the "push" of the low level of self-evaluation is translated into the "pull" of membership in the delinquent subculture; the manner in which an individual takes on the attitudes of a pre-existing delinquent group and thus comes to see himself as a delinquent. This process can be seen by examining the relationship of identification with a delinquent subculture to the level of self-evaluation.

Self-evaluation is basically a positive or negative attitude toward the self. It is made up of the individual's reactions to, and his judgments of, the opinions that significant others have of him. These opinions are based on the degree to which the individual fulfills the expectations of these others and the manner in which he fulfills them. The self-evaluation, then, is the individual's awareness of his degree of success or failure in carrying out those social roles which he identifies as his. Both the opinions and the resulting self-evaluations are often expressed as adjectives or modifiers attached to particular roles or identities, such as a *conscientious* student, *irresponsible* son, *inadequate* ball player, or *efficient* bookkeeper.

Nelson Foote has defined the process of *identification* as ". . . appropriation of and commitment to a particular identity or series of identi-

[1] William Healy and Augusta Bronner, *New Light on Delinquency and its Treatment,* New Haven: Yale University Press, 1936, p. 122.

[2] Sheldon and Eleanor Glueck, *Unraveling Juvenile Delinquency,* Cambridge: Harvard University Press, 1951; August Aichhorn, *Wayward Youth,* New York: The Viking Press, Inc., 1936; Fritz Redl and David Wineman, *Children Who Hate,* Glencoe, Illinois: The Free Press, 1951.

[3] For sociological explanations of delinquency, see: Albert Cohen, *Delinquent Boys,* Glencoe, Illinois: The Free Press, 1955; Albert Cohen and James Short, Jr., "Research in Delinquent Subcultures," *Journal of Social Issues,* 14 (1958, Number 3), pp. 20–37; Richard Cloward and Lloyd Ohlin, *Delinquency and Opportunity,* Glencoe, Illinois: The Free Press, 1960.

ties. As a process it proceeds by naming its products as ever-evolving self-conceptions. . . ."[4] The relevance of this process to delinquency has been observed by Daniel Glaser, who stated that *"a person pursues criminal behavior to the extent that he identifies himself with real or imaginary persons from whose perspective his criminal behavior seems acceptable."*[5]

At the same time that the individual comes to *identify* with delinquent others, he comes to *differentiate* himself from non-delinquent others. This dual process of identification and differentiation is basic to the validation of the identity. By engaging in this dual process, the delinquent learns who he is and who he is not. Since this learning process constitutes the announcement of a delinquent identity and a concomitant identification with a delinquent subculture, delinquents should, for example, want to associate with delinquent models (such as the individual who "horses around" or gets into trouble) and not associate with delinquent anti-models (such as the "brain" or the "square").[6]

In addition to specifying models and anti-models of association, the delinquent subculture, as a set of values, beliefs, and attitudes, determines the standards by which a member evaluates himself. The delinquent will judge himself by the degree to which he lives up to these standards. As the individual goes through this process of indentification, he comes to shift the bases of self-evaluation. Those standards, and the people representing those standards that provided the basis for the initial low level of self-evaluation, come no longer to be deemed important. It is in this way that the level of self-evaluation can be changed from low to high through the process of identification. It seems likely, therefore, that the delinquent who has a strong degree of identification with the delinquent subculture will tend to have a high level of self-evaluation while those delinquents with weaker degrees of identification will tend to have low levels of self-evaluation.

Two additional points need to be specified with reference to this process. First, since self-evaluation is determined in relation to a set of accepted standards, both non-delinquents and delinquents can have high levels of self-evaluation. The difference, of course, is that non-delinquents judge themselves by conventional standards and delinquents by delinquent standards. On the other hand, non-delinquents who fail to live up to conventional standards can have low levels of self-evaluation without necessarily becoming delinquent, and similarly delinquents

[4] Nelson Foote, "Identification as the Basis for a Theory of Motivation," *American Sociological Review,* 16 (February, 1951), pp. 14–21 (p. 17).
[5] Daniel Glaser, "Criminality Theories and Behavioral Images," *American Journal of Sociology,* 61 (March, 1956), pp. 433–444 (p. 440, emphasis in the original).
[6] See Roy G. Francis, "The Antimodel as a Theoretical Concept," *The Sociological Quarterly,* 4 (Summer, 1963), pp. 197–205.

with some degree of continuing identification with conventional standards can also have low levels of self-evaluation.

Second, given the presence of the above kinds of individuals within the universes of delinquents and non-delinquents and the usual method for selecting samples of delinquents, i.e. as a result of adjudication procedures, the state of the initial level of self-evaluation may be masked by the degree of identification. Therefore as long as the adjudication procedures constitute the basis of selection, *identification with the delinquent subculture will be a better predictor of delinquent behavior than self-evaluation.*

To explicate the observations made in the previous section of the paper, a three-point continuum of identification with the delinquent subculture or *delinquency orientation* was developed: (1) the "totally-committed delinquent" who is completely involved in only the delinquent subculture to (2) the "marginal delinquent" who is involved with and concerned with both the non-delinquent and delinquent spheres, to (3) the "non-delinquent" who is indifferent to and uninvolved with the delinquent subculture.

The totally-committed delinquent should show a complete, consistent, and integrated delinquent self-conception, because this type of delinquent has been stripped, either by choice or sanctions, of all but delinquent roles. More specifically, the totally-committed delinquent should (1) conceive of himself in terms of delinquency-orientated roles (delinquent identities), (2) possess negative attitudes toward parents, (3) place high value on delinquent associates and activities (delinquent peer group orientation), (4) reject middle class success orientations and accept exotic occupations and the "easy life," (5) perceive causes of crime as external to the person, and (6) place an accent on "kicks" and excitement as modes of self-expression. In addition, the totally-committed delinquent should have a high level of self-evaluation.

The marginal delinquent possesses both delinquent and non-delinquent identities. Compared to the totally-committed delinquent, his delinquency orientation is reduced both in qualitative and quantitative terms. Compared to the non-delinquent, the marginal delinquent maintains some prosocial identities and values but fails to realize them. The marginal delinquent experiences internal conflict as a result of these inconsistent and contradictory identities. Since he has not been able to completely detach himself from the conventional society and its representatives and make the delinquent peer group the primary reference point of self-evaluation, he should reflect a low level of self-evaluation.

To the degree that non-delinquency represents a commitment to "anti-delinquency," the non-delinquents should resemble the self-con-

ception of the totally committed delinquents in structure. There should
be a tendency for non-delinquents to possess an integrated self-conception and a high level of self-evaluation. This type should show
positive family relationships, non-delinquent associates, acceptance of middle class values and represent, in sum, the opposite of the totally-
committed delinquent.

Using this delinquency orientation continuum we will examine individuals classified essentially according to formal legal status (here-
after called delinquency classification) to establish the following two
hypotheses: (1) delinquency orientation is a better predictor of delinquency classification than self-evaluation and (2) there is a positive
relationship between delinquency orientation and level of self-evaluation among juvenile delinquents.

METHODS

The sample consisted of 23 non-delinquents, 26 self-reported delinquents, 39 delinquents on probation, and 42 delinquents placed in a
county institution (Total N=130, all males). The non-delinquents and
self-reported delinquents were randomly selected from four public
schools in Minneapolis. The self-reported delinquents were identified
by responses to two questions on the questionnaire indicating that they
had committed delinquent acts and also had friendships with delinquents.[7] The selected adjudicated delinquents had appeared before the
juvenile court for having committed one or more theft offenses. All
the boys were between the ages of 14–16, Caucasians, Minneapolis
residents, and from working class families.

A measure of identification with the delinquent subculture was developed by operationalizing the characteristics of the ideal type, the
totally-committed delinquent. Examples of this procedure can be found
in the appendix. On the basis of the set of possible alternatives to
questions about family relationships, peer group orientation, success
orientation and occupational choice, crime causation and perception,

---

[7] Until the analysis was begun, there were only three groups in the study, non-
delinquents, probationers, and institutionalized delinquents. However, preliminary
analysis of the non-delinquents revealed two different patterns of responses. The two
patterns became meaningful when it was discovered that twenty-six individuals
admitted, on the questionnaire, association with other delinquents *as well as* commission of delinquent acts. It was then decided to separate the total group into the non-
delinquent and self-reported delinquent groups.

By way of comparison, all but 2 of the 81 adjudicated delinquents answered
affirmatively to both questions. It is quite probable that some of the non-delinquents
who gave negative answers to the questions lied. Whatever error there might be in this
measure, however, would make it more difficult to observe any differences between
those subjects classified as non-delinquent and those classified as self-reported delinquents or adjudicated delinquents. Thus, it is reasonable to assume that any observed
differences represent an underestimation of true differences.

and excitement orientation, the responses were coded according to theoretical expectations into pro-delinquency and anti-delinquency patterns before the actual analysis was begun. These patterns of responses were then given scores which could be combined and thus provide summaries and indices for a comparison of degrees of delinquency orientation in a particular category. In addition, a sixth characteristic, identity, was determined from answers to the Twenty Statements Test (Who Am I?).[8]

Dichotomous scores of *1* and *0* were employed, for individuals whose summary score in a given category was above the median for the respective category (1), and those whose summary score was below the median (0). For the identity characteristic, those individuals who responded with at least one statement on the Twenty Statements Test indicating a pro-delinquency, antisocial, identity received a score of *1*, and all those who did not indicate such an identity received a score of zero. A general measure of delinquency orientation was derived by adding the scores on each of the six measures. Thus, the maximum score on the general measure was six, and the minimum zero. The measure is based on theoretical expectation and face validity and no data are available with respect to independent assessments of validity. With respect to reliability, the point biserial coefficients between the six measures that comprise the delinquency orientation scale and the total scale score are: family relationships, .59; peer group orientation, .69; success orientation and occupational choice, .54; crime causation and perception, .32; excitement orientation, .57; and delinquent identity, .49. These consistently high coefficients tend to indicate a very reliable index. It is, however, recognized that this procedure is rudimentary and arbitrary and does not necessarily reflect a true scale.

The other basic concept, self-evaluation, was measured by means of an adjective check-list on which each respondent designated how he perceived himself.[9] The respondent indicated, in terms of eighteen ad-

---

8 Manford H. Kuhn and Thomas S. McPartland, "An Empirical Investigation of Self Attitudes," *American Sociological Review*, 19 (February, 1954), pp. 68–76. See also Manford H. Kuhn, "Self-Attitudes by Age, Sex, and Professional Training," *The Sociological Quarterly*, 1 (January, 1960), pp. 39–55. This test can be used in many different ways to elicit self-conceptions, but for both theoretical and methodological reasons, it was used here as only *one* of six measures of delinquent self-conception. When planning the research, we assumed that many delinquents would resist presenting a delinquent self in their answers to the TST and that, therefore, additional measures of self-conceptions would be needed. For persons interested in using this test as a sole measure of self-conception, it should be further pointed out that neither our non-delinquents nor delinquents referred to peer groups in their responses. If this practice were accepted as fact, one would have to conclude that adolescents are not at all peer group-oriented. It is indeed doubtful that such a conclusion can be drawn.

9 The measure of self-evaluation was established by first selecting one hundred adjectives from a list of the 10,000 most common words, as reported by Thorndike and Lorge (Edward L. Thorndike and Irving Lorge, *The Teacher's Word Book of 30,000*

jectives or phrases, whether he was usually or not very often this kind of person. The nine positive and nine negative words and phrases (and their assigned scores) were as follows:

Weighted Values for Selected Adjectives

Positive		Negative	
1) Strong	1.48	1) Not smart	6.57
2) Popular	1.65	2) Afraid	6.39
3) Capable of doing		3) A failure	6.26
things right	2.17	4) Mean to others	6.09
4) Friendly	2.26	5) Selfish	5.91
5) Dependable	2.35	6) Ashamed of myself	5.70
6) Honest	2.48	7) Lazy	5.52
7) Lucky	2.52	8) Unhappy	5.43
8) Generous to others	2.64	9) Careless	5.04
9) Easy-going	2.65		

The check-list was scored by summing the weighted values of the adjectives which the respondent said he was usually like and dividing the sum by the number of adjectives so indicated. Like the delinquency orientation scale, the self-evaluation measure is based on theoretical expectation and face validity and there are no data on validity. With regard to reliability, it is not possible to use any of the standard measures to assess reliability since the score of any individual on the self-evaluation measure is the average weighted value of only the items he selected from the list of the eighteen alternatives. However, there is some evidence for assuming reasonable reliability on the basis of the complete agreement between the twenty-five judges and the twenty respondents in the pre-test on the classification of the adjectives into positive and negative categories.

RESULTS

HYPOTHESIS I.

Analysis of variance on the adjective check-list failed to establish significant differences between the means of the four groups with ref-

---

Words, New York: Teachers College, Columbia University, 1944). Next, twenty graduate students in sociology were asked to take the role of a fifteen year old working class boy and indicate on a seven-point scale whether each adjective was positive, negative, or neutral in regard to self-evaluation and whether it was a good indicator of self-evaluation. Third, on the basis of these responses, forty-five adjectives were selected from the list and the procedure was repeated. Fourth, the nine positive and nine negative adjectives on which there was the greatest consensus were chosen. These adjectives covered the range on the seven-point scale. Fifth, the mean rating of the judges on

erence to level of self-evaluation. Chi-square tests utilizing the tercile and median distributions of average scores and frequency distributions of the number of positive and negative adjectives applied to the self by the individuals were conducted in order to determine whether there were significant differences between the groups.[10] All proved to be statistically insignificant. The chi-square test using the median distribution is presented below (Table 1):

TABLE 1.

Delinquency Classification by Self-Evaluation

Self-Evaluation	Delinquency Classification							
	Nondelinquents		Self Reported Delinquents		Probationers		Institutionalized Delinquents	
	Number	Percent	Number	Percent	Number	Percent	Number	Percent
High	14	61	13	50	20	51	18	43
Low	9	39	13	50	19	49	24	57
Total	23	100	26	100	39	100	42	100

$\chi^2 = 1.94$ (3d.f.; P $<$ .70).

Examination of the table shows that more institutionalized delinquents than non-delinquents have levels of self-evaluation below the median (57% and 39%). Even though the result is not statistically significant, the possible relation between negative self-evaluation and juvenile delinquency cannot be dismissed because of the magnitude of the difference and the small sample sizes. There is a strong relationship between delinquency orientation and delinquency classification, as can be seen in Table 2. Observation of the table from left to right shows that the percentage of those who have high delinquency orientations rises from 26 percent in the non-delinquents, to the mid-40's for self-reported delinquents and probationers, to 69 percent of the institutionalized delinquents. It was expected that the percentages would rise from left to right but we also expected that there would be a linear trend. It is possible that the less-than-expected percentage of

the seven-point scale was assigned to each adjective so that each adjective checked by a respondent had a "positive" or a "negative" score. In a pretest, respondents were asked to indicate whether they thought the adjective when applied to them would be "good" or "bad." Using this dichotomy, the respondents on the pretest gave the same ratings as the judges.

[10] We are aware of the problems of interpretation when using a chi-square test in this research design, due to sample sizes and directional hypotheses. The test was used only as a rough means of measurement in an exploratory study.

probationers in the "high" category occurred because probationers are being re-socialized into the community as a result of family and probation department pressure or because probationers tried to present a pro-social image as a reaction to their visibility.

It seems more plausible, however, to assume that the responses are a function of the sampling technique. In order to gather the probation sample through the juvenile court, it was necessary to obtain written parental permission. It seems reasonable to assume that parents who agreed to let their children participate felt more secure about them and/or had more control over them. These children would be more likely than nonparticipants to respond in a non-delinquent direction. Follow-up phone calls to the parents of probationers who refused to let their children participate also indicate that refusals were frequently motivated by hostility and fear of authority. The children who were excluded were probably more likely to justify the parents' mistrust and would have reflected it in their responses. Table 2 shows that there is a

TABLE 2.

Delinquency Classification by Delinquency Orientation

Delinquency Orientation	Delinquency Classification							
	Nondelinquents		Self Reported Delinquents		Probationers		Institutionalized Delinquents	
	Number	Percent	Number	Percent	Number	Percent	Number	Percent
High	6	26	12	46	17	44	29	69
Low	17	74	14	54	22	56	13	31
Total	23	100	26	100	39	100	42	100

$\chi^2 = 12.11$ (3d.f.; P $<$.01).

sizable difference between the probationers and the non-delinquents (high delinquency orientation 44%–26%), and this difference also suggests that a more representative sample of probationers would increase the delinquency orientation in the expected direction. Tables 1 and 2 allow us to conclude that identification with the delinquent subculture is a better predictor of formal delinquency classification than is self-evaluation.

HYPOTHESIS II.

The data in Table 1 and 2 suggest that institutionalized delinquents have low self-evaluations and also have high delinquency orientations. Since this relationship was contrary to our expectations, we analyzed the relation between the self-evaluation and delinquency orientation without reference to the formal delinquency classification. The results are shown in Table 3.[11]

TABLE 3.

Delinquency Orientation by Self-Evaluation

Self-Evaluation	Delinquency Orientation				
	High		Low		
	Number	Percent	Number	Percent	Total
High	34	59	17	35	51
Low	24	41	32	65	56
Total	58	100	49	100	107

Note: This table excludes the scores of "nondelinquents."
$\chi^2 = 4.59$ (1d.f.; $P < .05$).

While the results are statistically significant (at the .05 level), the expected relationship is far from perfect, as indicated especially by the fact that 41 percent of the persons with a high delinquency orientation have a low self-evaluation. Some of the reasons for this can be observed in Table 4.

We expected that there would be a linear continuum beginning with a greater amount of low self-evaluation and low delinquency orientation among the self-reported delinquents and increasing to a greater amount of high self-evaluation and high delinquency orientation among the institutionalized delinquents, with the probationers being intermediate to the other two groups. Increasing delinquent involvement and identification should lead successively to raising the level of self-evaluation. However, differences among the types within and across the groups for the most part are not consistent or very great. The institutionalized group predominate in Type I (high orientation-high evaluation) and the self-reported delinquents are highest on Type III (low-low), as was

[11] Since we are concerned with establishing a relationship *for delinquents* between identification with the delinquent subculture and self-evaluation, non-delinquents are not included in Tables 3 and 4. This exclusion can be supported on the theoretical grounds stated earlier. We expected that the non-delinquents would show essentially opposite results, on these two dimensions, from delinquents; that is, non-delinquents would tend to have a high self-evaluation and a low delinquency orientation. The data of Tables 1 and 2 (and a four-fold classification of that data, not presented here) show that this is the case. Inclusion of the non-delinquents would lessen the expected relationship for delinquents; but since our hypothesized relationship pertains only to delinquents, inclusion of the non-delinquents would appear to be theoretically irrelevant and methodologically incorrect.

predicted. On the other hand, the self-reported delinquents have more of Type I, and the institutionalized group has more of Type III, than would have been expected. The probationers have fewer of Type I and much more of Type III than hypothesized. The probationers, in general, appear less delinquent than the self-reported delinquents.

TABLE 4.

Delinquency Classification by Self-Evaluation by Delinquency Orientation

Type	Delinquency Orientation by Self-Evaluation	Delinquency Classification						
		Self-Reported Delinquents		Probationers		Institutionalized Delinquents		
		Number	Percent	Number	Percent	Number	Percent	Total
I	High delinquency orientation High evaluation	8	31	10	26	16	38	34
II	High delinquency orientation Low evaluation	4	15	7	18	13	31	24
III	Low delinquency orientation Low evaluation	9	35	12	31	11	26	32
IV	Low delinquency orientation High evaluation	5	19	10	26	2	5	17
	Total	26	100	39	101	42	100	107

The divergences from expectation may have occurred because delinquency classification represents primarily a legal category rather than a sociological one, because the more extreme delinquents such as those in state institutions and those over the age of 16 are not represented in this study, leading to a low representation of delinquents with stronger delinquency orientations, or because the data-gathering situation influenced responses. The self-reported delinquents, by being anonymous and "invisible," may feel free to express themselves, while the institutionalized delinquents feel some constraint upon revealing themselves. The "true" delinquent nature of the institutionalized delinquents may therefore have been lessened due to the testing situation. It also should be noted that the response of the probationers might be a result of the selective process discussed previously.

DISCUSSION

The results indicate that the delinquency orientation continuum has some utility so that it is possible to empirically isolate representatives of the three points—totally-committed delinquents (Type I in Table 4), marginal delinquents (Types II and III in Table 4), and non-delinquents. For purposes of this discussion, we will concentrate only on the totally-committed and marginal types. The results demonstrate that increasing the delinquency orientation will have the effect of raising the level of self-evaluation, i.e. that there is a transition process from being a marginal delinquent to becoming a totally-committed delinquent. More specifically, we believe there is a transition from Type III to Type II to Type I. Type IV might be a transitory or situational delinquent who has engaged in delinquent behavior only through a momentary lapse of self-control or is now responding to persuasive changes in his environment toward non-delinquency.

Examination of the distribution of the types among the institutionalized delinquents gives a clear picture of the transition process. There is a steady increase of percentages from Type III to Type I, from 26 percent, to 31 percent, to 38 percent, and only 5 percent fall into Type IV. It should also be noted that Types III and IV occur more often among the self-reported delinquents and probationers than among the institutionalized delinquents, and that Types I and II occur more often among the institutionalized delinquents than among the other two categories. This trend shows that the greater the involvement as measured by adjudication criteria the more likely one is dealing with the types who have stronger degrees of delinquent identification. This trend then also lends support to the conception of the transition process.

There is, of course, a major limitation in our discussion of the transition process and that is that we have only been able to demonstrate it by cross-sectional means. It is necessary in order to establish the process rigorously that longitudinal research be conducted studying the changes occurring in identity as the individual moves from the status of being a non-delinquent to that of a totally-committed delinquent.

However, it still may be concluded that the concept of identification provides both theoretical and empirical utility in explaining the career of the juvenile delinquent mediating as it does between psychological and sociological concepts.

APPENDIX

Illustrative Questions and Weights for Summary Scores on
Delinquent Orientation

(1) Peer group orientation
    (a) peer group vs. family

Who do you like best to be with . . . (1st, 2nd, 3rd choice)

| mother 1 | alone 1½ | best friend 2 |
| father 1 | | group of friends 2 |

(b) reasons for association and models

I like being with my friends because:	Agree	Disagree
we do things that are "kicks"	2	1
we do things other kids don't	2	1

Which kind of guy would you *not* want to hang around with?	Agree	Disagree
the "brain" at school	2	1
the one who doesn't like to horse around	2	1

(2) Excitement orientation

	Agree	Disagree
I can easily make other people afraid of me and sometimes do for the fun of it.	1	
I have never done anything dangerous for the thrill of it.		1

(3) Attitudes toward parents

Do you feel your parents give you a "square deal"?

Mother		Father
1	most of the time	1
2	¾'s of the time	2
3	half of the time	3
4	¼ of the time	4
5	almost never	5

(4) Perception of amounts and causes of crime and delinquency

How many people break laws sometime during their life?

5 almost all	2 ¼
4 ⅗'s	1 none
3 half	

(5) Occupational choice and style of life preference

Suppose you could be any sort of person you wanted, which of these people would you wish to be? Write a "1" in front of your first choice, a "2" in front of your second choice, and a "3" in front of your third choice, for those that you wish to be. Which of these people would you *not* wish to be? Write an "X" in front of the three you would not wish to be.

doctor *1*   machinist *2*   millionaire *3*

(6) Anti-social identities (Twenty Statements Test)

Operationally, statements which indicated delinquent identities, such as "I am a juvenile delinquent," "a thief," "a Glen Lake bad boy," "I hang around with the baddest in the city"; acts and beliefs, such as "I like to fight," "I hate policemen," "I drink," "I hate school," "I like to skip school"; and other identities such as "fighter" and "dare-taker" were coded as being anti-social statements.

Suggested Further Readings

Bandura, Albert, and Richard H. Walters, *Adolescent Aggression,* New York, Ronald, 1959.

Korn, Richard R., and Lloyd W. McCorkle, *Criminology and Penology,* New York, Holt, Rinehart and Winston, 1959.

Langner, Thomas S., and Stanley T. Michael, *Life Stress and Mental Health,* New York, Free Press, 1963.

McCaghy, Charles H., James K. Skipper, Jr., and Mark Lefton, *In Their Own Behalf: Voices from the Margin,* New York, Appleton-Century-Crofts, 1968.

McCord, William, and Joan McCord, *Origins of Alcoholism,* Stanford, Calif., Stanford University Press, 1960.

Redl, Fritz, and David Wineman, *The Aggressive Child,* New York, Free Press, 1957.

Sykes, Gresham, and David Matza, "Techniques of Neutralization: A Theory of Delinquency," *American Sociological Review,* 22 (December, 1957), 664–670.

IV

Societal Reactions and Functions
of Deviance

Deviant behavior, as is true for all social behavior, occurs not *in vacuo* but in contexts variously shaped by other persons; the style of their formal and informal arrangements; and the extent to which values, meanings and norms are shared. This final part is concerned, therefore, with the fact that deviant behavior is not ignored but instead prompts various social responses which in turn may become significant ingredients in accounting for the continuation, control, or abrupt demise of the referent act or its perpetrator.

A major concern for specialty fields in sociology and social psychology is the nature and extent to which they contribute to general or comprehensive theories of human and social behavior. Lewis Coser, in his seminal article, "Some Functions of Deviant Behavior and Normative Flexibility," demonstrates the appropriateness of that objective by pointing to the role that deviance plays in reinforcing social solidarity by enabling social groups to more adequately define their norms.

The selection by Daniels and Daniels, "The Social Functions of the Career Fool," complements and supports Coser's argument regarding the functional aspects of deviance. This descriptive account of the interpersonal relations in a company of military recruits attempts to show in specific terms some of the functions that the deviant may perform for the group.

Kemper considers the function of deviance from still another perspective—that is, its special purpose and value for deviant actors themselves. His article examines deviance in the context of formal organization and discusses a set of conditions which tend to "legitimize" the performance of deviant acts.

The article by Lefton, Angrist, Dinitz and Pasamanick is concerned with the problem of social response and reaction to a specific form of deviant behavior—mental illness. These authors attempt to show that the expectations held by husbands regarding the post-hospital behavior of their wives are as much a function of the latters' actual role performance as they are reflections of independent and abstract social influences.

In also focussing attention on mental illness, Wolkon and Melzer emphasize a dilemma not very often recognized—namely, the practical implications of conflicting conceptions or models by which special forms of deviance are explained or acted upon. Their article, "Disease or Deviance: Effects of the Treatment Continuum," documents the difficulties engendered for mental patients as a result of two alternative and opposing perspectives regarding the purpose and aims of psychiatric treatment.

Gagnon and Simon raise another "hidden" problem with respect to society's reactions to and assessments of certain forms of deviance. In a candid and yet sympathetic portrait of the homosexual, they remind the reader that the deviant is a total human personality with needs, desires, and problems identical to those who judge and evaluate him. They argue that a preoccupation with the homosexual's perversion tends to ignore the special difficulties he has in fulfilling normal social roles and obligations.

In the final selection we return to a more abstract level and consider the issue of theorizing about deviance and the matter of asking the right questions. In his article, "Prospects for Theories of Criminal Behavior," Austin Turk suggests that criminologists have been addressing themselves to the wrong problem—he argues that the criminological problem is structural rather than behavioral. The problem revolves not around questions of why criminals act as they do, but rather the process by which society decides what particular acts are to be labeled as crime. This issue extends beyond that of crime and has important implications for the study of deviance in general. It forces students of the field to consider more closely the efficacy of their concepts, theories, and research hypotheses.

21

Lewis A. Coser

Some Functions of Deviant Behavior and Normative Flexibility

Most contemporary sociological theorizing about deviant behavior has tended to focus on mechanisms of social control. The analysis of instances in which behavior that violates institutional expectations may be considered functional for an ongoing social system has been largely neglected. This paper[1] tries to highlight some functions of deviance for social structures. This does not deny, of course, the dysfunctions of deviance, but only suggests that an exclusive emphasis on these may result in inadequate and distorted analysis.

CONSEQUENCES OF DEVIANCE FOR INTERNAL GROUP RELÅTIONS

We have known ever since Durkheim that crime alerts the common conscience and contributes to the revival and maintenance of common sentiments by arousing the community to the consequences of infringements of rules. "Crime," he wrote, "brings together upright

Reprinted from "Some Functions of Deviant Behavior and Normative Flexibility," by Lewis A. Coser, *The American Journal of Sociology,* **69** (September 1962), 172–181, by permission of The University of Chicago Press. Copyright by the University of Chicago.

[1] This paper was substantially completed during the author's stay at the Institute for Social Research, Oslo, Norway, under a Fulbright Senior Research Scholarship. I wish to express my appreciation to a number of European colleagues, too numerous to mention, whose critical reading of an earlier draft of this paper was most helpful. I owe a special debt to Johan Galtung, of the University of Oslo and the Institute for Social Research, Oslo, to Yrjö Littunen, School of Social Sciences, Tampere, Finland, and to Robert K. Merton, of Columbia University, who made a number of very valuable suggestions. Several propositions of this paper were adumbrated in the author's *The Functions of Social Conflict* (Glencoe, Ill.: Free Press, 1956).

consciences and concentrates them."[2] It will also be remembered that Mead wrote in a similar vein: "The criminal . . . is responsible for a sense of solidarity, aroused among those whose attitude would otherwise be centered upon interests quite divergent from each other." "The attitude of hostility toward the lawbreaker has the unique advantage of uniting all members of the community."[3] Durkheim and Mead both state that, though an individual criminal act elicits negative sanctions, crime also has positive consequences for the society or group since the breach of a norm calls attention to its importance for the common weal. Like bodily pain serves as a danger signal, calling for the mobilization of energies against the source of disease, so crime, these writers argue, alerts the body social and leads to the mobilization of otherwise inactive defense mechanisms.

Durkheim and Mead are often quoted in current theorizing, yet their pertinent insight on the functions of crime has been somewhat neglected. Thus Parsons focuses attention on mechanisms of social control which serve to check deviant behavior but fails to consider possible contributions that deviance may make to the system in which it occurs. He distinguishes types of deviance that "fall within the range of permissiveness which should be considered normal to people under certain strains" and "a vicious circle of gratification of deviant wishes [leading to the] undermining of the main value system."[4] But he does not consider those deviant acts which, though not considered "normal to people under strain," reinforce rather than undermine the social system. We shall see in a later part of this paper that different types of deviant behavior must be discussed in terms of their differential impact. Even if we should agree, for the purpose of discussion, that deviants are always motivated to defy the group's norms, nothing requires us to assume that such acts may not have the unanticipated consequence of strengthening those norms.

Durkheim and Mead see the functional consequences of deviance in the strengthening of the group which results from the collective rejection of the deviant. This assumption is indeed borne out by much of small-group research. An article summarizing much of the research findings in this field states, for example: "When a member deviates markedly from a group standard, the remaining members of the group bring pressures to bear on the deviate to bring him back to con-

[2] Emile Durkheim, *Division of Labor in Society* (Glencoe, Ill.: Free Press, 1947), p. 102.

[3] George Herbert Mead, "The Psychology of Punitive Justice," *American Journal of Sociology,* XXIII (1928), 557–602, esp. p. 591. Cf. also Marx's parallel formulation: "The criminal produces an impression now moral, now tragic, and renders a 'service' by arousing the moral and aesthetic sentiments of the public." Quoted in Bottomore and Rubel (eds.), *Karl Marx* (London: Watts & Co., 1956), p. 159.

[4] Talcott Parsons, *The Social System* (Glencoe, Ill.: Free Press, 1951), p. 512.

formity. If pressure is of no avail, the deviate is rejected and cast out of the group."[5] Statements such as these seem to imply, though the authors do not explicitly say so, that deviations from group standards lead to the mobilization of the group's energies. But small-group research has not adequately considered the possibility that the repression of deviance may not in all cases be functional for the group. Moreover, it has not been shown that all types of groups will reject deviance under all circumstances. These two variables—"strengthening of the group" and "rejection of the deviant"—call attention to four possible cases: (1) the deviant is opposed and the group is strengthened—the situation discussed by Durkheim and Mead; (2) the deviant is tolerated or even accepted and the group is strengthened; (3) the deviant is rejected and the group is weakened; and (4) the deviant is not rejected and the group is weakened. The last case is relatively unproblematical, but the other three have not been given sufficient systematic attention in sociological theorizing, although empirical evidence about them is available.

1. *The deviant is opposed and the group is strengthened.* In the process of uniting itself against deviance, the community not only revives and maintains common sentiments but creatively establishes moral rules and redefines "normal" behavior. "Each time the community brings sanctions against a detail of behavior . . . it sharpens the authority of the violated norm and redefines the boundaries within which the norm exercises its special jurisdiction."[6] Thus the criminal, the scapegoat, the mentally ill, in their diverse ways, allow the group to reaffirm not only its social but also its moral identity, for they establish signposts which serve as normative yardsticks.[7] Deviance "establishes the point beyond which behavior is no longer within acceptable reach of the norm, and in this way gives substance and authority to the norm itself."[8]

[5] Harold H. Kelley and John W. Thibault, "Experimental Studies of Group Problem Solving and Process" in *Handbook of Social Psychology*, ed. Gardner Lindzey (Cambridge, Mass.: Addison Wesley Publishing Co., 1954), II, 768.

[6] Kai T. Erikson, "Social Margins: Some Notes on the Sociology of Deviance" (paper read at the fifty-fifth annual meeting of the American Sociological Association, New York, 1960).

[7] W. E. H. Lecky wrote about the prostitute: "herself the supreme type of vice, she is ultimately the most efficient guardian of virtue" (quoted by Kingsley Davis, "Prostitution" in Robert K. Merton and Robert A. Nisbet [eds.], *Contemporary Social Problems* [New York: Harcourt, Brace & World, Inc., 1961], pp. 262–88). Davis shows the close connection between prostitution and the maintenance of traditional family patterns.

[8] Erikson, *op. cit.* Cf. also V. W. Turner's parallel formulation: "The norm derives strength and definition from condemnation of its breach in the public situations of ritual and law. The deviant, the haphazard and the contingent can only be recognized to be such where consensus to what is typical, orthodox, regular exists. And vice versa" (*Schism and Continuity in an African Society* [Manchester: Manchester University Press, 1957], p. 329). This is of course what Hegel meant when he asserted that "no step in philosophy was possible" unless it was recognized that the positive and the

Thus, definition of what is considered normal in the group takes place with reference to what is considered deviant, and morality is given its content through the contrast provided by that which is not moral. We touch here upon a dialectical relation which Gestalt psychology has discussed in detail with respect to perception. Figures cannot be perceived except in relation to grounds setting them off. In the same way, normalcy can hardly be perceived except against the ground of deviance; to be "good" makes sense only in relation to being "bad."

It is with the body social as it is with individuals: moral indignation against deviants serves to purge the righteous from a sense of their own sins and unworthiness and helps sustain their moral identity. Such indignation may well serve as a reaction-formation, securing the ego against the repressed impulse to identify with the criminal.[9] It is against the ground of their deviance that the righteous achieve the comforting affirmation of their normality. Inasmuch as "our" innocence is contingent upon "their" guilt, dereliction by others provides occasion for self-congratulations.

But dereliction by others also provides occasion for self-examination. Thus, when a crime is committed in the community, religious leaders use the occasion to exhort the congregation to re-examine themselves and "purify their souls." Deviance is taken as a warning that there is something foul in the state of Denmark that needs correction—correction not only on the individual level but in the social realm as well. Thus, Stewart and Helen Perry have shown that in the mental hospitals deviant patients may, by their acting out, "act as a fire alarm for the ward." By upsetting the social equilibrium of the ward, the "fire-alarm patient" may highlight such defects as understaffing, staff overwork, and the like and thus dramatize the need for remedial action.[10] Bureaucratic organizations are familiar with similar situations in which the failure effectively to control behavior in terms of official goals will be used by practitioners as a convincing means for appealing for increased resources. Thus many organizations (as well as many role incumbents) have a vested interest, though rarely acknowledged, in the very deviant behavior which they are set up to combat, for deviance provides the reason for their existence: Increases in deviance may help them to highlight the need for strengthening the organization (or the

---

negative gain their "truth only in their relation to each other so that each contains the other within it" (Wissenschaft der Logik, Lasson ed. [Leipzig: Felix Meiner, 1923], II, 54–56).

[9] Cf. Anna Freud, The Ego and the Mechanisms of Defense (New York: International Universities Press, 1946), pp. 117 ff.

[10] Stewart E. Perry and Helen Swick Perry, "Deviant Behavior, Function and Dysfunction on the Psychiatric Ward" (paper read at the Eastern Sociological Society meetings, April 23–24, 1960, Boston, Mass.).

department in the organization) to cope more effectively with disturbing behavior.

2. What has been said so far about reactions to deviance—be it a spontaneous, that is, a non-deliberate "pulling together" of group members, or deliberate policy—refers to those instances in which deviant behavior leads to its rejection. The second case is that of *tolerance or acceptance of the deviant with concomitant strengthening of the group*. There are groups in which deviants provide the occasion for a reaffirmation of values without incurring rejection. Thus in a seminal paper, Dentler and Erikson give illustrations from Quaker work camps and Army Basic Training Squads where deviants do indeed "become critical referents for establishing the end points (of the range of possibilities judged permissible within the group's boundaries)"—the figure-ground effect discussed earlier—and where "the deviant is someone about whom something should be done, and the group, in expressing this concern, is able to affirm its essential cohesion and indicate what the group is and what it can do."[11] However, in these cases the occasion for affirmation of cohesion does not come from rejecting the deviant but rather from protecting him: he "becomes the ward of the group. . . . In a setting in which having buddies is highly valued, he is unlikely to receive any sociometric choices at all. But it would be quite unfortunate to assume that he is therefore isolated from the group or repudiated by it: an accurate sociogram would have the deviant individual encircled by the interlocking sociometric preferences, sheltered by the group structure."[12]

It would seem that in some groups tolerance of deviance is a function of a specific value system: among Quakers, "tolerance" is a salient component of the ideology. In tolerating or protecting a deviant, they practice what they publicly profess. (It may even be said that such groups do, in fact, need social objects upon whom "tolerance" can be exercised because they provide the occasion for testing and confirming their values.)

If it is objected that tolerance of deviance in army units is merely a manifestation of opposition to official army goals, that is, part of a collective effort to "get back" at army authority, this only confirms the analytical point: by setting itself off against an intolerant environment, the group exercises tolerance precisely with regard to those individuals who would otherwise be the victims of the very environment whose values the group rejects. In both cases—Quaker camps and army units—acceptance of deviance is contingent upon the value system of the

[11] Robert A. Dentler and Kai T. Erikson, "The Functions of Deviance in Groups," *Social Problems*, **VII**, No. 2 (Fall, 1959), 98–107.
[12] *Ibid.*, p. 105.

group. What Kelley and Thibault say about the rejection of deviance applies to its tolerance as well: "Generally, the same factors responsible for the emergence of group standards will also in large measure be responsible for the motivations to enforce conformity to them."[13] Thus in the groups discussed by Dentler and Erikson, the practice of tolerance—whether positively stated as a "way of life" as among Quakers, or stated in opposition to the intolerance of army authorities as in army units—would seem to be a basis for the emergence or strengthening of group standards and would therefore be the guiding principle that motivates the responses of group members to non-conformity among them.

3. So far, the assertion has been made that deviants offer to group members the opportunity to reaffirm common values, be it by providing an occasion to oppose them collectively (case 1), or by bringing about a situation in which their acceptance or tolerance serves as an affirmation of beliefs held in common (case 2). In these cases, the groups were strengthened. There are groups, however, for whom *rigid and repeated rejection of deviants has serious dysfunctional consequences* (case 3). Rigidly structured sects or radical political organizations of the sectarian type provide examples in point. Even a cursory perusal of the history of the Trotskyist movement leaves no doubt about the fact that the lack of ability to tolerate deviance led to further and further fragmentation of the movement. Religious sects provide similar examples.

To be sure, in such groups each single case of negative sanctions against deviant behavior led, at the moment the act of sanctioning occurred, to a reaffirmation of values among those who remained faithful. Yet, rejection of nonconformity as an ongoing organizational activity was disruptive as a *process* in that in the long run it weakened the group in relation to its external environment.

This calls attention to the need to consider the relation between the group within which deviance occurs and the external context.

CONSEQUENCES OF DEVIANCE FOR GROUP RELATIONS WITH THE OUTSIDE

In the first two situations discussed—one of rejection and the other of tolerance of the deviant—our concern was with relationships within the group. It now turns out that what may be functional for the group in one respect—that is, the reaffirmation of its norms—may turn out to be detrimental in another respect, namely, in its relation to the outside. To consider only the internal consequences of deviance and of responses to it, that is, to limit analysis to the group processes within given subsys-

[13] Kelley and Thibault, *op. cit.*, p. 766.

tems without paying attention to the group's relations with the outside, is a common pitfall in sociological theorizing, especially in small-group research. In contrast to much of such research, Kelley and Shapiro set up an experimental group in a situation in which the group's norms were discordant with outside reality.[14] In this situation conformity to these norms tended to be detrimental to the success of the group. (Situations similar to those contrived in the laboratory are likely to occur when disparate rates of change impinge on a group and lead to cultural lags and dysfunctional resistances of vested interests.)

It turned out that in these experimental groups deviation from the norms did not call forth rejection. This case is, in this respect, more similar to case 2 discussed above, for here also deviance is accepted. While in the Quaker camps deviance may be *implicitly* welcomed as an occasion for group members to live up to professed values, in these experimental groups deviant behavior seems to have been *explicitly* welcomed as an occasion for better adaptability to outside reality. Indeed, it turned out that in these groups persons who deviated from the group's norms were also those who were judged to be highly acceptable as co-workers.

A consideration of the external environment for the understanding of internal dynamics of deviance and responses to it makes it possible to throw more light on the behavior of the Quaker camps and army units discussed earlier. There also the relation with the outside would seem to be one important determinant of inside responses: in Quaker groups and army camps alike, the norms that guide the behavior of members toward deviants seemed to consist in *countervalues* to patterns prevailing on the outside. Thus in Kelley and Thibault's groups, as in the groups studied by Dentler and Erikson, outside reality was an important determinant—whether as a spur for adaptation or for opposition to it—of the responses to deviant behavior within.

The evidence so far indicates that the widely accepted notion that groups always reject deviance is, at the least, open to question. To be sure, deviance may be *proscribed* as in the examples of criminal behavior used by Durkheim and Mead. Yet, a deviant redefinition of norms may be *permitted*, as when the value system of the group prescribes tolerance. It may be *preferred*, as when it is accepted as a means for better adaptability of the group.[15]

Deviant behavior may also be *prescribed*, as during periodic feasts when the participants are expected to infringe the norms of ordinary

[14] Harold H. Kelley and Martin M. Shapiro, "An Experiment on Conformity to Group Norms Where Conformity Is Detrimental to Group Achievement." *American Sociological Review*, XIX (1954), 667–77.

[15] These variations in social control have been identified and discussed by Robert K. Merton in his "Social Structure and Anomie," *Social Theory and Social Structure* (rev. ed.; Glencoe, Ill.: Free Press, 1957), esp. p. 133.

behavior.[16] These, however, are instances where it would be deviant not to deviate; that is, they are special instances of conformity which do not concern us here.

The recognition that departure from the norms may be preferred, permitted, or proscribed raises two related problems: (1) The license to deviate is differentially distributed among members of a group. For example, there is tolerance of deviance for special role incumbents such as the "star," the "stranger," or the "fool";[17] or there is some expectation of deviance for some group leaders who are supposed to be flexible and to depart from the norms to further the tasks of the group. (2) Another important problem raised by the differential response to deviance is the need to distinguish between different types of deviant behavior.

DEVIANCE AND INNOVATION

So far the concept of deviance has been used here in accordance with its definition in most contemporary sociological work.[18] An overarching concept of this kind has the distinct merit of drawing attention to the structural similarities of a variety of behaviors which might otherwise seem but little related. Yet at the same time, it has the disadvantage of obscuring distinctions which might be crucial in certain contexts.[19] Thus Merton distinguishes nonconformity from such other kinds of deviant behavior as crime or juvenile delinquency. Criminal behavior is impelled by private and self-centered motives which are by definition antisocial. Innovating dissent of a nonconforming minority, on the other hand, may be manifestly intended to serve group interests in a more effective manner than the conforming majority. "These kinds of 'deviant behavior' differ structurally, culturally and functionally."[20]

While both the nonconformist and the criminal defy normative ex-

---

[16] Roger Caillois, "Theory of the Festival" in *Man and the Sacred* (Glencoe, Ill.: Free Press, 1959).

[17] Georg Simmel, "The Stranger," in *The Sociology of Georg Simmel*, trans. and ed. Kurt H. Wolff (Glencoe, Ill.: Free Press, 1950); and Orrin E. Klapp, "The Fool as a Social Type," *American Journal of Sociology*, LV (1949), 157–62.

[18] Cf. Albert K. Cohen, "The Study of Social Organization and Deviant Behavior," in *Sociology Today*, ed. Merton *et al.* (New York: Basic Books, 1959), pp. 461–84.

[19] It was a distinct step forward to conceptualize the sick and the criminal as deviants from the institutionalized norms on the ground that both roles called forth social control mechanisms designed to restore "health." Nevertheless, as Vilhelm Aubert and Sheldon Messinger have recently argued ("The Criminal and the Sick," *Inquiry* [Oslo], I, No. 3 [Autumn, 1958], 137–60), these roles are also crucially dissimilar insofar as, among other things, the sick is conceived as one who cannot be held responsible for his failure to perform previously assumed roles, while the criminal is not perceived in terms of inability but rather as having been able to act differently had he chosen to do so.

[20] Merton, *op. cit.*, p. 360. Cf. also his "Social Problems and Sociological Theory" in Merton and Nisbet (eds.), *op. cit.*, pp. 697–737.

pectations, they are profoundly dissimilar: the nonconformist's dissent "is not a private dereliction, but a thrust toward a new morality (or a restoration of an old and almost forgotten morality). . . ."[21] I have argued elsewhere in a similar vein that "When all forms of dissent are [considered] criminal by definition, we are in the presence of a system which is ill-equipped to reveal fully the extent to which nonconformity, as distinct from crime, involves the striving forward on alternative moral basis rather than moral deviation."[22]

To be sure, the behavior of the nonconformist may bring forth community reactions similar to those occasioned by criminal violations of the norms, yet the innovations he proposes allegedly in the interest of the group's welfare are likely to be evaluated in their own right, if only by a minority. This is why, as distinct from the case of the criminal, there is likely to be buried under layers of hostility a certain measure of respect for the disinterested dissenter. Being oriented toward the collectivity, he is led to seek and to find an audience within it. The innovator sends a message intended to be picked up and diffused. His behavior proceeds, so to speak, in broad daylight in order to attract a maximum audience. While the criminal seeks to minimize the chances of detection, the innovator seeks maximum publicity for his message. One may argue with an innovator but hardly with a criminal.[23]

Just as with various types of deviance, the innovations which the nonconformist proposes for the consideration of the group may be prescribed or proscribed with various degrees of tolerance, depending on the structured and normative context. Moreover, they may be wittingly favored by the group or the group may unwittingly be favored by them.

When innovation is highly valued, as, for example, in scientific societies, innovating behavior must be considered a special type of conformity rather than deviation. In the context of the institution of science, innovations and discoveries, provided they satisfy the criteria of evidence, are highly valued variants that permit the goals of the group to be more adequately met—though even here the innovator may at first encounter the resistance of vested interests.[24]

On the other hand, in groups which place no value on innovation,

---

21 Merton, op. cit., p. 363 et passim.

22 Lewis A. Coser, "Durkheim's Conservatism and Its Implications for Sociological Theory," in Émile Durkheim, ed. Kurt H. Wolff (Columbus: Ohio State University Press, 1961), pp. 211–32. Cf. also Roger Nett, "Conformity-Deviation and the Social Control Concept," Ethics, LXIV (1953), 38–45.

23 Gandhi distinguished between criminal and civil disobedience in terms of the concept of publicity. Civil disobedience, to him, was by definition public action.

24 Cf. Robert K. Merton, "Social Conformity, Deviation and Opportunity-Structures," American Sociological Review, XXIV, No. 2 (April, 1959), 177–89, esp. p. 181. Cf. also Herbert Menzel, "Innovation, Integration, and Marginality," American Sociological Review, XXV, No. 5 (October, 1960), 704–13.

Societal Reactions and Functions of Deviance

an innovating response will be considered truly nonconformist. In contrast to the case of the criminal, however, at least some of the group's members might perceive that the innovator intends to perform a positive task for the group. This might then lead to a conflict within the group over the issue raised. If this happens, the innovator has transformed individual nonconformity into group conflict and has raised it from the idiosyncratic to the collective level.

Thus, pressures for innovation are likely to result in the emergence of social conflicts within a system. Such conflicts, as I have shown elsewhere, may be highly functional for that system.[25] Dewey has noted that "conflict shocks us out of sheeplike passivity, and sets us at noting and contriving . . . it is a *sine qua non* of reflection and ingenuity."[26] The innovator's behavior may serve to reduce the chances that adherence to the routines of yesterday render the group unable to meet the challenges of today. The innovator may thus be a pace-setter and a setter of new standards. By attacking vested interests in the habitual, the innovator helps insure that the group does not stifle in the deadening routines of ritualism.

What is said here of group process indeed applies to every fruitful interaction as well. Interaction does not merely consist of mutual filling of expectations but in ever renewed innovating contributions. In much current theorizing it is assumed that the equilibrium of a group is a function of the extent to which group members habitually conform to each other's expectations. The maintenance of complementarity between the interaction orientations of alter and ego is said to be the mark of a stable social system.[27] "This model seems to assume," Gouldner has noted, "that each of a sequence of identical conforming acts will yield either the same or an increasing degree of appreciation and satisfaction and will thus elicit the same or increasing amounts of reward."[28] Yet, "later conforming actions are worth less than earlier ones, in terms of the rewards or propensity to reciprocate which they elicit." When conformity is taken for granted, the propensity to reciprocate is weakened in the long run. Homans also states this principle of satiation, a version of marginal utility: "The more often a man has in the recent past received a rewarding activity from another, the less valuable any further unit of that activity becomes to him."[29]

The Finnish sociologist Yrjö Littunen has formulated an "optimal

[25] Lewis A. Coser, "Social Conflict and the Theory of Social Change," *British Journal of Sociology*, **VIII**, No. 3 (September, 1957), 197–207.
[26] John Dewey, *Human Nature and Conduct* (New York: Modern Library, 1930), p. 300.
[27] Talcott Parsons, *op. cit.*, pp. 204–5 *et passim*.
[28] Alvin M. Gouldner, "Organizational Analysis," in *Sociology Today*, pp. 423 ff.
[29] George Homans, *Social Behavior* (New York: Harcourt, Brace & World, Inc., 1961), p. 55.

frustration" hypothesis: "Persons who have to maintain a monotonous interaction pattern for a long period of time tend to become bored with each other. This phenomenon of *social fatigue* may be understood as a situation where there is no excitement in the interaction to maintain the cohesiveness, to increase liking."[30] Although sustained conformity may bring the reward of smooth adjustment to expectations, it also brings the penalty of boredom. That is why apathy and monotony may lead a person to "seek a frustration which his energy potential can adequately balance and overcome."[31] This hypothesis, which Littunen developed on the basis of the psychological research of Hebb and Thompson,[32] gains added theoretical relevance with Gouldner's recognition that a system built upon the habituation of conforming responses may be said to contain built-in tendencies toward a high level of entropy. It is high social entropy that the innovator, as an agent of change, helps to prevent.

NORMATIVE FLEXIBILITY AND INNOVATING ROLES

In monolithic structures role requirements may be so rigidly defined that only fully conforming role performance will be tolerated; in less rigid structures, on the other hand, a measure of diversity may be tolerated at various levels in the system.[33] For example, low-ranking deviants may perform important functions for the group. This was the case in the groups discussed earlier, about which Dentler and Erikson have argued that low-ranking members who deviate from the group's norms "become critical referents for establishing the end points" of the range of possibilities judged permissible within the group's boundaries.[34]

Such considerations direct attention to the relation between status, group structure, and the acceptance of innovation by the group.

Deviant behavior as well as innovation varies within different social

---

[30] *Income-Security Values at Different Levels of Frustration* (Transactions of the Westermarck Society, Vol. IV, No. 4 [Copenhagen: Ejnar Munksgaard, 1959]), pp. 234–35 ff. Cf. also Goethe's "Nichts ist schwerer zu ertragen als eine Reihe von schoenen Tagen."

[31] Littunen, *op. cit.*, p. 224. Cf. also Marx's statement: "The criminal interrupts the monotony and security of bourgeois life. Thus he protects it from stagnation" (*op. cit.*, p. 159).

[32] D. O. Hebb and W. R. Thompson, "The Social Significance of Animal Studies," in *Handbook of Social Psychology*, I, 532–61.

[33] Daniel J. Levinson, "Role, Personality, and Social Structure in the Organizational Setting," *Journal of Abnormal and Social Psychology*, LVIII (1959), 170–80. Cf. also Erving Goffman's discussion of "Role Distance" in his *Encounters* (Indianapolis: Bobbs-Merrill Co., 1961).

[34] *Op. cit.* Cf. also E. Paul Torrance, "Function of Expressed Disagreement in Small Group Processes" in A. Rubenstein and C. Haberstroh (eds.), *Some Theories of Organization* (Homewood, Ill.: Dorsey Press, 1960), pp. 250–57.

structures. Furthermore, the social structure puts pressure on some of its status-occupants to engage in innovating rather than in conforming behavior.[35] For example, as Veblen and Simmel,[36] among others, have pointed out, marginal individuals are likely to be highly motivated to engage in innovating behavior because they are structurally induced to depart from prevailing social norms. "With the least opportunity for full participation in the most valued activities of their own society,"[37] they may be stimulated to make new responses which depart from the habitually required. Being less tied to the system of wont and use which regulates the lives of insiders, they may see alternatives of action that escape the latter's attention. The structural circumstance of their exclusion from some of the prized values of the group may make the marginal man more sensitive to the lacunae which may well remain hidden from "well-adjusted" members of the group. If he wishes to gain acceptance among insiders, he will be motivated to propose innovating means designed to allow the group to reach its goals more effectively than before.

There are also other positions in a group than those of marginal men that motivate innovating departures from the norms. For example, the status of leader requires the ability to adjust to new circumstances. The rank and file may take the customary for granted, but a break of wont and use may enhance the reputation of the leader. The flexibility required in leadership roles may entail greater or lesser departures from otherwise expected behavior so that a certain amount of license to deviate and to violate norms is built into the very definition of leadership.

Homans, who had argued in an earlier work that "the higher the rank (or status) of a person within a group, the more nearly his activities conform to the norms of the group."[38] stated more recently, after discussing, among others, the above-quoted study by Kelley and Shapiro, that "we now have experimental evidence that it is not just the members of low status, but members of high status as well, who are prone at times to non-conformity."[39] It will be remembered that in

[35] Robert K. Merton, "Social Structure and Anomie," *op. cit.*, pp. 131–60.

[36] Georg Simmel, "The Stranger," *op. cit.*; and Thorstein Veblen, "The Intellectual Preeminence of the Jews," in his *Essays in Our Changing Order*, pp. 219–31.

[37] H. G. Barnett, *Innovation—the Basis of Cultural Change* (New York: McGraw-Hill Book Co., 1953), p. 404. Cf. also Karl Mannheim, *Man and Society in an Age of Reconstruction* (London: Routledge & Kegan Paul, 1940), esp. pp. 56–57, as well as Robert Park's "Introduction" to E. V. Stonequist, *The Marginal Man* (New York: Charles Scribner's Sons, 1937).

[38] Homans, *The Human Group* (New York: Harcourt, Brace & Co., 1950), p. 141.

[39] *Social Behavior*, p. 346. Recent experimental work throws doubt on the idea that the relation between status and conformity is ever a simple one. J. E. Dittes and H. H. Kelley showed, e.g., that individuals who felt acceptable in a group felt freer to express disagreements publicly, while those with a low sense of acceptance were much higher in their *public* than in their *private* conformity ("Effects of Different

these groups deviant behavior helped the group to adapt to the outside. This suggests that the pressure on the leader to engage in innovating behavior may derive from the structural circumstance that he is the group's representative to the outside. He stands at the point of interchange between in-group and out-group. A leader may be considered a special case of the marginal man: having the task to relate his group to the demands of the environment, he is oriented, at the same time as he is the group's representative, toward extra-group values.

In view of these requirements of leadership, it is not always clear whether the leader's innovation can be called "deviant" at all. Though it involves adoption of new procedures, innovation in this case still takes place within normative limits. Just as with groups in which innovation is highly prized, so in situations in which the leader's departure from institutionalized procedures is part of the system of expectations, what may be considered deviation from one point of view may well be considered conforming behavior from another.

Yet leaders are often also permitted some deviant behavior that neither increases the group's adaptation to the outside nor otherwise directly benefits the group in any way. Simply by virtue of otherwise showing prized qualities, a leader accumulates what Hollander has called "idosyncrasy credit."[40]

One would assume that the more task-oriented a group, the less its tolerance of deviant behavior that interferes with the attainment of the group's goal. This may well be so, but if a leader is seen as important for the attainment of these goals, or even for their partial attainment, the group may tolerate individual deviation when it is seen as balanced by positive contributions. A man may lose credit for deviations, but only when his credit balance is exhausted will he be removed. If he continues to amass credit in the eyes of the members through group-approved activities, he attains a threshold permitting deviations from common expectations. This may explain, at least in part, why a leader may be given greater leeway for deviating behavior than his followers: his having accumulated highly visible merit gives him a leeway in behavior not granted to less meritorious members; the group will take from "him" what it will not take from "them." Task orientation and tolerance of deviance are therefore not necessarily mutually exclusive.

The term "idiosyncrasy credit" readily brings to mind the image of a "would-be" innovator, who is tolerated because of other contributions,

---

Conditions of Acceptance upon Conformity to Group Norms," *Journal of Abnormal and Social Psychology*, **LIII** [1956], 100–107). Cf. also Herbert Menzel, "Public and Private Conformity under Different Conditions of Acceptance in the Group," *Journal of Abnormal and Social Psychology*, **LV** (1957), 398–402.

40 E. P. Hollander, "Conformity, Status and Idiosyncrasy Credit," *Psychological Review*, **LXV** (1958), 117–27.

yet whose innovating message is largely ignored by the group. This is not necessarily so. "Idiosyncrasy credit" because of high achievement does not merely imply tolerance of otherwise unacceptable behavior; it also implies that members of the group will listen more readily.

THE TIME DIMENSION OF INNOVATION

Innovations must not only be analyzed in terms of the structural circumstances under which they occur but also in terms of their impact over time. They must be located in social time as well as in social space.

A type of behavior which might at first be perceived by the group as an attack on its norms and values might at a later time be considered in a different light. If this happens during the lifetime of the innovator he is likely to experience a sharp change in status; he will then reap the rewards of an action which was at first negatively sanctioned. The innovator is then co-opted, perhaps even against his will, into the ranks of the upholders of conformity. If, on the other hand, he obtains recognition only after his death, the lifelong heretic becomes, in effect, a posthumous saint. The Catholic church, with its amazing flexibility, has been especially adept at this process of social transmutation in which, through a remarkable alchemy, its victims have been transformed into patron saints so that Joan of Arc in due time became Saint Joan. As Merton has observed: "In the history of every society . . . some of its cultural heroes have been regarded as heroic precisely because they have had the courage and the vision to depart from norms then obtaining in the group. As we all know, the rebel, revolutionary, nonconformist, individualist, heretic and renegade of an earlier time is often the culture hero of today."[41] The Jewish prophets, those holy demagogues, were feared, despised, and outcast by the religious and secular powers of their day. Yet, as Max Weber has noted, "it is completely inconceivable that without a profound experience of a confirmation of the prophetic words of doom . . . the belief of the people was not only unbroken by the fearful political fate, but in a unique and quite unheard of historical paradox was definitely confirmed. The entire inner construction of the Old Testament is inconceivable without its orientation in terms of the oracles of the prophets. These giants cast their shadows through the millennia into the present."[42]

[41] Merton, *Social Theory*, p. 183.
[42] Max Weber, *Ancient Judaism*, trans. and ed. Hans H. Gerth and Don Martindale (Glencoe, Ill.: Free Press, 1952), p. 334.

22

Arlene K. Daniels
Richard R. Daniels

The Social Function of the Career Fool*

Although many persons engage in "fool-like" behavior sporadically; a few individuals characteristically behave in this fashion, following a social career as fool. When they do so, they seem to be adopting a role that is a tolerated deviant type. Within the career fool's social world, the understandings and social rules that prescribe his conduct differ from those that govern others, although both sets of rules serve the function of allocating claims and duties, expectations and obligations in a systematic way. Sometimes social situations—rather than individuals—encourage the development of some tolerable deviant type, such as the fool. The requirement is especially pressing when formal understandings and expectations of a group or social world are so rigid and inflexible that the avowed purposes and functions of such groupings may be threatened unless a mediating principle is introduced to make the rules more viable. This paper describes the emergence of one career fool in such a rigid social system, and discusses the social functions performed by this and other deviant types in stressful situations.

In Air Force basic training, during the forties, the second author lived in a barracks which housed about sixty recruits who were designated as a "flight." The training schedule for each flight consisted of

From *Psychiatry*, **27** (August, 1964), 219–229. Reprinted by special permission of The William Alanson White Psychiatric Foundation, Inc., and the authors. Copyright by the Foundation.

* Sections of this paper were read at the Pacific Sociological Association meetings March 6, 1964. The authors are especially grateful to Erving Goffman and Warren Hagstrom for their criticism, comments, and ideas. Thanks are also due to Sally Cassidy, Alan Gowman, Jay Haley, and Thomas Scheff for their helpful advice during successive drafts of the manuscript.

thirteen weeks of close-order drill, firing range practice, field marches, and bivouacs. In addition, each week there were fifteen to twenty hours of lectures and films on diverse military topics.

The foreman of each flight throughout these various operations was, normally, either a corporal or a sergeant. He and the men who assisted him in giving drill instructions, managing the flight's schedule, and punishing minor infractions of the discipline were the "flight marchers." They also acted as barracks chiefs and occupied the one or two private rooms in each barracks.

The flight rather than the individual was treated as the basic unit of social control. The recruit soon learned that his success and comfort were determined by the grades of competence attributed by training instructors to the whole flight. For example, flight marchers advised their charges that the members of especially competent flights would be promoted en masse to private first-class grade at the end of training. The promotion was alleged to be imperative if the recruits' hope for pleasant duty assignments following basic training was to be realized. Furthermore, recruits were advised that although basic training was never an easy experience, it could be made unusually difficult for "foul-up" flights. Such units would receive more than their share of kitchen duty, heavy work projects, forced marches, and calisthenics. The clearest message of the basic training institution was that the individual could regard his enlistment optimistically only if he belonged to a highly rated flight.

To all but the few who had had R.O.T.C. training in high school or college, the unfamiliar routine seemed loaded with pitfalls. For instance, none but the experienced could avoid mistakes in the first close-order drill exercise. Nevertheless, the entire group seemed to feel that the flight could cover itself with honor if everyone were determined to succeed in the terms of the military value system.

However, a number of the recruits experienced considerable difficulty in contributing their share. Mistakes made in any of the training routines were certain to embarrass the offender and make him the object of prolonged taunting and "fool-making."[1] Everyone made such mistakes, so that it is accurate to say that, for a time, everyone had to play the fool; usually one escaped his discomfort easily because soon someone else would commit a foolish error, engaging the rather confined, censuring perspective of the group. As a simple matter of self-preservation, almost all recruits attempted to conform to the newly adopted military standards of the flight.

There was, however, one exception, Axel, who came from a small western town and was the only child of a protestant clergyman. In many

[1] Orrin E. Klapp, "The Fool as a Social Type," *Amer. J. Sociology* (1949) 55:157–162.

ways, Axel lived up to the stereotypic notion of both the preacher's son and the country youth. He seemed guileless, good-natured, and inexperienced in the bantering, somewhat coarse tone usually assumed in his age group (18–20 years). Evidently, however, he was intelligent and reasonably well educated. His score on the Army General Classification Test[2] was above 110, which probably placed him in the upper third of the flight. But Axel achieved a reputation as a slow learner of Air Force routines and seemed dull in consequence.

He was also unprepossessing in appearance, being stout and round-shouldered and an excessive salivator. His physiognomy was not genuinely remarkable in any sense, but combined with his lack of ability at repartee and his slowness, the total effect predisposed many recruits to keep away from him. During the first weeks of basic training his behavior was consistent with these impressions.

In the beginning, most of his peers were content to ridicule him for his many obvious failures to orient himself at the rate the recruits had established as minimal for their flight. In terms of comic relief, his response to hazing was very satisfactory. He was quite easily enraged, and flushed violently. Since he could not readily reply to others, Axel made ineffectual attempts to quell abuse with physical action. He was hopelessly out-pointed in this respect by any recruit in the barracks, and thus merely became more foolish. His awkward feints were sometimes answered with serious threats or genuine blows, which usually put an end to the incident. On one occasion, for example, ten or fifteen members of the flight thought it would be amusing to deprive Axel of his trousers and undershorts, and to lock him out of the barracks. Axel pounded on the door and threatened to throw rocks through the barracks windows—which would have gotten everyone in trouble—if he were not let in. The door was opened long enough to tell Axel how severe his punishment would be if he attempted anything of the sort, but he remained locked out. Eventually, near to tears from vexation, he sat down by the door and wailed to be let in. It was ten or fifteen minutes before he was allowed to return.

As the members of flight became better acquainted with one another during the course of training, a fairly definite, shared perspective toward Axel began to emerge. He was regarded condescendingly as someone who could not care for himself under these conditions of life. Those who had bunks near his were fairly charitable in their attitudes, and merely regarded him as unfortunately clumsy or careless. The other recruits took a less friendly attitude, which ranged from impatience to outright hostility, depending upon the nature of Axel's most recent of-

[2] The test was, at the time, a knowledge and skill examination administered to recruits in the sixth or seventh week of basic training and the results allegedly were used in determining subsequent job classification.

fense; he was viewed as a threat to their anxious attempt to become a first-class unit. Accordingly, considerable pressure began to be directed toward those who occupied bunks near him and those who marched in the ranks directly next to him. This pressure was the result of an understanding within the group that Axel's comrades would have to compensate for his irresponsibility and incompetence by zealous watchfulness.

Gradually, a regime of control began to take shape. Prior to the weekly standby inspection in the barracks, the men who bunked on either side of Axel allowed themselves enough time to put his area in order as well as their own. Axel made some attempt to manage this for himself, but invariably he neglected some of the many punctilious details which were required. His wardrobe would be improperly hung and disorderly, with buttons left undone, and his boots would be dirty or ill-polished. Furthermore, he was likely to keep forbidden personal belongings in his footlocker. The recruits' highly ritualistic, prescribed footlocker arrangement left little space for personal items. Want of sufficient storage area was a considerable problem to Axel, who was weighed down with the impedimenta of a pipe-smoker. He was also constantly hungry, and had to find room for a cache of fruit and candy bars. During one of the earlier standby inspections, a number of recruits, including Axel, were chastised by inspecting officers for untidily maintained footlockers, and the flight received a poor rating. As a result, most of the recruits eliminated many personal items in the footlocker and bunk area as the most simple solution to the problem. But Axel did not surrender his comforts readily. Before the next inspection, as Axel's area-mates were devoting themselves to putting final touches on his locker, bunk, and clothing, they discovered a quantity of pipes, tobaccos, and light snacks under the dust cover of his bunk. Axel had so cunningly arranged these items that there was no disturbance to the line of the dust cover. It was too late to rectify the matter. The recruits were barely able to replace the dust cover before the inspection party arrived. On this occasion, the inspectors were watching for soiled bed linen and unceremoniously threw back the dust cover on each bunk as they proceeded down the aisle. Axel's failure added many demerits to the few that the flight received for minor infractions.

Axel subsequently attempted to secrete his articles of personal comfort in the pockets of clothing hung on a clothes pole mounted on the wall near the head of his bunk, although clothing pockets were supposed to be empty and inspectors often searched for evidence of noncompliance. The men who were responsible for putting his area in order had become canny in anticipating his moves, however, and averted disaster. They showed Axel that above his bunk there was an unused duct section behind an easily loosened grille. Axel was taught how to slip the grille away and to use the space behind it for his storage. He afterwards kept his troublesome belongings there, and eventually became custodian for similar possessions of other recruits who required a last-minute hiding place for articles which they feared to place in the footlocker.

The recruits kept the barracks floors spotlessly clean. After a few weeks of regular and energetic scrubbing with strong soap, the pine boards had become nearly white. It was believed by the trainees that only a "white" floor could satisfy inspecting officers. Since it was difficult to avoid marking such lightened floors with the black rubber heels on service boots, the recruits adopted the practice of removing boots before entering the barracks. On inspection days, it was, of course, not possible to avoid wearing shoes in the barracks but the men took great pains to step carefully so as not to mark the floors. On one occasion just prior to an inspection, Axel forgot about this problem and left many black marks. Several recruits saved the situation by hurriedly scrubbing the marks away. Wash buckets, brushes, mops, and sinks then had to be cleaned, wiped dry, and restored to order at the final moment before the inspectors arrived. Axel, the cause of the crisis, had in the meantime been sent outside to prevent his making any further difficulty and did not take part in the last-minute flurry of work. The inspection was highly successful; the relief of the men at surmounting their difficulty was so general that they did not punish Axel. Axel's bunkmates regularly addressed themselves to his inconvenient and troublesome shortcomings partly out of a moral concern for his welfare, but chiefly to spare themselves and the rest the risk of poor inspection.

Axel had a few friends with whom he spent much of his time. His generally friendly and uncritical view of his fellow soldiers made him a relatively close companion to the few 'lower status' recruits in the flight, the four or five Mexican-Americans with language difficulties and with less ease in the cultural milieu. While there was no apparent discrimination from the larger group, the foreign-speaking minority tended to stay aloof and to await overtures from others rather than to initiate any friendly action. Since Axel was indiscriminately friendly, and since it was absolutely clear that anyone had access to him without fear of rebuff, this small group was somewhat more intensely involved with him than the rest and, accordingly, took more responsibility for him.

Outside of the barracks it was more difficult to secure control over Axel's nonconformist tendencies. He was especially likely to pass comments while marching—something strictly forbidden—and these remarks, often rather silly, would initiate a giggling in the ranks. Such behavior often resulted in extracurricular confinement of the flight to barracks or additional drill exercise. Because this impropriety was hard to control and led to collective punishments, the recruits once dealt very severely with Axel for it. The squad leaders and all the men present in the barracks gave him a "G.I. shower," a species of beating in which the denuded victim is first tossed under a cold shower and then belabored with stiff brushes. Compared to the punishments he usually received, the G.I. shower was immoderately severe. This was, however, the only time his excesses resulted in a serious break with the other men, and even on this occasion, the drubbing was not administered with the customary violence. Axel responded to this experience as one who knew he had gone too far. Ever after, his babbling in ranks could be stopped with ease; the man behind Axel reminded him that silence was wanted merely by stepping on his heels once or twice.

In summary, the effects of Axel's nonconformist activities were controlled in two ways. When satisfactory completion of an assigned task was involved, his deficiencies were compensated for by other recruits. The group simply excused him from many laborious duties which everyone else had to perform. However, when Axel's singularization in a public place risked the solid front which the recruits wished to maintain for their flight, he was given a direct, immediate, physical reprimand. Thus, in all cases when the flight was under official scrutiny, it could protect itself from his corrosive influence.

Axel's position in the flight was unenviable. He stood outside the social organization of the group in that anyone was understood to have the right to ridicule and insult him. He was open to any mischievous foray and had, therefore, even less privacy than the others in the barracks. His vulnerability was quite clearly established from the first week of training and many recruits worked out the frustrations of rigid group discipline by abusing him; however low one felt, Axel was lower still.

As noted above, however, in time Axel began to experience friendly relations with a number of the recruits. He was, in the main, a ceaselessly humble and good-natured fellow, and, to the extent of his capacity, generous in helping others with physical effort or loans of money. His establishment of friendly relations was helped by the fact that the men knew they had to live cheek-by-jowl for thirteen weeks whether they liked it or not. Thus, he was eventually able to turn his incidental characteristics of physical awkwardness, obtuseness, and ready amiability into a good thing. While at first reviled by the recruits outside his immediate circle of friends, he later became the more or less constant butt of far-from-hostile jokes, practical and otherwise. Throughout the flight, he enjoyed considerable limelight and, through his openness to attack, possessed entree into any circle in the barracks.

Axel's role was a positive asset to both the flight and himself. In the first place, he had a unique relationship with the flight marchers. These representatives of institutional authority lived in the barracks and could, and often did, interfere in the lives of their subordinates day

and night. Axel's stock rose considerably because of his ability to forestall or deflect their depredations against the men. From the beginning, the flight marchers had singled him out as the essence of recruit
stupidity; they liked to use him as a model in illustrating blunders and
inexperience. By making a fool of Axel before his comrades and using
his performance as an example of their gaucherie, the flight marchers
amused the recruits with their own weaknesses and, presumably, hoped
to embarrass them into improving. In time this practice resulted in
the development of a rudimentary joking relationship between Axel and
the two flight marchers. They tacitly encouraged his eccentricities for,
by commission of them, Axel afforded further pedagogical materials.
Thus, among other things, he was permitted to caper a bit, talk out of
turn, and make mild rejoinders to their denunciations of ignorance.
The effect of his levity was to turn situations of tension, which potentially could result in punishment for the whole group, into cathartic
situations in which the conflict between the group and its leaders was
reduced through comic relief.

Axel's function as a social go-between was apparently never given
much formal recognition by the rest. To the final day of training, he
was regarded as an essentially shiftless and undignified fool whose inept-
ness would prevent his ever amounting to much. However, the eventual
character of his relations with the other men indicated that a lack of
dignity does not always result in total disrespect. Indeed, by the end of
the training period, the attention to Axel was flattering. Frequent recol-
lections of his escapades by others helped him assume the status of a
small-time legend.[3] Axel was an important personage in the group with
which he trained. For one thing, he managed partially to convert a
rigid, tight, authoritative institution into one which could, at times, be
magnanimous. By joshing with the flight marchers, throwing precedence
to the wind in his familiarities, he narrowed the social distance between
the recruits and the noncoms. At other times, when the institution was
not so magnanimous, Axel's foolish conduct represented the quest of any
recruit for some release. In a sense, his mere existence as a fool showed
the vulnerability of the system that was supposed to be confining for all
within it. His continuing eccentricity and failure, as judged by the
standards applied to other recruits, showed that an individual could
survive without being automatically responsive to every whim of the

[3] This was emphasized long after the completion of training when recruits met
someone from their old unit, and Axel's name always came up. These encounters were
always a little troublesome because although the shared hardship had been unifying
at the time, the men often basically had little in common. The spell of embarrassment
could be broken usually by the mere mention of Axel's name and a reference or two
to his fumblings. Anecdotes about him were easily recollected, and memories of him
were often more vivid than memories of those who had been closest friends at the time.
To some, at least, his doings were a systematic and familiar adventure.

institution and its authorities. He was probably less changed by the basic training than any other recruit. His irresponsibility and incompetence, of which he was not too frequently made forcibly aware, cost him only his dignity.

Axel thus performed a valuable service for this group of recruits. In return, the men enabled Axel to give the appearance of meeting minimum requirements by doing for him what he could not do for himself. The exchange was one in which both parties benefited.

A case history of this type is suggestive of the career pattern through which a social type develops. We do not intend to suggest that the exigencies of life in such small groups necessarily press for or demand the development and identification of a fool type. Rather, we suggest that the capacity of some persons to function as social types, to make a "career" in one role or another, becomes very valuable to the group. The range of choice, however, is quite wide and the group can adapt to and make use of a variety of talents or characteristics which happen to be present or potential in individuals within the group.

An excellent example of this point is related by T. E. Lawrence in his account of his own basic training experiences in the R. A. F. under the name of Ross.[4] Some of the advantages which Axel brought to his company by playing the fool were brought to the company in which Lawrence served through his role as an older and educated man. He was respected and given a special place for qualities not immediately relevant to the activities of the group. The group found a way to use these qualities for its own benefit, even over Lawrence's objections and his desire to remain undifferentiated in the ranks and anonymous. An example appears in the following passage, which begins with Sailor, a fellow recruit, commenting to Lawrence, who has received an undeserved dressing down:

'But, mate, you let the flight down, when he takes the mike out of you every time. Give the ignorant shit-bag a fucking great gob of your toffology.'

Next day in the first stand-at-ease of first period:—'Short-arse you there, Ross, what's your bleedin' monaker:—what d'you know?' Such nonplussing questions are Poulton's favorite gambit for a hazing. *Spring to attention.* 'Sergeant,' I dutifully intone. He wouldn't stop. 'I arst you a question, you little cunt.' But I am not tired at this time of day: by Sailor's advice of priggery I made to drawl out 'Well, Sergeant, specifically of course we can know nothing— unqualified—but like the rest of us, I've fenced my life with a scaffolding of more or less speculative hypotheses.'

The rear rank deflated appreciatively, tired sounding, like the wind in wet trees. The Sergeant stared: then whispered to himself, 'Jesus fucking Christ.'

[4] T. E. Lawrence, *The Mint: A Day-Book of the R.A.F. Depot between August and December 1922 with Later Notes by 352087 A/C Ross;* Oxford, Alder Press, 1955.

At that Sailor let out a high, sudden, singing laugh. 'Flight—Attention' Poulton yelled, and the drill went forward, gingerly. 'My Christ' exulted James, thumping my back later, in the hut's safety, 'The silly twat didn't know if his arse-hole was bored, punched, drilled, or countersunk.'[5]

Ross served as a spokesman for the dissatisfactions of his comrades and as a symbol that successful evasion of heavy-handed authority could be effected. In this way he aided his group in much the same fashion as Axel did in his interchanges with the flight marchers.

One might argue, then, that a small group of persons in face-to-face interaction, visibly suffering under the same administrative rule, is quick to assess the possibilities of the membership for recruitment into positions or roles which will fill various requirements pressed upon the group. In Axel's unit, for instance, other types which developed were the elite and the housekeeper.

The elite were those four men who were both the tallest and the quickest to learn drill and drilling instructions. The men forming behind them depended upon their gestures to keep in orderly formation when wheeling about or changing step. These men could also most easily and quickly conform to other requirements in army routine. They became informal leaders and were even eventually given formal titles as squad leaders by the flight marchers.

The housekeeper started his career in laundering and ironing because the base laundering services were not rapid enough to enable recruits to keep their dress clothes in sufficiently clean and starchy array. Since he learned to soldier competently with the rest, no adverse comments about possible unmanly correlates of housekeeping interests were ever directed toward him and none of his comrades ever questioned him or joked about his comparative lack of masculine aggressiveness. To the contrary, he was highly esteemed because of his ability. Although he was paid for his services, he often good-naturedly helped out comrades without funds but in need of his laundering ability. As a result he himself had an opportunity to rail at the men for whom he performed services, eventually taking on some of the qualities of housemother as well as housekeeper.[6]

The types which have been suggested all emerge from the ranks rather than being introduced from above. They are, however, types which help to sustain the interaction among members of the group and which help to minimize the conflicts between the group and the powers above it. Other types developed by a group—such as the scapegoat,

[5] See footnote 4; p. 117.
[6] Lawrence has commented upon some aspects of this phenomenon, which also occurred in his unit. "White has turned himself into our hut tailor (his father and mother deal in worn clothes), and for a weekly tariff which suits our pay he creases everybody's trousers with the knife-edge that Stiffy demands." See footnote 4; p. 132.

which will be discussed later—are not necessarily so helpful. They may ultimately exacerbate difficulties within the group and between the group and outside influences.

Some groups produce both social types which are clearly useful and social types which are not useful in the functioning of the group. Such a commingling of types is often found in the family, particularly the large family. Bossard and Boll report that specialized roles are often found in large families.

Every family identifies at least one of its siblings as the responsible type, the one that is looked up to, the one that assumes direction or supervision of the other siblings, or renders service to them. The word "responsible" is the one used most frequently in referring to these siblings, but in some cases such words as dutiful, bossy, drudge, leader, helpful, martinet, and policeman are also used.[7]

In addition the authors identified the following: the popular, sociable, well-liked sibling; the social butterfly; the self-centered isolate; the irresponsible one; the sick type; the spoiled child; the student. Bossard and Boll's findings indicated that a family could only maintain one specimen in each slot: If one role or combination of roles was preempted by an older child, those that followed were forced into alternative roles.[8]

Miner has also observed that families tend to guide their children into slots. In the French-Canadian parish he studied, Miner noted that parents choose the inheriting son on the basis of which is the most capable and competent to manage the property and farm. They do their best to encourage other "specialties" among the rest. One is going to become a priest, another is "intellectual," and so on. In one family, the child who was chosen as the intellectual preferred the farm, so the father bought a piece of land for him and another son was promoted into the post of "intellectual." In another family:

Georges is a moron. He can go to church with the family and even was in the boys' choir for awhile until he proved himself incapable. At home he is ignored completely and cut out of all normal social contact with other members of the family. He eats with the younger children, but words are rarely addressed to him. His own statements may pass utterly unnoticed and unanswered. His mother is the only one who ever looks and smiles at him with any kindness. He is frequently sharply reprimanded; such reproaches making him cringe. This treatment has, of course, accentuated his deficiency and accounts for his love of animals, which treat him more humanely.[9]

[7] James H. S. Bossard and Eleanor Stoker Boll, *The Large Family System: An Original Study in the Sociology of Family Behavior;* Philadelphia, Univ. of Pa. Press, 1956; p. 212.

[8] See footnote 7; pp. 212*ff.*

[9] Horace Miner, *St. Denis: A French-Canadian Parish;* Chicago, Univ. of Chicago Press, 1939; p. 204.

On the basis of such instances taken from family life it can be argued that some of the strains and conflicts inherent within closely organized small groups of clearly interdependent persons may be contained through the development of social roles. It might even be argued that the role itself, rather than the actor filling it, serves to integrate the group when conflicts arise or tensions are great.

But if social processes such as role development are at work to resolve or at least mitigate the flow of recurring conflicts and tensions in the tightly knit small group, one is led to the question of how these processes are generated. In the instances taken from the family, it is clear that the formation of types is to a considerable extent imposed from above, though the allocation is influenced by historical accident and the wishes of the participants. The types can be positively or negatively colored; they can be clearly useful or indeterminate in their value to the ongoing life of the group. However, where types are the result of a more democratic process, some more elementary form of collective behavior, it is tempting to argue that they appear because the group really "needs" them: The fool, the elite, the older scholar, the housekeeper can all be seen to service the group in some way.

Since the perils of circular argumentation are well known, perhaps it would be better to avoid the question of why particular social types arise in small groups and to concentrate on one kind of problem which such groups often face: What kinds of roles are available within the group which can reconcile eccentricity or inadequacy in an individual with fairly rigid group expectations for individual behavior? Exploring this question will avoid the dangers of focusing upon the group's needs and permit, instead, an examination of the dialogue which occurs between certain kinds of individuals and their milieu as a 'place' is made for them.

The case history of the career fool illustrates the process through which a collectivity works out a scheme in which it can digest and even benefit from some of its less promising members. This case history also indicates that a wider range of 'tolerable' deviant behavior can exist in a tightly organized group than is suggested by an examination of the norms and the array of sanctions available for use against those who step out of line.

What are the circumstances which permit or even encourage the development of the career fool as a social type?[10] The examples of the

[10] For a general consideration of the sociological significance of foolish behavior possibilities inherent in the fool type, there is no better authority than Orrin Klapp. See especially "The Fool as a Social Type" (see footnote 1), and his recent work, *Heroes, Villains and Fools: The Changing American Character;* New Jersey, Prentice-Hall, 1962; pp. 68–69. In this work, Klapp surveys the variety of fools, such as the simpleton, the clever fool, and the comic butt, and elaborates the many kinds of functions the fool can perform in modern American society.

fool in literature,[11] like the fool in our case history, appear in small, rather tightly knit social worlds bearing some resemblance—in the intimacy of members and the nature of internal social controls—to "primitive" or *gemeinschaft* societies. It may well be that toleration of this form of deviancy is limited to such groups, and that many social worlds within the mass society would rebuke and not tolerate anyone persistently trying to play such a role. While situational fools or butts might still appear, most groups would find it difficult to meet the long-range expectations of career fools. In the first place, the role of career fool demands a long series of experiences in which the reciprocal expectations of the fool and the society supporting him can develop. Some kinds of groups, such as the family, foster such experiences. But in contemporary urban society opportunities to participate in such groups are rare. The example used in this paper is an exception in that the men involved were forced into one another's experience with little more power of choice than one has in choosing his own family; they were required to live wholly in the others' presence for a relatively extended period of time and, thus, to elaborate and maintain a stable set of relationships.

Perhaps there are a few such exceptional environments in modern society: Stablized career fools may be found in total institutions such as boarding schools, convents, and prisons. It may well be that a general characteristic of processing institutions is the imputation of collective responsibility to the inmates. If this be the case, it is easy to see how deviant social types may arise. As the description of the career fool suggests, the pressures of this kind of collective responsibility, and the ambivalent feelings which these pressures arouse, may be partially alleviated by one who can offer the group the catharsis of viewing a below-average performance. Perhaps in all extremely inflexible situations, the career fool can play a useful role as outlet and mediator. First, a feeling of comfortable superiority and confidence in one's own ability can emerge in situations where the fool is in the spotlight. Second,

[11] See especially: Hungry Smeed in Owen Johnston's short story, "The Great Pancake Record," pp. 730–743, in *An Anthology of Famous American Stories*, edited by Angus Burrell and Bennett Cerf; New York, Modern Library, 1936. H. H. Munro, "The Dreamer," in *The Short Stories of Saki;* New York, Viking Press, 1937. Fatty in Sinclair Lewis' *Arrowsmith;* New York, Harcourt Brace, 1925. The more obvious examples include: Cervantes' *Don Quixote*, Dostoevski's *The Idiot,* and the great fools portrayed in the drama, as summarized by O. M. Busby in *Development of the Fool in Elizabethan Drama;* London, Oxford Univ. Press, 1923. In addition, folklore abounds with fools and tricksters, such as the German Till Eulenspiegel or those mentioned in the collection of myths presented by Paul Radin in *The Trickster;* London, Routledge and Kegan Paul, 1956. Finally, historical accounts of various types of fools are offered by: Edith Sitwell, *The English Eccentrics;* New York, Vanguard Press, 1957. Barbara Swain, *Fools and Folly During the Middle Ages and the Renaissance;* New York, Duell, Sloan & Pearce, 1941.

vicarious satisfaction may accompany one's awareness that not everyone is broken or "processed" by the system, no matter how efficient or monolithic it may be. The fool can be the embodiment of each man's wish to escape from the full burden of responsibility which he carries.

In general, however, life in modern society does not encourage the development and maintenance of career fools and it is difficult to think of instances where such types can move freely through society. Nonetheless, a rudimentary type of career fool may be found in large-scale industrial, business, or educational organizations where jobs carry certain tenure connotations and the working atmosphere permits variation, or even negligence and incompetence in performance. The effects of career fools differ in different types of organizations. Some students, for example, may play the fool successfully through high school and then be cashiered in their first term at college.[12] It does seem that groups can encourage and train individuals to conform to expectations of a limited range of social types.

In organizations where variation is permitted, the question of motivation may be important. The evaluation of an individual as a legitimate or illegitimate deviant may influence the margin of toleration afforded him by the group.[13] In some situations where such evaluations may be made—such as basic training—group members will tolerate even "illegitimate" deviance because they are yoked together in a work situation from which it is impossible or difficult to escape or to expel others. It would be interesting to see if, analogously, some people are recognized and tolerated as fools within various departments and bureaus of civil service systems.

The toleration of this and similar social roles serves another function in providing a way in which societies can absorb certain unacceptable kinds of deviants that nevertheless must somehow be harbored. Schneider, in his study of the sick role in army life, has suggested that situations where rigid adherence to the rules of the group is required—for example, basic training—produce certain relatively acceptable deviant roles, such as the role of the sick man.[14] This alternative

[12] See Wayne C. Gordon, *The Social System of the High School;* Glencoe, Ill., Free Press, 1957.

[13] See Dorothy E. Smith, "Legitimate and Illegitimate Deviance: The Case of the State Mental Hospital," *Berkeley J. Sociology* (1959) 5 (Fall):17–20. For good examples of deviance which is illegitimate or intolerable and which results in the extrusion of the deviator, see Kai T. Erikson and David H. Marlow, "The Schizophrenic in Basic Training," pp. 99–131, in *The Symptom as Communication in Schizophrenia,* edited by Kenneth L. Artiss; New York, Grune & Stratton, 1959.

[14] David M. Schneider, "The Social Dynamics of Physical Disability in Army Basic Training," in *Personality in Nature, Society, and Culture,* edited by Clyde Kluckhohn, Henry A. Murray, and David M. Schneider; New York, Knopf, 1953. See also Parsons' analysis of the sick role: Talcott Parsons, *The Social System;* Glencoe, Ill., Free Press, 1951; Ch. 10.

gives those who cannot face the rigors of their new life a way out which is, to be sure, not highly valued, but which is at least not dishonorable. The limits and patterns of behavior accompanying the sick role are learned and perfected through interaction with other members of the group, who show the deviant what to expect and how to manage his position. The sick role, thus, is a legitimate kind of deviance built into the social structure, simultaneously protecting the social system against other kinds of deviance and providing a haven for the individual who cannot meet the demands of the system.

Another instance of legitimized or partially legitimized deviance in a family social role has been suggested by Vogel and Bell.[15] In their view, one child in a family often becomes the scapegoat if parental conflicts have no direct channel of expression. The child manifests emotional disturbance or some form of inadequacy around which the parents can marshal their disapproval. In the family system, the child is both punished and rewarded for his acquiescence and participation in the scapegoat role.

In the instances of the sick role and the scapegoat role, it should not be forgotten that the formation and development of such roles can often exacerbate the difficulties of the person playing the role, as well as fulfill social functions. In the sick role, an individual may 'save' himself only at the cost of moving out of the group, a maneuver which can leave a residue of ambivalence. In the scapegoat role, the individual plainly sacrifices himself by remaining in his position for the good of the group. The position of the fool, however, is more ambiguous. The social system does not view the role of fool as either predominantly positive or negative. The rewards and disadvantages for the participant in the role are such that the margin for negotiation, interpretation, and reinterpretation is great. Only after a lengthy process of interaction can the 'real' function or value of the fool be assessed.

The fool as a social type thus seems to illustrate a different level or intensity of deviancy from that involved in the sick or scapegoat roles. Organizations, subcultures, or even whole societies may find the fool "label"[16] a convenient one for the partly disabled, the weak, those uninterested in the conventional goals, and innovators. The low and ridiculed status of the fool serves as a prop to conventional decency;

15 Ezra F. Vogel and Norman W. Bell, "The Emotionally Disturbed Child as the Family Scapegoat," pp. 382–397, in *The Family*, edited by Norman W. Bell and Ezra F. Vogel; Glencoe, Ill., Free Press, 1960.

16 For a discussion of the way in which "tags" such as "bad boy" or "mischief maker" reinforce role conceptions of the individual, see Edwin M. Lemert, *Social Pathology*; New York, McGraw-Hill, 1951; pp. 76–77. See also Howard S. Becker, *Outsiders: Studies in the Sociology of Deviance*; New York, Free Press of Glencoe, 1963; Ch. 1.

persons so identified can to a certain extent be ignored.[17] At the same time, there is no need to punish such types severely, or to expel them or liquidate them, as may be necessary with extreme deviants.[18]

Considering social types of fools within the framework of tolerable deviation brings up the general question of what part deviant behavior may play in the problem of maintenance and control within any social organization. Dentler and Erikson, for example, have taken the view that deviant behavior is a positive thing which groups tend not only to permit but also to induce and sustain.[19] Groups channel and organize the deviant possibilities contained in the membership to maintain cohesion. Deviants help define the range and levels of group performance, they help define the boundaries of the group itself, and they highlight the comparison of rewards for deviant and conforming behavior. In Dentler and Erikson's view, groups not only permit deviation within them, but also resist any trend toward alienation of a member whose behavior is deviant.

To carry Dentler and Erikson's position somewhat further, it is possible to reinterpret many kinds of deviants and deviant actions as actually functional rather than dysfunctional for the social groupings in which they appear. The fact that societies or even smaller social groups

[17] The fool's role may be useful in softening the effect of conflict or subordinate status. American Negroes have, in the past, shared many jokes about the Negro as fool who wins over the white man by catering to his meanness or susceptibility to flattery. See St. Clair Drake and Horace R. Cayton, *Black Metropolis;* New York, Harcourt, Brace, 1945; p. 723. See also Samuel M. Strong, "Social Types in a Minority Group: Formulation of a Method," *Amer. J. Sociology* (1946) 52:23–30. Strong has pointed out that social types develop around the "axes of life," dominant themes of interest for specific social worlds or the community at large. Thus, for example, familiar, well-institutionalized types have arisen around the color line in the Deep South. And some of the types, such as the "Uncle Tom," illustrate a compromise between the needs and wishes of the subordinate group and the narrow structure provided by the super-ordinate group in which these desires may be expressed. The uneasiness of this particular compromise and the instability of the social type, with its underlying threat of rebellion (or repressed deviance from the viewpoint of the whites), is well expressed by Baldwin. "However inaccurate our portraits of them were, these portraits do suggest, not only the conditions, but the quality of their lives and the impact of this spectacle on our consciences. There was no one more forebearing than Aunt Jemima, no one stronger or more pious or more loyal or more wise; there was, at the same time, no one weaker or more faithless or more vicious and certainly no one more immoral. Uncle Tom, trustworthy and sexless, needed only to drop the title 'uncle' to become violent, crafty, and sullen; a menace to any white woman who passed by." James Baldwin, *Notes of a Native Son;* Boston, Beacon Press, 1955; p. 27.

[18] As Goffman points out, in mental hospitals the patients classified as inmates have paid the price in advance for their deviance. Their acts cease to threaten society, but the system contains the deviance at the price of the reputation of the deviants. Therefore, no further sanctions by social or physical deprivation are necessary. See Erving Goffman, *Behavior in Public Places: Notes on the Social Organization of Gatherings;* New York, Free Press of Glencoe, 1963.

[19] Robert A. Dentler and Kai T. Erikson, "The Functions of Deviance in Groups," *Social Problems* (1959) 7 (Fall):98–107.

do not have a single set of clearly delineated rules or models for social interaction has often been documented.[20] It seems reasonable to argue that rules and understandings in social groupings are contradictory because humans face so many contradictory pressures and demands. The contradictions arise because of the complex and overlapping combinations of social institutions and expectations for behavior within them, and also because many of the exigencies of life are unanticipated (what Sumner called "aleatory factors"). One can expect the formation of stabilized deviant roles as the precipitates of social interaction in which clashing interests may themselves be stabilized through the persons who play out the deviant roles.[21]

If one adopts this perspective, the fool as a deviant may be seen in a new light. He may occupy a low and ridiculed position in society, but it is a position which nevertheless possesses attractive possibilities both for him and for his society. For his part, the fool has a licensed freedom; he can do things others would not risk for fear of losing face because he has only a slight position to protect.[22] Attached to his license is a sort of negative celebrity which is something of an achievement, particularly in modern societies where only a few can be known for anything at all. Moreover, the fool's conduct can be in society's interest beyond its value as a form of boundary maintenance or cautionary tale for the less audacious. History is, after all, replete with inci-

[20] See Karl Llewellyn, "Remarks on the Theory of Appellate Decision and the Rules or Canons About How Statutes Are to be Construed," *Vanderbilt Law Review* (1950) 3:395–406. See also Robert Merton, George Reader, and Patricia Kendall (eds.), *The Student Physician:* Cambridge, Mass., Harvard Univ. Press, 1957; pp. 72–76.

[21] Gluckman has suggested evidence for the position that strains and stresses inevitably arise in society because individuals often must subordinate their own interests and desires to the end of preserving a social order. In the societies that he studied, institutionalized means for the expression of social tensions developed, so that members of the society could, through "rituals of rebellion," express their discontent. "A most striking feature of [the] organization [of these ceremonies] is the way in which they openly express social tensions: Women have to assert license and dominance as against their formal subordination to men, princes have to behave to the king as if they covet the throne, and subjects openly state their resentment of authority." Max Gluckman, *Rituals of Rebellion in South-East Africa;* Manchester, England, Manchester Univ. Press, 1954; p. 3.

In his examples, however, Gluckman deals mainly with primitive societies: illustrations from complex civilizations are scanty. Where many competing social worlds exist within a society, where many alternative explanations or evaluations of behavior are possible, it may well be that individuals must attempt to resolve inevitable social conflicts and tensions either within themselves or through the offices of those few who play somewhat institutionalized deviant roles, as in our example.

For some of the broader implications of this view for the development of new theoretical perspectives, see Pierre L. van den Berghe, "Dialectic and Functionalism," *Amer. Sociol. Review* (1963) 28:695–705.

[22] For examples of other ways in which individuals may seize upon opportunities to enlarge or expand their position beyond what is formally allowed to them, see Thomas J. Scheff, "Control Over Policy by Attendants in a Mental Hospital," *J. Health and Human Behavior* (1961) 2:93–105.

dents in which the fool triumphs over his low and ridiculed status; bohemian artists, mad inventors, crazy musicians, and absent-minded professors occasionally show in everyday life that they were right to have been "foolish." In the meantime, while society is not sure what verdict posterity will hand down, judgment can be held partly in abeyance. The status and general position of the fool within his social group illustrates one possible variation which does not represent conformity, yet is still tolerated, for the individuals who choose an outside position in society or find such a position thrust upon them.

23

Theodore D. Kemper

Representative Roles and the Legitimation of Deviance*

It is well-known fact of organizational life that organization members are frequently deviant.[1] They steal, come late, procrastinate, "goof off," fail to give proper service to customers and clients, forget to report details to superiors, and otherwise subvert the goals of the organization or deprive it of its rights, either in services or in material goods. Deviant acts of this type are violations of major rules of organizational life. These are not the "mock rules" described by Gouldner,[2] and the occurrence of

From *Social Problems*, 13 (Winter, 1966), 288–298, by permission of the author and the publishers.

* The author wishes to thank the following of his colleagues for their helpful criticisms of an earlier version of this paper: David Chaplin, Jerald Hage, Warren Hagstrom, David Heise, Gerald Marwell, Kenneth Reichstein, and David Schmitt. Research for this report was done while the author was supported in part by a grant from the Air Force Office of Scientific Research (AF-AFOSR 545–64).

[1] Deviant behavior is here defined as behavior which violates the more or less institutionalized expectations for performance of organizational roles set forth by the formal organization, i.e. those with the authority to make the rules and to sanction deviants. Not only are theft, lateness, and careless workmanship included in the concept of deviance dealt with here, but also ideological types of deviance as exemplified by the quota-restrictions of the "bank-wiring" room workers reported in Fritz J. Roethlisberger and William J. Dickson, *Management and the Worker*, Cambridge: Harvard University Press, 1939. See also Donald Roy, "Quota Restriction and Goldbricking in a Machine Shop," *American Journal of Sociology*, 57 (January 1952), pp. 427–442. Since informal systems can generate rules and norms which help the formal system accomplish its goals even while deviating from the norms of the formal system, only deviant behavior which manifestly harms the formal system or is intended to harm it will be considered here.

[2] Alvin W. Gouldner, *Patterns of Industrial Bureaucracy*, Glencoe, Ill.: The Free Press, 1954.

deviance in regard to these norms reduces either the effectiveness or the efficiency of the organization, or both.[3]

There are several approaches to the explanation of these phenomena in organizations. One of these would hold that individual members are insufficiently educated in their responsibilities as organization members, that the problem starts early in lack of adequate socialization in regard for the cultural decencies such as honesty, loyalty, a full day's work for a full day's pay, and the like.[4] This type of explanation may be termed *psychological* since it looks at the problem of deviance as an outcome of failure within individuals, i.e. some individuals were well-made at the proper point in time and others simply weren't.[5] There is no doubt an element of truth to this explanation, since there is also no doubt that some indivduals have received better training in honesty than have others.

But this explanation is not entirely satisfactory. It is atomistic and fails to take cognizance of the many conditions that must be present in order to trigger a deviant act. One of these is opportunity.[6] Another involves precipitating conditions in the social structure which can serve to legitimize deviance, from the deviant's point of view.

Sociologists have therefore sought for explanations of deviance in terms of the system or the organization itself. Thus, Merton's analysis of the disjunction between culturally approved goals and culturally approved means and the relatively low access to approved means by certain groups of the population points toward elements of social structure as the source of deviance rather than toward the individual and his conscience.[7]

Analyses by Granick and by Bendix of the Soviet industrial executive show clearly that it is virtually impossible for the executive to

[3] For discussion of *effectiveness* and *efficiency*, see Chester I. Barnard, *The Functions of the Executive*, Cambridge: Harvard University Press, 1938.

[4] We may infer that Talcott Parsons, for example, would phrase the answer to organizational deviance in this way. See, for example, his analysis of the role of the family in the preparation of individuals to play roles in the economy in Talcott Parsons and Neil J. Smelser, *Economy and Society*, Glencoe, Ill.: The Free Press, 1956. If individuals are deviant in their economic roles it is largely because of inadequate socialization while in the hands of the societal sector responsible for socialization in these matters, namely the family.

[5] Although, even from this perspective the "failure" is in the socializing agents, the explanation is still termed *psychological* because the deviance originates in the *individual* due either to ignorance of the institutional sub-structure of norms governing social life in general, or due to inability to control the desire for objects or activities requiring deviant behavior to enjoy.

[6] See for example Richard A. Cloward, "Illegitimate Means, Anomie, and Deviant Behavior," *American Sociological Review*, 24, 1959, pp. 164–176.

[7] Robert K. Merton, "Social Structure and Anomie," *Social Theory and Social Structure* (rev. ed.), Glencoe, Ill.: The Free Press, 1957.

meet all the demands placed upon him.[8] With respect to some member of his role set, or with respect to some code or standard propounded by the larger system, he must be deviant. In this instance the rules are often subverted in order to meet the goal. Field, also dealing with a Soviet functionary, describes the "structured strain" in the role of the Soviet physician.[9] Conflicting norms and expectations emanating from the state, from professional rules of conduct, and from citizen-patients frequently lead to a violation of one or another rule. In American industry, the role of foreman has similarly received attention as one which is structurally located at a point which almost necessitates deviance from the point of view of either management or workers.[10] Other structural features of organizations which lead to role conflict, deviance, and stress are described by Kahn et al.[11] This type of sociological analysis shows that there can be conditions within which not deviance, but the lack of deviance must be explained.

From the sociologist's point of view, individuals engage in deviant acts but the sources of deviance may often be found in the contradictory postures and requirements of the organization, i.e. in elements of its structure.

The purpose of this paper is to offer some additional thoughts on the subject of the organizationally-fostered impetus to deviance by organization members. The basic difference between the approach to the problem suggested here and previous approaches is that the earlier studies of "strain" and deviance were focused mainly on (a) contradictory or ambiguous demands or (b) impossible scheduling, while what is proposed here is an additional source of deviance, namely failures in the system of mutual expectations which bind together organizations and their members.

REPRESENTATIVE ROLES AND IDEALIZED EXPECTATIONS

Parsons suggests that social objects can be either persons or collectivities.[12] For analytic purposes there appears to be little distinction in the Theory of Action. In practice, however, there is much to be said for a somewhat different approach, namely one which holds that at any given level, the organization, i.e. its rules, claims, and demands, is

[8] David Granick, The Red Executive, Garden City, N.Y.: Doubleday, 1961. Reinhardt Bendix, "Industrialization, Ideologies and Social Structure," American Sociological Review, 24, 1959, pp. 613–623.

[9] Mark G. Field, "Structured Strain in the Role of the Soviet Physician," American Journal of Sociology, 58 (March, 1953), pp. 493–500.

[10] Burleigh B. Gardner and D. G. Moore, Human Relations in Industry (rev. ed.), Chicago: Irwin, 1950.

[11] Robert L. Kahn, Donald M. Wolfe, Robert P. Quinn, J. Diedrick Snoek, and Robert A. Rosenthal, Organizational Stress, New York: John Wiley and Sons, 1964.

[12] Talcott Parsons, The Social System, Glencoe, Ill.: The Free Press, 1951.

personified by those at the next higher level of authority. Thus, for the enlisted man, the Army, that is to say the *organization* which can direct his daily duties and activities, consists of all who give orders respecting his person. For the second lieutenant, the organization consists of all captains and above. In general, in any hierarchial group, for any member, the group and its will and purpose are manifested by and in those who have authority over the member[13]. To occupy a position of authority means, *ex officio*, to play a *representative role*.[14] Not only does each person at a given level represent the organization from the point of view of those below him, but these same persons cannot help but be aware that they do so. For one thing, those on lower levels treat them so, but, in addition, they are expected to represent the organization to those below by those above. It is suggested here that this kind of representative-role "altercasting" appears to be an inevitable feature of organizational life.[15] It is, however, exactly in the performance of the representative role which goes with authority, regardless of how slight, that we find additional sources of deviance. These are found in the nature of the expectations generated in lower organization members during enactment of the representative roles.

Probably the cardinal norm to be observed in the performance of such a role is that the group itself shall not be depreciated or betrayed. Facts will thus have a tendency to bow to ideology, and honesty to "public relations." The crucial point for the place of the re-

[13] Authority in the rational-legal Weberian sense is intended here, not simply naked power. Max Weber, *The Theory of Social and Economic Organization,* edited by Talcott Parsons, London: William Hodge and Co., 1942.

[14] In an earlier work Talcott Parsons, *op. cit.,* 1951, wrote: "When the special concern is with relations of the collectivity and its members outside itself, to other persons and collectivities, it may be called a 'representative' role." (p. 100) In a later work, however, Parsons wrote: "Because she is the primary link between the two systems, (the mother) plays a *representative role* on behalf of the family in relation to her child. Whatever different members of the family do empirically in relation to the child, by him she is 'held responsible' and, vice versa, the family holds her responsible for her treatment of the child." See Talcott Parsons and James Olds, "The Mechanisms of Personality Functioning with Special Reference to Socialization," in Talcott Parsons and Robert F. Bales, *Family, Socialization and Interaction Process,* Glencoe, Ill.: The Free Press, 1955, p. 204. (Italics in text.) It is in the latter sense of representative role, i.e. one which is played within an existing collectivity, in this case an organization, that the term is employed here. Erving Goffman who uses the concept, though not the term, generally confines himself to the former usage. See Erving Goffman, *The Presentation of Self in Everyday Life,* Edinburgh, Scotland: University of Edinburgh Social Science Research Center, 1958, p. 47. A curious instance of representative role playing involves the informal practice of sending life sentence prisoners in federal penitentiaries to other prisons when a new warden is appointed. The purpose apparently is to reduce the likelihood that a prisoner will come to represent the traditional authority of the particular prison due to his long acquaintanceship with it and its local precedents and previous administrations.

[15] Eugene A. Weinstein and Paul Deutschberger, "Some Dimensions of Altercasting," *Sociometry,* **26** (December 1963), pp. 454–466. To "altercast" is to act in such a manner to another person as to cause the other to assume a given role.

presentative role in the generation of deviance is that it leads to an idealization of expectations relating to the organization simply by virtue of the fact that idealization is what the role invites.[16]

Idealized expectations are of two major kinds. 1. First are those involving the *obligations* of the organization, thus implying the *rights* of organization members. This is the standard type of idealization practiced by public relations, personnel, sales, and marketing men when they represent the organization to the outside world. But to insiders as well, the requirements of representative-role-playing dictate a strategy of idealization of the organization—its goals, purposes, means, functional importance, quality and quantity of rewards, and the like. Among the problematic questions which each organization confronts as it attempts to reach its goals is that of the adequate motivation of its personnel. Even where knowledge of role requirements is granted, as well as the ability to perform the role, the motivational issue remains open. Obviously motivation is hinged to rewards, but very few organizations have the resources to provide immediate high level rewards for high levels of motivation. Thus the rewards are projected into the future, or, lesser rewards, available now, are dramatized and highlighted. This front of perfection which each level of authority presents to those inside who are below them in status serves certain integrative and morale functions, quite apart from its potency in obtaining high level motivation in the present as a means of obtaining rewards in the future.

2. The second type of idealization involves the *obligations* of organization members, thus implying the *rights* of the organization. Stand-

[16] Idealization must be seen as central to the performance of the representative role. This is true not only when the representative role is played internally, but, *a fortiori*, when it is played externally. Think for example of diplomats and negotiators who attempt to trade on the idealized images they convey about their groups. In some instances the idealization of the external representative role player leads to internal deviance. This can happen when a department manager promises his superiors that his department will do a job in record time, or when a military officer volunteers his men for an especially dangerous operation. Idealization can therefore be seen to suffer from the constraint imposed on all "extreme" solutions, namely that there is a tendency for regression toward the mean. The mean in this sense must be understood as a less than ideal performance. One of the possible strategies that may be employed by an external representative role player, especially when representing his group to higher authority, is purposely to *under*state the capacities of his group. This permits the group to comply with requirements with a minimum of strain. For a discussion of many different types of idealization practiced by individuals, see Erving Goffman, *op. cit.*, pp. 22–32. It is suggested here that idealization is the central distorting feature of the representative role. Other distortions are possible. For example, the structural position of the representative role player may prevent him from obtaining a complete or an accurate view of his subordinates' interests, capacities, and attitudes. When he distorts in this manner there is also the likelihood of a deviant response by subordinates who can resent requests and orders which fail to take account of their particular situation.

ards of punctuality, honesty, workmanship, loyalty and the like are set forth to each employee—explicitly in some cases—as representing the fair expectations of the organization. In most cases, these universalistic expectations apply to everyone in the organization indiscriminately. There are few instances today of a "higher morality" which reduces the burdens of upper levels and does not apply to lower levels. If such arrangements exist, they are very infrequently made public. In the universalistically oriented industrial-economic sector, in American society at least, it would be very difficult to sustain a public stand of differential morality for upper and lower levels in the face of a democratic ideology that relates to work.[17] Thus, even the incumbents of representative roles are constrained by the very obligations it is their duty to present to and demand of organization members. In fact, as representative role players, their own conformity to these obligatory expectations is the organization's warrant to each echelon that universalism, equity, and fairness are true organizational values. If there is a "higher morality" for public consumption, i.e. in the first sense of idealization, it is to the effect that those who exercise authority are models of punctuality, honesty, workman-like performance, and loyalty. Thus every representative-role player not only conveys verbally the organization's *obligations*, but in his person and behavior he himself is a model of the organization's *rights*. In two senses, then, the occupant of the representative role conveys idealized expectations which have their source in the organization.

But, just as inevitable as the idealization is the failure of the organization to live up to the ideal image which has been presented. This occurs in one of two ways: (1) The organization as an entity fails to live up to the expectations the idealized image has evoked—e.g. bonuses which were promised are cancelled because "business was bad"; or (2) someone in the line of authority—who represents the organization— is himself deviant, with or without the sanction of the organizational hierarchy.

When the organization as entity or the organization in the person of a superior fails to live up to the idealized expectations it has implanted in its members, it is itself being deviant. It is crucial to see that it is the organization which is considered deviant in either case, that is, whether the organization itself fails to meet its obligations to organization members or whether a representative role player has violated universalistic

[17] Other sectors of society are not quite as free of the implication of the inferiority of some that differential morality implies. The outstanding example in contemporary American society is the treatment of the Negro and other minorities. Differential privilege and morality is legitimated ideologically by the argument that the Negro (*et al.*) is inferior.

member obligations. The organization still is identified with the latter type of deviance, because of the nature of the representative role.

Deviance by the organization, which has made the rules and, through the representative role mechanism, conveyed them to organization members, opens up a major avenue for the legitimation[18] of deviance by those who now see the organization in its true light. Thus where there were no previous grounds for deviance, nor explanation for it except individual dishonesty, a rationale is created for all but the compulsive conformists, deviants in their own right.[19] In sum the argument we have woven is as follows:

(1) Organizations are personified at each level of authority to those below, and individuals at all levels, except the lowest, enact representative roles to those below.

(2) One aspect of playing the representative role is that the organization is defended and idealized.

(3) Two kinds of idealized expectations are involved here: (a) first are those involving the obligations of the organization, i.e. the rights of organization members; (b) second are those involving the obligations of organization members, i.e. the rights of the organization.

(4) These idealized versions of the organization become the basis for the expectations organization members have for the organization.

(5) Another aspect of the representative role is that the occupant is expected to perform in an exemplary manner according to the ideal expectations of the organization.

(6) Since the organization or the representative role player frequently fails to live up to the ideal image, the expectations are frustrated and deviance on the part of the organization's members is thereby legitimated.

We may analyze two kinds of deviance in this light. The first of these is *reciprocal* deviance and the second is *parallel* deviance.

[18] I have used the term *legitimation* generically to comprehend both deviant behavior which is publicly proclaimed as rightful as well as behavior which is covert but for which justification is claimed nevertheless. An example of the first is a "slowdown" on an assembly line as an answer to a "speedup." An example of the second is theft by warehouse employees who read about the price-fixing convictions of their higher-ups. This distinction follows Merton, who classifies deviant behavior as either "non-conforming" or "aberrant," depending mainly on the degree of legitimacy attributed to the deviant behavior. The definition used here departs from Merton in that legitimation is used for both kinds of deviant response, as long as the response is associated with a prior instance of organizational deviance. For other distinctions between aberrant and non-conforming deviance see Robert K. Merton, "Social Problems and Sociological Theory," in Robert K. Merton and Robert A. Nisbet (eds.), *Contemporary Social Problems*, New York: Harcourt, Brace and World, 1961, esp. pp. 723–729.

[19] Talcott Parsons, *op. cit.*, 1951, describes the deviance of the compulsive conformist. See also Robert K. Merton's "Social Theory and Social Structure," in his *Social Theory and Social Structure* (rev. ed.), Glencoe, Ill.: The Free Press, 1957, pp. 149–153.

RECIPROCAL DEVIANCE

When the organization either as an entity, or in the person of a superior, has defaulted on the obligations of the organization to its members, reciprocal deviance can result.[20] Reciprocal deviance is the deviance evoked as punishment.[21] There are several well-known types of organizational deviance which invite reciprocal deviance as a response.

1. *Failure to recognize merit.* This is perhaps one of the principal causes of deviance in organizations, especially among those whose positions allow them to exhibit merit. Organizational politics, supervisor cowardice or jealousy, a bad quarterly report, may all lead to failure to give sufficient recognition to meritorious service within the proper time limit for its notice. Here, the often ambiguous or vaguely worded organizational statements about the recognition of merit are helpful in giving those in authority latitude to avoid living up to the expectations the organization has generated. Initially the individual is usually told to expect handsome treatment for services well-performed. When these rewards are not forthcoming, i.e. when the organization is deviant, the individual in question is undoubtedly deflected from pursuing the goals of the organization with the same vigor as previously. The individual affront, however, is only part of the consequence. Peers at the same level who know the story are also given pause as to whether their exertions will be credited and rewarded. As a balm to ruffled feelings, the individual may indulge himself in extra days off, lateness, inattentiveness to matters requiring immediate attention, perhaps a higher expense account on the next trip, and so on.

---

[20] Talcott Parsons, *op. cit.*, 1951, in his analysis of deviance and social control discusses the dangers of reciprocity as a response to deviance on the part of alter. Non-reciprocity is listed as a control mechanism which prevents a spiraling cycle of deviance-reciprocal deviance-deviance, etc. While non-reciprocity of deviance is entirely plausible as a control mechanism, it is perhaps more applicable to the interpersonal realm than to the intercollectivity or inter-person-collectivity as is often the case in large scale organizations.

[21] Alvin W. Gouldner, in his article "The Norm of Reciprocity," *American Sociological Review*, 25 (April, 1960), pp. 161–178, deals with reciprocity as a "universal . . . element of culture" which is normatively specified or exists ". . . as a dimension to be found in all value systems and, in particular, as one among a *number* of 'Principal Components' universally present in moral codes." (p. 171) Gouldner also states that the norm ". . . makes two interrelated, minimal demands: (1) people should help those who have helped them, and (2) people should not injure those who have helped them." Gouldner does not go on to discuss what is perhaps a universal contra-normative imperative, namely, "hurt those who have hurt you." Forebearance, forgiveness, and turning the other cheek play as central a role as they do in various religious codes only because of the powerful urge to revenge wrongs done to one. Gouldner also does not discuss the *lex talionis* in what is perhaps its fundamental significance for society, namely as a form of social control. People have undoubtedly refrained from doing ill and have thus allowed society to hold together as much from fear of retaliation as from any positive motives.

2. *Increase in amount of work expected.* The "speed up" is a common cause for a visit to the plant superintendent by the union grievance committee. There is nothing inherently wrong, within limits, in the organization's demanding *at the outset* an amount of output equal, say, to $X+5$. But there is much that appears wrong with the organization's expecting, and leading others to believe, that the desired amount of output is only X, and then at some point, raising it to $X+5$. This is especially true at present when, theoretically, pay is hinged to productivity. Where any attempt is made to abrogate the pay-productivity ratio in a downward direction this is tantamount to deviance on the part of the organization. The consequence is the slow-down, or worse, a strike.[22]

In general, when obligations assumed by the organization in these and other areas *vis-à-vis* its own personnel are violated by the organization, a reciprocating process of deviance by organization members is initiated. Under three special conditions, however, reciprocal deviance will be avoided or minimized:

1. *Members have power to halt organization deviance.* In the case where organization members have the power to halt or reverse the deviance of the organization or of its representative engaging in deviance of the relevant type, the likelihood of reciprocal deviance is minimized. The true strength of a union is shown not only in how well it bargains during contract talks, but how well it deals with day-to-day grievances which are perceived as organizational deviance. A strike threat or the actual strike (if successful) represents the power of the union to reverse the effects of organizational deviance.

Procedures for "going over the head" of a deviant supervisor place a certain degree of power in the hands of lower organization members. The office of Inspector-General in the armed forces, for example, is a mechanism which gives some power to organization members to resist or reverse deviant plans, programs, and orders from higher authorities.[23]

2. *The representative role player is not viewed as a legitimate incumbent.* It has been suggested here that anyone in a position of authority assumes the mantle of the representative role to those below. While the position of authority is assumed in an instant, the actual acceptance of a new person in a position of authority may take some time. New supervisors are always on trial, in a certain sense, with the

[22] It is of interest to note that whereas the slowdown is simply deviant, i.e. there is no formal institutional support for it in labor contracts, the strike, which is a far more serious response, is not deviant, but fully institutionalized and formalized.

[23] There is growing sentiment for the institution of legal guarantees in private organizations involving such mechanisms as due process, right of appeal, etc. See William M. Evan, "Organization Man and Due Process of Law," *American Sociological Review,* **26** (August, 1961), pp. 540–547, and Richard Eells, *The Government of Corporations,* Glencoe, Ill.: The Free Press, 1962.

persons they supervise. Until they demonstrate their "right" to supervise, they are accorded less than full recognition as representatives of
the organization. Thus, when the new supervisor unwittingly orders a
change from an established and favored pattern, he can be excused
by the lower organization members as "new," "ignorant," "doesn't know
the score," etc. Reciprocal deviance will be withheld until the situation
proves unnegotiable. In the meantime, the organization itself is not
blamed for the errors of the new man, unless it is blamed for giving
him the position of authority in the first place. As may be seen this is
an unstable situation which changes to stability in a fairly short time;
the new supervisor, after a time, simply isn't new any more. His authority is now consolidated with organization authority and his actions
fully represent the organization. His deviance is then accorded reciprocal deviance, as long as no countervailing power exists to control his
deviance.

3. *The organization is non-profit.* In non-profit organizations there
may be a lesser tendency to respond with deviance to the deviance of
representative-role players. This should be true not only for reciprocal
deviance, but also for the parallel type of deviance discussed below.
In the non-profit organization all members are invoked to provide not
merely service, but, to greater or lesser extent, a moral commitment
to the goals of the organization as well. Even if the organization or a
representative-role player is deviant, the additional moral commitment
to the aims of the organization is thereby not usually abrogated, except
in extreme instances, where idealism turns to cynicism. This would
seem to be the case only when ultimate values are at stake, as in a religion or an all-embracing social movement.[24]

PARALLEL DEVIANCE

Parallel deviance, on the other hand, is not founded on motives of
revenge. It involves, simply, legitimated deviance at lower levels in
imitation of the deviance of upper levels. Legitimation stems from
the representative role aspects of the position of authority. The reasoning, reduced to its simplest format, is that "if the boss (read the
organization) can do it, so can I." By and large it is "homeomorphic" deviance, i.e. similar in kind.[25] Parallel deviance may be functional in that
it advances the ends of both levels, as, for example, the violation of

[24] For a distinction between economic and non-economic organizations which is
nearly co-extensive with profit and non-profit organizations see Amitai Etzioni, "Industrial Sociology: The Study of Economic Organizations," in Amitai Etzioni (ed.),
Complex Organizations, New York: Holt, Rinehart and Winston, 1961, pp. 130–141.

[25] Alvin W. Gouldner, *op. cit.,* uses the term "homeomorphic" to denote reciprocity in kind, and the term "heteromorphic" to denote repayment in other than the
same currency.

work rules in open conspiracy with foremen so that production goals can be met.[26] On the other hand, the deviance of both may be dysfunctional, as in the case of theft. When a boss gives his secretary an obviously padded expense account, the secretary may conclude that a bit of theft on her own part is therefore legitimate.[27] The parallelism of deviance between superiors and subordinates can be extended to a number of spheres. If the boss takes afternoons off to play golf, the office staff will be taking the afternoons off as well—as best it can; if the supervisor inspects parts in a careless haphazard manner, the work force will make them in a careless, haphazard manner, and so on.[28] As in the case of reciprocal deviance, the important consideration in instances of parallel deviance is the fact of its apparent *legitimation* by someone in authority who personifies the organization itself. Underlying this, of course, is an egalitarian social philosophy which grants no one the permission to stand outside the law. Thus, when a worker joins the work force and sees his peers acting in a deviant manner, he may, despite peer group pressure, resist joining them. He may feel that it is not right, and even after some practice, the deviant behavior is still recognized as *morally* wrong. But once let the boss show himself less than scrupulous with clients or with organizational resources, the worker's deviance is legitimated and the standards of compliance to organizational principle are shown to be simply myth and of no account.

In this regard it is said that there is more rejoicing in heaven when one sinner repents than when 10 righteous men enter the gates of heaven. Not so in society, for here the fall of one righteous man shakes the foundations of the whole system.[29]

It is of interest to note that while certain social structural features of organizations can provide a basis for deviance, once the deviance

[26] Joseph Bensman and Israel Gerver, "Crime and Punishment in the Factory: The Function of Deviancy in Maintaining the Social System," *American Sociological Review*, 28 (August, 1963), pp. 588–598. The authors clearly show that foreman and senior workers socialize newer men into the process of using illegal tools to do certain jobs.

[27] Cf. Erwin O. Smigel, "Public Attitudes toward Stealing as Related to Size of Victim Organization," *American Sociological Review*, 21 (June, 1956), pp. 320–327. Smigel writes: "Distrust and resentment of big business led 21 percent of the individuals who would rather steal from large business to apply the 'eye for an eye' principle in making their decision. They believed that big business robbed them either by outright theft, or by charging exorbitant prices. In either event, this 'behavior' on the part of large business provided justification for those who chose to steal from large business. . . ."

[28] Joseph Bensman and Israel Gerver, *op. cit.*

[29] Although no data are available, it is interesting to speculate on the possible increases in rates of theft and other forms of deviance at lower levels of the work force when major instances of white collar crimes are discovered. For example, the recent convictions of high level personnel of General Electric and other companies for price-fixing should, theoretically, have unleashed a rash of behaviors definable as parallel deviance.

occurs, psychological mechanisms may better explain what happens next.[30] For example, where a boss is deviant there may be either a greater or lesser tendency on his part to observe and control the deviance of his subordinates. Presumably if his own deviance must be psychically defended against, he will be overly concerned with whether his subordinates are meeting their obligations. If, on the other hand, his deviance is so acknowledged a fact that he is no longer threatened by it psychologically, there will be a relative laxity in enforcing conformity by subordinates. In some instances, where deviance by the boss is an open secret, there arises the possibility of either overt or covert collusion between boss and subordinates both to protect themselves and each other, and to profit from deviance. An extreme example of this kind involves the cooperative relations between corrupt prison guards and prisoners in whose employe they serve as much as they serve the penal institution. As can be seen, too, from this example, some partnerships in deviance strongly resist reversal. Thus, once a corrupt partnership is underway, the one who is by and large officially the more responsible, carrying either public or corporate trust, has the more to lose and consequently finds himself less free in the situation than those who are nominally his subordinates or in his charge.

SOME IMPLICATIONS FOR ORGANIZATIONS

Even given some of the proposed inevitabilities, e.g. idealization of the organization and subsequent disappointment, organizations are not entirely powerless to prevent deviance. For example, close supervision of material and money can reduce to a considerable extent instigatory and legitimating acts of deviance as well as their consequent reciprocals and parallels. There are, of course, limits to the amount of supervision that is possible without leading to serious dysfunctional consequences. For example, "frisking" every employee at the end of the day would generate serious problems of resentment.

The general question which needs to be answered has to do with the extent to which organization ideology and truth can be co-extensive. As proposed here, there will, inevitably, be slippage between ideology and practice, thus inviting either reciprocal or parallel deviance. However, the two types of deviance are quite different in motivation, although the general source is identical. This may be seen from the fact that only in the instances where reciprocal deviance is a potential consequence does the organization have options other than

[30] Gresham M. Sykes and David Matza, "Techniques of Neutralization," *American Sociological Review*, 22 (December, 1957), pp. 664–671. Sykes and Matza discuss five psychological release mechanisms which they suggest are operative in delinquent behavior. In different degrees they can be applied as personal rationalizations of any act of deviance.

close supervision at all levels. Where the slippage between ideal and practice is honestly regretted by the organization, there appears to be room for introduction of compensatory mechanisms, which may, in some instances, even foster higher morale and individual allegiance to the organization than existed before the instigatory act(s) of deviance occurred.

1. *Full Disclosure.* Honesty by the organization concerning its situation would appear to offer greater chance for success in controlling potential deviance than any other mechanism. The familiar story (if not practice) of the boss who is willing to tell the truth about the organization to his subordinates, who, in turn, are willing to do anything for him, is the case in point. At issue, though, is the question of whether the high level of allegiance to the honest boss is due to his honesty or his rarity. This of course is a researchable question.

Full disclosure may also have its drawbacks as may all of the mechanisms discussed here. The issue pivots on whether or not there is a likelihood that the organization is only temporarily discrepant, or whether the ideology is in the process of retreating to a lower level of reward potential so as to avoid the appearance of slippage in the future.

2. *Reduction of rewards to organization authorities.* Another way to establish confidence in the honest intentions of the organization and the men who represent it is to reduce the rewards of those who represent the organization at its highest levels. If salaries and benefits are to be cut, trimming at the very top provides assurances to those below that the organization takes responsibility for its own acts of deviance and does not, defensively, as it were, attempt to shift the consequences to others.

3. *Institution of limited-cost alternatives.* Where possible the organization may institute a series of low-cost alternatives to those that are being prevented by the slippage. These might include token raises to those who merit them or who have been promised them, even while reductions are instituted at higher levels. Needless to say, a minimax strategy must be employed here, lest reduction in differential rewards reach a dysfunctional point.

Even when the organization employs a compensating mechanism, there is danger to the organization. Excessive reduction of upper level rewards may depress motivation for achievement at lower levels; downward revision of the ideology for internal consumption may leak out and create difficulty with credit sources and threaten public or client confidence in the organization.

It should be noted finally that there is no way in which legitimated deviance can be eliminated entirely. The normal exigencies of existence will lead to some degree of organizational failure to live up to certain idealized expectations, and legitimated deviance is likely to occur.

24

Mark Lefton

Shirley S. Angrist

Simon Dinitz

Benjamin Pasamanick[1]

Social Class, Expectations and Performance of
   Mental Patients

Sociologists have recently turned their attention to what promises to be a fruitful avenue by which to substantiate their professional concern in the area of mental illness—namely, the clinical psychiatric process and its necessary consequence, case outcome. One of the more positive results of this recent emphasis has been the delineation of social class and class-related factors (as determining variables in such psychiatric procedures as diagnosis and treatment and in the post-treatment experiences of former patients. On one hand, the Hollingshead group has paid particular attention to class and diagnosis and treatment.[2] H. E. Freeman and O. G. Simmons, on the other hand, try to relate class and expectations to the performance levels of patients who succeed in remaining in the community following a period of hospitalization.[3] The

Reprinted from "Social Class, Expectations and Performance of Mental Patients," by M. Lefton, S. Angrist, S. Dinitz, and B. Pasamanick, *The American Journal of Sociology,* **68** (July 1962), 79–87, by permission of the University of Chicago Press. Copyright 1962 by the University of Chicago.

[1] This research was undertaken by the Research Division of the Columbus Psychiatric Institute and Hospial and was supported by a grant (M-2953) from the National Institute of Mental Health. During the course of this investigation, Shirley Angrist held a pre-doctoral fellowship from the National Institute of Mental Health, United States Public Health Service.

[2] A. B. Hollingshead and F. C. Redlich, *Social Class and Mental Illness: A Community Study* (New York: John Wiley & Sons, 1958).

[3] These authors have published a number of papers relevant to this issue: e.g., "Mental Patients in the Community: Family Settings and Performance Levels," *American Sociological Review,* **XXIII** (April, 1958), 147–54; "Wives, Mothers and the Posthospital Performance of Mental Patients," *Social Forces,* **XXXVII** (December, 1958), 153–59; "The Social Integration of Former Mental Patients," *International Journal of Social Psychiatry,* Vol. IV (Spring, 1959). Other papers will be cited when appropriate.

specification of these variables by Freeman and Simmons, as correlates of posthospital performance, is derived directly from their investigation of the experiences of 182 psychotic males in which the following findings were obtained: (1) a direct relationship exists between the class status of the patient's family and performance level[4] and (2) a direct relationship exists between the expectations of family members and performance level.[5] Interpreting these results they argue that (a) middle-class families are relatively less tolerant of deviant behavior than others and their poor performers are, therefore, more likely to have been returned to the hospital and (b) if congruence between expectations and performance is essential to the stability of an interpersonal system, low performance on the part of a patient must be complemented by low expectations on the part of his relatives in order for him to remain in the family.

Two separate questions or problems are raised by this work. First, to what extent are these findings which are based on a sample of chronic male patients applicable to the study of other types of mental patients (for example, acute cases, females)? Second, Freeman and Simmons fail to provide a demonstration of the relationship between social class and expectations.[6] The failure to do so is important for several reasons. To begin with, the absence of a clearly defined relationship between these variables makes it difficult to assess the relative influence of each as a determinant of posthospital performance. This issue is especially critical if one is to assume that class and expectations are independent of each other. If this is the case, two distinct problems emerge. First, the implied influence of class membership remains putative—that is, its status as a determinant still begs demonstration in terms other than those which first prompted its consideration. Second, by denying its association with a higher level construct, the efficacy of expectations as a generalized concomitant of performance is greatly restricted—expectations for performance become situationally determined and, hence, more likely subject to idiosyncratic interpretations.

If, on the other hand, it is assumed that class and expectations are highly correlated in the sense that the former implies the latter, and if performance fails to correlate significantly with either or both class and expectations, this would necessitate a reexamination of the

[4] "Social Class and Posthospital Performance Levels," *American Sociological Review*, **XXIV** (June, 1959), 345–51.

[5] "Familial Expectations and Posthospital Performance of Mental Patients," *Human Relations*, **XIII**, No. 3 (1959), 233–42.

[6] It should be noted that, in their discussion of social class and its relation to performance, Freeman and Simmons imply the importance of role expectations as a concomitant of class. Their discussion of expectations, however, although obviously significant in terms of delineating the relevancy of familial factors, makes no effort to explicitly examine what was previously implied. Instead both variables are presumed to be reflective of the same phenomenon—"tolerance of deviant behavior."

postulated direction of the relationships previously reported and of the criteria by which performance level is measured and evaluated.

This study is addressed to these problems and assumptions. Under investigation are the relationships between social class, instrumental role expectations, and the performance of former female patients who were discharged from a psychiatric institution. The major differences between the work reported here and that of Freeman and Simmons are: (1) the study group is composed of former patients who had manifested *acute* rather than chronic psychiatric difficulties; (2) these are married women and all returned to their husbands upon discharge from the hospital; (3) the patients themselves *and* their husbands were interview respondents; and (4), perhaps most significant, is the effort to examine social class and expectations as integral rather than as independent factors.

In the following the questionable postulate that class and expectations are critical determinants of the performance of these women will be examined. In this study previously neglected variables within the posthospital environment—namely, the disease manifestations of the patient and the manner in which she denies her role—have been taken into account.

STUDY GROUP AND METHOD

The subjects were sixty-two married women who were discharged from a short-term, intensive-therapy psychiatric institution between December, 1958, and July, 1959, and who had not re-entered this or any other medical facility for psychiatric treatment for a period of six months. These women represent 21.6 percent of the total number of females discharged in those eight months, 36.5 percent of all who were married, and 43.7 percent of the married women who had avoided re-entry into treatment and were still living in the community six months after hospital release.[7] Only those women were included who met the following criteria: (1) white; (2) functionally as opposed to organically impaired; (3) not addicted to either alcohol or drugs; (4) living with spouse; and (5) both the former patient and her husband had been interviewed.[8]

[7] For a description of the original study population see S. Dinitz *et al.*, "Psychiatric and Social Attributes as Predictors of Case Outcome in Mental Hospitalization," *Social Problems*, VIII (Spring, 1961), 322–28; S. Angrist *et al.*, "Rehospitalization of Female Mental Patients," *A.M.A. Archives of General Psychiatry*, IV (April, 1961), 363–70; and Dinitz *et al.*, "The Posthospital Psychological Functioning of Former Mental Hospital Patients," *Mental Hygiene*, XLV (October, 1961), 579–88.

[8] The decision to focus on married patients for the purposes of this paper and to control the factors indicated derives directly from experiences with the total subject population. Our earlier findings suggest that (1) the married women, as a group, perform far better than any of the non-married former patients and (2) that married

All sixty-two patients and their husbands were interviewed by trained psychiatric social workers six months after discharge. The interviews were designed to elicit from each of the husbands an index of his wife's actual performance in three separate areas of functioning—domestic activity (e.g., cooking, shopping, cleaning), social participation (e.g., visiting, entertaining), and psychological behavior. These measures consisted of five, nine, and thirty-two items, respectively.[9] Responses were scored according to arbitrarily assigned weights with the higher scores representing better performance. The scores were regarded as additive. In addition to the separate scores so obtained, a total performance index was derived as a composite of these three indexes.[10]

A separate section of the interview schedule was designed specifically to elicit the husbands' expectations of the role performance of

---

women are subject to and themselves express higher expectations for role performance than the others. These results, although related and important in and of themselves, are nevertheless prone to a number of substantive and methodological difficulties. Foremost among these are: (1) Many of the role performance and expectation items are more clearly applicable to wives and mothers than to widowed, divorced, and otherwise single females. Low performance, therefore, on the part of those in the latter categories could well be viewed with some ambivalence, i.e., either low performance per se, or the behaviors in question are simply irrelevant. (2) A variety of significant others (husbands, parents, children, siblings, friends, neighbors) introduces the issue of differential perception, knowledge, and/or concern and their effects upon reports of performance as well as on level of expectations. Although this particular problem is more severe for the non-married females, it is not entirely absent in the case of the married subjects.

In order, then, to adequately examine the effects of social class and expectations on performance, it was deemed necessary to control for those factors which had already introduced several interpretative difficulties and others which were likely to do the same.

[9] For a complete description of these instruments and a discussion of questions of reliability see Shirley S. Angrist, "Social Factors in the Outcome of Mental Hospitalization" (Ph.D. thesis, Ohio State University, 1960) (microfilm).

[10] The significance and implications of the results presented here, as well as those in related papers regarding the posthospital experiences of former patients, depend largely on the accuracy and validity of our performance measures. An attempt was made, therefore, to obtain professional psychiatric evaluations independent of those derived from the significant others. For this purpose a random sample of the original study population was asked to co-operate by presenting themselves for a psychiatric interview. Using a standard psychiatric rating instrument (the Lorr Multidimensional Scale for Rating Psychiatric Patients) each patient was rated by one of two staff psychiatrists. Despite some obvious differences in perception and insight between psychiatrists and the significant others and between the two physicians themselves, significant correlations were obtained between the Lorr Scale scores and the psychological performance scores derived from the reports of patients' relatives (for a discussion of these findings see B. Pasamanick and L. Ristine, "Differential Assessment of Posthospital Psychological Functioning: Evaluations by Psychiatrists and Relatives," *American Journal of Psychiatry*, **CXVIII** [July, 1961], 40–46). In addition, the fact that the three performance indexes used in this study—psychological, domestic, and social—are highly related lends plausibility to their use as indicators of the actual functioning level of the patients involved.

their wives. The twelve items which comprised this index are particularly pertinent to the women's domestic and social behavior and thus parallel, in part, their reports of actual performance. These responses were treated in a manner similar to that discussed above—the higher the score, the greater the expectation for performance.

While the former patients were not asked about their actual functioning, they were asked to indicate their own expectations with respect to performance. The items were identical to those used with their husbands' and were scored in a similar fashion.

The social class index used in this report was based on the Hollingshead Two Factor Index of Social Position.[11] The procedure consists of assigning the husband's occupational status a weight of 7 and his educational status a weight of 4. In accordance with current usage, Hollingshead's Classes I, II, and III are considered to be "middle class," and Classes IV and V to be "working class."[12]

FINDINGS

Social class and posthospital performance.—An earlier report showed that the married patients are better performers and are subject to higher and more consistent expectations than any of the women in several non-married categories included in the larger study population.[13] Therefore, by restricting our attention to married females, the posited relationship between social class and expectations, on the one hand, and posthospital performance, on the other, receives its severest test. The data presented in Table 1 show clearly that class fails to pass this test. The correlation coefficients as well as the mean performance scores computed for each of the major class groupings fail to demonstrate significant differences in performance by class.[14] As noted previously, a major factor inhibiting the discriminatory power of social class could logically be attributed to the fact that these women, as a group,

[11] A. B. Hollingshead, "Two Factor Index of Social Position" (1957) (mimeographed).

[12] See, e.g., M. L. Kohn, "Social Class and Parental Authority," *American Sociological Review*, **XXIV** (June, 1959), 352–66.

[13] Dinitz *et al.*, "Psychiatric and Social Attributes as Predictors of Case Outcome in Mental Hospitalization," *op. cit.*

[14] The authors wish to make known their recognition of some recent criticism regarding the Hollingshead Index of Social Position—i.e., that education alone may account for differences attributed to social class status. In this regard see S. M. Miller and E. G. Mishler, "Social Class, Mental Illness, and American Psychiatry," *Milbank Memorial Fund Quarterly*, **XXXVII** (April, 1959), 174–99; and H. E. Freeman, "Attitudes toward Mental Illness among Relatives of Former Patients," *American Sociological Review*, **XXVI** (April, 1961), 59–66. In line with this argument, separate analyses of education and occupation were made; the results reported in this paper were not in any way altered so as to warrant the abandonment of the Index as used.

are indeed high or at the very least adequate role performers—that is, the skewed nature of the performance curve, therefore, precludes a reliable differentiation by class.

The fact is, however, that not only are these former patients readily dichotomized into distinct and statistically significant performance

TABLE 1.

Pearsonian Correlations Between Hollingshead Two Factor Index of Social Position and Performance Levels of Sixty-Two Patients and Mean Performance Scores, by Class

| Index | | | Mean Performance Scores | | | |
| | | | Middle Class (N = 21) | Working Class (N = 41) | | |
	r	p			t	p
Domestic performance	.13*	N.S.	13.10	13.17	.14	N.S.
Social participation	.09	N.S.	58.52	58.93	.25	N.S.
Psychological performance	.05	N.S.	88.52	87.76	.51	N.S.
Total performance†	.12	N.S.	160.14	159.86	.16	N.S.

*Because of the reverse nature of the Hollingshead Index—i.e., the higher the score, the lower the class—a positive correlation would feature a negative sign. To avoid confusion and since all the correlation coefficients reported in this paper are positive, the negative sign is not used.

†Each of the three separate indexes of performance is positively and significantly correlated with the Total Performance Index—$p < .01$ in each case.

groups (the means for the high and low total performance groups are 167.55 and 152.42, respectively—the resulting t is 10.66, $p<.001$), but also the second of the variables at issue, role expectations, does significantly distinguish between high- and low-performing women.

Instrumental role expectation and performance.—It was stated at the outset of this paper that the expectations for performance on the part of significant family members have been regarded as a crucial concomitant of posthospital functioning. Not only is this concept essential to the work of Freeman and Simmons, but it illustrates one of the most fundamental of sociological propositions. When introduced in this way, the relationships depicted in Table 2 offer an intriguing pattern. The correlation coefficients reveal that, although the expectation scores of both patients and husbands are positively and significantly related to the total performance index, the level of expectation of the former patients themselves is by far the more critical correlate. This is evidenced not only by the differential magnitude of the coefficient with respect to total performance but especially by those obtained between expectations and psychological behavior and social participation. Furthermore, the relative stability of these relationships is markedly different. Whereas the expectations of the women relate strongly to performance, even when those of their husbands are controlled ($r_{12.3}=.42$, $p<.01$), precisely the reverse occurs with respect to the relationship between husbands' expectations and performance when those of their wives are partialled out ($r_{12.3}=.09$). On the strength

TABLE 2.

Pearsonian Correlations Between Patients' and Husbands' Expectations and Performance Levels

Index	Patients' Expectations		Husbands' Expectations	
	r	p	r	p
Domestic	.25	N.S.	.18	N.S.
Social	.31	< .05	.21	N.S.
Psychological	.38	< .01	.15	N.S.
Total	.48	<.01	.27	< .05

of these findings it seems appropriate to suggest at this point that the husbands' reports of actual performance and their expectations for such performance are to a considerable extent independent of each other.[15] In addition, and most important, the expectations held by these men for their wives' role performance are, in fact, dependent upon those registered by their wives. It is also to be noted that, if the correlation coefficient between patients' expectations and performance is to be attributed to an association between gradients, the source for such a relationship is to be found in the sphere of social participation rather than in the more purely domestic realm.

Two very important inferences are to be drawn from these findings: First, the husband's expectations as determinants of role performance are less important than was expected; and second, a shift in focus is required—that is, the former patient herself is revealed as a significant factor in structuring the normative pattern to which she must relate.

Social Class, expectations, and performance.—These findings make it necessary to ask the question: What factors account for the expectations held by these women? Within the context of this research, the

[15] Additional support for this contention is based on the fact that the correlation between husbands' expectations and patients' expectations is significantly greater than that between the latter and psychological performance ($t = 2.01$, $p < .025$ for a one-tail test). The formula used,

$$t = (r_{xz} - r_{yz})$$
$$\times \sqrt{\frac{(N-3)\ (1-r_{xy})}{2\ (1 - r_{xy}^2 - r_{zz}^2 - r_{yz}^2 + 2\ r_{xy}r_{xz}r_{yz})}}$$

search for an answer begins with a consideration of the relationship between social class and expectations. The relevant data show that, although these variables are differentially correlated with the reported performance of our subject group (expectations are positively and significantly related while class is not), they are positively and significantly related to each other (the correlations between the Hollingshead Two Factor Index and patients' and husbands' expectations are .33, $p<.01$, and .28, $p<.05$, respectively). This association is also obtained when class is treated as a discrete variable (Table 3). Further-

TABLE 3.

Mean Expectation Scores—Patients' and Husbands'—by Middle- and Working-Class Position

	Middle Class (N = 21)	Working Class (N = 41)	t	p
Patients' expectations (total)	33.67	32.12	2.56	< .05
Husbands' expectations (total)	33.57	32.39	2.09	< .05
Patients' expectations (social)	13.05	11.83	2.57	< .05
Husbands' expectations (social)	13.05	11.98	2.79	< .01
Patients' expectations (domestic)	14.71	14.49	N.S.	
Husbands' expectations (domestic)	14.52	14.27	N.S.	

more, it should be noted that whatever differential exists between the expectations of middle-class as opposed to working-class subjects is best accounted for by differences in the social as opposed to the domestic spheres of role performance. A similar finding was obtained with respect to the relationship between patients' expectations and performance (see Table 2).

Given these facts—(1) that social class and performance are relatively independent of each other and (2) that expectations correlate significantly with both class and performance—it seems reasonable to suggest that expectations are a function not only of class position but of performance as well. In an effort, therefore, to assess the nature of the class-performance relationship and to determine its influence upon expectations, a further analysis of the variables was undertaken.

The procedure for this analysis involved the construction of a four-celled bivariate typology. This typology was based on the dichotomization of social class into middle- and working-class categories and total performance into high and low levels. Mean expectation scores were then computed for each of the cells: middle class—high performance; middle class—low performance; working class—high performance; and working class—low performance. These results are presented in Table 4.

These data indicate several interesting and important relationships among the variables under consideration. In the first place, the mean expectation scores show that social class most readily accounts for the previously cited relationship between performance and expectations and at the same time accounts for a considerable amount of the unexplained variance in that relationship. The women of middle-class status tend to maintain high expectations despite low performance, while the

TABLE 4.

Mean Expectation Scores—Patients' and Husbands'—by Middle- and Working-Class Position and High and Low Total Performance Level

	Middle Class— High Performance (N = 12)	Middle Class— Low Performance (N = 9)	t	p
Patients' expectations	33.83	33.44	.54	N.S.
Husbands' expectations	33.92	33.11	1.05	N.S.

	Working Class— High Performance (N = 19)	Working Class— Low Performance (N = 22)	t	p
Patients' expectations	33.58	30.86	3.10	< .01
Husbands' expectations	33.47	31.45	2.39	< .05

expectations of the working-class women are highly congruent with their performance level.[16] *In short, the expectations which the middle-class women hold for themselves are independent of performance, while those of the working-class women appear to be a function of their ability to perform those very same activities.* Highly relevant to these results is the previously noted fact that the differences in expectation scores were due largely to those items concerned with social rather than the more strictly domestic activities. Not only is this point substantively significant but it adds an important measure of validity as well, that is, the findings clearly reflect the obvious and often documented class-related bias regarding the more purely social amenities of role performance. The results presented, therefore, are not only in accord with existing knowledge of the influence of social class upon role expecta-

[16] The t's reported in Table 4 for patients' expectations are supported by separate correlation coefficients between expectations and performance for the two class groupings. In the case of the middle-class women, $r = .41$, N.S. For the working-class patients, $r = .52$, $p < .01$. The correlations for husbands' expectations and performances were not significant for either class group.

tions but provide an empirical point of departure for a reassessment of the criteria by which the functioning of mentally ill persons has been examined and evaluated.

DISCUSSION AND CONCLUSIONS

The pattern of interrelationships found among the variables considered—social class, expectations, and the posthospital performance level of sixty-two married female mental patients—is consistent as well as inconsistent with both the findings and the inferences of other researchers in the area. On one hand, our findings strongly support the point of view that social class is a relevant factor in influencing the posthospital experiences of mental patients. On the other hand, however, our data indicate that, insofar as the subjects of this study are concerned, the influence is indirect rather than direct. That is, despite evidence which shows social class to be instrumental in accounting for relative discrepancies between expectations and performance, a demonstration of its influence as a determinant of performance was not achieved. This failure is far more significant than it would at first appear since it necessitates a closer examination of the nature and implications of the relationship between expectations and performance. The point of departure for such an examination is the finding that the poorly performing women of middle-class status, contrary to those of the working-class group, maintain this performance in the face of consistently high expectations. This finding, coupled with the fact that these women have been successful in avoiding rehospitalization, suggests four distinct but obviously interrelated propositions: (1) that middle-class families are more rather than less willing to tolerate low-level performance; (2) that the expectations to which middle-class women are subject are qualitatively different from those of the working-class women—that is, more complicated and demanding and, hence, more difficult to realize; (3) that the middle-class women are less realistic in judging their abilities and capacities; and (4) that expectations provide a questionable criterion by which to evaluate posthospital patient functioning.

While this study does not permit an intensive evaluation of the relative merits of these propositions, it does, however, provide a starting point from which to proceed. Of immediate interest are those data which show that the expectations to which these women were subject are of their own making—that is, the expectations reported by the husbands were largely dependent upon those expressed by their wives. As a result it is extremely difficult to view familial role expectations as a determinant of performance. If familial expectations were as instrumental in determining performance level as they have been posited to be, they would necessarily have to occupy the status of an independent rather than a dependent variable. Such was obviously not the case for these subjects. Furthermore, serious questions about the efficacy of role expectations as an indicator of greater or lesser familial tolerance are raised.[17] In short, the relative discrepancies between expectations and performance are largely a function of the expectations these women hold for themselves and to which their husbands acceded.

This latter point raises a more general question: To what extent are these findings uniquely relevant to the posthospital experiences of these former mental patients? More specifically, is the fact that these subjects are married women equally, or perhaps even more, important in accounting for the relationships found than is the fact of previous hospitalization? One significant answer to these questions is the information which shows that the expectations which most readily distinguish between the two class groups are those regarding social participation. In the case of the middle-class subjects these are uniformly high; in the case of the working-class women these expectations vary in accordance with performance. But in both instances it is the women who appear to determine the pattern to be followed. Since the husbands permit their wives to structure these particular normative standards for themselves, it seems reasonable to suggest that they reflect a cultural tendency. In other words, in the absence of clearly defined standards by which to determine, let alone evaluate, the substantive ways and means of social participation in the first place, the freedom of movement granted their wives in these matters seems not only logical but necessary.

Of greater importance, however, is the fact that the women themselves reflect the influence of social class position upon the differential importance attributed to the social aspects of role performance. In this regard the subjects are also in harmony with the normative standards accepted by women in the general population. There seems to be little reason, therefore, not to view their actual performance in a similar manner—that is, the role performance of these former patients may indeed be representative of never before hospitalized women, or at least, does not significantly differ in fact from the way in which role demands are met by other women.[18] This line of reasoning leads to

[17] It is to be noted that this criticism is applicable only if tolerance and role expectations are equated. It is not our intention to preclude familial "tolerance" as a factor in the experiences of mentally ill persons. It is our intention, however, to pose questions regarding the behaviors about which families are tolerant or intolerant.

[18] In order to empirically examine this assertion, a "control" group of 170 females who have not received any type of psychiatric treatment and their significant others have been interviewed in precisely the same fashion as the former patient population. The selection procedure involved matching each of the urban patients with a neighbor who resides ten house numbers away. The data obtained are currently being analyzed.

the conclusion that the role dimensions herein considered (domestic and social) are perhaps of secondary concern in the evaluation of the posthospital performance of these women. What could be of vital importance, however, is the fact that these former patients were hospitalized by and large for acute rather than chronic psychiatric difficulties. This suggests that the precipitating factor in their hospitalization lies primarily in the manifestation of severe, bizarre, or unusual psychiatric symptoms rather than disruption or breakdown in the more parochial spheres of role performance.

It is our contention, therefore, that the object of concern on the part of family members as well as the former patients themselves is not with whether the latter are capable of fulfilling their role obligations but whether those symptoms for which they had originally sought treatment have been effectively treated and minimized.

It is to be emphasized that we are not at all denying the crucial relationships between role performance and manifestations of disease. We are suggesting that these relationships are decidedly more complex than heretofore assumed or recognized. It could be reasonably argued, for example, that the degree to which questions of role performance assume importance is a function of the extent to which a discrepancy exists between the *capacity* for such performance and the normative demands. The more chronic the illness, the more the concern with questions of the appropriateness of role obligations and of the adaptation of abilities to the required norms. On the other hand, the more acute the illness, the greater the concern with the disease entity and its specific consequences and the less the concern with matters of role performance.

While the above is obviously a very tentative interpretation of our findings and their implications, one conclusion is clear and unequivocal: the appropriate test of the efficacy of social class and expectations as meaningful concepts in the study of the functioning of mentally ill persons awaits the formulation of an adequate frame of reference. Such a frame of reference must not only foster the recognition of the interaction of sociological and psychiatric variables but must also provide the means by which the relative importance of each may be weighted.

25

George H. Wolkon

Arden E. Melzer

Disease or Deviance: Effects on the Treatment Continuum*

The difficulties which attend a meaningful definition of "mental health" and "illness" have been discussed in many places.[1-5] The difficulties in definition are especially crucial for those persons who officially label others as "mentally ill" or "healthy" and then take action based on such labels.[6-9] Perhaps, the most important of these actions is the

This selection, written especially for this book, is published here for the first time. Copyright © 1967 by the authors and reprinted with their permission.

* Dr. Wolkon is Research Director of Hill House (Mental Health Rehabilitation & Research, Inc.), Cleveland and is presently an associate professor of sociology at Case Western Reserve University. Mr. Melzer is now an assistant professor at the School of Social Work, University of Pittsburgh. At the time of the study he was associated both with Hill House and Case Western Reserve University.

This research was supported in part by Grant No. MH-818 from the National Institute of Mental Health, U.S. Public Health Service. Gratitude is expressed to the administrations and staffs of Cleveland Psychiatric Institute, Cleveland State Hospital, Fairhill Psychiatric Hospital and Hawthornden State Hospital for their cooperation in this study and to Henry T. Tanaka for his comments on earlier draft of this paper.

[1] Jahoda, Marie, Current Concepts of Positive Mental Health, New York: Basic Books, Inc., 1958.

[2] Mechanic, David, "Some Factors in Identifying and Defining Mental Illness," Mental Hygiene, 1962, 46, 66–74.

[3] Szasz, Thomas, The Myth of Mental Illness, New York: Holker-Harper, 1961.

[4] Scott, William A., "Research Definitions of Mental Health and Mental Illness," Psychological Bulletin, 1958, 55, 29–45.

[5] Laing, R. D., "Is Schizophrenia a Disease?", The International Journal of Social Psychiatry, 1964, 10, 184–193.

[6] Hogarty, Gerard E., "Discharge Readiness: The Components of Casework Judgments," Social Casework, 1966, 47, 165–171.

[7] Weinstein, Louis, "Real and Ideal Discharge Criteria," Mental Hospitals, 1964, 15, 680–683.

[8] Szasz, Thomas, Law, Liberty and Psychiatry, New York: Macmillan Company, 1963.

taking of a person out of society to place him in a mental hospital and the subsequent decision to release him from the hospital and return him to the community.

A central problem in the attempt to define mental illness is whether mental illness is considered to be a disease entity which exists in absolute terms or whether it is a culturally classified type of deviance from societal norms. More important, however, for the purposes of this paper is the question of whether the gatekeepers of mental hospitals act in terms of a disease entity definition or a definition of relative deviance or social adjustment. Further, this paper will briefly consider what effects these different approaches have on the recipients of such treatment.

If the distinction between disease and deviance is more than hypothetical and reflects an actual conflict among practitioners it should be expected that: (a) Professionals primarily trained in terms of disease entities should have different criteria for hospital release than professionals primarily trained in the interpersonal, social, and cultural aspects of human behavior; (b) Decisions and opinions about persons who are within a "disease entity culture" (i.e., a hospital) will contain more indications of the disease entity and less of a deviance conception than will opinions about persons who are not within the culture of a hospital.

This paper contains descriptive data concerning the criteria for psychiatric hospital release and anticipated problems of post-hospital adjustment. It raises the following major questions: Is there general agreement among the gatekeepers of the mental hospital concerning criteria for hospital release, and anticipated problems of post-hospital adjustment; if not, do differences in professional training account for the lack of agreement? Further, is there a lack of consensus on the decisions and opinions concerning patients within a hospital and those outside of the hospital which reflects the assumed conflict between the concepts of "disease" and "deviance"; if so, what are the implications for programs for the recipients of service?

METHOD

As part of a larger study, all the social workers in four state supported psychiatric hospitals (34 workers) and all the psychiatric staff in three of these hospitals (40 physicians) were asked to state the major criteria they use in deciding to release patients or in recommending them for release from the hospital to the community. After responding to this open-ended question, they were asked for addi-

---

9 Mechanic, David, "Therapeutic Intervention: Issues in the Care of the Mentally Ill," *American Journal of Orthopsychiatry*, 1967, **37**, 703–718.

tional factors which they consider when evaluating a patient for release. They were then given a list of 11 factors which could be considered when releasing a patient and were asked to rank the factors and rate each of them on a 4 point scale in terms of importance (see Table 2 for the prepared list of factors). The respondents were then asked to state the most prevalent major problems for their recently released psychiatric patients. After responding to this open-ended question, they were asked to rank and rate 10 possible problems in terms of a 4 point scale of importance (see Table 2 for the list of prepared factors).

The responses to the open-ended questions were reliably coded into five categories (inter-rater reliability was 82 percent). They were: (1) pathology *per se*, (2) pathology in relation to the social environment, (3) the social environment *per se*, (4) finances and (5) jobs. The differences between the latter two categories are that "finances" is concerned with any form of monetary support except that derived from work. The category of "jobs" on the other hand, is a compound category which serves the patient in either a psychosocial or a financial manner. Although more subtle categories were desired and are desirable, intercoder reliability could not be obtained with such categories. Additional factors considered in deciding to release a patient (i.e., responses to general probes after the initial responses were given) were coded in the same manner.

RESULTS

RELEASE CRITERIA

As might be expected, in the responses to the openended questions almost all of the social service staff (94 percent) and the psychiatric staff (95 percent) considered the degree of pathology as primary criterion for hospital release (see Table 1). The responses to the prepared list of criteria also indicated that for physicians and social workers, the present degree of symptomatology and psychopathology were the most important criteria for release (see Table 2).

The data, however, further indicate that 70 percent of the psychiatric staff and 65 percent of the social service staff stated that pathology in relation to the interpersonal environment was a major criterion in releasing patients. Again, the responses to the prepared list of criteria were consistent. The four next most important criteria, after symptomatology and pathology, were all concerned with the immediate interpersonal environment. The word "immediate" is crucial. Indeed, despite the importance of the immediate environment, the prepared reason of "community attitudes" was considered to be of next to least importance.

It would appear, then, that there is a substantial amount of agreement that pathology must be understood in relative terms as well as absolute terms. To explore this point further, the responses to the open-ended questions were re-examined. The responses suggested that the absolute level of pathology and symptomatology required for hospital release is on the grossest level (e.g., such things as being "harmful to self and others" and "incontinence" must be absent). After such absolute minima of health or adjustment are established then such symptoms as hallucinations, apathy, etc., are thought of in relation to the extra-mural interpersonal environment of the patient who is being considered for release.

TABLE 1.

Percent of Respondents Using Coded Release Criteria and Post-Hospital Problems

Questions	Response Categories									
	Pathology		Pathology in Relation to Social Environment		Social Environment		Finances		Jobs	
	S. W.	M. D.	S. W.	M. D.	S. W.	M. D.	S. W.	M. D.	S. W.	M. D.
1. Release Criteria										
A. Primary	94	95	65	70	26**	5	21	10	24	20
B. Secondary	0	2	6	10	21	10	15	15	24	15
C. Total	94	97	71	80	47**	15	36	25	48	35
2. Post-Hospital										
Problems	59	68	56*	35	56*	22	12	8	44**	12

*p is $< .10$
**p is $< .05$

Despite the importance of the social environment when considered in relation to pathology, only 5 percent of the psychiatric staff and 26 percent of the social service staff mentioned the social environment *per se* as being of primary importance in deciding to release a patient. The expectation of professional differences was confirmed, that is, five times as many social workers as physicians thought the social environment to be of prime importance, although only one-quarter of the social workers initially mentioned this variable. Even when the secondary criteria for releasing a patient are considered, only one-half the social workers mentioned the importance of the social environment *per se*.

One possible reason for the unanticipated small proportion of social workers who mentioned the social environment *per se* is that they are in an ancillary position within a medical hierarchy and that the consequent organizational pressures militate against their prior training which attunes them to the importance of the social environment.

TABLE 2.

Importance of Criteria for Hospital Release and Anticipated Post-Hospital Problems[a]

Criteria and Problems	Release Criteria		Post-Hospital Problems	
	S.W.	M.D.	S.W.	M.D.
Employment	9	8	10	7
Patients' attitudes and expectations	3	3	1	1
Financial problems	8	7	6	8
Administrative feasibility	11	11	–	–
Potential recurrence of symptoms	7	9	9	10
Present degree of psychopathology	2	2	7	6
Present degree of symptomatology	1	1	5	2
Community attitudes	10	10	8	9
Level of social adjustment	4	4	4	3
Attitudes and expectations of closest relatives	5	5	2	5
Living arrangements	6	6	3	4

[a]Scores were derived from each of the rank and rate procedures by multiplying each respondent's rank of each item by his rating of each item. The sum of the products for all respondents for each item was obtained. The rank of the sum for each item is reported in this table. The lower the rank, the more important the item; e.g., rank of 1 indicates the most important item.

Perhaps more important than the reasons for the differences between professions are the reasons for such a low proportion of both professions mentioning the relevance of the environment *per se*. The social environment *per se* may in reality not be an important criterion for hospital release. Indeed, a disease residing in a patient can be "cured" or "arrested" independent of the environment. If the hospital's actual function is medical treatment of the patient's disease, then the environment should be of little or no concern. A second explanation suggests that inasmuch as the only "countable production unit" of a mental hospital is the number of hospital releases, the pressure to increase the units of production is great. Thus, as long as the environment will receive the patient, the quality of the environment is not a deterring factor to the staff.

Consistent with the notion that the social environment itself is not an important release criterion, only 21 percent of the social workers and 10 percent of the psychiatric staff saw "finances" as being important and only 20 percent of the psychiatric staff and 24 percent of the social workers mentioned jobs as being of primary importance.

ADDITIONAL RELEASE CRITERIA

After responding to the initial question concerning criteria for hospital release, the respondents were asked for any additional criteria they might use in making the decision to release a patient. Table 1 contains the percentage of an unduplicated count of responses classified according to the same criteria as the initial responses. The most salient finding from the responses to the general probes is the greater relative increase in the use of four of the five criterion categories by the psychiatric staff as compared to the social workers. This finding suggests that professional training is most influential in the selection of prime or necessary criteria for release rather than a full description of all relevant criteria for release. Indeed, if one considers only the rank order correlation (rho=.97) of the prepared list of reasons, the two professions seem to be in high accord concerning the importance of general release criteria.

POST-HOSPITAL PROBLEMS

An overall indicator of the amount of agreement between the professions is the rank order correlation of the prepared lists of reasons for the professions. The obtained correlation of .78 indicates there is general agreement between the professions concerning the prevalence of selected post-hospital problems. Specific disagreements, however, do occur and in conjunction with the responses to the open-ended questions are elaborated below.

The responses to the open-ended questions indicate that 68 percent of the psychiatric staff and 59 percent of the social service staff mentioned that psychopathology *per se* is a major post-hospital problem. In contrast to the similar proportion of each profession that considered the absolute level of pathology important, the proportion of social workers who considered pathology in relation to the social environment as a major post-hospital problem exceeded the proportion of physicians who did so by more than 20 percent ($X^2 = 3.24$, $p < .01$). In addition, the proportion of social workers who mentioned the importance of the environment in absolute terms exceeded the proportion of physicians who did so by more than 30 percent ($X^2 = 8.71$, $p < .01$). There are also marked differences between the proportion of the social service staff (44 percent) and psychiatric staff (12 percent) with respect to their expectations about the extent to which the lack of employment would pose a post-hospital problem ($X^2 = 9.32$, $p < .01$).

The responses to the list of prepared post-hospital problems given by the respondents support the above findings. It may be seen from Table 2 that the problem judged most prevalent by both the social service and psychiatric staff is the patient's attitude and expectations. For the social workers the next three items of importance may also be easily classified in the social deviance rather than disease categories; namely, attitudes and expectations of closest relatives, living arrangements, and level of social adjustment. With one exception, the psychiatric staff agreed with the above ranking: the physicians judged the present degree of symptomatology as second most important while the social workers judged this to be fifth most important.

An important distinction exists among the three categories of "present degree of symptomatology," "present degree of psychopathology" and "potential recurrence of symptoms." The list of potential problems given to the respondents, made a distinction between the present level of symptomatology and psychopathology. The difference between the two being that the symptoms are a particular class of behavioral responses to the environment which would be classified, under the disease orientation, as manifestations of underlying psychopathology. The physicians ranked symptomatology second and psychopathology sixth in importance. The difference in ranking may be interpreted in terms of the visibility of the disturbance and, even further, in terms of the amount of deviance within the immediate social environment. This distinction could not be made with the open-ended questions because of the general term "psychopathology" in the interview situation. It is clear from the above, however, that when levels of psychopathology are discussed it is done so in terms of symptoms. Thus, symptoms, even though they may result from a disease process, seem to be of concern only as they are deviant from social norms and affect social functioning.

The item concerning the potential recurrence of symptoms was ranked next to last by the social service staff and last by the psychiatric staff. In light of Freeman and Simmons's[10] conclusions that rehospitalization of mental patients occurs because they "get sick" again, how can this finding be explained? It is suggested that the rankings of post-hospital problems can be interpreted as meaning that if the more important items in the rankings are satisfactory, (i.e., given a benign environment) then a recurrence of symptoms will not occur. The finding may also be interpreted as a defensive response on the part of the hospital professionals (e.g., the effects of their treatment are not easily undone).

The item concerning community attitudes was not judged to be one of the more important post-hospital problems by either profession.

The fact the social workers thought that employment was the least important post-hospital problem on the prepared list appears to be

10 Freeman, Howard E. and Simmons, Ozzie G., *The Mental Patient Comes Home*, New York: Wiley and Sons, Inc., 1963.

inconsistent with the fact that 48 percent of them mentioned it as being a major problem in the open-ended questions. One explanation is, of course, that it is important but, relative to the other problems presented to the respondent it is merely less important. Or it may be that if the other environmental conditions can compensate in the financial and psychosocial areas, then employment is, in fact, not that important. The latter explanation can be expected only if the goal of the professionals is to prevent regressions rather than to promote socially desirable behavioral change.

RELEASE CRITERIA AND POST-HOSPITAL PROBLEMS

Do decisions and opinions about persons who are in the hospital contain more indications of the disease entity model and less of the social deviance model than the opinions concerning persons outside the hospital? As can be seen from Table 1, a lower proportion of both the psychiatric staff and the social service staff used the category "pathology *per se*" when considering post-hospital problems than when considering criteria for release. The findings for the social workers are more consistent than for the physicians. The same findings obtain when the category "pathology in relation to the environment" is considered. Here, however, the findings for the physicians are more consistent than for the social workers. These findings, taken together, indicate a general reduction in concern with criteria involving psychopathology when evaluating a person in the community as compared to when he is in a psychiatric hospital.

The use of the category "environment *per se*" is greater for evaluations of post-hospital problems than it is for evaluating someone for release from the hospital. For both professions, the findings are consistent when considering the use of this category as a prime criteria for release but not when the use of the category for secondary criteria is brought into the picture.

These findings indicate that the in-hospital professionals become more environmentally oriented when considering post-hospital problems as compared to criteria for hospital release. Although when the correlations between the rankings of criteria for release and the prevalence of post-hospital problems for each profession are examined, it is clear that the social workers (rho=.54) change more than the physicians (rho=.82).

It seems reasonable that in order for a patient to be released, he must have the financial resources to maintain himself in the community. The hospital staff thus attempts to become assured that at least minimum financial resources are available to the patient prior to his release from the hospital. Thus finances may not be, in reality, a prevalent post-hospital problem. There is great difficulty in interpreting the decrease in the use of the category of "jobs" from its use as a release criterion to a post-hospital problem because of the lack of specification within the interviews concerning which of the consequences of having or not having a job were meant (i.e., whether financial or psychosocial consequences). If financial aspects of having a job is the more important consequence, then the apparent inconsistency may be explained with the reason applied to the category of "finances"; i.e., if a job is important for financial reasons, it is likely to be obtained when the patient is still in the hospital. If psychosocial reasons stimulated the mentioning of the category of "jobs," then it may be that persons released from the hospital without a job have an interpersonal environment that is benign, accepting and tolerant of a non-productive person in the household. If the goal with the client is to promote socially desirable change (e.g., a "contributing citizen") rather than maintaining the *status quo*, this reasoning cannot be accepted as a rationale for "rehabilitation."

Discussion

The data reported herein indicate that the effects of having a disease model as compared to social deviance model of mental disturbance extend beyond theoretical arguments and indeed enter into the everyday operating decisions and evaluations with which in-hospital professionals are involved. The psychiatric staff (i.e., those trained in the disease approach) less frequently than the social service staff (i.e., those trained in the interpersonal social aspects of individual functioning) thought the social environment to be important both in deciding to release a patient from the hospital and in anticipating post-hospital problems. Not only are there differences between professions in the use of indicators of different models (i.e., disease versus deviance), but there are also differences in the evaluations of patients for hospital release as compared to the types of post-hospital problems that are anticipated. More indicators of the disease model and less of the deviance model occurred in hospital release evaluations than occurred in the considerations of post-hospital problems.

It may be argued that the obtained results are an overestimate of the real use of the disease model. For example, it was suggested above that the use of the work "pathology" in the interviews did not reflect a precise usage of the term but rather referred to overt symptoms rather than underlying psychopathology. Further, when the respondents judged a list of potential post-hospital problems, a clear differentiation was made between psychopathology and symptomatology. Thus, it may be said that although the language of the disease model is used, the meaning of language is concerned with the social deviance model. That is, medical language rather than a social behavioral language is used to describe adaptations which tend to interfere with the patient's functioning in the social environment.

The medical model and its language, by the professionals' own use, seems only slightly relevant for post-hospital problems though somewhat more relevant for hospital release decisions. Two issues are raised. First, why is the disease model so prevalent when it is not seen as most relevant throughout the different phases of the continuum of care? And, second, does the prominence and influence of the disease model throughout the different phases in the continuum of care maximize the potential benefits of the recipient?

Any attempt at complete answers to these questions is beyond the goals set in this paper. Briefly, however, historical precedent, including the mental health movement which attempted to reduce the stigma of mental illness by saying it was just like any other disease, contributes to the influence of the disease model. Another contributing factor to the disease model is that some of the uniquely medical interventions (e.g., chemotherapy and electric shock treatment) have been helpful in reducing symptoms. Symptom reduction is, after all, the goal of the classical disease model when a cure cannot be accomplished. If the goal of the continuum of care, however, is to restore the person to a functioning role in his social environment, the question must be raised as to the appropriateness of the disease model. Indeed, it is the lack of appropriateness of the disease model and the consequent in-hospital treatment that creates the incongruence between hospital release criteria and the anticipated post-hospital problems. The issue that is raised is whether the goal of psychiatric hospitalization is symptom reduction or preparation for living in the community. If it is the latter, the deviance model would seem to be the most appropriate overall model for the entire continuum of care with uniquely medical interventions being used when appropriate.

In addition, the existing inconsistency between the goals and models leads to a major discontinuity between patient roles and recently released patient roles[10,11] and creates an urgent need for transitional programs from the hospital to the community.[12,13]

[11] Wolkon, George H., "Effecting a Continuum of Care: An Exploitation of the Crisis of Psychiatric Hospital Release," *Community Mental Health Journal*, in press.

[12] Tanaka, Henry T., "Inconsistencies of Role Expectations Between Hospital and Community: A Problem of the Returning Mental Patient," Paper read at the National Conference on Social Welfare, May, 1963.

[13] Wechsler, Henry and Landy, David, "New Pathways from the Mental Hospital," *Journal of Social Issues*, complete 1960, 16, (2).

26

John H. Gagnon
William Simon

Homosexuality: The Formulation
of a Sociological Perspective*

The study of homosexuality today, except for a few rare and relatively
recent examples, suffers from two major defects: it is ruled by a
simplistic and homogeneous view of the psychological and social con-
tents of the category "homosexual," and at the same time it is nearly
exclusively interested in the most difficult and least rewarding of all
questions, that of etiology. While some small exceptions are allowed
for adolescent homosexual experimentation, the person with a major
to nearly exclusive sexual interest in persons of the same sex is perceived as belonging to a uniform category whose adult behavior is a
necessary outcome and, in a sense, reenactment of certain early and determining experiences. This is the prevailing image of the homosexual
and the substantive concern of the literature in psychiatry and psychology today.[1]

In addition to the fact that sexual contact with persons of the
same sex, even if over the age of consent, is against the law in 49 of
the 50 states, the homosexual labors under another burden that is commonly the lot of the deviant in any society.[2] The process of labeling

From *Journal of Health and Social Behavior*, **8** (September 1967), 177–185, by
permission of the authors and the American Sociological Association.

* A revised version of a paper presented at the 61st annual meetings of the American Sociological Association in Miami, August–September 1966. This research was
supported in part by USPHS MH grants #07742 and #12535.

[1] Irving Bieber *et al., Homosexuality, A Psychoanalytic Study*, New York: Basic
Books, 1962.

[2] Sex law reform occurred in the State of Illinois as part of a general reform
of the criminal code in 1961. For the manner in which the law's reform was translated for police officials, see Claude Sowle, *A Concise Explanation of the Illinois
Criminal Code of 1961*, Chicago: B. Smith, 1961.

and stigmatizing behavior not only facilitates the work of legal agencies in creating a bounded category of deviant actors such as the "normal burglar" and the "normal child molester" as suggested by Sudnow, but it also creates an image of large classes of deviant actors all operating from the same motivations and for the same etiological reasons.[3] The homosexual, like most significantly labeled persons (whether the label be positive or negative), has *all* of his acts interpreted through the framework of his homosexuality. Thus the creative activity of the play-wright or painter who happens to be homosexual is interpreted in terms of his homosexuality rather than in terms of the artistic rules and con-ventions of the particular art form in which he works. The plays of the dramatist are scanned for the Albertine Ploy and the painter's paintings for an excessive or deficient use of phallic imagery or vaginal teeth.

It is this nearly obsessive concern with the ultimate causes of adult conditions that has played a major role in structuring our con-cerns about beliefs and attitudes toward the homosexual. Whatever the specific elements that make up an etiological theory, the search for etiology has its own consequences for research methodology and the construction of theories about behavior. In the case of homosexuality, if one moves beyond those explanations of homosexual behavior that are rooted in constitutional or biological characteristics—that is, some-thing in the genes or in the hormonal system—one is left with etiological explanations located in the structure of the family and its malfunc-tions.[4] The most compelling of these theories are grounded ultimately in Freudian psychology, where the roots of this as well as the rest of human character structure is to be found in the pathological relation-ships between parents and their children.[5]

---

[3] David Sudnow, "Normal Crimes," *Social Problems*, 12 (Winter, 1965), pp. 255–276.

[4] A. C. Kinsey, "Criteria for the Hormonal Explanation of the Homosexual," *The Journal of Clinical Endocrinology*, 1 (May, 1941), pp. 424–428; F. J. Kallman, "Comparative Twin Study on the Genetic Aspects of Male Homosexuality," *Journal of Nervous and Mental Disorders*, 115 (1952), pp. 283–298; F. J. Kallman, "Genetic Aspects of Sex Determination and Sexual Maturation Potentials in Man," in George Winokur (ed.), *Determinants of Human Sexual Behavior*, Springfield: Charles C Thomas, 1963, pp. 5–18; and John Money, "Factors in the Genesis of Homosexuality," George Winokur (ed.), *Determinants of Human Sexual Behavior*, Springfield: Charles C Thomas, 1963, pp. 19–43.

[5] The work of Bieber *op. cit.* is the most recent of these analytic explorations, the central finding of which is that in a highly selected group of male homosexuals there was a larger proportion of males who had mothers who could be described as close-binding and intimate and fathers who were detached and hostile. The argu-ment proceeds that the mother has selected this child for special overprotection and seductive care. In the process of childrearing, sexual interest is both elicited and then blocked by punishing its behavioral manifestations. As a result of the mother's special ties to the child, the father is alienated from familial interaction, is hostile to the child, and fails to become a source of masculine attachment.

As a consequence of our preliminary work and the work of others, such as Hooker, Reiss, Leznoff and Westley, Achilles, and Schofield,[6] we would like to propose some alternative considerations in terms of the complexity of the life cycle of the homosexual, the roles that mark various stages of this cycle, and the kinds of forces, both sexual and nonsexual, that impinge on this individual actor. It is our

---

Regardless of the rather engaging and persuasive character of the theory, there are substantial complications. It assumes that there is a necessary relationship between the development of masculinity and femininity and heterosexuality and homosexuality. There is the assumption that homosexuals play sexual roles that are explicitly modeled upon those of the heterosexual and that these roles are well-defined and widespread. This confusion of the dimensions of sexual object choice and masculinity and femininity is based on two complementary errors. The first is that the very physical sexual activities of the homosexual are often characterized as passive (to be read feminine) or active (to be read masculine) and that these physical activities are read as direct homologues of the complex matters of masculinity and femininity. The second source of the confusion lies in the two situations in which homosexuality can be most easily observed. One is the prison, where the characteristics of homosexuality do tend to model themselves more closely on the patterns of heterosexuality in the outside community, but where the sources and the character of behavior are in the service of different ends. The second situation is that of public homosexuality characterized by the flaunted female gesture which has become stereotypic of homosexuality. This is not to say that such beliefs about the nature of homosexuality on the part of the heterosexual majority do not influence the homosexual's behavior; however, just because stereotypes are held does not mean that they play a role in the etiology of the behavior that they purport to explain.

Another major problem that exists for etiological theories of homosexuality based on family structure is the difficulty one finds in all theories that depend on the individual's memories of his childhood and that call upon him for hearsay evidence not only about himself, but about his parents. We live in a post-Freudian world and the vocabulary of motives of the most psychologically illiterate is replete with the concepts of repression, inhibition, the oedipus complex, and castration fears. The rhetoric of psychoanalysis permeates the culture as a result of a process that might best be called the democratization of mental health. One of the lessons of existentialism is that our biographies are not fixed quantities but are subject to revision, elision, and other forms of subtle editing based on our place in the life cycle, our audience, and the mask that we are currently wearing. Indeed, for many persons the rehearsed past and the real past become so intermixed that there is only the present. Recent research in childrearing practices suggests that two years after the major events of childrearing, weaning, and toilet training mothers fail to recall accurately their previous conduct and hence sound a good deal like Dr. Spock. An important footnote here is that persons do not always edit the past to improve their image in the conventional sense. Often the patient in psychotherapy works very hard to bring out more and more self-denigrating materials to assure the therapist that he, the patient, is really working hard and searching for his true motives.

[6] Evelyn Hooker, "The Homosexual Community," James C. Palmer and Michael J. Goldstein (eds.), *Perspectives in Psychopathology*, New York: Oxford University Press, 1966, pp. 354–364; Albert J. Reiss, "The Social Integration of Queers and Peers," *Social Problems*, 9 (Fall 1961), pp. 102–120; M. Leznoff and W. A. Westley, "The Homosexual Community," *Social Problems*, 3 (April, 1956), pp. 257–263; N. Achilles, "The Development of the Homosexual Bar as an Institution," in J. H. Gagnon and W. Simon (eds.), *Sexual Deviance*, New York: Harper and Row, 1967; and Michael Schofield, *Sociological Aspects of Homosexuality*, Boston: Little Brown, 1965.

current feeling that the problem of finding out how people become homosexual requires an adequate theory of how they become heterosexual; that is, one cannot explain homosexuality in one way and leave heterosexuality as a large residual category labeled "all other." Indeed, the explanation of homosexuality in this sense may await the explanation of the larger and more modal category of adjustment.

Further, from a sociological point of view, what the original causes were may not even be very important for the patterns of homosexuality observed in a society. Much as the medical student who comes to medicine for many reasons, and for whom the homogenous character of professional behavior arises from the experiences of medical school rather than from the root causes of his occupational choice, the patterns of adult homosexuality are consequent upon the social structures and values that surround the homosexual after he becomes, or conceives of himself as, homosexual rather than upon original and ultimate causes.[7]

What we are suggesting here is that we have allowed the homosexual's sexual object choice to dominate and control our imagery of him and have let this aspect of his total life experience appear to determine all his products, concerns, and activities. This prepossessing concern on the part of nonhomosexuals with the purely sexual aspect of the homosexual's life is something we would not allow to occur if we were interested in the heterosexual. However, the mere presence of sexual deviation seems to give the sexual content of life an overwhelming significance. Homosexuals, moreover, vary profoundly in the degree to which their homosexual commitment and its facilitation becomes the organizing principle of their lives. Involved here is a complex outcome that is less likely to be explained by originating circumstances than by the consequences of the establishment of the commitment itself.

Even with the relatively recent shift in the normative framework available for considering homosexuality—that is, from a rhetoric of sin to a rhetoric of mental health—the preponderance of the sexual factor is evident. The change itself may have major significance in the ways homosexual persons are dealt with; at the same time, however, the mental health rhetoric seems equally wide of the mark in understanding homosexuality. One advance, however, is that in place of a language of optimum man which characterized both the moral and the early mental health writings, we find a growing literature concerned with the psychological characteristics necessary for a person to survive in some manner

[7] Howard S. Becker, "Change in Adult Life," *Sociometry*, **27** (March, 1964), pp. 40–53.
Howard S. Becker, Blanche Geer and Everett C. Hughes, *Boys in White: Student Culture in the Medical School*, Chicago: University of Chicago Press, 1961.

within specific social systems and social situations.[8] In this post-Freudian world, major psychic wounds are increasingly viewed as par for the human condition and, as one major psychiatric theoretician observes, few survive the relationship with their parents without such wounding.[9] The problem becomes then, whether these wounds become exposed to social situations that render them either too costly to the individual or to the surrounding community. Accompanying this trend toward a reconceptualization of mental health has been a scaling-down of the goals set for men; instead of exceedingly vague and somewhat utopian goals, we tend to ask more pragmatic questions: Is the individual self-supporting? Does he manage to conduct his affairs without the intervention of the police or the growing number of mental health authorities? Does he have adequate sources of social support? A positively-balanced and adequately-developed repertoire for gratification? Has he learned to accept himself? These are questions we are learning to ask of nearly all men, but among the exceptions is found the homosexual. In practically all cases, the presence of homosexuality is seen as prima facie evidence of major psychopathology. When the heterosexual meets these minimal definitions of mental health, he is exculpated; the homosexual—no matter how good his adjustment in nonsexual areas of life—remains suspect.

Recent tabulations drawn from a group of 550 white males with extensive histories of homosexuality, interviewed outside institutions by Kinsey and his associates, suggest that most homosexuals cope fairly well, and even particularly well, when we consider the stigmatized and in fact criminal nature of their sexual interests.[10] Of this group, between 75 and 80 percent reported having had no trouble with the police, the proportion varying by the exclusivity of their homosexual commitment and their educational attainment (see Table 1). Following this same pattern, trouble with their families of origin tended to occur in a joint relationship with level of education and degree of homosexual commitment, with the less educated and the more homosexual reporting a greater incidence of difficulties. Only about 10 percent of the group reported trouble at work and less than five percent at school as a result of their homosexuality. Of those who had military experience, only one fifth reported difficulties in that milieu. In the military, possibly more

[8] Marie Jahoda, "Toward a Social Psychology of Mental Health" in Arnold M. Rose (ed.), *Mental Health and Mental Disorder*, New York: Norton, 1955, pp. 556–577.

F. C. Redlich, "The Concept of Health in Psychiatry," in A. H. Leighton, J. A. Clausen and R. N. Wilson, *Explorations in Social Psychiatry*, New York: Basic Books, 1957, pp. 138–164.

[9] Lawrence Kubie, "Social Forces and the Neurotic Process," in A. H. Leighton, J. A. Clausen and R. N. Wilson, *Explorations in Social Psychiatry*, New York: Basic Books, 1957, pp. 77–104.

[10] Extensive homosexuality is here defined as a minimum of 51 or more times and/or contact with 21 or more males.

than in civilian life, homosexuality is a difficulty that obliterates all other evaluations made of the person.

We do not wish to say that homosexual life does not contain a great potential for demoralization, despair, and self-hatred. To the contrary, as in most deviant careers, there remains the potential for a significant escalation of individual psychopathology. This potential is sug-

TABLE 1.

Reported Incidence of Social Difficulties by Education and Exclusivity of Homosexual Commitment

	High School		College	
	Exclusive Homosexual	*Mixed Homosexual and Heterosexual*	*Exclusive Homosexual*	*Mixed Homosexual and Heterosexual*
	%	%	%	%
Trouble with:				
Police	31	22	24	17
Family of origin	25	16	19	11
Occupation	10	8	7	8
(N)	(83)	(83)	(283)	(101)

gested by some other aspects of these same data. About one half of these males reported that 60 percent or more of their sexual partners were persons with whom they had sex only one time. Between 10 and 20 percent report that they often picked up their sexual partners in public terminals, and an even larger proportion reported similar contacts in other public or semipublic locations. Between a quarter and a third reported having been robbed by a sexual partner, with a larger proportion characteristically having exclusively homosexual histories. Finally, between 10 and 15 percent reported having been blackmailed because of their homosexuality (see Table 2).

There were further indicators of alienation and difficulty in the findings. For two fifths of the respondents the longest homosexual affair lasted less than one year, and for about one quarter kissing occurred in one third or less of their sexual contacts. In addition, about 30 percent reported never having had sex in their own homes. Accumulatively, such conditions add up to the two fifths of these men who indicated some serious feelings of regret about being homosexual, giving such reasons as fear of social disapproval or rejection, inability to experience a conventional family life, feelings of guilt or shame, or fear of potential trouble with the law. These figures require a more detailed analysis, and there are also uncertainties about sample bias that must be considered. However, it is our feeling that these proportions would not be substantially changed, given a more complete exploration of these factors. These data, then, suggest a depersonalized character, a driven or compulsive quality of the sexual activity of many homosexuals, which cannot be reckoned as anything but extremely costly to them.

Obviously, the satisfaction of a homosexual commitment—like most forms of deviance—makes social adjustment more problematic than it might be for members of a conventional population. What is important to understand is that consequences of these sexual practices are not necessarily direct functions of the nature of such practices. It is

TABLE 2.

Selected Negative Aspects of a Homosexual Career by Education and Exclusivity of Homosexual Commitment

	High School		College	
	Exclusive Homosexual	Mixed Homosexual and Heterosexual	Exclusive Homosexual	Mixed Homosexual and Heterosexual
	%	%	%	%
Proportion with 60% or more of sexual partners with whom had sex only once	49	43	51	45
Often pickup partners in public terminals	19	18	17	7
Ever been rolled	37	26	34	29
Ever been blackmailed	16	6	12	15
(N)	(83)	(83)	(283)	(101)

necessary to move away from an obsessive concern with the sexuality of the individual, and attempt to see the homosexual in terms of the broader attachments that he must make to live in the world around him. Like the heterosexual, the homosexual must come to terms with the problems that are attendant upon being a member of society: he must find a place to work, learn to live with or without his family, be involved or apathetic in political life, find a group of friends to talk to and live with, fill his leisure time usefully or frivolously, handle all of the common and uncommon problems of impulse control and personal gratification, and in some manner socialize his sexual interests.

There is a seldom-noticed diversity to be found in the life cycle of the homosexual, both in terms of solving general human problems and in terms of the particular characteristics of the life cycle itself. Not only are there as many ways of being homosexual as there are of being heterosexual, but the individual homosexual, in the course of his everyday life, encounters as many choices and as many crises as the heterosexual. It is much too easy to allow the label, once applied, to suggest that the complexities of role transition and identity crises are easily attributable to, or are a crucial exemplification of, some previously existing etiological defect.

An example of this is in the phase of homosexuality called "coming out," which is that point in time when there is self-recognition by the individual of his identity as a homosexual and the first major exploration of the homosexual community. At this point in time the removal of inhibiting doubts frequently releases a great deal of sexual energy. Sexual contacts during this period are often pursued nearly indiscriminately and with greater vigor than caution. This is very close to that period in the life of the heterosexual called the "honeymoon," when coitus is legitimate and is pursued with a substantial amount of energy. This high rate of marital coitus, however, declines as demands are made on the young couple to take their place in the framework of the larger social system. In these same terms, during the homosexual "honeymoon" many individuals begin to learn ways of acting out a homosexual object choice that involve homosexual gratification, but that are not necessarily directly sexual and do not involve the genitalia.

It is during this period that many homosexuals go through a crisis of femininity; that is, they "act out" in relatively public places in a somewhat effeminate manner; and some, in a transitory fashion, wear female clothing, known in the homosexual argot as "going in drag." During this period one of the major confirming aspects of masculinity— that is, nonsexual reinforcement by females of masculine status—has been abandoned, and it is not surprising that the very core of masculine identity should not be seriously questioned. This crisis is partially structured by the already existing homosexual culture in which persons already in the crisis stage become models for those who are newer to their homosexual commitment. A few males retain this pseudofeminine commitment, a few others emerge masquerading as female prostitutes to males, and still others pursue careers as female impersonators. This adjustment might be more widely adapted if feminine behavior by men— except in sharply delimited occupational roles—was not negatively sanctioned. Thus the tendency is for this kind of behavior to be a transitional experiment for most homosexuals, an experiment that leaves vestiges of "camp" behavior, but traces more often expressive of the character of the cultural life of the homosexual community than of some overriding need of individual homosexuals. Since this period of personal disorganization and identity problems is at the same time highly visible to the broader community, this femininity is enlisted as evidence for theories of homosexuality that see, as a central component in its etiology, the failure of sexual identification. The homosexual at this point of his life cycle is more likely to be in psychotherapy, and this is often construed as evidence for a theory which is supported by a missampling of the ways of being homosexual.

Another life cycle crisis that the homosexual shares with the heterosexual in this youth-oriented society is the crisis of aging. While American society places an inordinate positive emphasis on youth, the homosexual community, by and large, places a still greater emphasis on this fleeting characteristic. In general, the homosexual has fewer resources with which to meet this crisis. For the heterosexual there are his children whose careers assure a sense of the future and a wife whose sexual availability cushions the shock of declining sexual attractiveness. In addition, the crisis of aging comes later to the heterosexual, at an age when his sexual powers have declined and expectations concerning his sexuality are considerably lower. The management of aging by the homosexual is not well understood, but there are, at this point in his life, a series of behavioral manifestations (symptoms) attendant to this dramatic transition that are misread as global aspects of homosexuality. Here, as with "coming out," it is important to note that most homosexuals, even with fewer resources than their heterosexual counterparts, manage to weather the period with relative success.

A central concern underlying these options and the management of a homosexual career is the presence and complexity of a homosexual community, which serves most simply for some persons as a sexual market place, but for others as the locus of friendships, opportunities, recreation, and expansion of the base of social life. Such a community is filled with both formal and informal institutions for meeting others and for following, to the degree the individual wants, a homosexual life style. Minimally, the community provides a source of social support, for it is one of the few places where the homosexual may get positive validation of his own self-image. Though the community often provides more feminine or "camp" behavior than some individuals might desire, in a major sense "camp" behavior may well be an expression of aggregate community characteristics without an equal commitment to this behavior on the part of its members. Further, "camp" behavior may also be seen as a form of interpersonal communication characteristic of intracommunity behavior and significantly altered for most during interaction with the larger society. The community serves as a way of mediating sexuality by providing a situation in which one can know and evaluate peers and, in a significant sense, convert sexual behavior into sexual conduct.[11] Insofar as the community provides these relation-

11 Ernest W. Burgess makes this useful distinction in his article, "The Sociologic Theory of Psychosexual Behavior," in Paul H. Hoch and Joseph Zubin (eds.), *Psychosexual Development in Health and Disease,* New York: Grune and Stratton, 1949, pp. 227–243. Burgess says, "Accurately speaking the various forms of sexual

ships for the individual homosexual, it allows for the dilution of sexual drives by providing social gratification in ways that are not directly sexual. Consequently, the homosexual with access to the community is more protected from impulsive sexual "acting out" than the homosexual who has only his own fear and knowledge of the society's prohibitions to mediate his sexual impulses.

It should be pointed out that in contrast to ethnic and occupational subcultures the homosexual community, as well as other deviant subcommunities, has very limited content.[12] This derives from the fact that the community members often have only their sexual commitment in common. Thus, while the community may reduce the problems of access to sexual partners and reduce guilt by providing a structure of shared values, often the shared value structure is far too narrow to transcend other areas of value disagreement. The college-trained professional and the bus boy, the WASP and the Negro slum dweller, may meet in sexual congress, but the similarity of their sexual interests does not eliminate larger social and cultural barriers.[13] The important fact is that the homosexual community is in itself an impoverished cultural unit. This impoverishment, however, may be only partially limiting, since it constrains most members to participate in it on a limited basis, reducing their anxiety and conflicts in the sexual sphere and increasing the quality of their performance in other aspects of social life.

Earlier we briefly listed some of the general problems that the homosexual—in common with the heterosexual—must face; these included earning a living, maintaining a residence, relations with family, and so on. At this point we might consider some of these in greater detail.

First there is the most basic problem of all: earning a living. Initially, the variables that apply to all labor force participants generally apply to homosexuals also. In addition there are the special conditions imposed by the deviant definition of the homosexual com-

---

outlet for man are not behavior, they are conduct. Conduct is behavior as prescribed or evaluated by the group. It is not simply external observable behavior, but behavior that expresses a norm or evaluation."

[12] For descriptions of the content of other deviant subcultures see, Harold Finestone, "Cats Kicks and Color," *Social Problems*, 5 (July, 1957), pp. 3–13.

Howard S. Becker, *The Outsiders*, New York: The Free Press, 1963.

James H. Bryan, "Apprenticeships in Prostitution," *Social Problems*, 12 (Winter, 1965), pp. 278–297.

[13] The homosexual community does provide for an easing of strain by training essentially lower class types in middle class life styles and even middle class occupational roles to a greater extent than most people realize. In contrast, for those for whom homosexuality becomes the salient organizing experience of their lives there may be a concomitant downward mobility as their ties with commitments to systems of roles that are larger than the homosexual community decrease.

mitment. What is important is that the occupational activity of homosexuals represents a fairly broad range. The differences in occupational activity can be conceptualized along a number of dimensions, some of which would be conventional concerns of occupational sociology, while others would reflect the special situation of the homosexual. For example, one element is the degree of occupational involvement, that is, the degree to which occupational activity, or activity ancillary to it, is defined as intrinsically gratifying. This would obviously vary from professional to ribbon clerk to factory laborer. A corollary to this is the degree to which the world of work penetrates other aspects of life. In terms of influence upon a homosexual career, occupational involvement very likely plays a constraining role during the acting-out phase associated with "coming out," as well as serving as an alternative source of investment during the "crisis of aging." Another aspect bears directly upon the issue of the consequences of having one's deviant commitment exposed. For some occupational roles disclosure would clearly be a disaster—the school teacher, the minister, and the politician, to mention just three. There are other occupations where the disclosure or assumption of homosexual interests is either of little consequence or—though relatively rare—has a positive consequence. It should be evident that the crucial question of anxiety and depersonalization in the conduct of sexual activity can be linked to this variable in a rather direct way.

A second series of questions could deal with the effects of a deviant sexual commitment upon occupational activity itself. In some cases the effect may be extremely negative, since the pursuit of homosexual interests may generate irresponsibility and irregularity. Some part of this might flow from what we associate with bachelorhood generally: detachment from conventional families and, in terms of sex, constant striving for what is essentially regularized in marriage. Illustrations of these behaviors include too many late nights out, too much drinking in too many taverns, and unevenness in emotional condition. On the other hand, several positive effects can be observed. Detachment from the demands of domestic life not only frees one for greater dedication to the pursuit of sexual goals, but also for greater dedication to work. Also, the ability of some jobs to facilitate homosexual activity—such as certain marginal, low-paying, white-collar jobs —serves as compensation for low pay or limited opportunity for advancement. There may be few simple or consistent patterns emerging from this type of consideration, yet the overdetermination of the sexual element in the study of the homosexual rests in our prior reluctance to consider these questions which are both complex and pedestrian.

Similarly, just as most homosexuals have to earn a living, so must they come to terms with their immediate families. There is no substantial evidence to suggest that the proportion of homosexuals for whom relatives are significant persons differs from that of heterosexuals. The important differences rest in the way the relationships are managed and, again, the consequences they have for other aspects of life. Here also one could expect considerable variation containing patterns of rejection, continuing involvement without knowledge, ritualistically suppressed knowledge, and knowledge and acceptance. This becomes more complex because several patterns may be operative at the same time with different members of one's family constellation. Here again it is not unreasonable to assume a considerable degree of variation in the course of managing a homosexual commitment as this kind of factor varies. Yet the literature is almost totally without reference to this relationship. Curiously, in the psychiatric literature—where mother and father play crucial roles in the formation of a homosexual commitment—they tend to be significant by their absence in considerations of how homosexual careers are managed.

This order of discussion could be extended into a large number of areas. Let us consider just one more: religion. As a variable, religion (as both an identification and a quality of religiosity) manifests no indication that it plays an important role in the generation of homosexual commitments. However, it clearly does, or can, play a significant role in the management of that commitment. Here, as in other spheres of life, we must be prepared to deal with complex, interactive relations rather than fixed, static ones. Crucial to the homosexual's ability to "accept himself" is his ability to bring his own homosexuality within a sense of the moral order as it is projected by the institutions surrounding him as well as his own vision of this order. It may be that the issue of including homosexuality within a religious definition is the way the question should be framed only part of the time, and for only part of a homosexual population. At other times and for other homosexuals, to frame the question in terms of bringing religiosity within the homosexual definition might be more appropriate. The need for damnation (that rare sense of being genuinely evil) and the need for redemption (a sense of potentially being returned to the community in good standing) can be expected to vary, given different stages of the life cycle, different styles of being homosexual, and varying environments for enactment of the homosexual commitment. And our sense of the relation suggests that, more than asking about the homosexual's religious orientation and how it expresses his homosexuality, we must also learn to ask how his homosexuality expresses his commitment to the religious.

The aims, then, of a sociological approach to homosexuality are to begin to define the factors—both individual and situational—that predispose a homosexual to follow one homosexual path as against others; to spell out the contingencies that will shape the career that has been embarked upon; and to trace out the patterns of living in both their pedestrian and their seemingly exotic aspects. Only then will we begin to understand the homosexual. This pursuit must inevitably bring us—though from a particular angle—to those complex matrices wherein most human behavior is fashioned.

27

Austin T. Turk

Prospects for Theories of Criminal Behavior

This paper is addressed to the conceptualization of criminology as a scientific instead of an "applied" discipline—which implies that the field is thought of here as the study of crime per se without any necessary concern with controlling or changing behavior defined as "criminal" at some time in some jurisdiction. The objectives are (1) to indicate the evidence against the assumption that crime is a behavior class, a subcategory of deviant behavior; (2) to reject the view that it is mandatory, or even possible, for criminologists to produce theories of *criminal*, as distinct from *noncriminal*, behavior, i.e., theories explaining why and how specific individuals "deviated" in a legal sense and why and how other specific individuals did not so "deviate"; and (3) to suggest that success both in "scientific" and in "ameliorative" work presupposes that those interested in crime from either perspective will be more careful with the distinction between (*a*) assuming the criminality of some behavior and seeking to control or change it, and (*b*) trying to explain why the behavior is labelled "criminal" in the first place. The writer submits that criminology has not been focused upon the problems of explaining the *criminality*, the labelling, but has in fact been almost exclusively focused upon explaining behavior as such, in spite of Sutherland's statement of the criminological problem: "to explain the criminality of behavior, not the behavior as such."[1]

Reprinted with special permission from the *Journal of Criminal Law, Criminology and Police Science* Copyright © 1964 by the Northwestern University School of Law, Vol. 55, No. 4 (December, 1964), and by permission of the author.

[1] Sutherland, *Principles of Criminology* 4 (4th ed. 1947). Sutherland himself did not fully accept the implication of his statement by breaking away from a preoccupation

Is "Crime" Behavior?

The history of criminology is largely that of the search for criminal types—biological, psychological, or sociological. Students of crime have been preoccupied with the search for and explanation of distinguishing characteristics of "criminality," almost universally assuming that the implied task is to develop scientific explanations of the behavior of persons who deviate from "legal norms." The quest has not been very successful. Research has demonstrated the inadequacies of theories stressing biological determinants and appears to be doing the same for theories proposing fundamental, etiologically significant differences between criminals and non-criminals in regard to dimensions of personality. The study of the criminal as a social type and of his behavior as an analytically distinct system tends to dissolve into the study of variations in the life styles and opportunity structures of people located at different points in a given social structure.[2] Rather than developing theories of criminal behavior, the cumulative impact of efforts to specify and explain differences between "criminal" and "non-criminal" cultural and behavior patterns is to force serious consideration of the possibility that there may be *no* significant[3] differences between the overwhelming majority of legally identified criminals and the *relevant* general population, i.e., that population whose concerns and expectations impinge directly and routinely upon the individuals so identified. If in truth we are dealing not with individual departures from the norms of *their* groups but with subcultures wherein persons develop in ways more or less likely to get them into trouble with the Law, then we must inquire into the "criminality" of certain subcul-

---

with the behavior of offenders. The furthest advance in his thought appears to have been that "it is improper to view criminal behavior as a closed system, and participation in criminal behavior is not to be regarded as something that is determined exclusively by association with criminal patterns." Cohen, Lindesmith & Schuessler, *The Sutherland Papers* 36 (1956).

[2] Instead of theories explaining the *criminality* of some juvenile and adult behavior, the work of Cohen, Miller, Cloward and Ohlin, and other students of subcultural differentiation and opportunity structures promises explanations of behavior patterns and differences per se, explanations of tremendous potential value for the purposes of crime prevention and control. However, the "criminological problem" is scarcely touched.

[3] That is, significant from the standpoint of a psychologically and sociologically adequate criterion differentiating criminal from non-criminal attributes irrespective of the discriminatory enactment, interpretation, and enforcement of statutes. The "irrespective of" recognizes differences between scientific and legal classification as noted by legal scholars such as Jerome Hall and Karl Llewellyn. Hall, *Studies in Jurisprudence and Criminal Theory* 146 (1958), distinguishes between theoretical knowledge concerned with causes and practcial knowledge concerned with ends. Llewellyn, *Jurisprudence: Realism in Theory and Practice* 87 (1962), says the difference lies in the nature and handling of disputes, with the aim of scientific literature being "not debate, but co-operative thinking."

tures. At this point there are two alternatives: (1) to accept the laws in effect at a given time and place, and therefore *assume* the criminality of some subcultures; or (2) to question the laws, asking why there is some degree of association between subcultural variations and variations in crime rates. Historically, the great bulk of criminological thought and research has developed within the confines of the first alternative and is not, consequently, directly relevant to the problems of explaining *criminality*. It is, of course, very true that contributions to the theoretical and methodological progress of the behavior sciences have been by-products of efforts by criminologists who were actually studying behavior rather than criminality. Moreover, much useful descriptive and "applied" knowledge has come from efforts to locate offenders in social space and to explore connections between human experiences and criminality as defined in particular locales. The pragmatic value of research aimed at learning how to prevent or suppress certain kinds of behavior is incontestable; if one accepts the values reflected in particular laws, then he will seek knowledge that enables him to insure most effectively the survival and continued dominance of those values. On the other hand, from a more detached standpoint, the problem is to explain why some values *are* dominant while others are not. Criminological research has typically been carried out as if the values problem were no problem at all; the working assumption has been that *crime* and *not-crime* are classes of behavior instead of simply labels associated with the process by which individuals come to occupy the ascribed (not necessarily having anything to do with *actual* behavior) statuses of *criminal* and *non-criminal*. Efforts to determine *the* basic differences between crime and not-crime viewed as behavior and between criminals and non-criminals viewed as different kinds of people have contributed to eight kinds of evidence tending to destroy the very premise upon which such efforts have been based: that basic differences exist.

In each instance the evidence has been summarized as an empirical generalization. Opinions vary in regard to the relative importance of the several propositions and to the quality of the evidence represented by each. Taken in combination, however, the propositions do at least constitute a strong case against the assumption that the study of *crime* is synonymous with the study of a class or classes of *behavior*.

1. *There is apparently no pattern of human behavior which has not been at least tolerated in some normative structure.* The anthropology of law,[4] historical and comparative analysis of legal documents,[5]

---

[4] Hoebel, *The Law of Primitive Man* (1954).
[5] Hall, *Theft, Law and Society* (2d ed. 1952), and *General Principles of Criminal Law* (2d ed. 1960); Rusche & Kirchheimer, *Punishment and Social Structure* (1939).

research into subcultural differentiation,[6] and studies of the extent of "deviant" forms of behavior in general populations[7] have undermined the assumption that there are universally applicable distinctions between right and wrong.[8] If there is no behavior pattern which is universally defined as criminal, then research on the etiology of "criminal" behavior is inevitably culture-specific and time-bound, since the phenomenon under study will change from culture to culture and from time to time within essentially the same culture.

2. *The behavioral elements comprising an illegal act are not specific to criminal as distinguished from other human behavior.* Activities of the human organism—such as manipulation of material objects, display of violence, introduction of "illicit" substances into the body, indulgence in "perverted" sexual practices, frequenting of "off-limits" places, and "fraudulent" or "subversive" manipulation of symbols (e.g., numbers, words, gestures, facial expressions)—do not automatically sort themselves into the criminal and the non-criminal. The sorting is a matter of cultural definition and of the inclination and power to apply definitions in specific instances. "[Since] the muscular processes in criminal behavior are not unique, their study contributes nothing to the understanding of criminal behavior. Similarly the needs, values, goals, etc. in criminal behavior are not unique, and explanations cannot be made in terms of them."[9]

3. *There is selective and differential perception of every element (individuals, testimony, actions, sources and targets of actions, sequences of events, location and use of material objects, etc.) of a situation involving a criminal act.* Korn and McCorkle consider the assumption that the facts in each criminal case can be established as "probably the most important and the least demonstrable in all of the law."[10] The difficulties involved in efforts to arrive at "the truth" as perceived

[6] Whyte, *Street Corner Society* (enlarged ed. 1955); Becker, *Outsiders: Studies in the Sociology of Deviance* (1963); Miller, "Lower Class Culture as a Generating Milieu of Gang Delinquency," 14 *J. Social Issues* 5 (1958); Cohen & Short, "Research in Delinquent Subcultures," *id.* at 20; Cloward & Ohlin, *Delinquency and Opportunity* (1960).

[7] Porterfield, *Youth in Trouble* (1946); Wallerstein & Wyle, "Our Law-Abiding Law Breakers," 25 *Nat'l Probation* 107 (1947); Sutherland, *White Collar Crime* (1949); Clinard, *The Black Market* (1952); Kinsey *et al.*, *Sexual Behavior in the Human Male* (1948), and *Sexual Behavior in the Human Female* (1953); Nye & Short, "Scaling Delinquent Behavior," 22 *Am. Soc. Rev.* 326 (1957).

[8] This is not to say that social structures and cultures may not eventually be rated in terms of their viability, or that general value-assumptions derived from conceptions of prerequisites for viable patterns of living may not achieve a high degree of consensus. Levy, *The Structure of Society* 111–97 (1952); Northrup, "Cultural Values," and Bidney, "The Concept of Value in Modern Anthropology," in *Anthropology Today* 668–81, 682–99 (Kroeber ed. 1953).

[9] Cohen, Lindesmith & Schuessler, *op. cit. supra* note 1, at 38.

[10] Korn & McCorkle, *Criminology and Penology* 88 (1959).

by even the most honest of witnesses are compounded by the necessary reliance upon their recall of their perceptions.[11] Additional and largely unintended screening of the raw material of human affairs occurs as the police, prosecutors, defense counsel, judges, psychiatrists, and others attempt to sift and order the materials.[12] If even within a culture there is variation in the perceptions of those involved in determining the applicability of sanctions in specific cases, then the same behavior will sometimes be defined as crime and on other occasions be defined as not-crime, and different behavior will sometimes be labelled as identical behavior.

4. *An individual's range of behavior includes many more acceptable than illegal actions, objectives, and relations.*[13] The entirely vicious and treacherous individual who poses a continual and indiscriminate threat would be intolerable in any human group. Individuals who cannot or do not approximate the norms of their regular associates are eliminated in some manner—confinement, banishment, extermination.[14] If virtually all individuals identified as criminals within a jurisdiction are indistinguishable most of the time in most respects from non-criminals, then the expectation that there is some fundamental difference between these two categories is, to say the least, questionable.

5. *Criminal acts attributed to the same individual vary in terms both of the actual or imputed behavior on separate occasions and of the frequencies of particular acts.* Life histories,[15] analyses of arrest and other police contact records,[16] and studies of recidivism[17] indicate that variability rather than specialization is characteristic of known of-

[11] Davidson, "Appraisal of Witnesses," 110 *Am. J. Psychiatry* 481 (1954); Weinstein, "The Law's Attempt To Obtain Useful Testimony," 13 *J. Social Issues* 6 (1957).

[12] Frank, *Courts on Trial: Myth and Reality in American Justice* (1950); Arens & Meadow, "Psycholinguistics and the Confession Dilemma," 56 *Colum. L. Rev.* 38 (1956); Robinson, "Bias, Probability, and Trial by Jury," 15 *Am. Soc. Rev.* 73 (1950); Strodtbeck, James & Hawkins, "Social Status in Jury Deliberations," 22 *id.* at 713 (1957); Green, *Judicial Attitudes in Sentencing* (1961); Nagel, "Judicial Backgrounds and Criminal Cases," 53 *J. Crim. L., C. & P. S.* 333 (1962); Ferracuti, Perez & Wolfgang, "A Study of Police Errors in Crime Classification," *id.* at 113.

[13] In the theoretical limiting case where illegality exceeds legality, madness rather than criminality would most likely be inferred by fellows, legal authorities, and behavior scientists.

[14] *E.g.*, Hoebel, *op. cit. supra* note 4, at 90–91.

[15] Shaw, *The Jack Roller* (1930), *The Natural History of a Delinquent Career* (1931), and *Brothers in Crime* (1938).

[16] Current emphasis upon descriptive types of offenders and upon relatively stable records in terms of broad categories such as personal versus property offenses reflects the rehabilitative interest in changing behavior rather than the theoretical interest in learning how the adjective "criminal" comes to be applied to the individual and aspects of his behavior in the first place. Mayhew and Moreau are still very much with us. (Lindesmith & Dunham, "Some Principles of Criminal Typology, 19 *Social Forces* 307 (1941).) *E.g.*, Gibbons & Garrity, "Definition and Analysis of Certain Criminal Types," 53 *J. Crim. L., C. & P. S.* 27 (1962); Schrag, "A Preliminary Criminal Typology," 4 *Pac. Soc. Rev.* 11 (1961); Peterson, Pittman & O'Neal, "Stabilities in Deviance: A Study of Assaultive and Non-Assaultive Offenders,

fenders. The highly specialized psychotic whose timing, locale, victim, and mode of attack are almost invariable is an extreme rarity. Similarly, the code-conscious "professional" who is strictly limited to a field of criminal activity in which he exercises his skills with great discrimination is probably more a creation of journalism, romanticism, and commercialism than an empirically demonstrable social type. If the records of most individuals who have at times been assigned the status of criminal show that the acts attributed to them varied, then one may doubt that there is a detectable pattern in the officially and punitively recognized behavior of most sometime criminals. If there is no "career line" in the records of most of these persons, then there is little reason to expect theories of behavior to account for records of crime. Such records may or may not be valid indicators of the actual behavior patterns of particular individuals; to the extent that there is correspondence, it is in spite of rather than because of the processes by which crime records are produced.

6. *Most criminal acts do not become known and recorded.* Studies of self-reported offenses,[18] of offenses known to public and private organizations but not to the police,[19] of white collar crime,[20] and of variables related to differential crime reporting[21] make suspect any sample of presumptive non-criminals randomly drawn from the non-institutionalized or "no record" population. Indeed, Savitz's conclusion about the "non-delinquent majority" in socially disorganized urban areas may be generalized, it seems, to at least the American population as a whole: "Give them time. Most of them *will* be delinquent before it's all over."[22] If most criminally liable behavior is not recorded as crime, if the relationship between criminally liable behavior and recorded crime is not constant, and if most of the population within a

---

53 *J. Crim. L., C. & P. S.* 44 (1962); Hayner, "Characteristics of Five Offender Types," 26 *Am. Soc. Rev.* 96 (1961).

17 S. & E. Glueck, *Later Criminal Careers* (1937); England, "A Study of Post-probation Recidivism Among Five Hundred Federal Offenders," 19 *Fed. Prob.* 10 (Sept. 1955); Frum, "Adult Criminal Offense Trends Following Juvenile Delinquency," 49 *J. Crim. L., C. & P. S.* 29 (1958); Jacks, "Why Are Parolees Returned to Prison as Parole Violators?" 19 *Am. J. Correction* 22 (1957).

18 Porterfield, *op. cit. supra* note 7; Wallerstein & Wyle, *supra* note 7; Nye & Short, *supra* note 7.

19 Schwartz, "A Community Experiment in the Measurement of Juvenile Delinquency," *Nat'l Probation and Parole Ass'n Yearbook* 3 (1945).

20 Sutherland, *White Collar Crime* (1949); Clinard *op. cit. supra* note 7; Fuller, *The Gentlemen Conspirators* (1962); R. F. Kennedy, *The Enemy Within* (1960)—a report of white collar as well as of conventional offenses connected with the career of Hoffa.

21 Van Vechten, "Differential Criminal Case Mortality in Selected Jurisdictions," 7 *Am. Soc. Rev.* 833 (1942); Beattie, "Criminal Statistics in the United States—1960," 51 *J. Crim. L., C. & P. S.* 49 (1960).

22 Savitz, "Delinquency and Migration," in *The Sociology of Crime and Delinquency* 199–205 (Wolfgang, Savitz & Johnston eds. 1962).

jurisdiction do engage in such behavior more or less frequently, then conclusions about *basic* differences between the criminal and the non-criminal body, mind, personality, or subculture are highly suspect. When statistically significant differences are found in research comparing carefully selected recidivists and "no detectable record" controls, conclusions may be drawn about the attributes of persons who tend to become involved in the ascription process resulting in criminal status, i.e., we have clues toward an understanding of the *achievement* aspects —which may or may not be of overriding significance—of the status ascription process. In other words, we will know something about persons who get into trouble, but we cannot assume either (*a*) that their attributes alone explain their getting into trouble or (*b*) that the relative weight of personal attributes of offenders versus characteristics of the legal processing itself is constant.

7. *Not all persons known to have violated laws providing for penalties imposed by political authority*[23] *are subjected to punitive legal recognition.* At every stage in the law enforcement process decisions are made regarding what aspects of situations involving criminal acts will be emphasized. Whether or not one likes the fact, discretion is inevitable and to some extent necessary in the allocation of law enforcement resources.[24] If not everyone who is *known* to have engaged in criminally liable behavior is actually identified as a criminal, then the more appropriate question for criminology *qua* criminology seems to be not "Why did the criminal engage in certain behavior?" but rather "Why is one person who engages in certain behavior given the status of criminal while another who engages in the same behavior is not?"

8. *For most offense categories the rates are relatively high for lower class, minority group, young, male, transient, urban populations.* Allowing for the differential social participation of males and of females and for a fairly widespread cultural bias tending to favor females with respect to legal processing, the common attribute of the remaining populations seems to be their vulnerability when confronted by political authority. Only the most sanguine can continue to assume that legal processes exist apart from the conflicts intrinsic to social relations.[25]

---

[23] To restrict the concept to explicit political statuses and roles as found in contemporary large-scope societies is a matter of convenience at times, as noted by Llewellyn, *op. cit supra* note 3, at 31, but prohibits fundamental research on comparative legal processes. See Hoebel, *op. cit. supra* note 4, at 50.

[24] Newman, "Pleading Guilty for Considerations: A Study of Bargain Justice," **46** *J. Crim. L., C. & P. S.* 780 (1956); Goldstein, "Police Discretion Not To Invoke the Criminal Process: Low-Visibility Decisions in the Administration of Justice," **69** *Yale L. J.* 543 (1960); LaFave, "The Police and Non-Enforcement of the Law," 1962 *Wis. L. Rev.* 104, 179.

[25] Vold, *Theoretical Criminology* 203–19 (1958); Kirchheimer, *Political Justice* (1961); Jeffery, "Criminal Justice and Social Change," in Davis, Foster, Jeffery & Davis, *Society and the Law* 264–310 (1962).

If records of crime reveal with great consistency that higher crime rates are associated with relatively subordinate position within political structures, then the assumption that behavior variations among different categories of people are entirely, or almost always, responsible for differences in crime rates is open to question. Instead of assuming the criminality of some of the characteristic behavior patterns of persons in certain social categories and proceeding to investigate the sources of the behavior patterns in order presumably to explain their criminality— a neat circle—one may investigate (a) the tendency of laws to penalize behavior characteristic of the less powerful but not of the more powerful, and (b) the possibility that the more powerful can use the legal process to ascribe the status of criminal to members of the less powerful categories of a population *irrespective of actual behavior*.

WHAT HOPE FOR INTEGRATING THEORIES OF "CRIME" AND OF "CRIMINAL BEHAVIOR?"

A number of criminologists have attempted to resolve the conceptual difficulties generated by the dominant ameliorative, "offender" orientation of the field. Statements by Sutherland, Sellin, Tappan, Vold, Jeffery, and Korn and McCorkle are especially provocative. All of these writers have tried to provide a defensible scientific conception of criminology without giving up hope for theories of criminal behavior, and all have made signal contributions to criminological theory in the course of failing to accomplish their objective.

Sutherland and his colleagues and students have done criminology the great service of insisting and demonstrating that "criminal behavior is human behavior,"[26] but at the same time initiated a line of research that has now led to the conclusion that "human behavior is human behavior" regardless of the adjective *criminal*. The flaw in Sutherland's thinking does not lie in his assertion that scientific explanation of offensive behavior will be a specific application of a general theory of behavior, but in his assumption that the task is "to differentiate criminal from non-criminal behavior."[27] This differentiation is accomplished in the legal process, not by scientific classification. The real task for those concerned with behavior assumed to be offensive has been spelled out by Sellin, who has recognized the incompatibility between the languages and ends of law and of behavior science.[28] As he says, "etiological conduct research is not greatly interested in the legal label."[29] But even after rejecting Znaniecki's proposal to make *crime*

[26] Sutherland & Cressey, *Principles of Criminology* 75 (5th ed. 1955).
[27] *Ibid.*
[28] Sellin, *Culture Conflict and Crime* 24 (1938).
[29] *Id.* at 44.

synonymous with deviant behavior and reserving the term for "offenses made punishable by the criminal law,"[30] he proceeds to equate "crime" with "behavior" and "crime causation" with "conduct research."[31] It appears that at this point Sellin did not keep in mind the distinction, which he earlier recognized, between the procedures and aims of legal classification and of scientific behavior classification.

As the behavior scientists have rightly struggled to avoid letting legislators and other non-scientists define their basic terms of inquiry, so have the legal scholars, notably Paul Tappan, never relented in their just refusal to allow the behavior scientists to play fast and loose with the legal process as they sought a workable definition of criminal behavior.

"Our definitions of crime cannot be rooted in epithets, in minority value judgments or prejudice, or in loose abstractions."[32]
"In the developed society . . . criminal law and its correctional instruments become the ultimate regulators, though their effectiveness, like that of the mores, is circumscribed by public opinion and by the community reaction to constituted authority and to those who offend."[33]

Nonetheless, it is still the offender's behavior which is of central concern to Tappan;[34] to him the most fundamental problem for criminologists is "that of determining the specific connotations of the criminal universe."[35] Tappan's questions are "Who is the criminal, how large a social problem is he, and how can we best manipulate and control him?" Effective legal control mechanisms do require understanding of the etiology of human behavior, but to define criminal behavior as "in fact what the state through its legislature and courts says it is"[36] is not only to impose nonscientific definitions on the basic terms of behavior research but also to reify the state without getting at the distinctively criminological problem: to explain the *criminality*.

Vold's interpretation of the behaviorist-versus-legalist dilemma is that there is "always a dual problem of explanation—that of accounting for the behavior, *as behavior*, and equally important, accounting *for the definitions* by which specific behavior comes to be considered as crime or non-crime."[37] The dual problem does not exist, however, unless the investigator continues to assume that he must not only seek to explain criminality, the definitions, but offensive behavior as well *and using the same basic concepts of crime and criminal*. Vold, per-

[30] *Id.* at 32.
[31] *Id.* at 44–45.
[32] Tappan, *Crime, Justice and Correction* 10 (1960).
[33] *Id.* at 178.
[34] *Id.* at 10.
[35] *Id.* at 3.
[36] *Id.* at 7.
[37] Vold, *op. cit. supra* note 25, at vi.

haps more than any other single criminologist, has stressed the importance of the study of crime "as an aspect of the collision of and struggle for dominance among the groups and organizations of power in the community."[38] Yet, he hesitates to abandon the search for theories that will "serve to explain many kinds of impulsive, irrational acts *of a criminal nature* that are quite unrelated to any battle between different interest groups in organized society."[39]

Jeffery has reasserted the need for a sociology of criminal law that seeks to determine the conditions under which behavior is defined as criminal and to delineate the relationships between legal and other norms.[40] He emphasizes that "criminality exists not in the behavior but in the social system that controls and regulates the behavior"[41] and that "if you want to know something about crime you need to study social systems, not criminals."[42] In reference to socialization-acculturation theories of criminal behavior, specifically Sutherland's *differential association*, Jeffery has pointed out the inability of such theories to explain the origins of crime rates, correctly noting that they actually "explain how a person comes into contact with criminality if and when criminality is a part of his cultural system."[43] Unfortunately, Jeffery also has fallen into the trap of assuming that one must try to integrate the reformist and the scientific conceptions of criminology. It turns out that "the class 'criminal' is a class of objects included within a larger class 'social isolates' ", that "criminality is one of several ways in which a person can adjust to social impersonalization."[44] If one assumes that "law-violators" are necessarily a subcategory of "norm-violators"[45] whose "criminal behavior is an attempt to establish interpersonal relationships that have not been established in a socially acceptable way,"[46] then he is assuming that *legally* classified individuals are a subclass of a *scientifically* determined class of deviants—which is a restatement of Tappan's "legalistic behaviorism." While Jeffery has called for and contributed to work on basic criminological problems, he has vitiated his contribution by an empirically dubious attempted integration of "a legal theory of crime" with a psychologistic theory of "criminal" behavior.

[38] *Id.* at 13.

[39] *Id.* at 219. My italics.

[40] Jeffery, "The Structure of American Criminological Thinking," 46 *J. Crim. L., C. & P. S.* 658 (1956); "Crime, Law and Social Structure," 47 *id.* at 423.

[41] Jeffery, "The Structure of American Criminological Thinking," *supra* note 40, at 669.

[42] *Id.* at 671.

[43] Jeffery, "An Integrated Theory of Crime and Criminal Behavior," 49 *J. Crim. L., C. & P. S.* 533, 537–38 (1959).

[44] *Id.* at 539.

[45] *Id.* at 552

[46] *Id.* at 539.

Korn and McCorkle have come close to reconciling science and reformism in criminological theory.[47] Recognizing the critical significance of the legal process, they define a criminal as an individual "adjudged to be punishable by the authorities"[48] and crime as "an act or omission ascribed to a person when he is punished by the authorities."[49] They emphasize the point that the criminality of any act and the criminal status of any actor are determined through socio-legal procedures and "can only be conjectured about in advance."[50] Difficulties appear, however, when they try to integrate the socio-legal view of criminality with a social psychological theory of behavior. The main contribution of these writers is to indicate how role theory can be applied to understanding and changing the behavior of those who do commit criminal acts. Behavior, including criminal acts, tends to become patterned through a process in which the individual learns and is committed to behavior expected of him by others, both those who approve and those who disapprove.[51] Exploratory behavior that amounts to no more than a "tentative trying-on of roles"[52] tends to be taken very seriously if it results in personal or property damage or loss. The reactions of authorities and the public may help to reinforce the learning of disapproved patterns and to close off legitimate alternatives.[53] In this way, "criminal roles" are acquired. But to explain the acquisition of roles is, once more, not to explain the criminality of the behavior. In fact, the concept *role* itself may tend to exaggerate the degree to which most acts ascribed to offenders express systematic participation in networks of law-abiding and law-breaking relationships.[54] In any event, it seems highly probable that for those concerned with rehabilitation there inevitably *will* be "almost as many separate accounts as there are individual crimes or criminals."[55]

CONCLUSIONS

In considering implications of the foregoing for criminology, the writer is very much aware of two problems: (1) that he may appear to be indulging in a sweeping iconoclasm that denies the worth of "applied" interests in crime control, and (2) that he may be accused of

[47] Korn & McCorkle, *op. cit. supra* note 10, at 303–53.
[48] *Id.* at 45.
[49] *Id.* at 46.
[50] *Id.* at 47.
[51] *Id.* at 334–49.
[52] *Id.* at 349.
[53] *Ibid.*
[54] Korn and McCorkle are aware of the problem of varying degrees of "intensive" and "extensive" commitment. *Id.* at 341–43.
[55] *Id.* at 325.

attempting to dictate what is and what is not properly to be called criminology.

To those who view criminology as primarily an eclectic and applied discipline, it may seem that the writer feels that research into the social and psychological characteristics of offenders should cease. Such an interpretation would be in error, since the conception of criminology as a scientific discipline with its own analytically distinct problems by no means precludes an interest in changing behavior *on the basis of certain value assumptions*.[56] The point of the argument is that the differences between the reformist and the analytical interests, and the research problems of each, are fundamental and should be made explicit. It has been, is, and will continue to be misleading and confusing for social psychologists, legal scholars, corrections personnel, and others to assume or seem to assume that they can produce and use theories of *criminal* behavior. It is reluctance on the part of criminologists and non-criminologists alike to abandon the fruitless and unnecessary effort to reconcile reformism with the "scientific" view of criminology that perpetuates the confusion that is purportedly the science of crime.[57] Clarity, at least, will be gained if (*a*) those who assume *criminality* and support certain values and (*b*) those who study the ways in which values determine the application of the adjective *criminal* will unabashedly state precisely which category applies, and when, to them and their work.

As for the notion that this writer is interested in dictating the proper use of the word "criminology," it is not consensus on semantics but the *explicit* and *consistent* realization of the difference between two kinds of interests, both of which *happen* to be associated with the word "crime," that is the objective. If the primary aim of "criminological" research per se is not to develop theories of criminal behavior—if, indeed, any attempt to do so is doomed to failure—it follows that the traditional image of criminology as the scientific discipline that seeks to do just that is not an image which can be accepted by those who are interested in the distinctive problems of explaining *criminality*.[58] Similarly, those scientists and non-scientists who accept the

56 The foray of Jerome Michael and Mortimer Adler is 30 years in the past; not sweeping iconoclasm but a sharpening of conceptual and methodological tools is needed today. Michael & Adler, *Crime, Law and Social Science* (1933).

57 One eminent scholar recently concluded an excursion through Europe and the United States by declaring that "in the present state of knowledge, the very attempt to elucidate the causes of crime would be better put aside." Radzinowicz, *In Search of Criminology* 175 (1961).

58 There appear to be four kinds of distinctively "criminological" problems. To deal with any of them requires an understanding of the pervasiveness of social conflict in human affairs and implies an effort to relate the general phenomena of conflict to some major aspect of the legal process that defines right and wrong and determines

assumptions of a particular socio-legal structure and wish to apply their skills and experience to the problems of (1) reducing the incentives and opportunities for persons to engage in disapproved activities and (2) apprehending offenders and changing their behavior in desired directions are encouraged to make their values more explicit and to be more aware of differences between the roles of the reformer and of the scientist concerned with explaining "legal norms" without necessarily concerning himself with explaining the behavior of those who are defined as having violated some specific "legal norms" in some particular time and jurisdiction. The roles are equally important[59] and may to some extent be performed by the same individual, but he must remain aware of the activities and terminologies appropriate to each if he is to perform either effectively. Failure to keep the roles distinct has resulted in a conceptual morass that has both stunted the growth of a science of *crime* as such and hindered the effective application of sociological, psychological, and biological knowledge to problems of control and reform.

---

the criminal or non-criminal status of the actors within a given jurisdiction. The sets of problems are (1) to determine the conditions under which the very concept of law, of the rule of law, appears, varies, and declines; (2) to explain the enactment and wording of statutory law, i.e., the legislative aspect of the legal process; (3) to explain variations in interpretations of statutes; and (4) to specify relations among statutory law (involving the notion of "legislative intent"), court or "case" law, policeman's law, and "folk law" as these determine *de facto* criminality—which implies study of relations between (*a*) the actual behavior of persons and (*b*) the legal process, to determine the contributions of each class of variables to the probabilities of identification as criminal.

[59] The gross imbalance between the personnel and other resources directly and indirectly allocated to reformism and the resources available for research on the problems noted in footnote 58 must be reduced if theories explaining *criminality* are to be produced. Increasing interest in studies of various aspects of the legal process and in non-Western legal structures and concepts of law is a favorable sign, but practical efforts to revise curricula and the traditional "criminology" textbook and to channel research funds into projects of more significance for the study of *crime* but less relevance for the prevention and change of certain *behavior* have scarcely begun.

Suggested Further Readings

Friedson, Eliot, "Disability as Social Deviance," in *Sociology and Rehabilitation*, Marvin B. Sussman, ed., Washington, D. C., the American Sociological Association, 1966, pp. 71–99.

Goffman, Erving, *Stigma: Notes on the Management of Spoiled Identity*, Englewood Cliffs, N. J., Prentice-Hall, 1963.

Matza, David, *Delinquency and Drift*, New York, Wiley, 1961.

Parsons, Talcott, "Deviant Behavior and Mechanisms of Social Control," in *The Social System*, New York, Free Press, 1951, Chapter 7.

Scheff, Thomas J., *Being Mentally Ill: A Sociological Theory*, Chicago, Aldine, 1966.

Schur, Edwin M., *Crimes Without Victims: Deviant Behavior and Public Policy*, Englewood Cliffs, N. J., Prentice-Hall, 1965.

Wootton, Barbara, *Social Science and Social Pathology*, New York, Macmillan, 1959.

Author Index

Achilles, Nancy B., 351
Adams, Stuart, 202
Adler, L. M., 141
Adler, Mortimer, 373
Agger, Robert. E., 201
Aichhorn, August, 267
Allardt, Erik, 155, 157, 165
Anderson, Nels, 38
Angell, Robert C., 26
Angrist, Shirley S., 2, 67, 70, 142, 281, 327, 329
Archer, Jules, 121
Arens, Richard, 366
Aristotle, 6
Artiss, Kenneth L., 309
Attneave, F., 248
Aubert, Vilhelm, 290
Ausubel, David P., 67, 69
Ayler, Albert, 138, 139
Ayler, Donald, 138, 139

Bacon, Seldon D., 154, 155, 156, 157, 163, 167
Bain, Read, 4
Baldwin, James, 311
Bales, Robert F., 165, 317
Ball, Richard A., 187, 255
Bandura, Albert, 279
Barnard, Chester I., 315
Barnett, H. G., 294
Beach, W. G., 3, 14
Bean, Lee L., 91, 141
Beattie, Ronald H., 367
Becker, Howard, 68, 152, 159, 165
Becker, Howard S., 48, 50, 51, 52, 53, 54, 57, 58, 60, 61, 90, 106, 111, 130, 310, 352, 358, 365
Beebe, G. W., 142
Bell, Daniel, 203, 204, 218
Bell, Norman W., 310
Bell, Wendell, 247
Bendix, Reinhard, 170, 202, 315, 316
Benjamin, H., 105
Benoit-Smullyan, Emile, 201
Bensman, Joseph, 324
Berendt, Joachim, 135
Berg, I. A., 221, 224, 225
Beshers, James M., 154, 165
Bidney, David, 365

Bieber, Irving, 349, 350
Bierstedt, Robert, 120
Bilmes, Murray, 191
Bockoven, J. Sanbourne, 69
Bodenhafer, W. B., 4, 10, 13, 17
Boll, Eleanor Stoker, 306
Bond, E. D., 141
Boskoff, Alvin, 68
Bossard, James H. S., 3, 4, 6, 7, 8, 9, 10, 14, 15, 17, 19, 21, 306
Bottomore, T. B., 284
Braatoy, T., 141
Braceland, F. J., 141
Bredemeier, Harry C., 26
Brill, N. Q., 142
Bronner, Augusta, 189, 199, 266
Broom, Leonard, 70, 236, 242
Brown, C. W., 142
Brown, J. F., 229
Bruen, K., 155, 165
Bryan, James H., 91, 105, 358
Burchard, Waldo W., 96
Burgess, Ernest W., 23, 357
Burrell, Angus, 308
Busby, O. M., 308

Caillois, Roger, 290
Campbell, Ernest, 165
Cantril, Hadley, 256
Carstairs, G. Morris, 67, 142
Castillo, Cesar, 229
Cayton, Horace R., 311
Cerf, Bennett, 308
Cervantes, Miguel de, 308
Chassey, P., 247
Chein, Isidor, 198, 199
Child, I. L., 236
Christenson, Harold T., 165
Cicourel, Aaron, 50, 53
Clark, John P., 92, 168, 173
Clausen, John, 69, 75, 353
Clinard, Marshall B., 78, 90, 107, 166, 185, 365, 367
Cloward, Richard A., 78, 170, 185, 190, 198, 199, 236, 238, 267, 315, 363, 365
Coddington, J. W., 141
Cohen, Albert K., 57, 70, 74, 90, 159, 166, 173, 176, 177, 178, 181, 190, 199, 242, 262, 264, 267, 290, 363, 365

377

Subject Index

Abnormal, distinguished from deviant, 71–72

Abstinence background, and drinking behavior, 155–163

Achievement, emphasis on, and means, 236–238

Activism, political, and status consistency, 201–204

Adaptations to social order, 36–43

Adjustment model, in deviance theory, 20–23

Adolescents, goal orientation of, 168–184
   illegal behavior among, 168–184
   schizophrenia among, 189–199
   See also Delinquency

Adultery, 47, 54

African heritage, of jazz, 131–132

Age, and crime rates, 368
   and forgery, 224
   and goal orientation, 176
   and neutralization scores of delinquents, 257, 258–259
   and psychiatric treatment outcome, 143, 146, 147, 148
   and status integration, 99

Aggressiveness, and check forgery, 230

Aging crisis, of homosexual, 357, 359

Alcohol use, *see* Drinking behavior

Alienation, and alcohol use, 239, 250, 252
   index of, 258
   jazz as expression of, 130

"American dilemma," 27

Amish, norms of, 165

Anomia, Srole Scale of, 258

Anomie, and delinquency, 190
   dominant culture, 248, 249, 250
   as form of value conflict, 27–28
   and jazz, 130
   Merton's theory of, 32–43, 236–238
   and permissiveness, 162–165
   subcultural, 248, 249, 250
   types of, and alcohol use, 247–250

Anxiety, of adolescent schizophrenics, 197
   in sexual behavior of homosexuals, 354, 359

Apprenticeship period, in prostitution, 105–118

Army, response of deviants to, 287
   roles in, 317

Arrests, for drunkenness, 163
   of forgers, 224–225
   See also Criminal record

Arson, 173, 194

Aspirational reference framework, 33

Assault, 192, 194, 195, 223

Assimilationist stage, of jazz evolution, 134–135

Attitudes, of extreme right, 206–220
   See also Right-wing extremists

Autonomy, and delinquency, 179

Avant-garde jazz, and Black militancy, 137–140
   See also Jazz

"Behavior of organizations," 58

Behaviorist, versus legalist approach to crime, 369–372

Belief systems, as "social tranquilizers," 87–88

Biological theories, of crime, 46
   of mental illness, 80–81
   of social deviation, 8–9
   of social malfunctioning, 32

Black Arts Repertory Theatre, 137–138, 139

Black militancy, and avant-garde jazz, 137–140

Blackmail, of homosexuals, 126–127

Blockade, as deviance sanction, 65

Blues, classic, 133, 134

Body, norms relating to, in nudist camp, 119–128
   accentuation of, 127
   contact, 125–126
   covering of, 127

Bolshevik movement, 63

Bop movement in jazz, 135–137

Boycott, as deviance sanction, 65

Burglary, *see* Theft

Career fool, development of, 307–309
   social functions of, 297–313

Casework, situational bias of, 10–11

Catholic Church, 296

Catholics, church attendance of, 154
   drinking patterns of, 152

383